INDUSTRIAL RELATIONS AND
EUROPEAN STATE TRADITIONS

INDUSTRIAL RELATIONS AND EUROPEAN STATE TRADITIONS

COLIN CROUCH

CLARENDON PRESS · OXFORD

Oxford University Press, Great Clarendon Street, Oxford OX2 6DP

Oxford New York
Athens Auckland Bangkok Bogota Bombay
Buenos Aires Calcutta Cape Town Dar es Salaam
Delhi Florence Hong Kong Istanbul Karachi
Kuala Lumpur Madras Madrid Melbourne
Mexico City Nairobi Paris Singapore
Taipei Tokyo Toronto

and associated companies in
Berlin Ibadan

Oxford is a trade mark of Oxford University Press

Published in the United States by
Oxford University Press Inc., New York

First published 1993
First issued in paperback 1994
Reprinted 1996

British Library Cataloguing in Publication Data
Data available

Library of Congress Cataloging in Publication Data
Crouch, Colin.
Industrial relations and European state traditions / Colin Crouch.
Includes bibliographical references and index.
1. Industrial relations—Europe—History. I. Title.
HD8376.C76 1992   331'.094—dc20   92–14645
ISBN 0–19–827720–2
ISBN 0–19–827974–4 (Pbk.)

Printed in Great Britain
on acid-free paper by
Bookcraft (Bath) Ltd, Midsomer Norton, Avon

To the memory of

Charles Crouch
(1903–1990)
and
Doris Crouch
(1913–1990)

Preface

Over the decade that this book has taken to write, it has come to have three themes. Originally it was to be about the way in which industrial-relations systems changed over time, the different types of system one could identify, and the hypothetically different forms of behaviour and outcomes that might be associated with different types. This remains the predominant substance of the work, though my first intention to study the post-war development of France, Germany, Italy, and the United Kingdom changed into an account of fifteen western countries over 120 years, with a final glance over a far longer historical period.

The second theme concerns the unity and diversity of western European experience. This became an inevitable preoccupation given the period during which the book was written. I began to study European countries other than the United Kingdom in 1975, the year of the British referendum on entry into the European Economic Community, when I joined Alessandro Pizzorno's project on the resurgence after 1968 of industrial conflict in Europe. I finished writing the present volume as the political barriers that had hitherto defined western Europe's eastern boundary came crashing down and the geopolitical identity of Germany, Europe's most important state, changed yet again. And there are widespread expectations that the completion of the single European market by the end of 1992 will lead to an increasing homogeneity of European societies. The British, in particular, whether they are Europhiles or Europhobes, seem to feel that there is a monolithic Europe out there, from which Britain differs rather sharply. My own work has instead impressed upon me the persistent variety of western Europe— the plural 'traditions' in my title is very self-conscious—and the fact that the United Kingdom is just a part of that variety. On some points she is an outlier, but often she is more 'like', say, France or Germany than those countries are 'like' each other.

The year 1990, when my narrative ends, thus fortuitously saw the close of a chapter in the development of modern Europe. In the coming years Germany's economic and political record will take new paths, and anyone studying European historical

trajectories in future will have to take into account the experience under communist rule for so many years of the eastern part
of Germany, as well as, at least, Czechoslovakia, Hungary, and
Poland. The viability of 'western' Europe only as an object of
study will from now on be very questionable.

The third theme, which has become the most important to me,
concerns the boundaries of the political, and who are to be
counted as legitimate political actors, which in many respects is
what the whole debate about neo-corporatism has turned out to
be about. Anthony Black (1984) has described the way in which
the whole rich texture of medieval guild life, in which some of the
most creative and interesting political achievements of the pre-
modern period are to be found, was passed over in virtual silence
by contemporary political thinkers. Politics as a subject worthy of
attention was restricted to the formal and ultimately military
politics of nation-states, of kings and princes, working for essentially *purely* political ends, that is for the maximization of power
as such. Things have not changed much. Politics is today seen as
the business of career politicians, democratically legitimated, but
essentially using the substance of economic, social, and other
policy to maximize their achievement of a purely political end,
the maximization and prolongation of power. Those outside these
ranks are free to lobby, to try to influence, to engage in debate;
but they are supposed to remain, as the term lobby literally has
it, outside the chamber. If there is a suggestion that they have
become insiders, and have started to share in the internal task
of decision-making and administration, there is the smell of
something improper. (It happens of course, all the time; but we
are not good at understanding it as anything other than dubious.)

This is all part of a view that sees a clear distinction between
state and civil society, or state and the proper sphere of free
markets, or *état* and *citoyen individu*—the distinctions that have
been at the centre of Anglo-American and, differently, French
liberal political thought for much of the modern age, and which
Marxism and other socialist traditions in turn addressed. The
dominance of these national and philosophical traditions sub-
merged the suggestion of different possibilities being carried
forward in German, Swiss, Scandinavian, and Low Countries
political traditions—the possibilities of the functional representation of central social interests being a part of the legitimate

policy-making and public administrative systems in its own right, neither as a system of lobbies exceeding their entitlements nor as a quaint co-option to the formal political system through a 'house of industry'.

The rise of Germany as a major power after 1870 led to some changes in this perception, but commentators trained to concentrate on the state–society boundary tended to be preoccupied with the might of the Prussian state as such—whether they were observing the phenomenon itself or reading Hegel—and did not take much note of the functional representation that was a central aspect of its workings.

From 1914 onwards even this degree of attention to Germanic political models went into severe decline for obvious and understandable reasons, while the other polities that embodied similar features were too small to capture special interpretation. The outcome of the Second World War seemed finally to set the seal on what counted as major political traditions: those of France, Great Britain, the USA, and the Soviet Union, the four occupying powers of Berlin and Vienna after 1945. The first three offer different models of a strong state–society boundary; the last a kind of equivalent to a black hole for liberal political philosophy, the abolition of the boundary through the final conquest of society by the state.

So matters more or less remained. Germans, Scandinavians, and others shaped their study of politics around the Anglo-American, or, increasingly, American, tradition. Thus, when Stein Rokkan, the great Norwegian political scientist, wrote an article (1966) about his own society that even managed to include the term 'corporatist' in its title, he nevertheless approached that dimension through the concepts of pressure groups and lobbies that constituted the ethnocentric world-view of American political science and thus did not give full weight to the distinctiveness of what he was describing.

Since the early 1970s the growing literature on neo-corporatism has suggested an alternative way of viewing the polity, its boundaries, its component parts, and its participants. But, as I describe in Chapter 1, that came in oddly, so shaped were all our perceptions by the liberal state–society antithesis. The first articulated theory of the phenomenon (Schmitter, 1974) sprang from Latin-American experience; we chose a word oddly redolent with either nineteenth-century Roman Catholic social doctrine or fascism, or both; neo-corporatism was becoming a focus of attention at a time when difficulties in its management were leading to various state interventions, and so it became widely perceived as a form of state intervention in civil society when really it constitutes an alternative to that model of politics itself. Even (or especially) today, discussions of corporatism in the British mass media are likely to equate it to 'beer and sandwiches at No. 10'. That phenomenon is in fact the very reverse of corporatism, referring to crisis attempts at making contacts and compromises, whereas corporatism describes a stable set of relations that operate at a politico-economic level as a matter of routine. Any type of industrial-relations system—whether comprising normally corporatist behaviour, or pluralist collective bargaining, or ongoing conflict—may enter periods of crisis when something resembling 'beer and sandwiches', or *les accords de Grenelle*, or Harpsund diplomacy, will be needed to resolve problems.

We need an approach that can cope normally with what Keith Middlemas (1979) has called 'governing institutions', organizations going beyond the bounds of the officially 'political' which nevertheless can participate in the tasks of government. It is more easily done within the German tradition. One can work back from Böckenförde's (1977) striking concept of modern trade unions and business organizations as *staatsträgende Kräfte*; through Fischer's (1964) discussion of how pre-industrial forms of economic organization fed the institutional forms of industrial *Selbstverwaltung* in Germany and elsewhere in northern Europe; to Black's (1984) medieval urban polity of craft guilds. Now that the occupying troops have finally left Berlin, perhaps we can take more seriously a form of politics that, after all, has in both its modern and its medieval forms been preoccupied with the politics of economic life, which seems to be the principal concern of contemporary domestic politics.

C.C.

Trinity College, Oxford
June 1991

Acknowledgements

It is difficult to write about societies other than one's own without a good deal of help from natives, and over the years I have had the advantage of many good colleagues who have given such assistance. The main, though by no means the only, ones have been: Austria: Bernd Marin; Belgium: Armand Spineux; Denmark: Bruno Amoroso and Hans-Jørgen Nielsen; Finland: Voitto Helander and Heikki Paloheimo; France: Noëlle Burgi, Sabine Erbes-Seguin, Jean-Daniel Reynaud, and Denis Segrestin; Germany: Klaus Armingeon, Roland Czada, Otto Jacobi, Hans Kastendieck, Gerhard Lehmbruch, Walter Müller-Jentsch, and Wolfgang Streeck; Ireland: Bill Cox and Niamh Hardiman; Italy: Guido Baglioni, Ida Regalia, Marino Regini, Michele Salvati, and Tiziano Treu; Netherlands: Tinie Akkermans, Anton Hemerijck, and Jelle Visser; Norway: Paul Knutsen and Pål Foss; Portugal: Mario da Silva; Spain: Jose Maria Maravall and Victor Perez Diaz; Sweden: Victor Pestoff, Gøsta Rehn, and Birger Viklund; Switzerland: Lorenzo Parri; just about everywhere: Alessandro Pizzorno, Phillipe Schmitter, and Wolfgang Streeck again; and for warnings against trying to do clever things with crude statistics: Michael Shalev.

Since my wife Joan and I share most of each other's work problems, she has had more than her fair share of this project. My sons Daniel and Ben can hardly remember a time when this book didn't hang like a pall over the family. And I have promised my 1981 model BBC 32K micro-computer *requiem aeternam* if it will just see these acknowledgements through.

Chapter 2 incorporates material from my chapter in W. Grant (ed.), *The Political Economy of Corporatism* (London: Macmillan, 1985), 'Corporatism in Industrial Relations: A Formal Model', and from that in B. Marin (ed.), *Governance and Generalized Exchange* (Frankfurt am Main and Boulder, Colorado: Campus and Westview, 1990), 'Generalized Political Exchange in Industrial Relations in Europe during the Twentieth Century'. Chapter 3 also makes use of the chapter in Grant's book. An initial outline of some of the material in Chapters 4 to 7 appeared in the chapter in Marin's book. A shorter, preliminary version of Chapters 9 and 10 was published in my chapter, 'Sharing Public Space: States and Organized Interests in Western Europe', in J. A. Hall (ed.), *States in History* (Oxford: Blackwell, 1986).

Considerable help was given in the very early stages of this project by a year's leave from teaching duties secured partly by a Morris Ginsburg Fellowship at the London School of Economics and Political Science and partly by a Nuffield Foundation grant. I am grateful to both for the only leave from which this project has benefited, apart from a term's sabbatical from Trinity College in 1989.

Contents

Figures

Tables

Abbreviations

A	Austria
B	Belgium
BDA	Bundesvereinigung der Deutschen Arbeitgeberverbände
BDI	Bundesverband der Deutscher Industrie
BdI	Bund der Industriellen
BEC	British Employers' Confederation
CAF	Centrala Arbetsgivarförebund
CBI	Confederation of British Industry
CCI	Conseil Central de l'Industrie
CC.OO	Comisiones Obreras
CCTI	Conseil Central du Travail Industriel
CDI	Centralverband der Deutschen Industriellen
CEOE	Confederación Española de Organizaciones Empresariales
CGdL	Confederazione Generale del Lavoro
CGIL	Confederazione Generale Italiana del Lavoro
CGPF	Conseil Général du Patronat Français
CGPME	Conférence Générale des Petites et Moyennes Entreprises
CGT	Confédération Générale du Travail
CGTB	Confédération Générale du Travail Belge
CGTP-IN	Confederação Geral dos Trabalhadores Portugueses–Intersindical Nacional
CH	Switzerland
CIU	Congress of Irish Unions
CNPF	Conseil National du Patronat Français
CNT	Conseil National du Travail (Belgium); and Confederación Nacional de Trabajadores (Spain)
CNV	Christelijk-Nationaal Vakverbond

CS	Commission Syndicale
CSC	Confédération des Syndicats Chrétiens
D	Germany
DA	Dansk Arbejdsgiverforening
DAF	Deutscher Arbeiterfront
DGB	Deutscher Gewerkschaftsbund
DIHT	Deutscher Industrie- und Handelstag
DK	Denmark
DsF	De samvirkende Fagforbund
E	Spain
E(E)C	European (Economic) Community
EFO	Edgren, Faxén, Odhner
ER	Erhvervsøkonomisk Rad
F	France
FBI	Federation of British Industry
FEB	Fédération des Enterprises de Belgique
FfA	Fællesforening for Arbejdgivere
FGTB	Fédération Générale des Travailleurs de Belgique
FIB	Fédération de l'Industrie Belge
FIE	Federation of Irish Employers
FIM	Federation of Irish Manufacturers
FNV	Federatie Nederlandse Vakbeweging
FUE	Federated Union of Employers
GAV	Gesamtarbeitsvertrag
GK	Generalkommission
GNP	Gross National Product
GPE	Generalized Political Exchange
HAÖI	Haupstelle der Arbeitgeberorganisationen der Österreichischen Industriellen
I	Italy
ICTU	Irish Congress of Trade Unions
IG Metall	Industriegewerkschaft Metall

IRL	Ireland
ITUC	Irish Trades Union Congress
LO	Landesorganisasjon i Norge; Landsorganisation i Danmark; and Landsorganisation i Sverige
MHP	Federatie van Middelbaar en Hoger Personeel
N	Norway
n.a.	not available
NAF	Norsk Arbeidsgiverforening
NEDC	National Economic Development Council
NKV	Nederlands Katholiek Vakverbond
NL	Netherlands
NOU	Norges Offentlige Utredninger
NVV	Nederlands Verbond van Vakverenigingen
ÖGB	Österreichischer Gewerkschaftsbund
P	Portugal
PBO	Publiekrechtelijke Bedrijfsorganisatie
PK	Paritätische Kommission
PSI	Partito Socialista d'Italia
RDI	Reichsverband der Deutschen Industrie
S	Sweden
SACO-SR	Sveriges Akademiken Centralorganisation
SAE	Sveriges Allmännexportförening
SAF	Svenska Arbetsgivarförening
SAJ	Suomen Ammatliittojen Järjestö
SAK	Suomen Ammatliittojen Keskusjärjestö
SD	Socialdemokratisk Parti
SER	Sociaal-Economische Raad
SF	Finland
SGB	Schweizerischer Gewerkschaftsbund
SHIV	Schweizerisches Handel- und Industrieverein
SID	Specialarbejderforbund i Danmark
SMUV	Schweizerisches Metall- und Uhrverband

STK	Suomen Työnantajain Keskusliitto
TCO	Tjänstemännens Centralorganisation
TUC	Trades Union Congress
UGT	União Geral de Trabalhadores (Portugal); and Unión General de Trabajadores (Spain)
UIMM	Union des Industries Métallurgiques et Minières
UK	United Kingdom
USA	United States of America
USI	Unione Sindacale Italiana
VDA	Vereinigung der Deutschen Arbeitgeberverbände
VF	Verkstadsförening
VNF	Verbond van Nederlandse Fabrikantenverenigingen
VNW	Vereniging van Nederlandse Werkgevers
ZSAO	Zentralverband Schweizerischer Arbeitgeberorganisationen
ZU	Zentral der Unternehmerverbände

PART I

ORGANIZED INTERESTS
IN ECONOMY
AND POLITY

1

Organized Interests in the Economy: Diversity in Western European Experience

Centralisé et centré sur la situation économique de l'industrie, le système allemande repose sur la forte homogénéité sectorielle et sur l'autorité des organisations patronales et syndicales sur leurs membres. Décentralisé et centré sur les luttes de marché du travail dans les firmes, le système français correspond à l'hétérogénéité du tissu industriel et à la faiblesse structurelle des organisations syndicales et patronales.

(Maurice, Sellier, and Silvestre, 1982: 214)

One often hears talk of a 'European' approach to affairs. It may be people close to the European Community mistaking aspiration for accomplished reality. It may be North Americans losing sight of detail when looking across a large institutional as well as geographical distance. It may be the British, still equating European with 'Continental' and still seeing the latter as virtually equivalent to 'French'. This last point is in fact likely to be shared by all three of these distorted perspectives on European reality. The Napoleonic state, with its rationalized and formal legal code, its continuing conflict with the Catholic Church, and its generally jealous approach to its own autonomy and sovereignty, is frequently seen as embodying the archetypical attributes of the modern (meaning here primarily post-1789) European political tradition.

An alternative view, increasingly encountered as the decades since the Second World War lengthened and the western part of Germany finally acquired a stable political presence, is to see a European generality in German specificities. Here, 'modern' means primarily industrial, implying particularly the patterns of industrial organization and industrial politics that developed after the great recession of the 1870s and which found their most clear expression in the German Reich of that time. The emphasis is therefore on organized co-operative relationships between state, financial capital, and industrial capital; and, in the post-war years, labour too.

The French and the German are two very different political traditions; there is as yet no European synthesis between them. It is possible, with some distortion, to regard the various other continental European traditions as being of either the French or German type, but a better starting point is with the diversity of experience among them all, with subsequent consideration of whether any identifiable groupings really exist. The movement towards greater integration on which most western and probably some eastern European nations have now embarked may well fashion a more coherent and definable 'European political model', but if so that model will have to emerge from past and current diversity.

This book is an attempt to trace and analyse that diversity as displayed in a particular area of political practice: the organization of employers and workpeople and the relationships of these organizations to government. The patterns that we find may not be capable of generalization to all aspects of relations between state and society—the politics of agriculture, for example, may often be different. But it is an area of importance in its own right and one where political practice does seem to correspond to what is often presented as being generally representative of a particular society. Such a study as this must be both generalizing and particularizing. While an important aim is to draw attention to the specificity of national experiences, nothing is served by insisting on minute differences when these conceal an underlying and interesting similarity, particularly one that distinguishes a group of countries. To take this middle path requires concepts somewhere between those that enable us to talk about industrial societies in general (such as the concepts of basic economic theory) and those that are suited to individual historical narratives. In particular I shall make use of a distinction among different kinds of organizational politics that emerged from the literature of the 1970s and 1980s: a threefold division between contestation, pluralism, and corporatism. These concepts must first pass the test of usefulness; does their application to the analysis of cases tell us anything about differences in behaviour, in outcomes, as well as in styles and patterns? To pursue this we need to return to the debates of the period that gave rise to classifications of this kind.

VARIETIES OF INFLATIONARY EXPERIENCE

The high inflation of the 1970s and recession of the early 1980s brought an hysteria to discussions of democracy that had been absent from the complacent 1950s and 1960s. Evidence of vigorous interest-group activity, earlier lauded as the pluralism that separated the liberal democratic West from state socialism, was often seen as evidence of ungovernability. Samuel Brittan (1975) even voiced concern that democracy itself might be incompatible with a healthy capitalist economy. Most other commentators stopped short at that, but found more convenient scapegoats, such as the trade-union movement (Beer, 1982; Rose and Peters, 1977).

The tirade was most shrill in the United Kingdom and Italy, where indeed both inflation and workers' militancy were particularly high; but the theme was general throughout the Western world. Relatively minor disturbances in Germany gave rise to complaints about a *Gewerkschaftsstaat* or trade-union state—a phrase that had not been heard since Hitler's Nazi Party coined it in the late 1920s (*Gewerkschaftliche Monatshefte*, 1974; *Die Zeit*, 1974). Of course, strict monetarists claimed that trade unions could do neither good nor ill by themselves; if monetary authorities refused to increase the money supply that financed wage increases, then general price rises could not follow, and a consequent rise in unemployment would soon deal with the militancy. But governments often seemed unable to take action of appropriate toughness, which is why the issue was seen as one of ungovernability, not just economic malfunctioning.

An image of a frenzied race for higher incomes in order to compensate for higher prices, but which could end only in further price rises, dominated political, popular, and academic debate alike. Stand still and one would be overtaken by everyone whose earnings were hitched to the inflationary spiral; join the race and one would contribute to making it all even worse. The prisoner's dilemma became the favourite game-theory concept of political economists of the period. In the terms of an earlier tradition this was also a Hobbesian image of man. Leviathan seemed to be present, in the form of the late twentieth-century interventionist state, trying to regulate, control, secure agreements to good behaviour, construct consensus, develop incomes policies, and manipulate fiscal and monetary variables. But a democratic state can never be a convincing Leviathan. As Lindbeck (1976) noted, democratic politicians are endogenous to the societies they govern. And so government was commonly depicted as prey to a welter of interest groups which it needed to appease as well as discipline; it had to sustain full employment while also seeking to reduce inflation. Such a state only reflected or even magnified the prisoner's dilemma.

From this impasse emerged, both in theory and in practice, two contrasted policy options. One was to free Leviathan from social pressures so that he could play the true Hobbesian role usually associated with a non-democratic state and impose a logic of market forces so that unemployment and the fear of it might put an end to the inflationary spiral. Pessimistic conservatives were unable to see how this could be achieved if the state remained democratic. A good example was Michael Parkin (1975), who erroneously predicted an ineluctable escalation in inflation as a result of both political and economic factors, partly because he left out of account the possibility that the polity might respond to such dire predictions themselves. Such observers reckoned without both the incipient unpopularity of governments that failed to halt inflation and the ability of more resourceful conservative politicians to construct a populist appeal that could compensate for the inherent unpopularity of much of what they would do in order to break the inflationary log-jam. This option was pursued most vigorously in the United Kingdom and the United States, and to a lesser extent in Denmark and the Netherlands. The alternative was to replace the plethora of pluralistic interest groups with an orderly, concentrated, and internally disciplined set of organizations. These would share responsibility with the state, using their internal organizational authority to supplement that of the government in bringing order to the competitive struggle. This is a strategy opposite to that of Hobbes, since far from drawing into itself all political authority—

as do both the interventionist and the free-market states in their different ways—the state here tries to succeed by *sharing* its public-order function, sharing political space, with organized groups in civil society who thereby become what Germans call *Ordnungsfaktoren*. In exchange for having certain of their private arrangements virtually acquire the status of public authority these groups help bear the burdens of the state; in another German phrase, they become *staatstragende Kräfte*, 'state-bearing forces' (Böckenförde, 1977: 244).

Attempts at using devices of this kind were made by most western European governments during the 1970s, and, at the end of the Carter presidency, even by the United States administration (Harrison, 1989). But sustained success was achieved only in Austria, Germany, the Netherlands, Norway, Sweden, Switzerland, and possibly Belgium and Denmark.

The theoretical analysis of this alternative model was varied. Some authors, especially Scandinavians (e.g. Korpi, 1978; Korpi and Shalev, 1979) and those who based their models primarily on Scandinavian examples (Hibbs, 1978; A. Martin, 1979; Stephens, 1979) saw it in terms of an essentially social-democratic stability. Organized labour co-operated either because it recognized a social-democratic government as its 'own', or because under such a government social spending increased and workers were therefore less anxious to secure big wage rises. These theories had some difficulty when changes of government failed to produce changes in the conduct of organized groups, and they made rather ambitious assumptions about the political consciousness of unions and their members. Less vulnerable to such criticism was Stephens's (1979) argument that strong labour-movement political parties were likely to produce a centralization of union structures as priority was placed on the national task of mobilizing voters; this in turn produced unions capable of behaving in a strategic way. This theory has one major problem in that one of the world's largest and most successful Labour parties, the British one, has been associated with a distinctly decentralized union movement. However, Stephens provided a valuable bridge between the foregoing and the second group of theories: neo-corporatism.

Writers in the revived school of corporatist analysis concentrated more on the organizational characteristics of organized groups than on their political orientation. Indeed, it was an interesting element in the personal itinerary of many of these writers that in the early 1970s they started out (if they departed at all from value neutrality) rather disliking corporatist arrangements and deliberately evoking the fascist connotations of the term; but by the end of the decade they had become advocates of them, seeing them as far from fascist and rather embarrassingly hoist on the petard of the word that they had rescued from oblivion.

My own case serves as an example. In 1970 I wanted to analyse what was happening to the politics of industrial relations in Britain, starting from the perspective of the voluntarist pattern of free collective bargaining epitomized in the work of the Donovan Commission (1968). I wanted a concept that would describe a situation in which governments were challenging this essentially liberal model in order to require trade unions to help them with the task of disciplining workers (mainly over wage demands, but also over work practices). I eventually found what I needed in a casual reference to corporatism in an essay someone had written about the Trades Union Congress. Besides being analytically useful, this carried the veiled implication of fascism that conveyed the antiliberalism I wanted to capture. However, by 1975 I had become convinced that it was only under the discipline of such arrangements that strong trade unions and collective bargaining could be made compatible with economic growth and stability. I developed adjectives to limit different types of corporatism, distinguishing most of them from any association with a fascist form (Crouch, 1977).

A similar journey, though literally through different geography, is discernible in the work of Philippe Schmitter. His essay, 'Still the Century of Corporatism?' (1974), which has become a *locus classicus* of the neo-corporatist literature, was originally published in a collection dealing with Latin America, and his own immediate background was work in Argentina and Brazil, including under the politically highly ambiguous regime of Peron. However, soon he had noticed, as had several other scholars, that in western Europe corporatist structures were more likely to be associated with social democracy than with fascism; and by 1981 was comparing such societies favourably with those that lacked these organizational characteristics (Schmitter, 1981).

In addition to social-democratic and corporatist theory was a theory of rational collective action that distinguished between the behaviour of large organizations whose actions had a discernible macro-effect and small ones whose actions would have an infinitesimally small impact on the wider whole. The latter corresponded closely to the kinds of organization common in the pluralist models that were running into difficulties in the 1970s; the former to neo-corporatist structures. As with corporatist theories as such, the main theoretical contribution to this analysis was rather accidental and the opposite of the author's original intentions. Mancur Olson's (1982) study of collective action was primarily designed to demonstrate the efficiency-inhibiting impact of the organization of interests. This has indeed been its main economic policy message, and as such his work has been an important part of the intellectual case for deregulation, freeing markets, and breaking down organized groups that was such a central feature of neo-liberal politics in the 1980s. He did however allow an interesting if somewhat grudging exception, largely in recognition of the way in which organizational life had been conducted in the Scandinavia of his own family origins.

For Olson the problem with the typical organized group, which is seen as constituting a very small part of the whole society, is that it can gain by interfering with market forces without facing the negative consequences as these are general in impact and can therefore be externalized, and sufficiently small for them not to matter. It is only as the impact of a mass of such groups builds up that the uncontrollable negative consequences appear. However, if an organization becomes so large that its membership includes a significant proportion of the 'public', it is forced to internalize part of that externality, and has an impact sufficiently large to be discerned. Olson calls these organizations 'encompassing', a word so useful in describing the phenomenon concerned that it passed immediately into general academic currency. To illustrate with the simplest and most relevant example, a small work group that negotiates a rise in its pay that can be financed through price rises which in turn have no substantial effect on demand for the goods or services produced need have no regard to the contribution thereby made to general inflation in the society at large. In contrast a trade-union confederation negotiating on behalf of virtually the whole manual workforce of a country cannot but have regard for such consequences.

Olson's argument, even though almost a parenthesis to his

central thesis, has had an enormous impact in making more rigorous the logical strength of all subsequent writing on neo-corporatist organization, though it should be appreciated that the central thrust of the argument was anticipated by a couple of years in the early work of Wolfgang Streeck (1979). Also, Olson and many other authors concentrate on the way in which encompassing organizations can achieve collective goods in the negative sense of avoiding collective bads (e.g. helping to reduce the inflationary implications of their action). But the same theory should work more constructively too. We are dealing with a model of organizations that are so structured that they can, or even must, internalize public goods. This is, it will be noted, an economic version of the political concept of *staatsträgende Kräfte* discussed above. As such these organizations may help secure goods not attainable through market forces. Streeck later applied this to the particular and important issue of training (1985 and 1989). In a normal market situation employers have a disincentive to train, in that companies that do not do so will have lower costs and be able to recruit trained workers from those firms that do; training is a semi-public good. The problem might be resolved through the state providing training and levying employers for it, but often more effective is action by associations of employers, sometimes acting alongside trade unions, using organizational sanctions to ensure that training is carried out, or at least financed, by firms themselves.

Finally, as the North American pluralist tradition ran into trouble when the behaviour it had become accustomed to cel-ebrate became stigmatized as ungovernability or as 'pluralist stagnation', its members scattered. Many, perhaps a majority, became neo-liberals, considered everything to have got out of hand, and sought tough market constraints on the freedom of groups to lobby and exercise power (e.g. Beer, 1982; Crozier *et al.*, 1978). A minority however, which happened to include two of the most significant theorists of 1950s pluralism, Robert Dahl and Charles Lindblom, turned, like Olson but more wholeheartedly, to their Scandinavian ancestry. Dahl (1982 and 1985) saw the more tightly and centrally organized structures of Sweden and Norway as likely not only to afford more order than a characteristic United States pluralism, but also to give organized labour greater influence. A similar argument was made by Lindblom (1977), who in particular departed strongly from the assumption of much of the literature of the period that somehow it was labour groups that benefited most strongly from the pluralist pattern anyway. His concern was that business interests benefited excessively by virtue of governments' dependence on them for economic success.

In recent work these four streams of writing on organizations have combined. The 'social-democratic' and neo-corporatist schools have, with some surprise, recognized their similarity, amalgamated with 'revisionist pluralism', and taken advantage of the theoretical elegance and rigour to be achieved by casting their arguments in terms of rational action and exchange theory (e.g. Lange and Garrett, 1985; Crouch, 1985; Bruno and Sachs, 1985; Dell'Aringa, 1990).

For practical political even more than intellectual reasons, it is particularly important to note what has happened en route to pluralism and its evaluation. As already stated, in the 1950s this was a model that celebrated the mutual compatibility of democracy and capitalism. This was not only because it made possible a very favourable comparison of political life in the open capitalist societies of the West with the rigid, intolerant regimes of communism, but because of the harmonious analogy of pluralism to the free market. In the pluralist polity, as in the market economy, any number of actors could participate on a basis of 'win some, lose some', and no one was in a position to exercise undue influence on the system as a whole.

However, devices for disciplining the pursuit of ends, provided in the economy by market forces, were far less clearly developed in the polity; there was no ready equivalent of bankruptcy. By the 1970s academic, and by the 1980s political, advocates of free markets had therefore come to oppose richly developed organizational politics, and to seek measures to reduce the number, power, and role of organized interests. And the model of organizational life deemed to be compatible with economic growth and stability contrasted with the analogy of the free market as much as the 1950s and 1960s models had approximated to it.

Neo-corporatist and pluralist theories have often been set against each other as rival *accounts* of the political process (e.g. Berger, 1981; Martin, Ross, 1983). This is however quite unnecessary. They certainly describe very different *forms* of organization, but there is no reason for the theories to be rivals. Patterns of organized groups may conform to either account, and there is no need to reduce either to the other. Much of Andrew Cox's (1988) criticism of neo-corporatist claims falls away once writers in that school concede this point. It is also possible to reconcile both the free-market and the neo-corporatist accounts, as Olson does, by positing a U-curved relationship between the scale of interest organization and economic efficiency: A growth of organization of economic interests, interfering with market forces for their own benefit, is likely to be associated with declining efficiency, until the point where a high density of organization implies concentrated structures of the Olsonian encompassing kind. Thus several studies present a bimodal distribution of conditions for economic efficiency: either free markets with weak organizations or regulated markets with encompassing organizations (Crouch, 1985; Lange and Garrett, 1985; Calmfors and Driffill, 1988).

ASSESSING THE EVIDENCE

Most scholars engaged on studies of this kind made either a simple distinction between corporatist and pluralist industrial-relations systems or constructed a scale of corporatism. As Dell'Aringa (1990) has recently pointed out in a survey of this literature, there has not been universal agreement on the meaning to be given to these terms, but included in the operational definition of corporatism is usually some combination of centralization in the decision-making capacity of organizations (part of the criterion for Olson's 'encompassingness') and an indicator of social consensus or cohesion.

These are both problematic. A 'centralized' organization may well be one in which a remote central bureaucracy is out of touch with active forces on the ground; in later chapters, developing themes in Kjellberg (1983), I shall replace this with the idea of an *articulation* of local with central power. 'Consensus' is an even bigger problem, since there is both substantive doubt whether it is a precondition for corporatist behaviour or an outcome of it, and methodological doubt whether it can be identified except in a form that might also be taken for an output. Some of these issues will be addressed in later chapters. For present illustrative purposes I shall consider the evidence on the less problematic centralization rankings alone. Some examples are summarized in Table 1.1, which is based on but extends a similar table in Dell'Aringa (1990).

Schmitter (1981: 294) produced a rank order of what he called 'societal' corporatism, based on a combined ranking of trade-union centralization (interpreted in terms of the powers of confederations) and associational monopoly (the extent to which confederations were without rivals). Despite this pure industrial-relations base, he was able to apply this to measures of ungovernability that extended to civil violence, government instability, and fiscal ineffectiveness, leading to conclusions that corporatist patterns of interest organization were associated with high levels of stability, though probably at the cost of some institutional sclerosis and with considerable doubts over their ability to respond to emerging new political issues and identities.

In Crouch (1985) I produced a simpler dichotomy between corporatist and liberal industrial-relations systems, based partly on similar measures as Schmitter and partly on assessments of the degree of national co-ordination in the collective bargaining system as a whole. I was able to use this successfully to test the hypothesis that symptoms of economic malfunctioning during the crisis associated with the 1973 oil shock (industrial conflict, unemployment, increases in inflation levels) would be positively associated with levels of trade-union membership in liberal systems but not in corporatist ones. In other words, those authors worried at the potential instability of highly *pluralist* systems might well be right; what they might be missing were the potentially stabilizing implications of the extensive organization of interests when this took a corporatist form. Similar conclusions were reached by Calmfors and Driffill (1988), using a fully ranked scale. Bruno and Sachs (1985) used a version of Crouch's index to develop a rank order and observed superior performance in mastering problems of inflation and unemployment in corporatist systems. Similar scales, based on similar measures emphasizing centralization, and with similar predictive success,

TABLE 1.1. *Rank-orderings of countries by levels of centralization of industrial relations, various studies*

Schmitter (1981)	Bruno and Sachs (1985)	Tarantelli (1986)	Calmfors and Driffill (1988)	Blyth (1979)	Dell'Aringa (1990)	Crouch (1985) Neo-corporatist*	Crouch (1985) Liberal*
Austria	Austria	Austria	Austria	Austria	Austria	Austria	Australia
Norway	W. Germany	Japan	Norway	Norway	Norway	Denmark	Belgium
Sweden	Netherlands	W. Germany	Sweden	Sweden	Sweden	Finland	Canada
Denmark	Norway	Denmark	Denmark	Denmark	Denmark	Netherlands	France
Finland	Sweden	Finland	Finland	Finland	Finland	Norway	Ireland
Netherlands	Switzerland	Norway	W. Germany	New Zealand	W. Germany	Sweden	Italy
Belgium	Denmark	Sweden	Netherlands	Australia	Netherlands	Switzerland	Japan
W. Germany	Finland	Netherlands	Belgium	W. Germany	Belgium	W. Germany	New Zealand
Switzerland	Belgium	Belgium	New Zealand	Belgium	Switzerland		UK
USA	Japan	France	Australia	Netherlands	Australia		USA
Canada	New Zealand	Australia	France	Japan	Japan		
France	UK	Italy	UK	France	France		
UK	France	UK	Italy	UK	UK		
Italy	Italy	Canada	Japan	Italy	Italy		
	Australia	USA	Switzerland	USA	Canada		
	Canada		USA	Canada	USA		
	USA		Canada				

* Alphabetical order.

were produced by Tarantelli (1986), Blyth (1979), and also by Newell and Symons (1987) (not set out in Table 1.1). More recently, Dell'Aringa (1990) has made his own assessment.

Those authors who combined measures of centralization with those of the questionable concept of 'consensus' did so better to express their understanding of corporatism as a richer concept than centralization alone. MacCallum (1983) and Paloheimo (1984 and 1990) used a low level of strikes as their main indicator, though other authors had used this as one of the main indicators of stability that might be an output of an orderly industrial-relations system. Others again (Cameron, 1984; Lehner, 1988; Paloheimo, 1984) found their indicator of consensus in an absence of ideological conflict between governments and unions—meaning in effect participation in government by labour-movement parties, thus leaving the role of employers unresolved. Most of the literature in fact treated employers as non-problematic; it was assumed that they had no great problems in organizing should they choose to do so (Offe and Wiesenthal, 1980), and that they would favour the kind of stability that neo-corporatist arrangements could produce, even if their preference might be for purer market systems. (Marxist authors often argued that in the stage of late capitalism, employers preferred corporatist to market means of incorporating labour (e.g. Jessop, 1978).)

In much of the literature it becomes difficult to determine whether one is looking at a corporatist mechanism, or simply the success of social democracy in achieving a society in which workers secured sufficient social gains to make disruptive behaviour in the labour market less *necessary* for them. As noted earlier in this chapter, several authors took this view (Hibbs, 1978; Korpi and Shalev, 1979), some later contributions both covering a more recent historical period and investing the party–union relationship with a more sophisticated game-theoretical logic (Lange and Garrett, 1985).

Most of the explicitly corporatist studies were mainly concerned to discover to what extent the corporatism variable explained variations in performance. Calmfors and Driffill (1988) however followed the suggestion in Crouch (1985: 119) that corporatism's achievement might be to offset the potentially disruptive consequences of a highly organized labour market.

Using a simple index of centralization, they found a U-shaped relationship between this and economic performance as measured by inflation and unemployment levels in the years before and after the 1973 oil shock. In other words, while highly centralized systems performed well, so did those approximating more closely to a pluralist model of decentralized, competitive interest groups. The really poor performances came from those in a midway position, which might be defined as those too co-ordinated and perhaps politicized to be controlled by pluralist mechanisms, but not enough to be subordinate to corporatist discipline. Similar results are reported by Dell'Aringa (1990) and by Kendix and Olson (1990).

Soskice (1990) queries the finding of Calmfors and Driffill here by questioning their allocation of France, northern and central Italy, Japan, and Switzerland to the non-corporatist pole. He does this partly by substituting co-ordination for corporatism, which allows him to interpret the French state as a co-ordinating mechanism. As following chapters will show, he is on strong ground with Switzerland, and Dore (1990*b*) would agree with him on Japan. His point on France is, however, rather different, and the exceptionally strong performances of Japan and Switzerland suggest the possibility that their cases are explained by both a strong level of corporatism and weak unions.

This raises the question: do corporatist union movements do anything other than counteract the effect of their own organization (Crouch, 1985: 139)? That they do not is of course what Marxist writers have consistently argued (e.g. Jessop, 1978; Panitch, 1976). Castles (1987), however, adduces evidence to suggest that what they receive is a far lower level of unemployment and a higher level of social welfare spending—a finding implicit in a number of the other studies (e.g. Cameron, 1984; Crouch, 1985), strongly suggested in the work of Wilensky (1976), and demonstrated with some sophistication in Glyn (1991) and Wilensky and Turner (1987). This again confirms the link between neo-corporatism and social democracy. Most of these studies concentrated on inflation and unemployment measures around the period of the late 1960s to early 1980s, or in the case of those using industrial-conflict data as indicators of the output of an industrial-relations system, the years extending back to the 1950s. Some, primarily considering unemployment, were able to extend findings of the superior performance of corporatist countries into the mid-1980s (Lange and Garrett, 1985; Bean *et al.*, 1986; Lehner, 1987; McCallum, 1986; Newell and Symons, 1987; Schmidt, 1987).

However, as the Calmfors and Driffill (1988) study showed, in the 1980s it became increasingly difficult to perceive any superiority among the corporatist cases in inflation performance. These results, alongside a similar pattern for economic growth, have been confirmed by Dell'Aringa (1990). If anything, the highly corporatist countries (especially in Scandinavia) are performing relatively poorly among member countries of the OECD, though the countries with extensive corporatism but relatively weak labour movements (Switzerland, Germany, Japan) continue to perform best of all, while Austria, Norway, and Sweden continue to provide far lower levels of *unemployment* than all low-corporatism countries (Pekkarin *et al.*, 1992; Glyn, 1991). There are two potential explanations of this. First, as has been suggested by a number of authors, while corporatist systems may have been effective at the macro-economic crisis management of the 1970s, they have been less successful in the restructuring tasks of the 1980s, which have required action at the level of the firm, not the economy or branch, and which have implied change, rapid adjustment, and job losses. Against the strong logic of this argument stands the evidence from Streeck (1985) and others that neo-corporatist arrangements have been particularly important in giving workers and shop-level union representatives confidence that co-operation in restructuring can be risked without the threat of major unemployment. In addition, corporatist networks were important in sustaining training and other public goods aspects of restructuring during the difficult years of the early 1980s, though these arrangements do not always involve unions.

A second explanation may lie in the changing structure of employment. Crouch (1990*a*) has noted an association between the strength of industry-level unions in the exposed sector of the economy and the effectiveness of corporatist mechanisms. The reasoning is as follows: the Olsonian argument explains a general sensitivity among encompassing organizations to externalities; but there will be exceptional sensitivity among organizations who have little choice but to recognize the effect their actions may have on the ability of their industry to compete in international markets. Domestic political lobbying can do little to alleviate these constraints. This becomes a particularly important variable to consider when it is appreciated that the larger constituent organizations of an encompassing organization are not themselves encompassing across the whole economy, and, as Rasch and Sørensen (1986) argue (mathematically, though with some reference to Norway), may seek to commit the wider organization to the defence of their narrow interests, a point on which Olson (1986) readily agrees. But the ability of these bodies to behave in this way may depend crucially on whether they can resolve their own problems within the wider unit being embraced by the encompassing organization (usually a nation-state) or must face external competition which they cannot avoid.

In order to add this dimension to the theory it is useful to note that Olson's 'encompassingness' can exist at different levels, and should be defined in terms of the scope of the group concerned. An organization is encompassing to the extent that its reach, that is the membership over which it has effective authority, is coterminous with the population that will bear any adverse consequences of its actions. For example, if it is possible for the organization of labour to be confined to the level of the firm, that is to 'company unionism', then such a union will probably act in an encompassing way, avoiding action that may threaten the viability of the firm. This is highly relevant to a study of the behaviour of Japanese labour, and to many firms in the United States. Within western Europe it is relevant in some individual firms and, in a much amended way, to the operation of the dual-representation systems of Austria, Germany, and the Netherlands, or the particular form taken by a highly articulated decentralization in Switzerland.

Also compatible with this idea of alternative macro and micro 'horizons' for labour is the Calmfors and Driffill (1988) argument that optimal economic behaviour may be associated with either highly centralized or highly decentralized bargaining. For the most part European labour has effectively organized itself at the national level, but sectors have been important even in movements of the Scandinavian or Austrian type where bargaining is mainly carried out by confederations. An analysis distinguishing between the exposed and protected sectors of the economy was indeed developed originally in Norway in the 1960s (see Aukrust, 1977) and later incorporated within the model developed in Sweden by Edgren, Faxén, and Odhner (the so-called 'EFO' model) which for many years guided centralized negotiations between capital and labour in Scandinavia (see Edgren, Faxén, and Odhner, 1973; for a discussion of the practical application of these models in these and other countries, see Flanagan, Soskice, and Ulman, 1983).

The exposed sector in these models comprises firms producing goods and services traded in international markets. The protected sector includes central and local government, public utilities, railways, postal and telegraphic services, and also construction. It should be noted that it is not the ownership of public services that matters, but whether or not they are internationally traded under competitive conditions. These two sectors are seen as being vulnerable to very different sets of market pressure. If there are rising prices in world markets, wages in the competitive sector may rise in line with them and be followed by wages in the protected sector which are unable to be financed by rising world prices, leading to the importation of inflation. Alternatively, if wages rise in the protected sector and spread to the exposed sector in the absence of rising world prices, exposed-sector firms may be priced out of both export and home markets. Those responsible for national bargaining need to take account of the relationship between price levels in the two sectors when reaching collective agreements.

Following Olsonian logic, unions representing workers in these two sectors can be seen as being under very different degrees of compulsion to avoid externalizing the negative consequences of their economic disruption. Those in the exposed sector are likely to be more concerned with problems of international competitiveness than those in the protected, more concerned with economic indicators of likely patterns of demand in product markets, and less able to treat the consequences of their actions as something that can be absorbed within a general national development. This does not necessarily mean that wage demands will always be more moderate in the exposed sector; if world prices are rising more rapidly than domestic ones, unions in this sector may take the lead in making demands; the point is that, *ceteris paribus*, their actions will be more constrained by concern for product-market developments and will also be more concerned to ensure competitiveness in, for example, manning practices. Further, developments in one labour market influence those in others, and at least within centralized union confederations the behaviour of one union influences others. Differences in behaviour should therefore be evident between *national systems* with different union structures. To the extent that a trade-union movement is dominated by industrial unions in the export sector, 'foreign-trade-conscious behaviour' should characterize the movement as a whole.

It is important to be clear what is meant by 'unions in the exposed sector'. A union's total membership may lie within the sector, but they may represent only a small part of any individual industry within that sector, such that the union can always externalize the consequences of its bargaining to other sections of the work-force. This will be the case with many 'craft' unions; these are not encompassing unions within a sector. Alternatively, a union may have members across a wide number of industries, never constituting a large proportion of any given work-force despite the possibly large overall size of the union itself. Again, such a union can externalize, and moreover does not have its own fate bound to the future of any individual industry. General and white-collar unions come in this category. Our attention remains limited to industry-level unions.

Union movements dominated by exposed-sector, industry-type unions should therefore represent the type most capable of facilitating the actions of a centralized confederation trying to internalize national economic *desiderata*. The evidence, which will be discussed in more detail in later chapters, shows that exposed-sector unions have lost their dominance of European labour movements as changes in occupational structure and the strong unionization of public-service workers have become increasingly important, though there are exceptions in Germany, the Netherlands, and Switzerland where particularly large metal-industry or general-industry unions still dominate their confederations. These changes seem associated with the declining effectiveness of neo-corporatist arrangements in the Scandinavian countries in particular.

CONCLUSION

Looking back, the whole neo-corporatist debate has made a contribution at a number of different levels. For economic policy there has been a demonstration of some of the circumstances in which impure markets might lead to optimal outcomes. For industrial-relations theory there has been a model of action to add to the typology bequeathed by the Webbs (1897) of unilateral action, legal regulation and collective bargaining. For sociology there has been, with considerable assistance from economics, a contribution to theories of organizational behaviour and of class relations. For political science there has been a major extension to the theory of pluralism and the role of interest groups, as well as to theories of the state and the concept of state sovereignty.

More recently questions of a different kind have been raised. Researchers in the 1970s encountered neo-corporatist policies as responses to the inflationary crises of those years. Certainly for British researchers, there was a sequence: in (or at least near) the beginning was collective bargaining and pluralism; then came inflationary crisis and intensified industrial conflict; neo-corporatist strategy appeared as a rational state response to that. But when attention shifted to other countries it was notable that some—the Scandinavians, the Austrians, the Dutch, probably the Germans—had had such structures for several decades. What was the rational choice combination at their outset? And why did some countries seem to develop these structures far more richly than others?

Rational-choice and social-exchange theories could explain why and how, given certain environing conditions, actors would choose one path rather than another, but how do we explain the environing conditions? How do we indeed define them? The enduring nature of different societies' varied organizational characteristics makes the question an important one. Relevant here is a certain limitation of exchange theory when applied to complex structures and multiple actors. Even powerful leaders in such situations are very rarely able to make true strategic choices. There are usually many actors, and for a system to have an overall coherent character, something must have led them to act congruently (though not necessarily in agreement). Also, at any one time only a few elements in a situation can be determined or altered; the rest must be taken for granted. Finally, actors often have little idea of the likely consequences of their actions; their rationality is bounded by their knowledge, and knowledge of the behaviour of large-scale social structures is very limited.

Rational-choice theory has to operate within some theory of historical processes. Olson (1982) propounds one, but by staying very close to rational choice as such. He sees time as a source of repeated interactions, sees interactions changing in character as a result of massive repetition, and sees major exogenous events that break up organizational structures as sources of variation in the impact of time. But this is limited and sometimes leads him astray, most notably in his treatment of Germany and Japan (pp. 75–80). German and Japanese institutions were broken down, initially by their own dictators and then by their victorious enemies after 1945. For Olson this implies that they have weakly developed interest-group structures, which fact in turn accounts for their post-war economic success. But it is difficult to square this with accounts that demonstrate the extraordinary density and historical continuity of the organized economic interests, especially on the side of business, that those two countries continue to possess. We shall have ample opportunity to demonstrate this for Germany in subsequent chapters; for Japan see Dore (1990*b*). We need a theory of collective rational choice; but it must exist alongside an account of historical forces liable to favour particular choices and exchanges.

2

A Theory of Exchange in Industrial Relations Systems

Kooperation selbst [ist und bleibt] konfliktreich.
(Marin, 1983: 332, on co-operation in Austrian social partnership)

The first step in the systematic comparison of industrial-relations systems is the construction of a theoretical framework against which empirical systems can be described, analysed, and contrasted. The approach used here will be that of rational exchange or choice. The starting point of such theories is the concept of the 'pure' exchange, pure in the sense that every item in the exchange has a calculable value. It is important to be clear on the status of the priority accorded to this kind of calculation. It is not historical; there is no reason at all to believe that somehow precisely calibrated exchanges have some primeval quality. Neither are they 'natural' in the sense that Hayek (1973) considers pure market exchange to be—that is, the way people will behave unless they are 'unnaturally' interfered with. As Durkheim (1893) observed long ago in his debate with Herbert Spencer, to engage in a precise system of pure exchange requires a very sophisticated mechanism of shared values and means of enforcement.

The priority of pure exchange is not at all ontological but consists in its transparency solely *for the theorist*. It is the form of relationship most amenable to precise study. Its priority is therefore methodological. At the same time exchange in a more general sense is a very useful tool in social analysis: in any relationship (from love to hate) something is given and something taken. We can make progress by defining the field of exchange generally and by then locating different types of exchanges more precisely within that field. Figure 2.1 expresses such a definition diagrammatically. Social relationships between two actors are

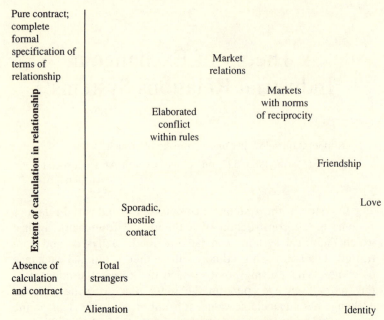

Source: Crouch 1990d: 70.

FIG. 2.1. Forms of variation in social exchange

here considered in terms of two variables. (The actors may be anything from human individuals to collectivities on the scale of nation-states or even larger.) First is the degree of separateness between the actors, rated on a scale ranging from alienation to identity. The limiting case at the former end will be total strangers who never actually meet and who therefore do not even establish relations of hostility. We then move through sporadic, hostile contact, through regular but rather formal contact, then increasingly friendly relations, until we meet the limiting case where the identity of the actors is so close that they are experienced as the same self. (The latter is unlikely outside poetry, as in the moment in Act II of *Tristan and Isolde* when he calls her Tristan and she him Isolde.)

The second variable is the extent to which the exchange possesses the specific, calculated qualities of contract, ranging from total absence of calculation to pure contract, that is to complete formal specification of the terms of the relationship. The location of a relationship on the vertical axis will be determined by the extent to which the actors make explicit arrangements in order to conduct the relationship. At the high extreme is the clearly specified bargain, either a straight equivalent swap or a precisely calibrated price, in major transactions accompanied by detailed formal documentation to provide guarantees of performance and redress in the case of non-compliance. For even small transactions there is in most societies a complex structure of law to support contract exchanges—the law of contract in the English legal system. At the bottom of the vertical axis these characteristics are absent: there are no guarantees of equivalence, no calibration, no documents, probably not even a legal basis.

We can hypothesize that, should two actors begin to move to the right along the horizontal axis away from alienation, the degree of contract in their relationship will first rise and then again decline. This is because relations between strangers are characterized by extreme mistrust: if I offer you something, how do I know you will reciprocate? I shall offer only if there is a prospect of an immediate equivalent return. The most primitive form of trade is of course barter, where there is not even enough trust to accept money tokens as exchange. If the parties come to deal with each other regularly, they may develop enough mutual confidence to articulate rules of exchange that make possible more complex transactions. This is the development of contract that takes us to the apex of the curve. If alienation is transcended further still, real 'trust' may be established; repeated interaction reveals the partner to be reliable, and both have a mutual interest in maintaining the relationship. In this case, the formal specification and precise calculation of pure contract gradually becomes otiose. On the left-hand side of the curve pure contract is impossible for the parties; on the right it is unnecessary.

Human relations will therefore tend to follow the curve implicit in Fig. 2.1, with the degree of pure contract in a relationship being maximized at a certain 'middle range'. Mortal enemies cannot make contracts; lovers do not need them; salesmen have little else. Love and hate, as emotional states, occupy similar positions of low degree of contract, but of course strongly contrasted positions on alienation/identity. Pure markets, often seen as the archetypical forms of exchange, can be seen as occupying a rather limited space on the total exchange map. They are extremely high on the contract scale, but come midway on an alienation/identity ranking. The position of a particular relationship on the curve can change dramatically. An intimate relationship may collapse back into alienation, with a period of elaborate contract facilitating the move. This is most commonly seen in divorce. It is also possible for movement between extreme states to be so rapid that there is no intermediate contract stage.

Changes may be wrought by moves on either axis: an increase in identity will reduce the need for exchange specificity because identity necessarily implies trust. To the extent that I know your interests are identical to mine, I can trust that your attempts to maximize your own interests will also maximize mine. This is of course open to enormous abuse. History is full of examples of people using claims to shared identity to win a trust that they then proceed to betray; from the confidence trickster who wields symbols of identity and respectability to the war leader who makes cynical use of patriotism—hence the rationale for Dr Johnson's often-quoted remark about patriotism being the last refuge of the scoundrel. If one has no viable personal claim to plausibility but wishes to gain and then betray the trust of large numbers of people, there are few more potent appeals than patriotism in a society where nationhood is a major source of general identity.

But, despite so much evidence to the contrary, human beings persist in according trust on the basis of claimed shared identities because it has an underlying logic: the reason I cannot trust you is that you are not me and therefore may have conflicting interests; however, the more you display characteristics that resemble my own in relevant respects, the more that gap can be narrowed. Appreciation of this logic is the key to an understanding of hostility between ethnic groups (Banton, 1983). Closer to the theme of the present study, Fox's (1974) great study of the role of trust in industrial relations points out the frequently ambiguous use of the expression 'trust me' precisely in contexts where a factual basis for trust is missing. What is really happening here is that the people being appealed to (say workers being called upon to trust their employer) are being asked to demonstrate their capacity for what is seen as a desirable human quality (a willingness to trust), in the absence of a genuine claim to trustworthiness by the person making the appeal.

Alternatively, the mere frequency of interactions can produce a reduced need for contract because trust can be built up on the basis of experience—assuming of course that there is no betrayal. Also, as the number of interactions intensifies, it ceases to be worthwhile weighing each exchange. One may be willing to take losses one day because there will be a chance of gains another day. Hoping to gain back on the roundabouts what one has lost on the swings makes increasing sense the longer one intends to stay at the fair—provided past experience has suggested that it is a fair fair. Further, as this process proceeds one becomes less likely to withdraw from the relationship, as one has unrealized 'investments' therein that would thereby be sacrificed. After a time the relationship may itself become a source of shared identity and perceived as a good in itself.

All this is independent of the relative *power* of the actors. This can be defined in terms of their ability to exit, to find alternatives to the relationship, though if shared identity has developed, loyalty may inhibit this (Hirschman, 1970). But in general changes in the power relationship can be quite exogenous to the model. They may well result in great shocks to the system, but they are a separate dimension.

As in Parsonian theory, this model can be applied to different levels of aggregation of social actors. For sociology, the lowest level is the single human individual. From there we proceed up through groups of increasing scale and complexity until ultimately we reach humanity in general as the highest level, though this is not an actor that normally engages in social relationships with others. Identification of the intermediate levels at which most social interaction takes place will be determined empirically by the substantive area being considered. The actors at successively higher levels are of course comprised of units that might themselves be actors in social relationships at lower levels. One major source of complexity in social relations is that actors may stand in different relationships with each other on the alienation and contract dimensions at different levels. To take an example from industrial relations: individual workers may be in a fairly high-trust near-identity relationship with their individual managers, but both may be part of unions and employers' organizations which are engaged in low-trust bargaining at every step—or, of course, *vice versa*. A related problem is that the relevant level of action might change as groups and organizations form and fragment.

EXCHANGE IN INDUSTRIAL RELATIONS

Such a model can be applied to many areas of human interaction, but I want here to limit it to the place of labour within the politics of industrial relations. These relations are capable of occupying a wide range of spaces on our map of exchanges: from states of alienation so extreme as to include the physical liquidation of opponents to degrees of identity so close that one can hardly talk of industrial relations at all. The levels covered range from individual workers, managers, and employers to national-level labour movements and employers' organizations. There is also an international level of interaction. In practice this last is of growing importance but unfortunately, for reasons of length and complexity, it has to be omitted from the present study.

My starting point is the problem central to relations between employees and employers under any economic system that separates those who perform work from those who control its performance. On the one hand the employers need pure contract in their relations with labour, so that effort and its reward can be bound closely together; but they also want workers to co-operate like willing partners. For their part, workers do not want to give any more than they are being paid for, but also want to be treated like reasonable human beings. The issue has received illuminating treatment in a number of texts (e.g. Bendix, 1956; Baldamus, 1961; Offe, 1970; Fox, 1974; F. Hirsch, 1977). As a question of individual relations, this is an important theme in industrial sociology. Somewhat different issues are raised when we consider relations between organizations of employees and employers (the latter including large firms). Interpersonal relations may still be important, as in the many recorded cases of employers and trade-union leaders seeking a personal *rapprochement* to help resolve their organizational conflicts. Our concern here however is with the superpersonal and organizational. What is the range of possible relationships between such entities? In particular, are there circumstances under which they move clockwise through the arc in Fig. 2.1, past pure contract and towards zones normally limited to relations between individuals?

The only collective relations usually seen as embodying a high level of identity and a relative absence of calculated exchange are those described as community, but it is only by an abuse of that term that it can be applied to relations between industrial-relations bureaucracies. Streeck and Schmitter (1985) have proposed treating 'association' as a form of social order differing from both market and community (and also from the state, which raises slightly different questions). The difference between the relationships produced by community and those by association is that between mechanical and organic solidarity identified long ago by Durkheim (1893). Community rests on similarity and shared experience. Associations can approximate the solidarity of 'community' only through close interdependence, by entering into so many exchanges with each other that they cease to calculate each one and begin to trade demands and concessions across a lengthy time horizon. This considerably reduces their incentive ever to leave the relationship. The organizations become engaged in a rapidly multiplying network, in which they keep seeking out new areas for transactions, so that they might increase further their scope for trading concessions. They acquire a commitment to the relationship itself; it becomes part of their identity, and some movement is made from alienation to identity, not so much towards *alter* as towards the relationship itself or the institutional context within which *ego* and *alter* are both defined.

The model does not cease to be one of exchanges, nor is the question of alienation transcended. The partners remain aware of separate interests; they are trying to maximize those of their 'side', and they may engage in open conflict from time to time. It is essential not to mistake this model of action for the claim that 'everyone is on the same side really', or what Fox (1966) called a 'unitary' model of industrial relations. It does however also differ sharply from bargaining in a purely contractual sense.

For most people's working lives these matters are all contained at the level of the firm, with them as individual employees facing their employer's representatives. Many factors discourage the formation of workers' collective organizations. There are the problems of organizing collective action (Olson, 1965) and the fact that life is often tolerable enough without it; in many other cases either the employer or the state prevents, or at least makes very difficult, any attempt to do anything about it; or either employer or state may provide a system of collective representation controlled by itself. However, despite these various obstacles, it is a matter of historical fact that in many countries the phenomenon of autonomous representation of employed persons through organizations transcending the individual firm has occurred and become a matter of economic and political importance. Workers have found this escape from domination by the firm and its identity helpful in maintaining their personal sense of identity and bringing new power resources to bear on their employment contract.

In many cases the logic of collective organization has ended at that point, but very often workers have gone on to find that such organizations, having been constructed, can be used to bring other, more general resources to bear to help them be more powerful. Labour organizations have fought for the extension of the suffrage, for changes in the law affecting employment, for certain kinds of economic and social policy. In other words, employment relations have acquired a public, political dimension. In most countries only a minority of the working population has been part of such structures, and many workers only passively so, but influence of such organizations has extended beyond the scope of the membership as such.

It would be possible to make a study of trust and exchange in work relations across the whole gamut from the individual to the international. But I already wish to range over time and across countries, and the study must have some limits. I am therefore concerned solely with what happens when work relations result in the formation of autonomous employee organizations that reach the *public* domain. This is because my interest is in the ways in which different political practices have interacted, between countries and over time, with the underlying abstract dynamic of exchange and trust to produce industrial-relations systems as we know them. But one must always remember the continuing existence of the other levels. What if, for reasons nothing to do with these variables, employers in a particular country have a means of relating to workers in individual firms so that they approach the contract relationship in a particular way? I do not mean phenomena like Japanese company unionism, because that is a general system characteristic that would be picked up by any analysis at the level of national systems. I mean a series of *ad hoc* company responses, unrelated to national specificities, that just happen to accumulate. Their impact is beyond the scope of my analysis. Our central concern is a process of publicly oriented behaviour emerging from the work encounter and interacting with the various more formally political arrangements of society. It is from that encounter that industrial-relations systems develop.

A FORMAL MODEL

Our starting point is the relationship between two actors in a capitalist economy—organized labour (L) and (organized) capital (C), which is a subset of the wider relationship between labour and capital. The parenthesis around 'organized' in the case of capital indicates that capital may appear as an individual firm, not necessarily as a group or association of firms, while labour is always collectively organized, at least informally, if it is taking part in an exchange going beyond the simple wage-effort bargain that binds individual employees to their jobs. This reflects part of the fundamental imbalance between capital and labour, in that capital automatically possesses power by virtue of its role in the employment relationship, while labour does so only if it organizes. (For a fuller account of this inequality, see Offe and Wiesenthal, 1980; and Crouch, 1982*b*: ch. 2.) The question of the levels at which C and L operate will be left indeterminate until a later stage. This has considerable advantages in enabling us to build up the relationship from its simplest components.

Contestation

For theoretical purposes L and C initially encounter each other as strangers, though in practice there will be considerable inter-ference with this situation from carry-overs from the individual work relations in which the structure is rooted. They are there-fore alienated, their relationship is unformed, interaction is likely to be thin on the ground and to take the form of conflict. Issues enter the relationship because one side (usually labour) is dissatisfied. The simplest form of relation between L and C is therefore a zero-sum game, i.e. a change to the benefit of one party can be achieved only through a concomitant change to the disadvantage of the other:

$$\Delta c + \Delta l = 0 \qquad (1)$$

where c, l = shares of C and L respectively. When industrial relations take this form we can speak of contestation. Neither party can be expected voluntarily to concede such gains to the other. C may be able to achieve improvements to its share under such a system because of its position of authority in the general capital–labour relationship, but L will be able to pursue its interests against C only by waging conflict that imposes costs on C greater than the costs C would incur by making concessions to L. That is, L will secure an improvement in its share only when:

$$b_c > \Delta l \qquad (2)$$

where b_c = the cost imposed on C by conflict, and where it is assumed that Δl represents an improvement in L's position that L regards as worth having. Most conflicts will impose costs on both parties, such that $b = b_c + b_l$, where b = total conflict costs, but so long as L has some expectation that $b_l < \Delta l$, it will find the conflict worthwhile.

The implication of this is that cases of contestation are in fact *negative* sum games: the costs of conflict impose a net loss on the aggregate share of the two parties, whatever happens to any individual party:

$$\Delta c + \Delta l = 0 - (b_c + b_l) \qquad (3)$$

The more frequently the two interact, the greater the range of issues covered in their interactions; and the more important those issues, the greater become these losses from conflict:

$$\Delta c + \Delta l = 0 - (b_c + b_l)n \qquad (4)$$

where n = the density of interactions between the parties, 'density of interactions' being a compound expression denoting frequency, extent, and importance of interaction.

This might imply that, despite the zero-sum nature of the substantive distributive relationship, the two parties share an interest in reducing conflict costs. However, there are several reasons why such an interest may not be realized. First, either C or L might believe that in the long run it will succeed in getting more concessions and a lower share of conflict costs than the opponent. Second, even if this is not the case, either (though in practice probably only C) may believe that in the long run such heavy costs will be imposed on the other by conflict that the other will lose the capacity to struggle, and that therefore it is worth tolerating heavy conflict costs on its own side while awaiting that outcome. Third, by the same token one side might believe that an overall reduction in conflict costs will only help the other side maintain a capacity for conflict that it could not otherwise afford. Where at least one side acts on at least one of these three assumptions, there will be no co-operation in a mutual reduction of conflict costs, though of course each side will try constantly to reduce its own share of these costs. Every conflict will have to be fought right through until one side acknowledges defeat; this is pure contestation. It also follows that, interactions being mainly conflictual, both sides will adopt a general strategy of avoiding each other as much as possible; they remain united in their preference for mutual alienation and have no wish to encourage intimacy.

The reason that employers are more likely than organized labour to pursue a strategy of maximizing conflict is that it is quite realistic for them to envisage a world without trade unions. Labour can envisage a world without employers only if it maintains a belief that a radically transformed social order is possible. This probably explains why labour movements in conditions of extreme alienation are attracted to doctrines like Marxism and syndicalism. Records of industrial relations in France from the late nineteenth until the late twentieth century are replete with examples of this combination of characteristics: highly limited interaction; an important presence of revolutionary doctrines; and bargaining that takes a tacit form, aimed at achieving temporary truces rather than anything constructive (see Perrot, 1974b: 426; Shorter and Tilly, 1974). However, even in these cases conflict is unlikely to be entirely unrestrained. In reality few conflicts are truly unrestrained, even wars, as Simmel long ago noted (see Coser, 1956). (Simmel's point is that even warfare implies a degree of interaction and certain interdependencies, for example, over the treatment of prisoners. Interactions of this kind mark a primitive form of contract.)

If, say, L is using pressure to secure a wage increase, then it must be willing to accept temporary truces and resumptions of normal working. Within an individual dispute, L will expect C to concede at the point where C's losses through continuing conflict become greater than the cost of making a concession to L adequate to stop the conflict, that is $b_c > \Delta l$. It does not make sense for L to continue the struggle beyond the point where C has made its maximum concession, because on those terms C will never concede; C might as well save the cost of the concessions if it must bear a conflict cost irrespective of whether it makes them or not. This is obvious, but in real life it is often far from obvious when maximum concession points have been reached. Workers' representatives have to make a judgement about this as best they can, and there will often be disagreement among them and between them and their members. The negotiators will be able to make deals with employers only if they can undertake to call off conflicts at points where they judge maximum concessions to have been reached. This implies a modicum of *discipline* within the workforce. Even under contestation there will therefore be occasions when workers' representatives act in the manner normally associated with corporatism, urging their members to go back to work or cease some kind of disruption. However, this is of the most minimal kind.

In general, the amount of discipline that representatives need over their members to end a conflict depends on the relationship between the different estimates made by the workers and by their representatives respectively of the likely outcome of prolonging the conflict. If these estimates are identical, they will agree when to end the struggle and the matter is simple:

$$\Delta l_e - b_e = \Delta l_r - b_r \qquad (5)$$

where subscripts $_e$ and $_r$ indicate the expectations of outcomes held by workers and their representatives respectively. But several factors may lead to these expectations differing. We shall deal here with just one of them: the more that the role of representatives differs from that of ordinary workers, the more likely it is that their expectations will differ. For example, if the representatives are simply fellow-workers who from time to time are called upon to act as spokesmen, we might expect the gap to be smaller than if they are specialized, full-time union officers.

Therefore, *ceteris paribus*, the difference between the expectations of workers and their representatives is given by:

$$\Delta l_e - b_e = (\Delta l_r - b_r)x \qquad (6)$$

where x = some function of the difference in experience of representatives.

If the workers are more optimistic than their representatives concerning the outcome, the latter will be able to secure an end to conflict only by the imposition of a degree of discipline (the content of which we shall discuss in due course) sufficient to bridge the gap between their respective expectations:

$$\text{where } (\Delta l_e - b_e) > (\Delta l_r - b_r), \quad \Delta l_e - b_e = (\Delta l_r - b_r) + d$$
$$(7)$$

where d = discipline. (If members are more pessimistic about chances of success in conflict than their representatives, (7) of course reads:

$$\text{where } (\Delta l_e - b_e) < (\Delta l_r - b_r), \quad \Delta l_e - b_e = (\Delta l_r - b_r) - d$$

That is, conflict will be ended by workers *breaking* union discipline—which will be trying to maintain the conflict—and ending the dispute.) Since under contestation, there is little specialized role for representatives (that is, x is low), then *ceteris paribus* there is little difference between their expectations and those of the workers and there is therefore only a very small role for discipline.

Pluralist Bargaining

Let us now assume that for some exogenous reason the density of interactions rises. This could be the result of simple accumulation over time, or of an increase in the power of labour that enables it to make more demands or express more grievances than before, or of a multiplication of levels or points of interaction. In such a situation both capital and labour are likely to decide that, in the long run, they would stand to gain from a reduction in conflict. For employers this might still lead to the conclusion that they should therefore smash organized labour once and for all; for workers this remains less feasible, still implying revolutionary action, and may appear increasingly unattractive compared with the gains flowing from increased interaction). It is important to bear this employer option in mind. Puzzling lurches in employer strategy from conciliation to ruthlessness can sometimes be observed; these may be very logical. In both cases the goal is peace in the workplace; but at times the easiest route to that end lies in crushing workers' organizations, and at others in coming to terms with them by developing institutions and structures for negotiation. But in the long run a choice between these strategies has to emerge and become dominant, as each undermines the conditions for the other. Changes then become likely only along-side major shifts in environing conditions (such as the rise or fall of democratic or dictatorial rule in the general polity).

The beginning of the alternative to crushing as an employer strategy is the development of procedures for conducting conflicts with labour in such a way that mutually damaging action is avoided: for example, the development of rules for deciding how disputed matters should be resolved, and having recourse to conciliation and arbitration services. The agreement to set up procedures constitutes a growth in contract, and the functions of the institutions established is always to frame contracts for the parties, whether through facilitating bargaining between them or with third-party help. For each side these procedures constitute restraints on their own freedom of action, but they accept these because of the mutuality of the arrangement. The function of the procedural restraints is to reduce conflict costs, such that the conflict relation summarized in (4) may now be expressed as:

$$\Delta c + \Delta l = (b_c + b_l) - (p_c + p_l)n \qquad (8)$$

where p_c and p_l are the procedural restraints adopted by C and L respectively. It will be seen that this arrangement does not diminish the zero-sum conflict at the heart of the relationship, but merely reduces the negative sum imposed on the parties by the need to resort to open conflict to resolve their disputes.

There will not necessarily be less aggregate conflict than under contestation; that will depend on the size of b_c and b_l, and on the capacity of the parties to enter into conflict. C may be unwilling to develop procedures because L's capacity to engage in conflict is too low to make the exercise worthwhile; this will lead to an enduring contestation model, though with actual outbreaks of conflict probably being only sporadic. But, for a given level of b_c, b_l, conflict will be lower under pluralist bargaining than under contestation.

Procedures not only enable conflicts to be played out *in parvo*. Some operate by insulating conflicts from one another, by preventing an aggregation of disputes into major cleavages. Particularly important in the history of modern capitalism has been the containment of industrial conflict so that it does not spill over into the political realm. This was a dominant theme in the literature on the institutionalization of conflict (Dahrendorf, 1959; Harbison, 1954). Similarly, theories of pluralist politics (e.g. Dahl, 1961) stressed that in such polities no one group of actors is able to become involved in a large range of issues, and that most of the time most issues are not in play (see also the general statement of the pluralist theory of industrial relations in Clegg, 1975).

There is therefore an interesting distinction among the procedures which help to make pluralism. Some, those we have called p, bind the parties together through a procedural positive-sum game; others separate the parties from each other by disaggregating their interactions over substantive matters. In other words, these latter operate by reducing the density of interactions (n) which, as we saw above, increase conflict losses. We can therefore improve (8) by writing it as:

$$\Delta c + \Delta l = 0 - (b - p)\frac{n}{s} \qquad (9)$$

where s = devices for insulating conflict, and simplifying the specification of b and p for ease of reading.

This is paradoxical. Increased interaction begins to overcome alienation but increases the risk of conflict through increasing points of contact. Fear at the implications of this leads to the deliberate erection of blocks to intensified contact. This helps explain the opposition of many moderate union leaders to worker participation, as when the post-1945 generation of United States' union leaders, known for their anti-Marxism, warned their German counterparts of the dangers of becoming too close to employers through *Mitbestimmung*.

We now have a full statement of a pluralist relationship between C and L. It is a system that requires more from representatives than does contestation. The actors in procedures are representatives alone, and procedures work only if the representatives are able to convince their members that their experience of these serves as a better guide to the balance of power than any attempt by the members to play the matter out for themselves in 'real' conflict. As this divergence in experience develops, so, in terms of (7), more discipline is required if the representatives are to be able to deliver consent. This requires a higher level of aggregation and organization than the sporadic stuff of contestation. But it must not be *too* highly aggregated, as that would threaten institutionalization by bringing too many issues together, and also by threatening to raise the general, public—and therefore political—implications of what is going on. We thus find that the main theoretical model of pluralist industrial relations (that of Dunlop (1958)) insists on a rather fragmented structure of competing labour organizations, and explicitly rejects centralized organizations as incompatible with pluralism (Crouch, 1990*b*).

Within such a structure relations become less sporadic, more continuous, and contracts become richer in content, though individual bargains are still discrete exercises. A major motive in the construction of procedures is acceptance of the long-term nature of the relationship; neither side seeks to eliminate the other as a conflict force. This means that during each bargaining round each side is aware of the probability of future rounds and may therefore convey signals which it hopes will affect the behaviour of the opponent in the future. These signals may be negative; that is, they may try to stress how little will be available for concessions in the future. But they may be positive: one side may attempt to provide small, apparently gratuitous gains to the opponent; these are designed to act as *douceurs*, creating good-will that may moderate the behaviour of the opponent in the next bargaining round. Within pluralism, therefore, we have the nascent development of minor substantive positive-sum exchanges, often facilitated by intertemporal bargaining.

Bargained Corporatism

If there is scope for positive-sum games, why do not all partici-pants always introduce them on a large scale, until they dwarf the negative nature of zero-sum bargaining? This is what the wider public often asks of the two sides in industrial relations. There are in fact several good reasons for the reluctance. First, there may be a limited supply of such issues. We must remember that the C–L relationship is that subset of all capital–labour relations that has been subjected to negotiation between organized actors, usually because a union has raised questions as issues. Unions will rarely bother to raise non-contentious matters. For its part, capital will rarely want of its own accord to place them within the negotiating relationship; if it can unilaterally allocate positive-sum advances between itself and its work-force, why should it share the credit by enabling a union to be seen to have helped secure these gains? Also, even if both sides stand to gain from a development, there may still be conflict about the division of the spoils. Again, management may prefer to forgo the chance to negotiate the positive-sum issue in order to protect its ability to determine the relative shares of any mutual gains which it is unilaterally able to secure.

Second, and especially for the workers' side, there is consider-able difficulty in determining whether an issue really is a joint one. If a false identification is made, and a zero-sum issue is treated as positive-sum, unions run the risk of failing to defend their members' particular interests. Given this dilemma of lack of knowledge, workers' representatives often respond by treating all issues as zero-sum games, regarding any positive-sum gains as windfalls, implying nothing for long-term relations. British shop stewards may often be heard to remark that, since they never really know what management is up to, they play safe by follow-ing the rule, 'if the bosses are for it, we must be against it'. Managers less often have this dilemma, as they normally possess better knowledge; but if they feel uncertain about the likely outcome of situations, they may also follow a policy of restricting negotiations to matters of win-or-lose.

Third, it should not be assumed that the pursuit of joint interests will proceed 'innocently'. Once labour, in particular, has accepted a specific goal as common, capital may try to induce it to believe that its pursuit of other, conflictual goals nullifies or at least jeopardizes the chances of achieving the joint goal. (This is so obvious a tactic that employers almost routinely use it.) However, there will be circumstances where the two sides start to grapple with these problems and try to play their conflicts in the context of the pursuit of certain joint interests. They then begin to depart from a pluralist system towards that which we call neo-corporatism or bargained corporatism.

To explore this we need to consider more precisely what is involved in positive-sum bargaining. Except in the most trivial cases, the pursuit of joint interests is not painless. We must assume that, if the two sides could achieve something together from which they would both gain without costs, they would do it immediately, and the issue would not remain on the agenda long enough to become involved in complex interactions. More often, positive-sum bargaining starts with one side (say C) saying to the other, 'If you accept sacrifice k_l, you will attain gain g_l, which will be greater than k_l; and I shall gain g_c.' L will probably refuse this until it can negotiate a considerable reduction in g_c, because C is asking to share the gain without making any sacrifice. The issue is thus likely to include many elements of a zero-sum conflict after all. It is therefore more likely that C's offer will take the form: 'If you incur sacrifice k_l and I incur sacrifice k_c, you will attain gain g_l, and I shall attain gain g_c, both g_l and g_c being greater than k_l and k_c respectively.' Alternatively, it may be L that proposes k_c to C. The balance of g and k values on each side now being fairly incommensurable, it is more likely that an agreement will be reached, such that:

$$(g_c - k_c) > 0; (g_l - k_l) > 0 \qquad (10)$$

A typical example might be: C offers to share strategic decision-making (k_c) with L if L will agree to a change in manning practices (k_l); from this L will gain better wages for its members because of improved efficiency plus the chance to share in strategic decision-making (g_l); C will gain from increased profits following the change in manning practices (g_c). It should be noted that such an exchange by no means excludes conflict. Either party may become resentful that somehow the other side always seems to achieve a better balance of g and k. However, they are both unlikely to take their dissatisfaction to the point of relinquishing the entire g, k exchange so long as they continue to gain from it more than they could reasonably expect to gain in its absence.

Often, although both sides gain more from prolonging an arrangement than from breaking it, the gains are unequally shared. This may eventually strain the tolerance of the weaker party, although it remains in its interest to try to renegotiate the arrangement rather than to wreck it. An important example was the way in which the Swedish unions' solidaristic wage policy benefited capital. From the mid-1970s the unions developed their policy of wage-earner funds as an attempt to change the terms of the relationship *within* the general framework of Swedish incomes and industrial-relations policies (A. Martin, 1979).

Matters are made more complex by the fact that typically the parties are asked for sacrifices now in exchange for gains in the future. In estimating their g, k balance they must therefore discount the gains by a factor representing the risk that they will not be achieved. Looking at it from L's point of view, the deal is worth while only if:

$$(qg_l - k_l) > 0 \qquad (11)$$

where q = the probability that the gains will be achieved. The total gains available to L under these conditions are, at first sight, a sum of the gains from pursuing common interests plus the fruits of continuing pursuit of conflict:

$$\Delta l = ((g_l - k_l) + (z_l - (b_l - p_l)))\frac{n}{s} \qquad (12)$$

where z_l = L's gain from conflict.

But we must now recall that often the k_l being demanded is the forgoing of a zero-sum demand. In a case of that kind, L is confronted with a choice: continued pursuit of conflict demands (z_l) will reduce its co-operative gains (g_l), in the extreme case to nothing. Where $k_l = fz_l$ we can rewrite (12) as:

$$\Delta l = ((g_l - fz_l) + (z_l - (b_l - p_l)))\frac{n}{s} \qquad (13)$$

where f = the factor by which pursuit of conflict goals destroys the achievement of joint goals. Therefore, L's position as it contemplates becoming involved in this kind of bargaining contains the following unattractive elements: to achieve the newly attainable goals it must give up some zero-sum goals, from which C will clearly gain; and the identity of an issue as zero-sum or joint will often be obscure and subject to manipulation by C. We must now add to these problems the relationship between L as representative and its membership.

Statement (7) gave us the role played by organizational discipline if representatives were to persuade their members to accept their version of the point at which conflict should be ended in the minimal case of representation under contestation. In the kind of bargaining we are now considering, the representatives are usually asking their members to accept an immediate and therefore *known* sacrifice in exchange for the representatives' *estimate* of the gains that will come in exchange. The members have to make their own estimate of the quality of the representatives' estimate, without having been involved themselves in the negotiations:

$$(q_e g_l - k_l) = (q_r g_l - k_l) + d \tag{14}$$

Given that the members are making an estimate of the credibility of the representatives' own estimate of g, it is probable that q_e will be lower than q_r, placing an increased strain on d. To anticipate some later arguments, this problem is lessened if the gap between members' and representatives' perceptions is reduced by the involvement of members of the latter in negotiating, conciliating, administration, and other industrial-relations activity.

One might conclude that, in the light of all these points, unions would be well advised to stay clear of all entanglements with positive-sum issues and stick to conflict, even if that means the sacrifice of some indefinable positive-sum gains. Such, for example, was the majority view of the British Trades Union Congress in 1977 when it rejected the proposals of the Bullock Committee for a system of worker-directors. Many unionists saw a great risk of the worker-directors being lured by management into discussing probably bogus mutual interests to the point where they discouraged fellow-workers from pursuing conflict issues (for a discussion, see Elliott, 1978).

However, in some situations exogenous factors may give actors, whether L or C, little choice over their willingness to venture out from either simple zero-sum bargaining or contained, institutionalized exchanges. For example, L's power may increase to a point where an increasing number of issues enters the relationship, making it impossible to contain it within the non-public realm of collective bargaining. Alternatively, either C or L, or both, may have organizational capacities at a general level that automatically render their actions a matter of public concern (such as an employers' organization capable of bargaining solidarily across a whole nation or major sector of the economy). In such situations, n is likely to be high and s low.

We need to consider four main possibilities, as shown in Fig. 2.2. We have two variables: the power of L, expressed as some measure of its ability to secure concessions from C; and the level of organizational articulation of both C and L. By organizational articulation is meant the capacity of C or L to act strategically, with central leaderships able to commit memberships to a course of action (high d in terms of the current discussion). The asymmetry (considering only L for one variable but both for the other) is justified. It is only when L acquires power that industrial-relations situations become interesting; and, as later chapters will show, organizational capacities on both sides are usually similar.

In case I, with L weak and both sides lacking strategic capacity, pluralist bargaining (or even contestation) is likely to be preferred and to be unproblematic. Under II (L strong but both sides

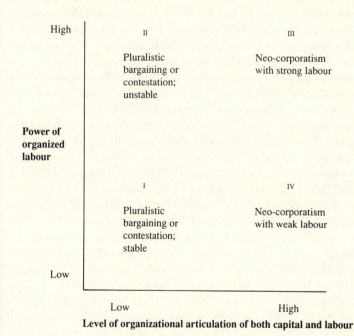

High

II

Pluralistic
bargaining or
contestation;
unstable

III

Neo-corporatism
with strong labour

**Power of
organized
labour**

I

Pluralistic
bargaining or
contestation;
stable

IV

Neo-corporatism
with weak labour

Low

Low   High

Level of organizational articulation of both capital and labour

FIG. 2.2. *Varieties of industrial-relations system*

lacking strategic capacity) relations are likely to become unstable. C will attempt to produce positive-sum exchanges to reduce L's tendency to use its strength to threaten conflict, but there will be constant difficulties in persuading workers to accept this unless clear short-term gains are made available to compensate for the lack of *d*. Unless the economy is flourishing there will be inflation or inefficiency. Under III (L strong and both sides possessing strategic capacity) the necessary conditions exist for sustaining a positive-sum system. Although labour is powerful, both sides have the structural capacity necessary for high levels of *d*. We have here the conditions for neo-corporatism described in Chapter 1. Case IV (L weak but both sides possessing strategic capacity) is odd; how does L come to possess a well-structured organization while remaining weak? Assuming however that it is possible—and subsequent chapters will show that it is—and that C bothers to work with L under such circumstances, the chances of success for a positive-sum system are actually greater than under the more obvious case of III. There is less risk of shop-floor rebellion as labour is in fact being accorded a position and status in excess of its real power capacity. Indeed, the main threat to the viability of the model comes from C simply not bothering with it any more and preferring to risk occasional conflict.

Cases II, III, and IV all produce action having the *appearance* of bargained corporatism, but while III and IV are viable, II is not, as it is constantly threatened with internal collapse.

If we can assume that the neo-corporatist dynamic is attempted, the pursuit of mutual interests does present opportunities for mutual gain. In what ways can, say, L reduce the risks and difficulties of trying to realize them? The main basic problems are an inability to trust C, inadequacy of information available to judge the character of an issue, and the contingent, future nature of gains in comparison with present sacrifices. L can try to reduce these, (*a*) by extending its share of control over aspects of its exchange with C, (*b*) by similarly extending its access to relevant information, and (*c*) by developing a dense network of exchanges with C so that both sides become caught in a continuous flow of contacts. This last is particularly important in reducing the imbalance of timing between sacrifice and gains. There is no need to put all weight on one big exchange, and at any one moment each side is receiving gains from past commitments as well as making and receiving further present and future commitments. Each side acquires a vested interest in demonstrating its own trustworthiness because it stands to gain from the continuation of the relationship.

All this leads in a common direction: a dense multiplication of the links binding C and L, an extension of the new issues which they try jointly to regulate, or about which they at least share available knowledge. This of course threatens an important element of pluralist bargaining summarized in (9), in which conflict was limited by insulation devices, s, which limit the number, extent, and importance of interactions between C and L. Bargained corporatism is therefore risky: if the zero-sum issues after all prove more important, the conflict will be intense. The inner dynamic of industrial relations under bargained corporatism can therefore be summarized as follows: in order to realize common interests, the parties are constrained to restrict their pursuit of zero-sum gains and also to expand the scope of their interactions. The equivalent of (9) for bargained corporatism is thus:

$$\Delta c + \Delta l = ((\cdot g - (fz_c, fz_l)) - (b - p))\frac{n}{s} \qquad (15)$$

In addition, as we have seen, particular strain is placed on the relationship between representatives and members.

Such a system is not assured of success. It remains possible for the net gains expected from conflict by either party to become greater than those from pursuit of the joint aims, making it rational for them to break loose from the strains towards conflict avoidance that the above implies—with concomitant risks of major conflict because of the inbuilt weakness of insulation devices. And in practice it remains impossible to resolve all problems of mistrust and of the correct identification of zero- and positive-sum issues.

However, once such a system becomes established, it contains certain self-reinforcing elements. The dense nature of the web of exchanges eventually enables commitments to be traded over time in the complex way anticipated above in general discussion of the implications of repeated interactions. Even zero-sum matters may acquire the appearance of positive-sum ones as concessions made at one point may be regarded as credits available to be 'cashed' at a future date, confidence in adopting which approach becomes possible when the flow of exchanges has become very dense, with a high expectation of its indefinite continuation. The system itself becomes a positive-sum game: at any one time each side has a stock of cashable credits; the practitioners on each side become experts at working the system; and they derive status from being associated with its achievements. There is therefore a very high premium on maintaining the system, and all involved will be very reluctant to pursue any course likely to put it in jeopardy. This itself considerably reinforces the pressure to reach agreements and to avoid conflict.

We therefore have an example of clockwise movement from pure contract in terms of Fig. 2.1. The explosion of interactions being described is associated with a big rise in contract activity as the volume of exchanges increases, but with greater density contracts come to require less specificity.

Does 'trust' develop? Within industrial relations unmerited trust is most likely to be encountered in situations of deference; when the authority of employers is imbued with a paternal character which is believed by workers to lead employers to restrain the ruthlessness of their pursuit of labour-market advantage. Merited trust is more likely to be the result of experience with elaborate interactions over a period of time of the kind described above—though not necessarily involving union representation. The potential confusion between these two—a point missed by Fox (1974), who tends to identify trust with the latter form—will be part of the day-to-day reality of industrial relations, with employees not always being sure whether the trust they are expected to exercise is of the former or latter kind; and indeed the mix may vary.

We may label the two forms of trust 'naïve' and 'experience-based'. If the former is sufficiently strongly accepted by a workforce, it is likely to be associated with feelings of identity towards the employer: no distinct interests are perceived, nor danger of betrayal. What suits *alter* suits *ego*, because *ego* am part of *alter*. It is not necessary for us here to judge whether this amounts to false consciousness, merely to recognize it as different from the product of experience-based trust. The latter will not lead to anything like complete identity. A separation of interests is still perceived, but elaborate means are provided whereby the gap may be bridged to make co-operation possible. Trust is here the willingness to make use of those means in order to accept risks in making commitments.

Authoritarian Corporatism

This raises the question of what happens if the actors C and L develop their relationship to the point where zero-sum games disappear altogether. Conflict costs would then be nil. In other words, why not progress towards:

$$\Delta c + \Delta l = gn \tag{16}$$

If corporatist relations become more stable and less risky the greater the proportion of total transactions that are positive as opposed to zero-sum, then surely the end-point of corporatist stability must be the reduction of all transactions to positive-sum games only. This implies the identity of capital and labour.

The problem with this reasoning is as follows: since there are real conflicts of interest at many points between capital and labour, how are persisting zero-sum games to be suppressed? If they are simply ignored by the corporatist representatives, then other representatives will spring up to deal with them, and the corporatist system will be weakened. Perhaps legal, police, or other measures could be used to stamp out any attempt at raising conflict issues, at disturbing the corporatist peace. But if all difficulties caused by labour for capital are simply squashed, why should capital bother to go into the corporatist exchange at all? If C can be confident that L will never raise awkward and expensive conflicts, it need waste no time developing a dense web of relations with L designed to maintain good relations between them. As we saw earlier, much of the elaboration of the bargained corporatist network is needed precisely to contain the irreducible core of conflict. Once that core disappears, the network becomes irrelevant.

Coercive elements have, it will be noted, been introduced to squash conflict in such a model; it should therefore be distinguished from bargained corporatism by terming it authoritarian corporatism. The only other possibility is that there will be sufficiently strong shared interests between C and L that they will more or less spontaneously give greater weight to co-operative rather than any conflictual elements in their relationship. This was indeed the aspiration of the late nineteenth-century doctrines of industrial relations that adopted and gave to the world the name of corporatism (Black, 1984; Williamson, 1985). These were doctrines of identity *par excellence*. The appeals to unity were based on the shared identity of employers and workers within a religious community (usually Roman Catholic, sometimes Calvinist) or a nation. But this never proved realistic enough to overcome conflict, until it took the form of fascism and added to powerful identity appeals the apparatus of the authoritarian state.

This helps explain two important points. First, it has been noted (Williamson, 1985) that the corporatist edifices of such countries as fascist Italy and Portugal were largely bogus, elaborate façades that did little. Corporatism entered fascism as a useful ideological device for demonstrating how the conflicts of pre-fascist society could be ended; but once the fascists had liquidated the autonomous labour movement, there was no real need for such institutions. As Martinez-Alier and Roca (1988: 128) put it, with particular reference to the Spanish case: 'state corporatism should be considered a political ideology without historical reality'. Second, one can understand how it is vital to actors in bargained corporatist systems that they retain their sense of separate identities, that they continue to rally their 'side' and develop its symbols, and that they cling tenaciously to the core of zero-sum conflict in their relationship, no matter how far they compromise it in practice. Were the two sides to lose their sense of conflict and separateness, the whole system would become unnecessary and the representatives would lose their function.

This is therefore another of the risks taken by bargained corporatism: the actors must in everyday practice constantly compromise the separate identities whose strength and separateness are the *raison d'être* of the system. Occasional major outbreaks of conflict, such as the Swedish general strike of 1980, or even recent rituals like the Swedish employers' annual march through Stockholm to protest against the wage-earner funds, therefore perform a function similar to that played by crime and its punishment in the Durkheimian theory of social integration.

At a far less dramatic level than fascist, authoritarian corporatism, many employers daily practise, at a non-political, enterprise level, a mix of punishing and repressing dissidents and depriving them of their livelihood, and encouraging feelings of identity in the rest of their work-force. It is probably the most common form of industrial relations within the capitalist indus- trial world in general; it is certainly the predominant form in the world's leading capitalist country, the United States of America. It is not a form of corporatism, because it does not make use of organized groups; it is not fascist because it does not have an extensive political strategy and is compatible with a high degree of civil liberty in non-work areas of life; it does not need a special name because it is simply the normal form taken by capitalist employment relations in the absence of powerful unions. It is an interesting irony that, while the main thrust of pluralist and institutionalized conflict theory has been concerned with con- taining and coping with workers' ability to express their demands and to organize, the most dramatic contrasts between institu- tionalized and heavily politicized industrial relations appear when employers manage to conquer autonomous labour organization. If they do that without extensive political recourse and while keeping everything contained within the occupational sphere, one has normal US-style liberal-democratic capitalism; if they do it through national political organizations, one is in the world of Hitler and Mussolini.

3

Rational Action, Political Space, and Historical Reality

It is probably right to insist, following Max Weber, that no substantive definition of the realm of the political can be given, and that any *general* attempt to define 'the political' must be satisfied with a formal concept (such as coercive, collective regulation or territorial sovereignty, or the authoritative allocation of values). Nevertheless, it is possible to specify which substantive concerns are politicized at any given moment in a particular society. If everything can be the object of political transaction at some point, not everything can be political at the same time. In a given polity there is always a relatively stable evaluative framework according to which interests are recognised as such.

(Offe, 1987: 66)

We must now consider in more detail what is meant by the increasing density of the network of relations that characterizes bargained corporatism and distinguishes it from pluralism. This discussion will also enable us to introduce the state into our analysis. Relations between capital and labour can extend across two dimensions: horizontally, to embrace new issue areas (e.g. moving from central questions of labour's wage-effort bargain to include the overall level of employment in the economy, or labour's social benefits); and vertically, to embrace new levels in the scope and hierarchy of decisions (to move upwards through the capital–labour relationship is to move from shop floor, through company, economic branch, possibly region, to nation-state and perhaps to supra-national bodies).

Interest groups are not at liberty to move around this space at will. They are constrained by their capacity to bring people together at a certain vertical level and around a certain set of (horizontal) issues, and by their ability to take effective action at the point in question. These two aspects are linked: the willingness of people to adhere to the interest organization will depend on its effectiveness, and its effectiveness will depend on its ability to mobilize support. Effectiveness can for our purposes be seen as a function of a group's ability to forge relationships with other interests capable of exercising power over the issues in question. To 'forge a relationship' in this sense means to be recognized as a force to reckon with, to possess the capacity to wield sanctions in the issue area concerned.

Interests tend to have a 'base' point within political space. For trade unions this is obviously located horizontally within issues affecting pay and conditions of work for employed labour; vertically it will be at whatever point (shop, firm, branch, etc.) it has been easiest to organize workers. One can similarly identify the base points for organizations of capital. Clearly, the further an interest moves from its base point across the space, the more difficult it finds it to forge effective relationships. In addition, irrespective of 'distance travelled', there may be institutional barriers inhibiting the formation of certain relationships and therefore entry into certain parts of the space.

Within capitalist societies there are severe limits on the capacity of labour organizations to affect issues going beyond their exchange with given units of capital unless they can forge effective relations at the level of the nation-state. It is at this level that crucial macro-economic variables can be manipulated, and the state has unique opportunities for reaching out to all parts of the society through its capacity to make law. Sometimes unions and employers organized at national level can determine macro-economic variables together; they might also reach agreement on certain desirable legal changes. (The latter sometimes occurs in countries with parliaments that are deadlocked over non-economic issues, but in which national agreements are possible between organized labour and capital. Not surprisingly, Belgium has provided several instances—see Molitor, 1978: 34–5.) But for this to be effective they must have, in the former case, at least the tacit approval of the state, and in the latter at least its willingness to accept their proposal. For an interest group to make an effective vertical move to the level of the state is therefore also to facilitate a range of horizontal moves. In its relations with organized interests the state acts something like the hand on the cork of a bottle containing an imprisoned genie: if the hand can be persuaded to lift the cork, there is no knowing what the genie may do.

Usually genies are released in the hope that they will perform some task. So far we have spoken as though the organized interests are striving to reach state level in order to extend their own influence. Equally, the state may want to encourage groups to perceive some version of a national interest, which they will be able to do only if invited and enabled to raise their organizational capacities to the state's level. The state then faces the risk that they will seek to exercise influence in ways other than those envisaged.

Clearly, there are on this question considerable differences in the structural constraints and state policies compatible with pluralism and corporatism respectively. The ability of interests to transcend their initial institutional confines is a central variable determining those devices for insulating issue areas (s in the language of the previous chapter) on which the two systems occupy different positions. In an ideal-typical pluralist society, the centre of gravity of the labour movement comes at a point considerably short of the nation-state. It is not highly decentralized, because an important element of the procedural rules for conflict minimization that are crucial to pluralist bargaining is the avoidance of uncontrollable 'guerrilla' conflicts. Also, access to wider political influence is not entirely prevented; pluralism is a system without rigid barriers to entry, so organized interests will have lobbying influence, via the nation-state, over areas of interest close to them. However, the insulation constraints limit the network of relations that might develop from this; they also keep the interests within the institutionally separate 'lobbying' role and inhibit a share in administration.

In contrast, under bargained corporatism the emphasis is on the establishment of an extensive network of relations. Not only does activity at state level enable this, but this is also the level at which interests have access to the macro-economic variables that give them some mixture of control, predictability, and information that they need if they are to commit themselves to corporatist exchange. Further still, the national level is particularly appropriate for the search for common interests. To recall from Chapter 1 the argument based on Olson (1982): groups operating effectively at or near an 'encompassing' national level are unable to externalize the negative consequences of their actions and are therefore likely to recognize responsibility for them. Groups that are small in relation to the overall system, on the other hand, can look after their own immediate interests and ignore externalities.

Elaborate bargained corporatism is therefore likely to grow in systems where organized interests (including labour) are able—or even encouraged—to range over an extensive political space, binding the exchanges they make there into their general expanding network. This process is at the heart of the concept of generalized political exchange developed by Marin (1990*a*). He contends that in neo-corporatist systems (especially as seen in his own country, Austria) a small group of persons from the various political and functional interest organizations engages in a mass of transactions, extending over a wide range of issues. He describes this in exactly the same way as the account in Chapter 2 of bargained corporatism: multiple exchanges are happening, stretching over time; there ceases to be a discrete calculable contract. See also Traxler (1990).

Marin develops this idea in explicit contrast with Pizzorno's (1978) concept of political exchange. This was based on the Italian situation in the early 1970s which was essentially an attempt to shift from a contestation system straight to bargained corporatism. It took the form of attempts to produce one big bargain: indeed, when temporary success was achieved, in 1983, the agreement reached was known as the *Maxitrattiva*. According to Marin, one big exchange can never acquire the stability of the Austrian mass of exchanges continuing over time. The relationship remains too much at the contract pole and allows no chance for trust and identity to develop. It is also a case of putting all the eggs in one basket. Marin's thesis is central to an understanding of how neo-corporatist institutions at national level, as analysed in Chapter 2, work in practice. If the central *modus operandi* of contestation is the strike or lock-out, and that of pluralism collective bargaining, then that of neo-corporatism is generalized political exchange. Such a model (henceforth to be called GPE) is often mistakenly seen as 'consensus'. But consensus means an absence of disagreements, a unity of views; GPE accepts and takes for granted a mass of conflicts, but processes them in such a way that, unless and until something goes drastically wrong with the balance, the likelihood of recourse to open conflict is reduced, and actors enabled to trade gains in one arena for losses in another. Consensus may sometimes be the outcome of such a pattern: it is not a precondition.

There is still however something unsatisfactory about the emphasis on action by very small peak élites at national political level in Marin's scheme. An important theme to emerge from Chapter 2 is the considerable strain that corporatist bargaining imposes on relations between representatives and members. As noted in Chapter 1, many analyses have used sheer centralization as a proxy for neo-corporatism. Authors have simply taken for granted either the solution of these problems by exercise of authority or the fragility of neo-corporatist arrangements. Schmitter's original (1974) formulation placed stress on the hierarchical and non-competitive nature of even societal (as opposed to state) corporatist arrangements. But little of this is compatible with the reality of existing systems.

An important point is made by Kjellberg (1983 and 1990) who, while accepting that industrial relations in his native Sweden are centralized, also points to the important part played by local, plant-level, union activists. In no senses are Swedish unions centralized in the way in which the term is often used in relation to post-war French or Italian communist unions: a decision-making centre that has little to do with a rank and file which has only small capacity for serious action. But Kjellberg's model of a simply bipolar union movement, with points of activity at both centre and periphery, does not by itself solve the problem of how tensions between members and representatives of the kind considered in Chapter 2 can be resolved. Indeed, it reads very similarly to the account given by the Donovan Commission (1968) of the bipolar and therefore quite dislocated industrial relations of Britain during the 1960s.

Stable bargained corporatism requires the very opposite of dislocation, and for that reason I shall use the term *articulation* to describe the requirements of internal structures of labour (and to a lesser extent capital) organizations if they are to be compatible with such stability. An articulated organization is one in which strong relations of interdependence bind different vertical levels, such that the actions of the centre are frequently predicated on securing the consent of lower levels and the autonomous action of lower levels is bounded by rules of delegation and scope for discretion ultimately controlled by successively higher levels. If such conditions exist, they provide a context within which neo-corporatist arrangements can overcome the tensions considered in Chapter 2 without taking on the strict hierarchical discipline described by Schmitter (1974) which is difficult to reconcile with the principle of voluntary association. How such forms of interdependence and articulation are developed in practice is something for which we shall search in empirical analysis of organizational structures.

HISTORICAL SPECIFICITIES

This discussion still leaves us in rather abstract territory. A variety of patterns of industrial relations seems possible, but the question, raised in Chapter 1, which launched this theoretical discussion was why and how does any one pattern dominate at a particular time and in a particular place? How do individual real-life examples of these patterns develop and how do they change? Certain approaches within the existing literature on the development of industrial-relations systems might be pressed into service to provide hypotheses for answering these questions.

An initial and simple account, one that needs to add very little to the bare bones of rational exchange theory, can be derived from Olson's (1982) theory: given security over a lengthy period, groups will resolve their collective-action problems, come to terms with each other and establish stable bargaining relations. Thus, patterns of relations will differ primarily in terms of the density of their network, and development and change will be a function of time—that is, time free of major disruption. We shall call this the simple Olson theory. It should be pointed out that Olson himself is not primarily interested in whether an increasing density of relations produces any qualitative change in their form, so this is therefore not 'his' theory. The idea of pure exchange becoming generalized political exchange is not part of his thesis. That of encompassing organizations, embracing a major shift in the level of exchanges from small-scale competitive market actors to oligopolistic organizations, is important to his discussion, but it is exogenous; he does not claim to explain why this phenomenon sometimes exists. Such a theory has to seek explanation primarily in the passage of time. An exchange-based theory that stays at the level of relatively unspecified actors has little else to use. This is clearly too simple to stand as an adequate theory, but it serves a useful heuristic purpose as a limiting case, a theory that has no recourse to historical specificity.

As we have seen, it is possible and necessary to introduce concepts of differential power into an exchange model. Employers need to engage in a bargaining exchange going beyond simple contract only when labour has developed effective power. How might different power balances between workers and their employers affect the development of exchange systems? This adds a new variable. While there is scope here for considerable variety in argument, we can simplify available theories into three mutually exclusive groups, according to whether workers' power is seen as being efficiently maximized in (1) contestative relations, (2) collective bargaining, and (3) neo-corporatism.

Thus the second set of theories we can discern are those held by advocates of position (1). These comprise primarily orthodox Marxists and pure syndicalists. To them any institutionalization of the class conflict constitutes a weakening of the drive for revolutionary transformation. It will therefore be seen as a manipulation of class consciousness, a corruption of working-class leaders, or something similar. From this point of view neo-corporatism is even worse than collective bargaining, because the institutionalization is that much heavier, the implication of workers' representatives in managing the system that much greater.

Third come those who take position (2), the main pluralist Anglo-American industrial-relations school, of which Dunlop remains the theoretical doyen. The transmutation of open contestational conflict into bargaining is seen as an achievement of organized labour—by observers who of course do not share Marxist eschatology and who therefore place some premium on the stable functioning of the economy. Such writers, however, are often suspicious of political and especially neo-corporatist entanglements, which they may well view in terms similar to Marxists as suborning workers' own authentic autonomy. For this school, then, workers' power is optimized with the attainment of stable collective-bargaining arrangements. Either side of that there is a slide into weakness.

Pluralists are therefore unlikely to share the assumption of an evolutionary development from contestation to GPE via collective bargaining, based on the idea of a densening web of exchanges. This can be seen most clearly in Dunlop (1958). Dunlop does not have workers' power as his primary independent variable, but rather the inverse—the strategies of industrializing élites (for a criticism of this, see Scoville, 1973). However, one can easily interpret this mirror image. The élite which he sees as pursuing pluralist or collective bargaining relations with employees is the liberal bourgeois élite of market capitalism. Since this is a pluralist model it can also be interpreted as an optimal position for labour too. Essential ingredients of the Dunlop model are relatively decentralized bargaining, a plurality of mutually competing unions, and an avoidance of political entanglements. This is of course entirely consistent with the market capitalist base of this élite's *modus operandi*.

Within both industrial relations and political science, pluralism amends classical market liberalism by allowing organized groups to be the actors. They are assumed still to be competitive, but without pure market constraints. (It was the apparent failure of the polity to provide an equivalent constraint that led to fears of overloaded government and to political theories of inflation in the 1970s. Pluralists then moved in the two directions indicated in Chapter 1: to advocacy of a more 'pure' market economy or to neo-corporatism—in Olson's case to both, depending on the circumstances.)

Dunlop's other two main élites are the dynastic-feudal and the revolutionary intellectual. The former is associated with very weak, barely tolerated unions, and a very strong state that dictates the terms of industrial relations. Revolutionary intellectuals cultivate numerically strong, well-resourced, but entirely heteronomous unions, with again a centralized, politicized centre of gravity. There is strictly no place in this model for GPE or neo-corporatism, as the possibility is excluded of unions being at once centralized, political, strong, and autonomous. Such patterns could be interpreted by Dunlop only as uncomfortable halfway houses; seen in evolutionary terms, they would be systems that had not yet achieved the decentralization and internal competition that marks a mature industrial-relations system of collective bargaining. Therefore, while Dunlop would share the account given in Chapter 2 of a transition from contestation to pluralism, he would depart sharply in seeing pluralism as a culmination of historical development—in addition to being an optimization of workers' strength.

Finally, there is the school which treats neo-corporatism, or something resembling it, as marking a high point for workers' power (e.g. Esping-Andersen, 1985; Rothstein, 1987; Glyn, 1991; Korpi, 1978; Stephens, 1979). The argument can be seen as starting from broadly Marxist premises about class struggle, but differs from the various orthodox Marxist theories by making the key assumptions that class struggle may be a prolonged, more or less peaceable, process, and that it may take the form of everyday political power-brokering as much as (or more than) the street fighting and barricade storming usually assumed. 'The state as a locus of class struggle' is the phrase used by some writers in this tradition (e.g. Esping-Andersen *et al.*, 1976). One implication of such a view is to treat the conduct of large, centralized, political union organizations bargaining over national economic policy as being an advance, in terms of workers' power, from limited collective bargaining over wage rises. The concern of this school is with both power *per se* and power as condensed in organizations with a central strategic capacity.

To the extent that these theorists remain Marxists, such arrangements are seen as temporary or transitional, but for others there is at least a tacit acceptance that matters may be more durable. I shall call these theories 'Scandinavian', as their authors tend to be Scandinavian or to have based their theories primarily on Scandinavian societies. This is not surprising since, as we have seen in Chapter 1, the Scandinavian countries provide the main examples of both self-evident union power and neo-corporatism.

Finally, combining the effect of changing power relations with Olsonian 'stable time' assumptions, we might argue that, given prolonged stability and no untoward disturbances, as the web of exchanges intensifies it will both transcend the trust barrier (becoming generalized political exchange) and begin to spread 'upwards' to more embracing levels. In other words, generalized political exchange ought to be the eventual form taken by every pattern of industrial-relations exchanges that has sufficient time to develop, does not encounter particular obstacles on the way, and allows labour to develop growing power. Such potential obstacles remain exogenous, but we have here an essentially evolutionary model of the development of industrial-relations systems that sees GPE, if not as an ultimate end point, at least as a more 'advanced' form than either collective-bargaining systems or managerial consultation schemes, which are in turn more advanced than contestation systems. We shall call this the 'modified Olsonian' theory.

OPERATIONALIZING THE THEORIES

Chapter 2 gave us what looked suspiciously like such an evolutionary progression from the destructive conflict and primitive institutional structures of contestation, through the thickening but insulated, apolitical, and still negative patterns of pluralism, to the constructive co-operation of neo-corporatism (with the nasty aberration of authoritarian corporatism as an avoidable byway on the evolutionary path). But is there really a *logic* of development that drives systems through such a path as the theory seems to imply? Or is there a *history*, or rather series of national histories, that inclines countries to different positions on that continuum? Can we judge whether neo-corporatism is in fact better suited than pluralism (or indeed contestation) to minimizing conflict and achieving positive-sum gains, perhaps for different given levels of power, for organized labour?

We shall examine these questions by assessing the institutions of a number of western European countries as they have developed since the early days of the organization of labour. Attention will be focused on fifteen countries, though one of these, Portugal, plays only a minor part in the account. My aim has been to take the whole of what was, for most of the post-war period, non-communist Europe, less Greece and the very small countries (Iceland and Luxemburg). The period analysed runs from 1870 until 1990, but this is covered, not as a continuous narrative, but as a series of 'snapshots', moments at which we take stock of the state of institutional development and various other indices. With the exception of the first interval, from 1870 to 1900, these snapshots are at distances of around a dozen years.

While there is some narrative, the snapshots primarily take the form of consideration of certain standardized, operationalized variables relating to principal characteristics of industrial-relations systems and related matters. Where possible, quantitative indicators, such as membership levels and strike frequency, have been used, but there is clearly much that is qualitative, and reliance has had to be placed on estimations and narrative accounts of situations to be found in the literature. There are clearly problems in this; we cannot be certain that estimations of, say, how centralized trade unions are in a particular country are equivalent to similar estimates made by observers of a second country. But we have little choice.

A further problem is that matters as complex as the characteristics of an industrial-relations system are usually multidimensional. For example, trade-union power is the product of a number of different components. I have not followed the common path of reducing such indicators to numbers which are then combined to provide an aggregate score, as this only deceptively resolves through arithmetic the task of assessment of relative weights that needs to be done substantively. Were we to be considering sufficient cases for proper statistical analysis to be appropriate, this arithmetical solution would have to be chosen. Given the small number of cases and variables, it is in fact more accurate to remain at the level of conscious assessment. When presenting the data based on these variables in the following chapters, I have tried to avoid the extremes of both an unjustified conflation into simple scales and surrender of the attempt at any quantitative assessment. Countries are therefore loosely ranked in terms of the variables under discussion, and where it is difficult to discriminate among them they have been put in rough groups.

The central variable is the state of *institutional development of the industrial-relations system*, defined in a way that will enable us to distinguish between contestative, pluralist, bargained corporatist and authoritarian corporatist systems, and (given what has been said concerning the need for actors to be so structured that they can participate in the manner demanded by the logic of the system in which they find themselves) including relevant characteristics of employers' organizations and trade-union movements. For some purposes (when we are explaining the development of systems) this is the dependent variable; when we are considering theories that assert that different kinds of system will be associated with different typical outcomes, it becomes the central independent variable.

Systems will be modelled in terms of the extent and intensity of relations that are formed within them. Extent is largely a matter of plotting the basic levels at which interaction takes place: plant or company, locality or region, economic branch, nation, state. There are distinctions between both plant and company, and locality and region, that we shall discuss when we encounter them. An economic branch (often called an 'industry' in Britain, but 'branch' will consistently be used here) is a rather arbitrary construct. Sometimes we speak of the metals sector, sometimes of the motor industry, sometimes of the truck-making industry within that. However, as a matter of fact industrial relations has often placed particular emphasis on branches as defined in Group II of the International Standard Industrial Classification of the United Nations Organization. These constitute a broad aggregation of labour, product, and raw materials markets, and the term 'branch' will here usually refer to this level. National and state levels are distinguished in that the former refers to action by organizations of functional interests at the level of the nation-state, but without the state's active participation. State-level action occurs when the government initiates the contact and remains a major actor.

Intensity is more difficult to assess because it is more *ad hoc*. One cannot deduce the potential range of issues embraced in interaction. We shall need to specify the particular decision-making fields involved, and also state whether the action takes the form of consultation, bargaining, participation in mediation and conciliation activities, or participation in the administration of services, successive forms indicating more intense levels of interaction. Where a description of a system in terms of these features reveals sparse institutions with few points of contact, we shall speak of contestation. Where there are elaborate mechanisms for handling conflict and promoting interaction, but an absence of mechanisms other than consultative ones at national and state level and for aggregating issues across levels, we shall speak of pluralist collective bargaining. Where there is a dense web of exchanges, binding employers and unions across levels, especially involving national political co-ordination, extending over a wide range of issues going beyond industrial relations *per se* and involving in particular the joint administration of policy areas as well as bargaining relations, we shall speak of neo-corporatism and generalized political exchange. Where there is an attempt by the state to impose a system ostensibly having these characteristics but on the basis of heteronomous organizations, we shall speak of authoritarian corporatism.

To consider the compatibility of representative organizations with the systems of which they are a part, we shall need data on labour and business organizations. Given what has been said about the problems of relations between members and representatives in anything other than purely contestative systems, there is particular interest in the degree and type of *articulation of trade-union movements*. We consider this by examining certain characteristics of both confederations and individual unions. How extensive is the reach of major confederations, as a proportion of all union members and of the total labour force? How many unions are members of the confederation (a small number of unions is both evidence of the relative ease of decision-making at central level and an indicator of prior central strength in having been able to reduce the number)? What powers can confederations exercise over constituent unions? Where individual unions are concerned we need to know: are they of branch, craft, general, or other type? What powers can they exercise over constituent lower levels? What form does their shop-floor organization take? Because of the hypothetical importance of exposed-sector unions to the behaviour of confederations, data are separately calculated on the relative size of such unions.

For *organizations of capital* we need to know the levels at which employers organize and the scope of the organizations that exist; and also the kinds of co-ordinating powers over affiliates that organizations at various levels possess. An important difference between employers and workers is that the former often organize for trade as well as for labour purposes. Assessment of this conduct can be combined with that of industrial-relations organization as such to give a fuller picture of what Streeck and Schmitter (1985) call the 'associative' behaviour of business.

According to the model set out in Chapter 2, *the power of*

organized labour determines whether employers will be required to come to terms with labour as a bargaining partner; the argument summarized in Fig. 2.2 gives labour strength a place alongside the articulation of systems in determining their overall character; and some hypotheses concerning the likely outcomes of different systems are stated in terms of given levels of this variable. We therefore need data that will enable us to assess this strength. It will here be appraised in terms of: membership (expressed as a proportion of both the total labour force and the total number of employees or dependent labour force); major events, such as legal changes, that may have affected organized labour's position; the level of unemployment; the political position of parties friendly to unions (i.e. what their share of the vote is, and whether they are in government); and any other general political events that may have affected labour's position. In considering the forces that might have shaped systems, we need some means of assessing *periodization*, in terms of states of economic and political development. This is important to the Olsonian, modified Olsonian, and Marxist theories.

Finally, various potential outcomes (industrial conflict, inflation, unemployment) will be assessed to enable some test of the hypotheses concerning the effectiveness of different kinds of system.

Details of the sources used in compiling each of these tables will be found in the Appendix. Presentation of the tables and their detailed discussion comprise Part II of this book.

PART II

A CENTURY OF INSTITUTIONAL DEVELOPMENT

4

1870–1914: On the Threshold of Organized Capitalism

The best thing the foreigners could do would be to organize themselves into trade societies similar to ours and endeavour to get their wages up to the same rates as ours and then we could begin to discuss questions with them.

(The British Amalgamated Society of Engineers, responding to overtures to associate with the International Workingmen's Association, 1871, quoted in Richter, 1973: 33)

Par tous les moyens, même légaux!

(Guesde, French syndicalist leader, around 1880)

NEAR THE BEGINNING: AROUND 1870

To provide a point of reference for subsequent organizational development, we begin our account with the state of industrial relations in western Europe around 1870. Shortly after the unification of Italy and the impact of the American Civil War; the time of the unification of Germany, the Franco-Prussian War, the Paris Commune; shortly before the great recession of 1873 and the gradual overtaking of the United Kingdom by the United States of America and Germany in gross industrial production—this was a period of considerable ferment in European societies and economies. For many regions industrialization was in its very early stages, and industrial relations in the modern sense barely existed. What evidence there is of autonomous labour organization and collective bargaining is entirely limited to the skilled crafts. While in Britain, France, Belgium, and parts of Germany this included the textile industry, coal mining, and some engineering, in general it referred to trades that in some form or other pre-date the industrial economy:

the building crafts, baking, brewing, tailoring, traditional metal working, and, above all, printing. Organization and bargaining, such as they were, were both essentially *local* in scope.

Few firms were large enough to have developed a company level of industrial relations, especially as nearly all the skilled crafts made a point of organizing themselves at a supra-company level to stress their autonomy and independence. On the other hand, poorly developed forms of transport and communications and the low level of workers' living standards prevented much effective organization beyond the local level. With one or two exceptions in the United Kingdom, and the German book-printing industry, there was no national bargaining at this period. Neither—with a rather odd regional exception in Catalonia—had political authorities begun to establish state-level industrial-relations institutions beyond *ad hoc* inquiries. (The Catalan exception was a legally established bipartite conciliation system, a *jurados mixtos*, for the textile industry, set up in 1873; but by all accounts it hardly functioned (Abad de Santillàn, 1967).)

Institutional Development, 1870

Table 4.1 represents this thin institutional structure. Local collective bargaining in skilled trades was fairly well developed in the United Kingdom and less so in Switzerland. It was fragmentary in newly united Germany, Austria-Hungary, and Denmark; about to develop in the Netherlands, Norway, and Catalonia; but virtually non-existent elsewhere. In general all these systems apart from the British and Swiss should be defined as contestative in so far as there were any collective labour relations at all. Attempts at action by workers in most sectors in most countries would be treated with considerable repression by employers and, often, the police.

Workers' and Employers' Organizations, 1870

As might be expected, it is not worth producing a table on the articulation of union movements at this period. In 1870 organizations purporting to be national centres existed only in Germany, Spain, Switzerland, and the United Kingdom; one

TABLE 4.1. *Institutional development of industrial relations, c.1870*

Main pattern of industrial relations	Country	Level		
		Plant	Locality	Branch
Collective bargaining in skilled trades	UK		Bargaining well established in skilled trades	
	CH	Some bargaining	Bargaining established in skilled trades	
Fragmentary collective bargaining in skilled trades	D	Some bargaining		Book industry only
	DK			
	A		Some bargaining *Genoßenschaft*-type bargaining in some skilled trades; unions not permitted above local level	
Incipient collective bargaining	NL, N, E*		Very little bargaining	
Contestation or nothing	F, B	Sporadic strike activity only		
	Elsewhere: virtually nothing			

Notes: UK includes Ireland. German Reich excludes Alsace-Lorraine. Austrian Reich excludes Hungary and Bosnia-Herzogovina.
*Catalonia only.

had appeared and disappeared in Denmark and one would be founded in the Netherlands in 1871. But only in the United Kingdom did this organization survive more than a few years (and has indeed remained in place ever since). Even then, the Trades Union Congress at this stage cannot really be considered as a peak organization: it was an annual meeting that by the early 1870s had set up a minor central office in order to carry on continuing lobbying of Parliament. On the other hand, the TUC's ability to provide some sort of framework for about a million of the country's 1.2 million trade-unionists was a unique achievement. Elsewhere union organization was overwhelmingly local; where supra-local organizations existed they were little more than loose federations.

Business organization presents a more interesting picture, not so much for employer-association development as such, which is extremely thin outside the United Kingdom, but for the evidence of other associative activity by business (Table 4.2). It is on the basis of this activity that we can classify countries. The differences among them are quite striking: hardly anything in most countries, but a variety of developments elsewhere. Swiss capitalists were in many respects in a class of their own, since the organizational deficiencies of the Swiss state required business groups to take on a number of public administrative functions normally carried on by state agencies. In exchange for this the state would subsidize their organizations. As a result, Swiss business had national organizations from a very early stage. This was mainly concentrated on trade and manufacturing activities, not on the employer role as such (Gruner, 1956).

Also worth consideration are the organizations in Austria, Denmark, and Germany. In Austria the middle classes had won the right to compulsory *Kammer* for trade, crafts, and agriculture as part of the settlement of the crisis of 1848. These were genuinely representative but not autonomous, being part of the state structure; as such they had administrative powers over certain functions (Traxler, 1986: 78 ff.). Some of the German states had had similar *Kammer*, others had adapted Napoleonic institutions to a more participative German model, and others again had developed the extensive business associations of the Hanseatic League (Fischer, 1964). As in Austria, these organizations were representative, but not in the external 'lobbying'

T ABLE 4.2. *Organizations of capital, c.1870*

	Scope[1]	Power[2]	Other associative business activity[3]
CH	Local and branch level	Largely informal	Trade associations receive state funds for carrying out delegated public tasks; *Genoßenschaften* take on training role; SHIV, 1870, as national co-ordinating body
DK	Fællesrep, 1871, at national level	Weak; building employers loosely organized to fight strikes	Trade associations involved in trade regulation and training
A	Branch level only	Weak; some anti-union organization at local levels	Elaborate structure of *Kammer* and other organizations represent trade interests to state as part of formal system of non-parliamentary representation
D	Branch level only	Weak; some anti-union organization at local levels	Elaborate structure of *Kammer* and other organizations at local and regional levels organize training; these structures pre-date the unified German state
N	Virtually nothing	None	Trade interests involved in advisory councils of non-parliamentary state
UK	Branch level only	Weak; but in some areas important in either encouraging or breaking unions	Very little; some consultation
F	Very little	Nothing	Comité des Forges on margin of legality; little else

TABLE 4.2. *Continued*

	Scope[1]	Power[2]	Other associative business activity[3]
S	Some local activity	Virtually nothing	Compulsory trade associations replace guilds, 1864, but are later made illegal
NL	Very little	Nothing	Guild legacy still operative
B	Very little	Nothing	Weak, unstable; discouraged by government
All other cases: no serious organization or activity			

Note: Country boundaries as in Table 4.1.

[1] Extent of organization of employer interests.
[2] Resources available to employer organizations to co-ordinate action.
[3] Activity directed at trade rather than labour issues.

sense understood by United States pluralist theory: they were part of the extended state and carried out some 'public space' functions in administering government trade policies. They had, in the years preceding our 'snapshot', provided the base for pan-German business organizations that had *pre-dated the German state*, having adopted some public functions, in a rather Swiss pattern, in that context. Also rather distinctive was Danish business organization. Here a smooth transition from earlier guild activity to the small-scale business activities of modern Denmark meant that commerce and industry retained an organizational life throughout the 'competitive' period of capitalism (Bruun, 1931*b*).

A notable feature of this associative activity among businessmen in some parts of Europe is its antiquated character. Even where modern forms of bureaucratic organization had begun to appear (Germany, Switzerland), they were rooted in post-medieval structures.

Power of Organized Labour, 1870

Indicators of the power of organized labour also present a thin picture (Table 4.3). In terms of sheer membership, the United

TABLE 4.3. *Power of organized labour, c.1870*

	Total known union membership		Major industrial-relations and political developments affecting position of organized labour within industry	Other major political developments affecting wider position of organized labour
	as % of labour force	as % of dependent labour force		
UK	8.32	11.32	Major legal hindrances to union activity removed by negative immunities approach, 1871	Very restricted suffrage, but some skilled workers have vote
B	2.42	3.62	Organizations permitted since 1866	No working-class suffrage
D	0.39	0.55	Rights to organize in various states since 1860s; all Reich, 1872	Extensive male suffrage since 1871 (social democrat vote 3.2%)
CH	n.a.	n.a.	No legal problems to labour organization	Extensive male suffrage
DK	0.54	1.81	Unions emerge from guild structures	Fairly extensive male suffrage, but excluding farm labourers
F	0.20	0.33	Right to strike, 1864; to organize (with permission), 1868	Extensive suffrage but workers' organizations broken after defeat of Paris Commune, 1871
A	0.28	0.42	Right to organize at local level, 1870	No working-class political participation
NL	n.a.	n.a.	Right to organize, 1871	Unions allied with liberals but very little working-class suffrage

TABLE 4.3. *Continued*

	Total known union membership		Major industrial-relations and political developments affecting position of organized labour within industry	Other major political developments affecting wider position of organized labour
	as % of labour force	as % of dependent labour force		
N	n.a.	n.a.	No handicaps for organization	Unions allied with liberals but very little working-class suffrage
E	n.a.	n.a.	Unions allowed if on 'mutual' basis since 1861 in Catalonia only	No suffrage; frequent repression
S	n.a.	n.a.	No handicaps for organization	No working-class political participation
I	n.a.	n.a.	Virtually no organization	Limited suffrage
P	n.a.	n.a.	Virtually no organization	No suffrage

Note: Country boundaries as in Table 4.1.

Kingdom unions are in a class of their own. There had been a certain amount of development in a further group of countries (Belgium, Denmark, Germany, and Switzerland), though of very small proportions of both the total and the dependent labour force. There is even less in another group: Austria, France, the Netherlands, Spain (mainly Catalonia), and Scandinavia outside Denmark; and virtually nothing in Italy, Portugal, and the rest of Spain.

In most countries the right to organize had been gained only sometime between 1861 and 1872 and was still often precarious and vulnerable to police action. The fact that labour had been gaining rights is an indication of its growing significance, though in many cases those granted were very limited. No union movement had yet developed the capability to organize its own political party; even where both suffrage and industrialization had progressed some way, the level of organization was cripplingly low. However, the German social democrats were on the eve of launching themselves (in 1871), when they would secure just 3.2 per cent of the poll; and in some countries—Denmark, the Netherlands, Norway, and the United Kingdom—liberal parties showed an interest in adopting labour's causes.

As already noted, organization at this stage was almost entirely limited to the skilled crafts, with the important exception of mining, where distinctions over skill are less easy to determine. In terms of Fig. 2.2, there is no difficulty in allocating all our countries at this period to category I: low articulation of structures, low power of organized labour—though the United Kingdom and also Denmark, Germany, and Switzerland are showing signs of more interesting possibilities. The last three countries and Austria (but not the United Kingdom) have fairly rich patterns of public-space occupancy by business, though not specifically employer, associations.

Economic and Political Development, 1870

Table 4.4 presents evidence of the state of economic and political development. The well-known economic precocity of the United Kingdom is clearly shown, and the relatively advanced state of her industrial relations thereby 'explained' in a common sense way—though it is useful to be reminded of the retarded state of British democracy at this time. The relatively advanced positions

TABLE 4.4. *Indicators of political and economic development, c.1870*

	Agricultural work-force as % of total work-force (1880)	GNP p.c. (1960 US$)	Electorate as % of adult male population	Leading economic sectors
A	55.6	305	none	Agriculture
B	30.3	571	8.5	Textiles, steel, coal, capital equipment, finance
DK	50.3	340	72.9	Agriculture, small trades
F	40.0	437	87.0	Textiles, mines, engineering, agriculture
D	45.0	426	80.0[1]	Textiles, coal and steel, agriculture
I	56.7	312	8.9	Agriculture, public utilities
NL	n.a. (relatively high)	506	11.3	Agriculture, some urban crafts
N	n.a. (high)	421	21.0	Shipping, agriculture
P	n.a. (high)	n.a. (very low)	none	Agriculture
E	n.a. (high)	329	none	Agriculture, textiles in Catalonia
S	51.5	246	20.0	Agriculture, wood, textiles
CH	37.4[2]	549	79.0	Metal industries and watchmaking
UK	10.4[3]	628	31.4	Textiles, coal, steel, engineering, finance

Note: Country boundaries as in Table 4.1.

[1] But government not responsible to Reichstag.
[2] 1888.
[3] 1891.

in industrial-relations institutional development of Germany and Switzerland are also well 'explained' by evolutionary theories of development.

However, if economic development accounts for the development of collective bargaining, Belgium and France are a puzzle: why did these countries, particularly the former, exhibit so little institutional development in the early 1870s? One recalls the splendid description in Shorter and Tilly's monumental study, *Strikes in France* (1974: ch. 3), of the early French version of collective bargaining, whereby workers would parade around the town with placards declaring their demand, and if the employer wished to make a concession he would simply post a notice outside the factory announcing a changed wage rate. The two sides never spoke to each other. It is a pure instance of the fragmentary, marginal contact described in Chapter 2.

The rest of the list contains few surprises, though it is worth noting the political heterogeneity of Scandinavia at this period and in particular the poverty of Sweden.

Industrial Conflict, 1870

If there is some support for evolutionary explanations of the development of systems at this early stage, what evidence do we have of the socio-economic outcomes that might be explained by the state of system development? Unfortunately the data for these and many subsequent years are not available to permit much of a test. There are no good statistics on inflation and unemployment, and industrial-disputes statistics exist for too few countries at this period to make possible a proper analysis. We do know of certain major outbreaks of conflict: in Austria, parts of Germany, the United Kingdom, and, mixed up with more general social agitation, in Paris and Catalonia. But the number of persons involved in these events, spectacular though some of them were, was small and their incidence sporadic. The great majority of workers were simply not involved in a world of action at all. Outside the skilled trades they were simply working—most of them in the fields—as individuals or family groups, for a meagre living. In the terms of Chapter 2, employers could afford the contestative model because it cost them little in extended conflict. Indeed, contestation is really a misnomer for the situation in this period.

This initial 'snapshot' is primarily the 'before' phase of a before-and-after sequence. Little, apart from the underdevelopment of Belgian and French institutions and the curious way that trade unions in the United Kingdom developed faster than political democracy, causes us to depart from a simple developmental thesis.

ORGANIZED CAPITALISM: AROUND 1900

The first generation of sociologists in the mid-nineteenth century was concerned with the way in which modernization broke down traditional collective bonds of community, kinship, village, and guild. But by the end of the century a new preoccupation had joined this. The new industrial society began to appear less that of the atomized individual and more that of a new kind of collectivity: the large, bureaucratically co-ordinated organization. The state, the company, the mass political party, the modern army, were all examples of the phenomenon. Max Weber's essay on bureaucracy (1919) is the most important piece of scholarship on the theme, but there were many others: the work of Weber's pupil, Roberto Michels, on the mass party and trade union (1911); the cynical analyses of mass political organization by Mosca and Pareto (see Meisel, 1965). Émile Durkheim (1893) tried to console his pessimism at the passing of old forms of social solidarity by seeing trends to new forms of organizational interdependence in industrialism—to the extent that he virtually advocated works councils as a cure for high suicide rates (1897).

It was the years between 1870 and the turn of the century that produced the outlines of a society based on large organizations, though the extent to which these were eventually to grow could then be only dimly perceived. This was the period that Hilferding (1910) dubbed organized capitalism (Winkler, 1974). After the crash of 1873 the growing capitalist economies adopted a defensive aggressiveness. In several countries large banks emerged, caught up in a close, non-market relationship with client firms—for Hilferding this was the key development. He called it *Finanzkapitalismus*, by which he meant not dominance by the financial sector at the expense of the industrial in the British sense, but a close integration of financial and industrial concerns. An increasing number of economies embraced either outright protectionism or at least a general avoidance of competition, with firms forming cartels and associations to manage these. Departments of state grew in order to keep up with the tasks of managing even a non-interventionist complex economy. Companies grew large and developed large managerial hierarchies. And labour, once it had weathered the weakening of its organizations wreaked by the depression, began to develop its trade unions towards the end of the century.

These changes were helped by new production methods that introduced the early stages of mass production and dramatically increased the economies of large-scale output. At the same time they threatened the rigid old distinctions between skilled and unskilled workers and rendered many of the latter, now herded into large factories for the first time, available for unionization, either in organizations of their own or in former craft unions that were recognizing the likely fate of continued isolation from the rest of the workforce.

While the period saw the countries of western Europe at very different stages of development, the industrializing world of that period was sufficiently integrated for no country to be unaffected. Once large-scale production, or integrated banking, or extended government departments had been developed somewhere, others would note the advantages and try to imitate them. Sometimes they would succeed in so doing and steal a march on the pioneer country in examples of Gershenkron's advantages of historical backwardness (1962). This process does not necessarily impart convergence: to do the same thing as another country at a different stage of development may well be to produce very different outcomes. Or sometimes an apparent imitation will be little more than a superficial institutional copying without real roots. For example, during the 1890s nearly all European trade-union movements that did not already have trade-union confederations established them; in some cases these were ineffectual bodies of just a few thousand people, in others the seeds of durable and important organizations.

With some exceptions, by 1900 most states—though by no means most employers—had at least temporarily relinquished the use of repression as the main means of coping with organized labour. Two developments were of particular significance. The German government, which in 1878 had introduced its famous ban on socialist organizations, the so-called *Sozialistengesetz*, allowed it to lapse in 1889; and in the following year the Pope issued the encyclical *Rerum Novarum* that criticized individualistic capitalism and legitimated the idea of autonomous workers' organizations provided they were true to the Church and repudiated class conflict. This initiated Christian democratic political parties and Catholic trade unions—to the chagrin alike of ruling élites who had relied on the Church to oppose democracy, and of socialist organizations seeking a unified working class.

Institutional Development, 1900

How far had the arrival of the age of organization at the end of the century affected the development of industrial-relations systems since we examined them in 1870? Table 4.5 presents a bald summary. With the exception of Belgium, France, and southern Europe, a local level of collective bargaining had got off the ground everywhere, though it was very thin in the Netherlands and Sweden. (In Norway there was actually some decline in bargaining institutions after the turn of the century.) There are also interesting and varied cases of plant- or company-level action: a form of shop-steward or *tillidsman* system in much of the United Kingdom and Denmark respectively, extensive company-level bargaining in Switzerland; elected safety delegates in French and British coal mines; some works-council experiments in Austria, Germany, and the Netherlands—sometimes involving union or elected representatives but sometimes being employer-appointed and thus examples of heteronomous collectivism. There were also developments at supra-local levels: industry-wide bipartite conciliation and arbitration in a few British industries, and a national version in France, where, however, the law did not receive so much support and was virtually a dead letter.

But by far the grandest development at this stage was the *Hovedafteling* or Basic Agreement for regulating conflict worked out in Denmark between the Fællerforening for Arbejdgivere (FfA) and De samvirkende Fagforbund (DsF). This was the first

TABLE 4.5. *Institutional development of industrial relations, c.1900*

Main pattern of industrial relations	Country	Level				
		Plant	Locality	Branch	Nation	State
Developing collective bargaining	DK	*Tillidsmænd* in commitment to co-operation with employers	Collective bargaining general in all skilled trades		Mediation system under *Hovedaftaling*, 1899	
	UK	Some bargaining	Bargaining well established in skilled trades; some growth among unskilled. Also growth of conciliation	Bargaining beginning to develop strongly at this level		
Collective bargaining in skilled trades; state involvement of workers'	CH	Plant to branch: Bargaining well entrenched				State support for union and employer association activities
	D		Bargaining	Book industry		Government

Table 4.5. *Continued*

Main pattern of industrial relations	Country	Level				
		Plant	Locality	Branch	Nation	State
organizations			growing; growth of *Ortskrank-enkaßen* with elected worker representatives	only		arbitration service, 1901
	A	Worker participation in employer-dominated *Betriebskaßen*, 1890	Bipartite *Kaßen* (2/3 worker), growth of bargaining			*Vereinskaßen* (all worker), *Arbeitsrat*, both 1898

	F	Délégués de sécurité for mines	Bipartite caisses de retraite for miners
Sporadic collective bargaining			
	N	All levels: mainly strike action as only form of collective industrial relations	
	B	Locality to nation: some bargaining but declining after 1900. Major lockouts	Some bargaining; bourses de travail, 1899	Bipartite conseils d'industrie, but for workers, not unions
	NL, S	Some bargaining		
Contestation or nothing	I, P, E	Police repression of strikers; occasional sporadic representation of workers		

Note: Country boundaries as in Table 4.1.

agreement of its kind at such a level and involving matched confederations. Denmark is of course a small society, and perhaps one should treat as of similar standing the not dissimilar agreement reached at national branch level within the British engineering industry two years previously. On the other hand, the fact that the Danish agreement was national and multi-industrial gave it a general and public status which meant that it occupied political space. It is notable that neither the British nor the Danish agreement was the product of amicable consensus: both were preceded by lock-outs of particular severity. It is also important to note the limitations of both: the organizations agreed in effect to mind their own business and just engage with each other for wage bargaining from time to time. The agreements embodied merely a mechanism for mediating disputes; nothing was said about agreed criteria, aims, or desiderata for such mediation. They do'enable us to talk unambiguously about the emergence of collective bargaining as opposed to pure contestation (sectorally limited in the United Kingdom), though the Danish *Hovedafteling* departs somewhat from the rules of Dunlopian pluralism in its centralization. Denmark is one of three countries which can now be characterized as having developed collective-bargaining systems, the others being Switzerland and the United Kingdom.

Some interesting institutions set Switzerland together with Austria and Germany apart as a group having institutions not readily embraced at this 'stage of development' by the analysis in Chapter 2, though they are indicative of something more general but very weak at this time: states taking initiatives to involve autonomous workers' organizations at the margins of public life—something unthinkable in previous decades. The British government began to appoint union representatives to occasional committees on labour matters, and bipartite conflict arbitration in Denmark and France was a government initiative. But the Swiss government went beyond this and subsidized the establishment of a secretariat for the *Arbeiterbund*—an umbrella body covering a number of separate workers' peak organizations. This was highly distinctive and marked a clear departure in the treatment of labour by Swiss governments, but it was an established Swiss policy where other economic interests (industry, handicrafts, agriculture) were concerned. The Swiss state, lacking as it was in bureaucratic resources of its own, had developed the habit of subsidizing the conduct of tasks such as the collection of official statistics or the provision of expert advice by organized groups; it had long done this for employers (Parri, 1987*a*).

The Austrian and the German *Reich* took the remarkable step of instituting elected commissions of workers to run (or share the running of) the pensions and social insurance schemes—at company, branch, and national levels—that they had instituted during the 1880s (Traxler, 1982; Heidenheimer, 1980; Weitbrecht and Berger, 1985). In both cases this followed abruptly on an earlier policy of repression and exclusion. The same device was also followed in France, but limited to the mining-industry scheme. An ostensibly similar but in the long run rather different development took place in Belgium where, starting in the city of Ghent and eventually adopted as national policy, trade unions were given responsibility for running the public unemployment insurance system.

We thus have an interesting state of affairs: collective bargaining was still largely restricted to the skilled trades and operated largely at a local level, and most systems can be summarized as comprising overall a combination of pluralism and contestation. However, at state level governments were simultaneously engaged on strategies clearly intended to go beyond bargaining and to bind workers' representatives into some form of national integration. In no sense did these initiatives amount to anything that might begin to be described as neo-corporatism; there was here no dense network of relations, but a few, isolated, sometimes anomalous initiatives. But the motive in establishing these devices was often to try to induce in workers a sense of national loyalty—in terms of the model in Fig. 2.1, to encourage a form of identity going beyond that implied by contract. Such was certainly the motive of the Berlin- and Vienna-based empires. It was possibly a nascent form of authoritarian corporatism. These two states are difficult to classify in terms of an evolutionary scheme of thickening institutional textures.

Articulation of Labour Movements, 1900

By the end of the nineteenth century there is enough information available on the structure of union movements to enable consideration of their form of articulation (Table 4.6). By 1900 four

TABLE 4.6. *Articulation of trade-union movements, c.1900*

| | Unions affiliated to main confederation | | | | Dominant types of union | Individual unions | |
| | Membership as % of | | No. | Powers of confederation re affiliates | | Characteristic internal authority structure over local groups, individual members, etc. | Characteristic shop-floor organization |
	known unions	labour force					
DK	79.99	7.01	n.a.	DsF has weak strike fund	Craft	Weak, local	*Tillidsmaend* active but committed to co-operation by *Hovedafteling*
UK	59.35	7.42	191	TUC has no authority	Craft; new general	Weak in craft unions, where power is local; more central in general unions	Shop stewards in craft unions, but not active in bargaining
D	80.00	2.72	c.55	GK has some authority	Craft, but gradually amalgamating	Weak in craft unions, where power is local; more central in industrial groups	Very weak

N	24.00	0.25	n.a.	LO has strike fund, 1899	Craft; new general unions forming	Strong, but unions very small	Some shop-floor organization
S	87.15	2.21	21	LO has little authority	Craft and branch; some general; unions seeking to merge	Strong	Semi-autonomous *Verkstads-klubbrörelsen* active in metal industry
A	66.77	0.73	17	GK, 1893; Catholics and nationalists then form separate organizations	Attempts at centralization	Weak	Limited; very weak
CH	26.00	0.64	15	SGB, 1896; weak	Branch	Power at local levels	
F	48.57	1.45	3,000	CGT, 1895, but inchoate	Federations of local branch unions; trend to branch unions but also local cross-branch organization	Loose, weak	Very weak
B	29.82	0.98	n.a.	Workers Party acts as union centre, 1898	Federations of local branch unions	Varied	Very weak

TABLE 4.6. *Continued*

	Unions affiliated to main confederation				Individual unions	
	Membership as % of		No.	Powers of confederation re affiliates	Dominant types of union	Characteristic internal authority structure over local groups, individual members, etc.	Characteristic shop-floor organization
	known unions	labour force					
NL	n.a.	n.a.	n.a.	Centres formed: Liberal, 1871; Protestant, 1877; Catholic, 1888; social democratic, 1895	Craft	Strong in craft unions	Very weak
E	n.a.	n.a.	n.a.	UGT, 1885	Local	Loose	Non-existent
I*, P*						Loose, local	Non-existent

Notes: Country boundaries as in Table 4.1.

* No confederations.

movements had produced confederations that made some claim to co-ordinate overall strategy: Denmark, Germany, Norway, and Switzerland. Within a couple of years they would be joined by Austria-Hungary and Sweden. However, only Denmark and Germany were dealing with memberships of any size, and nowhere could there be any claim to encompassingness. In the United Kingdom, of course, the TUC was already very well established, but it had now been overtaken by these others in terms of having a co-ordinating role; it was still merely a forum from which unions might lobby parliament.

Looking at the structure within movements, some have started to try to build organizations with a national and branch-level scope: Austria, Belgium, Germany, Norway, and Switzerland, though these were largely just small, loose federations of local and craft groupings within the branch in question, or, as in Norway, tiny. Only Danish and British unions had begun to generate a shop-floor structure of union representation and activity; most other systems depended on local union offices outside the plant.

In summary, the Danish movement is in a class of its own in having developed by this early stage the skeleton—though no more than that—of an articulated union movement. After it come the German and British organizations, which are on an impressive scale but as yet unarticulated. The Austrians, Norwegians, Swedes, and Swiss, in contrast, had more articulated structures but with few members inside them. Outside these cases one can hardly speak of structure. The French, Belgian, and Dutch movements had produced organizations, but there is little evidence that these engaged seriously in whatever fragmentary industrial-relations activity was in progress.

Employer Organizations, 1900

Table 4.7 summarizes the state of employer organization. Looking first at their role strictly as employers, we find the Danish DA equipped with funds to help finance strikes and lock-outs—funds extensively used in 1898—and making some claim to co-ordinate employer behaviour whether in conflicts such as that of 1898 or peace agreements such as that of 1899 (Bruun, 1931*b*). Three other countries had developed similarly strong organ-

TABLE 4.7. *Organizations of capital, c.1900*

	Scope[1]	Power[2]	Other associative business activity[3]
DK	Rapid growth of specific employers' associations; sometimes negotiate, sometimes combat strikes; FfA, 1885	FfA acquiring authority to act in relations with unions; central strike fund, 1896	Trade associations involved in trade regulation and training
D	Strong growth of employers' organizations, some to help bargaining, others to stop it, as aspect of trade-association activity	CDI strike insurance fund; also co-ordinates lock-outs	Elaborate structure of *Kammer* and other organizations at local and regional levels organize training; cartels and CDI increasingly drawn into sharing responsibility for industrial policy (CDI, 1876; BdI, 1895)
CH	Growing network	Employers' associations with well-developed strike funds	Trade associations receive state funds for carrying out delegated public tasks; *Genoßenschaften* organize training; Vorort, 1881
S	Rapid growth of associations; CAF co-ordinates except in metal industry (VF independent); merger as SAF, 1902	Some co-ordination of bargaining and strike-breaking	SAF works closely with government on export policy
N	Growth of associations; NAF, 1900	NAF organizes many lock-outs; seeks to impose centralized	Trade interests involved in advisory councils of non-parliamentary state

A Branch level only	bargaining on LO Limited	Elaborate structure of *Kammer* and other organizations
UK Branch-wide organizations in engineering, 1896, and ship-building, 1890	Limited co-ordination power, mainly during major conflicts	Very little; some consultation
F Very little	UIMM and Comité des Forges try to organize, but little success	Very little
B Fragmentary	Very weak; mainly combating social legislation	Rise of Catholic organizations in agriculture etc. but weak Guild legacy still operative
NL Some anti-union organization and lock-outs; VNW, 1899	Weak	
All other cases: no serious organization or activity		

Notes: Country boundaries as in Table 4.1.

[1] Extent of organization of employer interests.
[2] Resources available to employer organizations to co-ordinate action.
[3] Activity directed at trade rather than labour issues.

izations, with at least some strike-fund role, but less coherent organization. Swiss, and to a similar extent German, employers were highly organized for both industrial-relations and trade-association political work as discussed for 1870. (Leckebusch, 1966; Gruner, 1956). These two are now joined by Sweden, a country whose industrial-relations institutions were fairly rudimentary. There were increasing similarities in the industrial structures of Germany and Sweden. In both there were strong divisions between largely domestic industries, mainly comprising small firms, and the large companies in such export industries as steel. Organizations of the former were likely to want amicable relations with unions; those in the latter sought a tougher line, though only in Germany did major employers seek to destroy unions. But in all cases firms sought the strength of an organizational base.

Behind these stand Austria and Norway. Norwegian employers were beginning to build structures similar to those in the rest of Scandinavia, but the development was not very advanced. Austrian employers could work through their *Kammer* structure to co-ordinate policy, but had not taken many independent initiatives.

The strength of branch-level employers' organizations in the United Kingdom puts that country in a class of its own. Employers' organizations existed in the Netherlands, but had little in the way of effective structure for industrial relations, while in France the biggest sectoral organization (the Union des Industries Métallurgiques et Minières), rather like the Engineering Employers' Federation in the United Kingdom, tried to co-ordinate a broader employers' front, but met with considerable reluctance from firms (Lefranc, 1976). In the remaining countries employer organization was fragmentary.

If we now look at other associative activity by business, we find a similar rank order. The relatively unbroken transition from guild to industrial organization in Denmark that we noted in 1870 had by 1879 produced an extensive organization, the Fællesrep, which was active in the organization of training, etc. (Dybdahl, 1982). Swiss organization had followed a not dissimilar path, and was perhaps more strongly developed than in Denmark because of the need (already noted in 1870) to fulfil functions not carried out by the limited Swiss state. As with labour, but on a much larger scale, the government passed funds to business organizations who then organized training, the collection of statistics, etc. Furthermore, Swiss industry was highly protectionist, and business organizations organized the protection (Gruner, 1956). The Vorort had already appeared as a powerful co-ordinator in 1881.

German business no longer had the problem of compensating for an absent state, as it had before 1870, but it had maintained and intensified the elaborate organization built up at that period and, like the Swiss, was deeply protectionist. This was perhaps the prime case of organized capitalism, with tight relations between a small number of large banks and a cartellized industry. Sweden was never as protectionist as Germany, but its small number of export-oriented firms were distinctly collusive and by the 1880s had turned to protection. It is important to note here a Danish–Swedish contrast: in Denmark (and in Norway) the logic of business organization was that of small firms seeking the security of organization (whether against labour or international competition); in Sweden, as in Germany, that pattern combined with that of branches dominated by large firms who found collusion easy because of their small numbers.

Apart from these countries and the Austrian *Kammer*, there is not much associative activity of importance, except for the protectionist arrangements in parts of southern Europe. It is important to distinguish these from the German and Swiss cases. The latter countries used protection as a shield behind which associations, governments, and firms pursued a dynamic modernization strategy; in southern Italy, Portugal, and Spain—and perhaps Austria—surviving guild structures protected ancient crafts from internal and external stimulus.

In general, therefore, with some precocity among Swedish employers, the organization of the 'sides' of industry runs congruently with the industrial-relations institutions. Systems and organizations alike are equipped for either contestation or incipient collective bargaining, though there are signs in some instances (Austria, Germany, Sweden, and Switzerland) of some overarching and political structures not strictly compatible with the pluralist model.

Power of Organized Labour, 1900

Indicators of trade-union power (Table 4.8) suggest Denmark and the United Kingdom as the most advanced union movements. Union membership and mobilization capacity are fairly straightforward data, but comparison of the political position of labour is made complicated by the variety of forms it took. Belgium and Switzerland were countries with autonomous labour-movement parties and democratically accountable governments, while the Danish and German governments were not responsible to their national assemblies. The Austrian government had a similar position, but the assembly was itself not democratic but comprised a number of appointed status-based *Kuria*, the fifth of which contained trade-union representatives sitting as such.

In a number of other countries liberal or similar parties had adopted some of organized labour's causes: in France the socialist Millerand, who had some union connections, was included in a liberal cabinet in 1899; in Italy the liberal Giolitti government that came to power in 1900 was expected to be favourable to labour. Norwegian liberals had campaigned jointly with labour for reforms to the suffrage, though that having been achieved in 1898 and labour having shown weakness in certain industrial conflicts, the liberals were in fact about to shift away from that alignment. Liberals also shared some labour causes in the Netherlands, Sweden, and the United Kingdom. Only Spain and Portugal—non-democratic and with very small working classes— stood completely outside this pattern of labour political progress.

Small though labour movements were at this stage, the growth in both suffrage and the working class, together with labour's capacity for disruption in certain sectors of the economy, was making established parties sensitive to labour interests. They might still respond—as they all did from time to time—with repressive measures against strikes; but they were also aware of a need to avoid alienating this potentially vast section of the electorate. In some countries beset by problems of national cohesion governments had additional motives for not excessively alienating labour. For the Hapsburg empire the social democrats and trade unions, while troublesome, were at least dominated by ethnic Germans, by and large accepted the empire and were therefore not part of the clamour for national determination that was threatening its stability. In Norway labour was clearly part of the nation that was struggling to free itself from the last vestiges of domination by a Swedish administrative élite. French governments, aware of the weak labour movement's capacity for disruption, sought to integrate workers through the establishment of *bourses de travail* that became important institutions for union organization.

It is impossible to rank the relative importance of these differences. All that one can conclude is that, looking at all aspects of union power, Denmark and the United Kingdom stand out as particularly strong, and Portugal and Spain as exceptionally weak. The others stand somewhere in between. The Swiss, German, and Belgian movements are probably stronger than the rest, but from the vantage point of 1900 that is not clear.

In terms of Fig. 2.2, in historical perspective all these countries remain safely within quadrant I (weak organizational articulation; weak labour), but Denmark has made steps in a north-easterly direction, towards the distant neo-corporatist quadrant III. The United Kingdom's movement is in the direction of the unstable (but still distant) II. Austria, Germany, and Switzerland have possibly moved towards IV.

Economic and Political Development, 1900

Table 4.9 shows indicators of economic and political development at this period. The extraordinary position of the United Kingdom as exceptionally developed economically but backward democratically continues to be evident, but the former is enough to 'account' for its advanced industrial-relations pattern. The undeveloped state of Belgian and Dutch industrial relations is not at all explained by their position here; in particular their contrast with the relatively advanced industrial-relations institutional development, at least at state level, in Austria-Hungary is difficult to understand. Denmark is an anomaly: fairly wealthy and advanced in democracy, but still heavily agricultural: if we are seeking an answer to the question of why Denmark was the first country to develop a bipartite national institutional structure of industrial relations, we do not find it here. True, Danish agriculture was not a peasant or latifundia system, but one of small land-owners and independent farmers, but they had little to

TABLE 4.8. *Power of organized labour, c.1900*

	Total known union membership		Major industrial-relations and political developments affecting position of organized labour within industry	Other major political developments affecting wider position of organized labour
	as % of labour force	as % of dependent labour force		
UK	12.50	16.49	Major union defeat in engineering industry lock-out, 1897–8; but growing organization and militancy of unskilled workers	Unions growing in importance as component of Liberal Party
DK	8.76	12.31	Major iron industry lock-outs, 1895, 1899; latter marks breakthrough in union recognition	Social democrats win 19.3% of vote, 1901
D	3.40	3.84	Crimmitschau textile strike, 1902, major defeat for unions	Social democrats win 27.2% of vote, 1898
B	3.29	4.79		Major suffrage struggles, 1890s; Workers Party wins 22.5% of vote, Catholic Party 51.1%, 1900
CH	n.a.	n.a.	Major strike wave, 1895–6	State support for union secretariat
I	3.07	6.45	Waves of rural dissent, 1887, 1893, 1897; unions restricted to north	Liberal Giolitti government, 1900, expected to be favourable to labour

F	2.99	5.01	Strike waves in new manufacturing industries	1884 law requires prefects to help both sides of industry to organize; *bourses de travail* founded; arbitration law, 1891; socialist leader Millerand in Cabinet, 1899
S	2.53	3.64		Venstre (Liberal) Party helps labour
N	2.30	3.90		Labour Party wins 3% of vote, 1900, and is part of national campaign for autonomy from Swedish rule
A	1.00	2.39	Growing displays of labour militancy	Union leaders gain places in nominated *Kuria*; German labour a relatively loyal component of fragmenting empire
NL	n.a.	n.a.	Some major strikes	Social democrats win 9.5% of vote, 1901
E	n.a.	n.a.	Unions illegal since crushing of republic, 1874, but existence tolerated	
P	n.a.	n.a.	Virtually no organization	No suffrage

Note: Country boundaries as in Table 4.1.

TABLE 4.9. *Indicators of political and economic development, c.1900*

	Agricultural work-force as % of total work-force	GNP p.c. (1960 US$)	Electorate as % of adult male population	Leading economic sectors
A	60.9	361	82.7*	Agriculture; but some important industrial development
B	21.9	721	90.7	Textiles, steel, coal, capital equipment, finance
DK	47.5	633	87.4	Agriculture, small trades, rapid growth of tertiary sector
F	41.8	604	87.9	Textiles, mines, engineering, agriculture
D	36.0	639	80.0*	Coal and steel growing in dominance, textiles
I	59.4	335	26.5	Agriculture, public utilities, textiles
NL	30.8	614	51.0	Agriculture, some urban crafts
N	41.3	577	89.7	Shipping, agriculture, forest products
P	n.a. (high)	n.a. (v. low)	none	Agriculture
E	n.a. (high)	351	none	Agriculture, textiles in Catalonia
S	49.8	454	25.1	Agriculture, wood, textiles
CH	31.0	785	78.9	Metal industries, watchmaking
UK	7.7	881	61.5	Textiles, coal, steel, engineering, finance

Note: Country boundaries as in Table 4.1.

* But government not responsible to Reichstag.

do with the Basic Agreement, which was between craft unions and industrialists in rather small-scale, traditional manufacturing and handicrafts.

Industrial Conflict, 1900

For this period statistics on industrial conflict are available for a few countries (Table 4.10). Of these Denmark clearly experienced the greatest overall levels in the final years of the nineteenth century, though where worker involvements and days lost are concerned this is almost entirely because of the Great Lock-out of 1898, which constituted, relative to the size of the work-force, the single biggest industrial dispute in Europe of the nineteenth century. The Basic Agreement the following year certainly did not have consensus as its precondition.

Looking more specifically at the central datum, working days lost per 1,000 union members, three countries had historically very high conflict levels (Austria, Denmark, and the United Kingdom). France, Germany, and probably Belgium were also high. Comparing this information with the evidence on institutional development in Table 4.5, there is at this 'thin' stage of labour-movement growth little trace of the inverse relationship between institutional development and conflict levels that most theories expect to find. As conflict became significant, employers and governments sought to construct institutions that might contain it; elsewhere, workers' ability to disrupt was too sporadic for employers to bother. Contestation remained an inexpensive strategy.

Conclusions, 1900

Developments in the latter part of the nineteenth century continue to provide support for the Dunlopian thesis that collective bargaining will flourish best under bourgeois liberal élites, the best instances being Britain and Denmark. There might be a question over Germany, surely a dynastic élite but with some elaboration of bargaining. However, at this early stage it is still possible to claim that, given the size and organization of both labour and capital, it was remarkable how extensively bargaining was being avoided. France is surprising here, being a 'liberal'

TABLE 4.10. *Industrial conflict, 1896–1900*

	Strikes per 1,000		Workers involved per 1,000		Days lost per 1,000	
	dependent labour force	trade-union members	dependent labour force	trade-union members	dependent labour force	trade-union members
A	0.05	1.97	6.45	270.16	210.08	8,801.20
B	0.06	1.16	17.83	372.32	n.a.	n.a.
DK	0.14	1.14	19.12	155.30	1,080.55	8,776.64
F	0.05	0.97	11.32	225.69	169.52	3,380.57
D	0.06	1.47	4.48	116.75	129.70	3,377.83
I	0.04	0.59	11.01	170.74	107.66	1,670.30
S	0.06	1.76	2.76	75.83	145.31	3,987.20
UK	0.06	0.63	16.92	172.83	566.69	5,790.00

Note: Country boundaries as in Table 4.1.

polity but with little institutional development in industrial relations. The thesis that the development of systems will be a function of union power also receives some support, and there is a hint in the Danish, though not the British, case that increasing power causes increasing articulation.

Employer organization follows broadly similar and therefore expected patterns to that of unions, but *business* organization outside industrial relations is more puzzling. If the United Kingdom is the most advanced economy of the late nineteenth century, why have the Germans, Scandinavians, and Swiss (and in a different way the Austrians) built themselves such formidable organizations? It cannot be a simple argument about historical backwardness. The Swiss were among the most advanced nations by any standards; as were the Danes in terms of wealth though not industrial development; and Germany, though often seen as backward, had by 1900 become a very serious industrial power.

THE EVE OF THE FIRST WORLD WAR

Since the World Wars were to have such a major impact on the political structures—even the geographic and demographic identities—of the countries under review, it is important that we survey them before and after these events. Although less than fifteen years elapsed between the start of the century and the outbreak of the First World War, they were years of some change in industrial relations. We also acquire another country, as in 1907 the Grand Duchy of Finland secured sufficient autonomy from the Russian Empire to organize its own government. Autonomous trade unions had existed there for longer, though they were very small. To improve the chances of comparison I begin to include Finland in the survey only at this point.

Institutional Development, 1914

Table 4.11 summarizes the state of industrial-relations institutions around 1914. Branch-level collective bargaining had spread in a number of countries: the growing interest of employers in

Table 4.11. *Institutional development of industrial relations, c.1914*

Main pattern of industrial relations	Country	Level				
		Plant	Locality	Branch	Nation	State
Continuing strengthening of collective bargaining	DK	*Tillidsmænd* in commitment to co-operation with employers	Collective bargaining general in all skilled trades	Developing	DA and DsF agree on mediation scheme	Labour Court established
	CH	Bargaining well entrenched	Bargaining growing			State support for union and employer association activities; GAV law, 1911, including provisions for *Friedenspflicht*
	UK		Bargaining well entrenched and spreading to new groups of workers	Bargaining well entrenched and spreading to new groups of workers		Increased government consultation of unions; legal basis strengthened by 1906 Act

S	Recent growth in collective bargaining; state mediation schemes			Bargaining growing	Bargaining growing; LO/SAF mutual recognition agreement, 1906	Union involvement in state mediation schemes
N				Bargaining growing in metal industry		Union involvement in state mediation schemes
D	Some collective bargaining; limited state involvement of workers' organizations	Some development of works councils, sometimes as anti-union device	Bargaining growing		Union role in pension fund management; bargaining growing	Limited consultation of unions
A		Some development of works councils, sometimes as anti-union device	Growth of bargaining in some branches		Union role in pension fund management	Limited consultation of unions

TABLE 4.11. *Continued*

Main pattern of industrial relations	Country	Level				
		Plant	Locality	Branch	Nation	State
Thin collective bargaining	NL	Some development of works councils, sometimes as anti-union device	Some bargaining	Bargaining growing but still rare; employers seek 5–7 year agreements		
	B	All levels: little change since 1900				
	SF	Locality to state: some bargaining between unions and *ad hoc* groups of employers; fierce conflict				
Fragmentary bargaining; contestation	F	As 1900		As 1900		Government tries to encourage bargaining
Contestation	I, P, E	All levels: police repression of strikers; some bargaining in northern Italy and Catalonia				

Note: Country boundaries as in Table 4.1. Grand Duchy of Finland, including Karelia, is semi-autonomous part of Russian Empire.

'yellow' (i.e. employer-dominated) unions suggests an increasing concern on their part not to leave matters to the individual labour contract, and state involvement was growing. Overall however the main pattern was still of local bargaining with skilled groups. The Danish Basic Agreement and the particularities of Swiss arrangements still stand out for the extent of their institutional-ization. The United Kingdom probably had still the most ex-tensive overall level of pure collective bargaining as such. These three are the only ones that can be said to be characterized more by collective bargaining than by contestation.

The rapid development since 1900 of collective bargaining at branch level in Norway and Sweden is notable, in particular the mutual recognition agreement between LO and SAF in the latter country. These countries were beginning to follow Denmark, but count as a separate group with incipient collective bargaining, as developments were at an early stage and not very extensive. In Sweden the employers, led by those in the key metal sector, had succeeded in weaning the craft-based unions away from local to branch-level agreements, but despite some major national conflicts (1904, 1912) over suffrage, the unions were neither able nor willing to move to a more centralized level (Hadenius, 1976). It should be noted that the employers wanted to erect national-level institutions. No such development was possible in Norway at that time.

The institutional structures of Austria and Germany were less straightforward, since, as we have seen for 1900, while collective bargaining was not particularly well developed, the degree of administrative involvement by unions, at political or politically initiated levels, was much greater than in the United Kingdom or Denmark—though similar to Switzerland. These are as difficult to classify as in 1900; are they an incipient neo- or authoritarian corporatism?

In 1911 British unions could have taken advantage of arrange-ments for participation in the administration of social insurance similar to those established in the two German *Reich* two decades previously. The Liberal government offered union participation in social insurance schemes, and for a while it took place. But the unions' main concern was in running their own pensions funds, and they lost interest in any role in the co-management of state schemes (Heidenheimer, 1980).

Showing thin signs of a development of collective bargaining are Belgium, Finland, and the Netherlands, but there are few such in France, which almost joins Italy, Portugal, and Spain as cases to be labelled, if anything, purely contestative.

Articulation of Labour Movements, 1914

Degrees of articulation are shown in Table 4.12. A comparative assessment is difficult as countries were moving in qualitatively different ways. We can at least group them, if not rank the groups. Denmark and, less prominently, Germany and Norway were developing articulated movements embracing a high proportion of unionized labour, though only Denmark extended this to a union shop-floor organization. The Norwegian labour movement was so small in absolute terms that it is not clear that very much was being articulated at all. Also developing some kind of structured, co-ordinated national organization, though within tiny movements and therefore classified separately, were the Austrians and the Dutch.

The United Kingdom's TUC remains a major problem: it was the nearest thing to a genuine economy-wide movement—though only in relative terms—and yet almost entirely uncoordinated and not particularly successful at gathering all unions within the one confederation, undemanding though it was. Comparing Norway, Finland, and perhaps Germany, with the United Kingdom at this stage, one sees force in Dunlop's (1958) argument that a *lack* of centralization is the hallmark of maturity. But it is the advantage of our multinational comparison that we can examine such generalizations more widely. If centralization correlates with immaturity, Spanish and French labour must at that stage rank as more highly developed than Danish or German. One might hazard a curvilinear thesis, that very primitive movements are decentralized, acquire a rather empty centralization and then mature like good British (and American) localized collective bargainers. The problem here is that the British movement did not go through a centralized 'stage'. We are already beginning to see, as we contrast the development of the French, Italian, Portuguese, and Spanish movements with the Nordic cases, a point of considerable importance: labour movements tend to acquire either fragmented or articulated structures from early on and then reinforce these early trends. Later years will show this even further.

A rather inchoate pattern of development is revealed by two early industrializers, Belgium and Switzerland, and two very late ones, Finland and Sweden, with elements of both fragmentation and the development of an articulated movement. It is in fact difficult to rank these very diverse movements against each other, though they clearly contrast with the extremely weakly organized movements in the remaining countries. Of these, Italian labour was somewhat more articulated than France, Spain, and Portugal, but all were essentially very fragmented with confederations having very notional roles.

Employer Organization, 1914

In employers' organizations (Table 4.13) we can now identify two different forms of co-ordination among those which have developed some organizational capacity. In both forms employers were grouped in strong, centralized associations that had become (or were associated with trade associations that had become) considerably involved in dealings with government. But in one group—the Scandinavians—these associations insisted that the unions try to bargain with them at a national, cross-branch level, while in the other—Switzerland, the two German-speaking *Reich* and the Netherlands—they either kept bargaining at local levels or tried to stop any dealings with unions at all.

It should not be assumed from this distinction that the Scandinavian employers were particularly friendly towards organized labour. They engaged in very tough struggles, calling nation-wide lock-outs to enforce their demand for centralization (especially in Denmark and Sweden; as we have seen, Norwegian labour was already more clearly centralized). But they seemed to take the existence of labour's organizations for granted and were confident they could cope best with highly centralized relations. But there was variety within Scandinavia. In both Denmark and Norway employers' organizations were dominated by small, formerly handicraft, firms, while Swedish industry was becoming dominated by the large-scale export sector, though forest-based industries were significant in both Norway and Sweden. Danish employers had organized in response to the industrial conflict of

TABLE 4.12. *Articulation of trade-union movements, c.1914*

	Unions affiliated to main confederation				Individual unions	
	Membership as % of		No.	Powers of confederation re affiliates	Dominant types of union	Characteristic internal authority structure over local groups, individual members, etc.	Characteristic shop-floor organization
	known unions	labour force					
DK	77.9	10.14	c.50	DsF controls strike fund but not bargaining	Craft, general	Relatively centralized	Strong role
N	78.0	6.65	32	LO controls strike fund but not bargaining	Craft, general	Relatively centralized	Little role
D	65.0	7.40	49	GK controls some strike funds but not bargaining; rival Christian and other organizations	Craft, but grouped in branch-level structures	Relatively centralized	Little role
A	58.5	2.78	19	GK controls some strike funds but not bargaining;	Craft, but grouped in branch-level structures	Relatively centralized	Little role

NL	30.2	3.69	20	rival Christian and other organizations (Christian peak body, 1906) NVV firmly established, 1905; controls strike funds but not bargaining; rival Christian organizations	Craft, general	Relatively centralized	Little role
UK	64.7	14.62	207	TUC has very little power over affiliates	Craft, general	Power very localized, but growing role of national leaderships	Some role in skilled trades
S	63.6	4.54	27	LO has very little power over affiliates; rival white-collar organization	Craft, general	Relatively centralized	Little role
B	48.8	3.64	c.50	CS encourages amalgamations of	Growth of *centrales*, of	Growing strength	Very weak

TABLE 4.12. *Continued*

	Unions affiliated to main confederation					Individual unions	
	Membership as % of		No.	Powers of confederation re affiliates	Dominant types of union	Characteristic internal authority structure over local groups, individual members, etc.	Characteristic shop-floor organization
	known unions	labour force					
				local unions into *centrales*; rival Christian CSC formed	branch and general types		
SF	75.0	2.51	30	FL has very little power over affiliates	Craft, general	Power very localized	Little role
CH	64.36	3.66	15	SGB has very little power over affiliates; rival organizations	Branch	Power very localized	Very weak
I	76.9	3.05	*	CGdL, 1906; very little power over affiliates; small rival organization	Craft, general	Power very localized	Very weak

				(USI, 1912); also Christian unions			
F	51.5	0.99	*	CGT has very little power over affiliates	Craft, general	Power very localized	Very weak
E	n.a.	n.a.	n.a.	UGT and CNT co-operate, but both weak and fragmentary	Various, mainly local	Power very localized	Very weak
P	n.a.	n.a.	n.a.	Weak and fragmentary	Local	Loose	Non-existent

Note: Country boundaries as in Table 4.11.

*Signifies a complex pattern of local cells of the confederations alongside individual economic-branch unions, giving a very large number of units, many of which were, however, parts of the confederation itself.

TABLE 4.13. *Organizations of capital, c.1914*

	Scope[1]	Power[2]	Other associative business activity[3]
DK	Employers try to impose national bargaining scheme	DA has authority to act in relations with unions	Trade associations involved in trade regulation and training
N	Small employers and hydro-electric industry organize more strongly against unions in wake of post-1905 political realignments	NAF continues to seek centralized bargaining	Trade interests involved in advisory councils
S	Continuing growth of associations; SAF, 1902	SAF exercises tight control over employers' bargaining and co-ordinates tough lock-out strategy	Growing importance of export-sector organizations, especially in metal industry
CH	ZSAO, 1908	As 1900	As 1900
D		BdI and CDI form specialized employers' associations to try to centralize bargaining; these merge as VDA, 1913	As 1900
A	HAÖI, 1907	Central bodies fund strike resistance, 1912	As 1900
NL	Some anti-union organization and lock-outs; VNW	Weak	As 1900
SF	Small but combative national organization, 1907; becomes larger STK, 1914, but excludes VF	STK establishes strike support on Swedish model	

	[1]	[2]	[3]
B	Growth of organizations in metals, mines, etc.	Very weak; mainly combating social legislation	As 1900
UK	Continuing growth	Limited co-ordination power, mainly during major conflicts	Increasing engagement with government as war looms
I	Some organizations in north only		
F	Very little	UIMM and Comité des Forges continue to experience little success	Very little
E, P	Very little activity		

Note: Country boundaries as in Table 4.11.

[1] Extent of organization of employer interests.
[2] Resources available to employer organizations to co-ordinate action.
[3] Activity directed at trade rather than labour issues.

the last years of the nineteenth century; Norwegians in the aftermath of the collapse of the all-class coalition struggling for independence in 1905; and the Swedes in the wake of the great general strike to achieve the suffrage in 1904. Despite these different points of origin, they were all able fairly speedily to achieve a tight level *and similar form* of organization, with strike-support funds and a degree of discipline. In several respects the Norwegians and Swedes were consciously imitating their southern neighbours (Galenson, 1952*a*).

Swiss employers differed from those in the above countries in that, while strongly organized and having close dealings with government, they were not at all centralized in their relations with labour, though during the early years of the twentieth century they developed considerably the trade-association and cartel-management role of the Vorort, which became almost an instrument of the confederal government (Gruner, 1956).

Finnish employers, who were organized as virtually a mirror image of the Swiss, are a class of their own. They were developing, in direct imitation of the Swedes, centralized power, but had few dealings with a government that was mainly concerned with issues of national independence and agrarian policy (Mansner, 1981). In the remaining countries business organizations in general were relatively unimportant, though Britain stands, with northern Italy, as having stronger *employers'* organizations. French employers continued to be extremely suspicious of attempts by UIMM to co-ordinate them.

It is possible at this juncture to note an oddity of time sequence. We are often told how employer organization has historically followed that of labour, and in several respects this is true; employers do not have to bother to organize *qua* employers unless and until labour does. But one must enter two reservations. First, once goaded into action by labour, employers often set the pace for subsequent organizational development. In Scandinavia they quite openly pressed unions to get themselves organized on a far tighter national basis before they would deal with them seriously. In Sweden in particular the national decision-making capacity of labour that eventually became such a hallmark of Swedish social democracy was initially demanded by the SAF from a highly reluctant group of unions—the LO hierarchy itself was more interested—and grudgingly conceded over a period of thirty years (Hadenius, 1976). (Half a century later the SAF was trying to put the development into reverse.) In Germany too, though rather more negatively, it was the imposing edifice of organized capital that pushed labour into establishing those centralized bureaucracies that Roberto Michels (1911) misleadingly saw as intrinsic to *labour* organization *per se*; a view he would not have reached had his starting point been British trade unions (Roderick Martin, 1978).

The second point is that, although the first steps of employers' organization *followed* union mobilization, those employers who organized most speedily and effectively were those who *had already achieved* some associative capacity for trade purposes, especially in their relations with the state. The rapid development of specifically employer organization, overtaking the unions to whom it was responding, in the Netherlands, Norway, and Sweden during the pre-war years may be explained by this fact. These employers had also organized, as it were, in advance of industrial-relations institutions, and would appear to have an 'excess'—or perhaps anticipatory—capacity for managing an elaborate industrial-relations system.

Power of Organized Labour, 1914

Turning to indicators of union power (Table 4.14), most labour movements were still small and their associated parties weak. Unemployment was generally high, but at this stage available statistics were still neither comparable nor sufficiently reliable to make use of them worthwhile. In spite of their weakness, most union movements had managed some major mobilizations, though often these had ended in major defeats. Working primarily from membership strength, we can form four broad groups.

In terms of the standards of the later twentieth century, none of these movements had a large membership, though the United Kingdom unions had already secured a higher proportion of the work-force than has ever been achieved by their French counterparts. Labour movement *parties* in Finland and Germany had also reached historically high levels of electoral success. Three countries (Denmark, Germany, and the United Kingdom) can be picked out as having unions with an above-average membership

TABLE 4.14. *Power of organized labour, c.1914*

	Known union membership c.1910–14, as % of		Major industrial-relations and political developments affecting organized labour within industry	Share of popular vote[2] %	Participation in gov't[3] %	Other major political developments affecting wider position of organized labour
	labour force	dependent labour force[1]				
UK	22.59	26.89	Major strikes; Trade Disputes Act, 1906, favourable to unions	6.4 (44.2)	0.25	Liberals very dependent on Labour Party support
DK	13.02	19.72	Labour Court law, 1910	29.6		
D	11.38	17.24	Some loss of union freedom as Reich prepares for war	34.8 (16.4)		
N	8.53	13.75	Rise of militant syndicalist groups	26.3		
S	7.14	12.51	Arbitration law, 1906; big defeat for LO in 1909 national strike	30.1		
NL	12.19	16.24	Major conflict 1903–5	18.5 (46.5)	0.25	
B	7.45	11.23	Suffrage strikes 1902, 1912	9.3 (51.1)	0.25	

			GAV law, 1911		
CH	5.68	9.47		0.25	
A	4.75	10.25	Some loss of union freedom as Reich prepares for war	10.1 (21.2) 15.9	German-speaking labour of value to Reich in context of national discontents
SF	3.35	11.76	Unions suffer many defeats in conflict	43.1	Social democrats central to new nation; had formed first Finnish government, 1906
I	3.97	6.3	Most strikes broken by police	17.6	
F	1.93	3.45	Major conflicts (e.g. mines, 1906); defeats		Unions committed to syndicalism by Congress of Amiens, 1905
E	n.a.	n.a.	General strike, 1911		
P	n.a.	n.a.	Strikes in support of democracy		Many unions committed to syndicalism

Note: Country boundaries as in Table 4.11.

[1] For Finland, percentage of non-agricultural labour.

[2] In most recent general election, secured by parties primarily allied to trade unions; parties with a union wing but primarily committed to other interests (e.g. Catholic parties) in parentheses.

[3] 0.25 = by party/ies not primarily labour but with union wing.

for the period and a prominent political presence, though Denmark is the sole clear-cut case. Germany looks similar, but the Reichstag in which labour had representation was unable to control the executive. British labour, though by far the most powerful industrially, was dependent for most of its political influence on the Labour Party's alliance with the Liberal Party, which was also linked to non-labour interests; but the liberals did form the government, so British labour was the only movement at this period with major and substantive government influence.

The Norwegian and Swedish movements, and in more complex ways the Austrian, Belgian, Dutch, and Swiss, lagged behind these, but were showing signs of strength. The membership weakness of Austrian unions was largely a function of the large peasant economy; within the modern sector they were more important. And, as we have already noted, although it had continuing difficulties with the Hapsburg regime, the General-kommission's commitment to the identity of the existing Austrian state gave social democracy a place of some significance in an empire where nationalist struggles often loomed larger than class ones.

The Belgian and Dutch movements (like those in Austria, Germany, Switzerland, France, and Italy) were made complicated by a division between socialist and Catholic unionism, and in these two countries the Catholic minority was particularly large. Catholic unionism has been a very ambiguous phenomenon, as we shall see in discussions of later periods. On the one hand it was a source of disunity weakening labour; although socialist complaints that Catholic unions were virtual 'yellow unions' were often inaccurate, there have in all countries been important moments when they have supported the employers' position. A Catholic union dealing with Catholic employers should have a source of solidaristic identification with the employer other than that won through the establishment of exchanges based on a power relation. If such unions are dealing with predominantly non-Catholic employers, of course, the situation might be very different, and the role of Catholic unions in Wilhelmine Germany and the pre-war Netherlands, and of Catholic groups within United Kingdom unions, has differed from that in Italy or Belgium. But neither Catholic unions nor Christian democracy were necessarily welcomed by employers, who often preferred no unions and no democracy. And even if Catholic unions were trying to demonstrate that there was no need for a class war, they had to do so by demonstrating to workers that they could nevertheless achieve something for them, which meant a distancing from employers.

Further, to the extent that political and economic élites welcomed these unions as alternatives to the socialists, they had to provide a space for them and the causes they represented. A Catholic pro-democracy party could never adopt the hostile stance to labour's demands for union rights and welfare policy that could be risked by purely conservative, or even certain kinds of liberal, regimes. In the late nineteenth and early twentieth centuries, when radical political struggle was often against old traditional, often Church-based, élites and for an extended suffrage, labour's allies were more likely to be found among liberals. But after the achievement of extended suffrage, as Christian democracy grew and as liberalism became preoccupied with the protection of economic freedoms against a state intervention that was increasingly motivated by welfare policy, this alignment was often completely reversed. The process was not straightforward, and depended partly on the extent to which the new Christian democracy became the preferred vehicle for conservative groups.

Even within such broad groupings as we have here, Finland clearly stands alone. The extreme industrial weakness of labour is partly explained by the exceptionally peasant character of the economy, but the Social Democratic Party was the strongest in Europe and, as early as 1906, had become the first European socialist party ever to hold government office. (Thus, European socialism first came to power in the country with the smallest industrial working class.) It thereby stands at the opposite extreme from the British labour movement.

Four union movements (those of France, Italy, Portugal, and Spain) are easily classified as the weakest. France is notable for having no real political component to its labour movement. The unions mistrusted the socialists and were devoted to anarcho-syndicalism. It was an ironic development for unions in one of the first countries to develop both modern unions and popular participation in politics to become alienated, marginalized, and resembling their counterparts in the economically and politically 'backward' parts of southern Europe. In fact, if the north of Italy could be taken as a separate country it would be seen to have a unionism considerably stronger than the aggregate of the French movement. In both the industrial cities of the north-west and the agriculture of the Po Valley there was a vital unionism, brought down in the national scale by the very weak situation in the latifundia economy of the south (Barbadoro, 1973*a* and *b*).

What seems to have happened in France is that the odd combination of early democratic advance but retarded industrialism in a country whose agriculture was dominated by land-owning peasants imparted to organized labour a pessimistic view of the opportunities presented by democracy. At the same time the dominant secularism of the Third Republic did not give even the Christian-democratic wing of the labour movement much hope. Anarcho-syndicalism, otherwise associated with countries with very bleak democratic possibilities (Spain, Portugal, parts of Italy, and Latin America) is thus found in the first of the European democracies. This stance was formally asserted by French socialists at the conference at Amiens in 1906, and while in theory it was repudiated in the 1920s, it lives on.

In Portugal and Spain democratic interludes were brief; unions had few or no connections with established political parties and embraced anarcho-syndicalist or similar strategies as virtually the only available ones in the circumstances—though these were strategies that encouraged neither organizational nor political growth.

Thus, on the eve of the First World War, union power seems to correlate well with institutional development at the extremes (Denmark, Germany, the United Kingdom; France, Italy, Portugal, and Spain). While there had been considerable change since the beginning of the century, countries do not occupy very different positions in terms of Fig. 2.2.

Economic and Political Development, 1914

A glance at comparative levels of economic and political development reveals some interesting details (Table 4.15). If one starts from a simple expectation that industrialization, growing wealth, and democracy advance together, there are two principal surprises. First, countries with major problems of national inte-

T ABLE 4.15. *Indicators of political and economic development, c.1914*

	Agricultural work-force as % of total work-force	GNP p.c. (1960 US$)	Electorate as % of adult male population	Leading economic sectors
A	56.9	490	94.5[1]	Agriculture; but some important industrial development
B	22.4	891	91.6	Textiles, steel, coal, capital equipment, finance
DK	42.7	862	87.8	Agriculture, small trades; rapid growth of tertiary sector
SF	71.5	520	88.5[2]	Peasant agriculture
F	42.7	689	90.5	Textiles, mines, engineering, agriculture
D	35.2	741	94.1[1]	Coal and steel dominant; textiles
I	55.5	441	89.8	Growing division between industrializing north and peasant south
NL	28.4	734	67.0	Agriculture, some urban crafts
N	39.2	749	70.3	Shipping, agriculture, forest products
P	n.a. (high)	292	none	Agriculture
E	n.a. (high)	367	none	Agriculture, textiles in Catalonia
S	45.6	680	76.5	Agriculture, wood, textiles; growing metal industry
CH	26.8	964	75.8	Metal industries and watchmaking
UK	8.1	965	62.4	Textiles, coal, steel, engineering, finance

Notes: Country boundaries as in Table 4.11.
    Work-force data for France 1906, Germany 1907, Netherlands 1909.

[1] But government not responsible to Reichstag.
[2] Percentage of male and female adult population.

gration (Austria and Italy, though not Belgium) or in contrast recent major triumphs of national autonomy (Finland and Norway) have high levels of democracy in relation to their level of economic development. And countries with reputations for advanced levels of liberalism have the most restricted democracies (the Netherlands, Switzerland, and the United Kingdom, but not Belgium). Belgium's position, as a liberal economy but a country with linguistic problems of integration, perhaps explains its doubly exceptional character.

The negative association between democracy and liberty may perhaps be understood in the sense that, the more rights over the state that the suffrage secures, the more reluctant will political élites be to grant it. If so, it is no coincidence that the countries with the two most advanced suffrages (Austria and Germany) were two with governments not responsible to parliament. It should also be noted that in Belgium property owners had double votes.

However, it is not easy to make sense of a relation between either economic or political development and industrial-relations development. Southern Europe (Italy, Portugal, and Spain) is perhaps to be understood in general 'undeveloped' terms, and Britain and Switzerland as 'advanced'; but it is difficult to see any pattern beyond that point.

Industrial Conflict, 1914

Data on conflict indicate this to have been a particularly turbulent period. Four of the fourteen highest examples of annual working days lost per 1,000 union members during the twentieth century occur at this time, and no country had conflict levels less than moderately high in historical terms. Contestation was beginning to show its potential, but with the possible exceptions of Denmark and Switzerland there was little evidence of the expected inverse association between degree of institutional development and level of conflict. On the other hand, these two countries are the only two to have at that period a degree of institutionalization at both shop-floor and national level. It is perhaps not surprising that, by the end of the War, employers and governments in many countries seem to have decided that contestative systems were not so cheap after all.

TABLE 4.16. *Industrial conflict, 1910–1914*

	Strikes per 1,000		Workers involved per 1,000		Days lost per 1,000	
	dependent labour force	trade-union members	dependent labour force	trade-union members	dependent labour force	trade-union members
A	0.09	0.88	14.79	144.29	263.45	2,570.24
B[1]	0.07	0.62	21.72	193.41	n.a.	n.a.
DK	0.08	0.41	11.99	60.80	297.66	1,509.43
SF[2]	0.10	0.85	19.81	168.45	524.86	4,463.10
F[3]	0.12	3.48	25.49	738.84	306.47	8,883.19
D[4]	0.14	0.81	19.09	110.73	616.72	3,577.26
I	0.11	1.75	31.74	503.81	406.48	6,452.06
NL	0.16	0.99	15.92	98.03	302.28	1,861.33
N	n.a.	n.a.	27.59	200.65	771.02	5,607.42
S	0.07	0.56	7.24	57.87	226.81	1,813.03
CH	0.05	0.53	3.58	37.80	n.a.	n.a.
UK	0.06	0.22	52.36	194.72	1,044.86	3,885.68

Note: Country boundaries as in Table 4.11.

[1] 1910–13 only; big suffrage strikes, 1912.
[2] Figures relate to manual workers only.
[3] Figures based on 1906 labour force statistics.
[4] Figures based on 1907 labour force statistics.

Conclusions, 1914

By the outbreak of the Great War we do not find any trade-union movements capable of shaping national industrial-relations systems, though the importance of labour issues was producing both political and industrial responses. Theories expecting a clear relationship between 'development' and the institutionalization of industrial relations have difficulties. Of the most clearly 'advanced' systems, the United Kingdom's was highly disaggregated, Denmark was primarily a rural country and Germany, though it had some collective bargaining, still had many employers wanting to wipe out autonomous labour representation altogether. France's presence, as an advanced economy and polity, at the lower end of a scale of institutional development, was surprising, but otherwise the group of Italy, Portugal, and Spain makes sense, as does Finland if the rather special circumstances of its labour movement's political rise are taken into account.

Given the absence of any real articulation among unions at this period, it is not surprising that we can discern nothing resembling neo-corporatism, though a 'premature' articulation among weak unions and an articulation of capital's *trade* interests even more than its *employer* interests give a surprising guide to later twentieth-century developments. The range of forms among western European industrial-relations systems lies between sporadic contestation (when labour can rise to anything at all) and limited collective bargaining, with just a few incipient developments going beyond the latter. It is notable that in the three German-speaking countries (Austria, Germany, and Switzerland), and to some extent in Belgium, institutions for incorporating labour in a public administrative role have developed at state level without much prior development within industrial relations. This throws into doubt any theory one might construct about gradual upward accretions of institutions from the industrial-relations base.

5

Organized Industrial Relations between the Wars

Der Staat ist heute zum guten Teil ein sehr gewichtiger und wirkungs-voller Träger der proletarischen Bestrebungen geworden und darum hängt deren Fortschritt sehr wesentlich auch von dem Gedeihen des Staatsganzen ab ... da die Erregtheiten der gegenwärtigen Zeit und die Kleinheit unseres Staates jede Lohnbewegung, sei sie auch die wenigst umfangsreiche, weit mehr zu einer Sache der Allgemeinheit machen, als es ehedem der Fall war.

> (Generalkommission, Vienna, 1920, quoted in Traxler, 1982: 109)

Vi har ofret nogle principper, men vi har reddet landet.

> (Thorvald Stauning, Danish trade union leader and Prime Minister, 1934, quoted in Hansen and Henriksen, 1980a: 291)

Immediately after our 'snapshot' of 1914, the countries of western Europe were engulfed in a World War, either as participants or as affected neutrals. National integration became an overwhelming issue. States faced a major need to develop identity and transcend alienation at the level of the nation, and the manner in which total war defines people in terms of their national location facilitated this. There were differences within and between nations; indeed one might predict from the foregoing discussion the way in which the majority of the German labour movement moved more readily than the French to accept a patriotic role.

In general, labour movements became important to governments and were incorporated in a manner that dramatically changed their relations with the state. Barriers between political space and civil society were broken down. In the main combatant countries (Austria, France, Germany, and the United Kingdom) labour and employer organizations were drawn into wartime

planning. Even the liberal economies of France and the United
Kingdom became co-ordinated, market processes were partially
suspended, and where workers were concerned there was a particular need to shore up their identity with and loyalty to the
state. In the neutral countries and occupied Belgium (to the
extent that that country continued to exist), concerns for maintaining national unity and for organizing production and distribution were not much less. Only Italy (late to join the War),
Portugal, and Spain seemed relatively unaffected. As primarily
peasant agricultural economies they were less integrated in world
trade.

The main exception was however Finland, where the Russian
Revolution raised enormous conflicts. Opposition to Tsarist
Russia had brought together Finns of all political opinions, but
when the Russian regime was a workers' revolutionary one the
labour movement's position became ambivalent. A civil war of
considerable ferocity was unleashed, lasting beyond the end of
the World War, leaving labour beaten and broken and inducing a
sharp shift to the right in Finnish politics.

In most countries the immediate aftermath of war continued
the momentum of the incorporation of labour into grandiose
plans for a new tripartite capitalism, the most tangible international manifestation of which was the formation of the International Labour Office under cross-national tripartite control in
Geneva. In recognition that the social conflict was potentially as
vast as the military one, the Treaty of Versailles included clauses
establishing the ILO (initially a potential international corporatist
institution) and committing the nations to a new incorporation of
labour. In Austria, Belgium, France, Germany, the Netherlands,
and the United Kingdom national industrial conferences were
called and plans made for the incorporation of labour through
works councils in the factory and through various consultative
agencies at national level. Among the most elaborate were
British plans for joint consultation bodies at all levels and in all
sectors, the so-called Whitley Councils.

Governments were clearly seeking gestures to signify a desire
to overcome working-class alienation through the elaboration of
institutions for national dialogue. Their anxiety seemed well
justified. The Russian Revolution had awakened proletarian
ambitions; the Red Flag had been flown from public buildings in

Berlin, Munich, and Budapest. Millions of men only recently disarmed were returning from the horrors of the trenches where many had been poorly led by high-status officers. And strike levels had been running high in several countries during the last years of the War.

An institutional snapshot of 1919 would demonstrate an extraordinary general shift towards unambiguously corporatist institutions. However, the impact of all this did not necessarily reach far down into subnational or subpolitical levels. Wartime measures were an emergency, temporary imposition on existing institutions; and the extent to which the immediate post-war aspirations for change subsequently survived depended on how closely they suited existing institutional patterns.

As early as 1920 the first post-war recession had affected most European economies. From being scarce and crucial to the war effort, human labour was now in surplus. The contrast was swift and stark, and enabled employers rapidly to reverse the rise of labour and concomitant institutionalization of industrial relations that had occurred. The shallow, bolt-on nature of the wartime changes and war-related character of the state's earlier accessibility made matters that much easier for them. Unions usually wanted to keep their wartime positions, but their declining strength could often no longer sustain them. Meanwhile labour movements at the political level underwent a major schism as within each country groups responded differently to the challenge thrown down by the leaders of the Bolshevik revolution of 1917 to join an international communist movement. In Finland, France, Germany, Italy, Portugal, and Spain very large parts of the movement accepted this challenge and broke with their colleagues who persisted in seeking a parliamentary road to socialism. In Norway, though only temporarily, the whole movement did so; elsewhere only minority factions, though often important ones. The schism affected the union wing of the labour movement, either by producing equivalent breaks in its own organizations or by setting up tensions within unions.

The change was most abrupt in Italy, with the accession of a fascist regime encouraged by industrial and rural employers fearful of labour's militancy in the immediate post-war years. By 1925 Italy lacked an autonomous labour movement of the kind we are studying here, so that country temporarily leaves our analysis. In its early years, of course, Italian fascism made much of its plans for achieving national integration and overcoming class conflict through the erection of a grand *soi-disant* corporatist edifice. For each industry or occupational sector bipartite institutions were established to which a good deal of policy-making authority would be delegated, with a national assembly of corporations comprising a parliament for functional interests. But first, existing autonomous labour organizations were destroyed. Shortly afterwards the wing of the fascist movement that represented an autonomous labour organization was also liquidated. In line with the expectations of the argument in Chapter 2 concerning authoritarian corporatism and heteronomous organizations, the whole structure soon became lifeless and lacked any substantive significance. However, in the turbulence of the inter-war years the fascist adaptation of nineteenth-century corporatist ideas was attractive, at various times, to several groups in a number of countries, including elements of labour movements.

Democracy survived, but the labour movement suffered rapid reverses, in France, the Netherlands, and the United Kingdom, where the grand schemes of 1919 had virtually disappeared from the agenda by 1922. British progress stopped in its tracks with the erection of Whitley Councils in several parts of the public service; the private sector avoided the development altogether. In Belgium socialists took part in a post-war government of reconstruction, but a return to 'normalcy' rapidly followed its fall in 1923.

The story is rather different in the two defeated German-speaking *Reich*, where the discrediting of established élites propelled labour movements to a leading position in the polity. Here, while labour was in rapid retreat in the victor countries, labour-led coalitions set about both advancing labour's rights and entrenching the labour movement as an important representative of the national interest. This made for a rapid advance in both institution-building and political access within the context of the awesome task of national reconstruction. But after a few years this proved to be an enlarged, nightmare version of the 'premature' promotion of labour elsewhere. There remained a discontinuity between labour's sudden political importance and growing centralization on the one hand and its labour-market position and therefore real organizational strength on the other, the latter being weakened by both the general recession and the particular dislocation of the defeated economies. The labour movement became a paper tiger.

This was by no means the only source of instability that beset those two ill-fated republics, but it was certainly among the sources. Labour was politically prominent and exposed while being vulnerable to its enemies should it seek to use any of its apparent political strength. However, as of the mid-1920s, when we take our first snapshot after the First World War, the fact remains that immediate pre-war and wartime trends towards an increased participation by organized labour were temporarily being maintained only in the two countries which had seen the apparent abrupt discontinuity of defeat in war, regime collapse, and, in the case of Austria, major geographical dismemberment.

THE MID-1920S

Border changes have affected the identity of some of our cases between 1914 and 1925: Austria has lost its Slav lands and is pressed back into the German-speaking territories around Vienna and the Alps, the loss of both rural and Slav populations greatly enhancing the relative weight and internal unity of labour within the infant republic. Germany lost Alsace-Lorraine to France, and also ceded parts of Poland. The United Kingdom lost the major part of Ireland, predominantly a peasant economy. The last change gives us a new case to consider: the new Irish Free State, later the Republic of Ireland. And Finland finally secured independence from now revolutionary Russia. At the time of our 'snapshot', 1925, Ireland and Finland were both still in the midst of internal conflict surrounding their constitutional status.

Institutional Development, 1925

The state of institutional development is shown in Table 5.1. There has been the gradual 'thickening up' of institutions that would be expected by simple evolutionary theories: considerable development of bargaining and mediation arrangements, increasingly at branch rather than local level, and a considerable extension of government consultation with unions. We encounter,

Table 5.1. *Institutional development of industrial relations, c.1925*

Main pattern of industrial relations	Country	Level				
		Plant	Locality	Branch	Nation	State
Incipient neo-corporatism with collective bargaining	CH	Collective bargaining	Collective bargaining	Union involvement in administration of public policy		Union involvement in administration of public policy; also consultation
State-determined (neo-)corporatism; little collective bargaining and considerable contestation	A[1]	Statutory *Betriebsräte* with some administrative powers	Extensive bargaining and consultation	Bipartite consultation; union role in pension fund management	Centralized collective bargaining (resisted by many employers)	Formal involvement of unions and employer associations in economic advice
	D[2]	Statutory *Betriebsräte* with some administrative powers	Extensive bargaining and consultation	Bipartite consultation; union role in pension fund management	Centralized collective bargaining (resisted by many	Formal involvement of unions and employer associations in

Industrial Relations between the Wars   131

				...employers)	economic advice
E	Collective bargaining alongside severe conflict	*Comités paritarios* for bargaining and consultation at all levels			Unions participate in national administrative agencies
DK	Some collective bargaining	Extensive bargaining	Extensive bargaining but severe conflict	Union involvement in mediation and running social funds	Unions in consultation arrangements
UK[3]	Some collective bargaining	Extensive bargaining	Extensive bargaining; union involvement in mediation; but post-war institutions collapsing		Unions in small number of consultation arrangements
S			Extensive bargaining but severe conflict	Union involvement in mediation	Unions in consultation arrangements

TABLE 5.1. *Continued*

Main pattern of industrial relations	Country	Level				
		Plant	Locality	Branch	Nation	State
	NL		Some bargaining and union involvement in mediation schemes	Some bargaining and union involvement in mediation and pension schemes		
	N		Some bargaining and union involvement in mediation schemes	Extensive bargaining but severe conflict		
Collective bargaining developing with state support	B		Collective bargaining	Some growth of *commissions paritaires*		Unions in consultation arrangements

Contestation	F	Some limited bargaining	Union involvement in mining pension scheme; much conflict elsewhere	Strike-breaking by employers' 'Export Peace' movement
	SF	Some limited bargaining	Some bargaining	
	IRL	Some bargaining	Some bargaining	
Authoritarian corporatism	I, P	Autonomous unions illegal; fascist unions of workers and employers have formal consultation role at all levels		

[1] Territory of Restösterreich.
[2] Territory of post-Versailles Germany.
[3] Excluding Republic of Ireland.

as already with pre-war Austria and Germany in Chapter 4, a problem of how to rank gradual developments in collective bargaining in relation to the establishment by government of elaborate institutions not necessarily rooted in relations among the social partners.

Only in Switzerland was there a *combination* of union institutional involvement at national political level as well as developed collective bargaining. At neither level were developments particularly strong, but they formed a kind of incipient neo-corporatism with union leaders and employers being involved with each other and public agencies at a variety of levels (Parri, 1987*a*).

In Austria and Germany there was apparently the kind of institutional integration that, when combined with appropriate organizational characteristics, might be expected to have encouraged neo-corporatist arrangements and exchanges transcending collective bargaining. That had of course been the language talked by industrial spokesmen in the wake of 1918; but by 1925 many sections of industry were resisting this legally imposed system, were not working within the institutions, and were returning to their earlier preference for repressing labour instead (Maier, 1975; Talos, 1981).

The options available in these countries therefore seem to have been the stark alternatives of either a shift into an elaborate generalized political exchange or a complete dismantling of institutions. Labour had managed to establish itself more firmly in these countries in 1918 than in the victor nations because it had rushed to fill the institutional vacuum left by the defeat and discrediting of old élites. It was therefore difficult to dislodge when economic circumstances changed and the threat of the spread of Bolshevism receded. But the old élites were no less determined than their British, French, and other counterparts to regain power. For that reason the incipient neo-corporatism here is best regarded as fragile or brittle.

An essentially politically generated high level of institutional development also took place suddenly and anomalously in Spain at this point. The dictatorship of Primo de Rivera, having made enemies among traditional conservatives, the Church, the liberal bourgeoisie, and the strong anarchist and communist movements, turned to the socialists and their associated trade union, the

Unión General de Trabajadores (UGT), for support (Ben-Ami, 1985). They gave it reluctantly and grudgingly in exchange for an ostensibly extraordinary degree of institutional incorporation. A structure of *comites paritarios* was established, running from shop-floor to national-political level, in which workers and employers were represented. The *comites* dealt with matters ranging from what the British would call joint consultation, through collective bargaining, to participation in national administrative agencies. It was the early Weimar and Austrian Republic blue-prints or the British Whitley Council model on a very ambitious scale. The major limitation on it was that it did not extend to the rural sector, which was at that stage by far the majority of the Spanish economy.

The self-confessed similarity of Primo's regime to those of Mussolini and Salazar raises the question of whether we should be considering these structures as aspects of autonomous labour representation. In fact the UGT did remain in control of itself throughout—to the extent that eventually it was able to be one of the organizations that helped bring down the regime. However, anarchist organizations were suppressed; Catholic, liberal, and even 'yellow' ones ignored. There was therefore a privileging of a particular form of autonomous labour movement, but auton-omous it remained. The case helps us comprehend the com-plexity and ambiguity of organizational structures during the inter-war years, with fascist, socialist, communist, Christian social, and liberal ideologies producing overlapping policies for the institutions of an organized industrial society.

Labour was also being incorporated at a wider range of levels in Denmark, but building up from the industrial base that had been established at the turn of the century rather than the political base being used in German and Spanish lands: less dramatic but also far less exposed. At this point the Danish system had not changed markedly from what had been estab-lished at the turn of the century, and it therefore ranks here as an established collective-bargaining case alongside two others: Sweden (where both organized labour and the previously back-ward manufacturing economy were growing rapidly) and the United Kingdom (which saw mainly a combination of orthodox collective bargaining with some involvement in mediation and consultation with government). The Netherlands and Norway differ from this group through the relative absence of national-level institutions.

A development surprisingly similar to Primo's in Spain, and from the perspective of 1925 difficult to distinguish analytically from it as potentially a form of authoritarian corporatism, was being furthered at the same time in liberal-democratic Belgium, where the government began to set up *commissions paritaires*. These were bipartite institutions established by the state, initially in only a few industries, and charged with the task of both collective bargaining and representing the interests of the branch to government. The development was small at this stage, but it is significant coming as it did in a country not affected by massive conflict and without a marked legacy of encouraging strong organization. Indeed, Belgian industrialism, the earliest on the European continent, had typically followed a liberal model, and briefly during the 1923–5 period Belgian élites seemed to be following the British and French preference for expelling labour from important influence.

The position of France as a country of contestative, low institutional development, already noted in 1914, now becomes even clearer, as progress in the establishment of collective bargaining took place very haltingly. Ireland and Finland, the two 'new' countries, also have low levels of development and join France as essentially contestative cases. The former inherited institutions of the British kind, but within a small modern sector in a primarily peasant economy. Finally, Italy and Portugal had fascist regimes which, unlike that in Spain, abolished autonomous institutions before erecting an unambiguously authoritarian corporatist structure.

Articulation of Labour Movements, 1925

Developments in labour's articulation are shown in Table 5.2. There has been a general shift to a concentration of numbers and powers within national unions and confederations. Austria and Norway appear as the most centralized, the former having gained since 1914 from the reduction in heterogeneity in the shift from Austria-Hungary to *Restösterreich*. Neither can really be said to be *articulated*, as they lacked an integrated shop-floor presence. The Norwegian LO was particularly weak, accounting for barely

TABLE 5.2. *Articulation of trade-union movements, c.1925*

	Unions affiliated to main confederation					Individual unions	
	Membership as % of		No.	Powers of confederation re affiliates	Dominant types of union	Characteristic internal authority structure over local groups, individual members, etc.	Characteristic shop-floor organization
	known unions	labour force					
A	86.67	26.92	52	GK monopolizes strike calls and funds, but rival Christian confederation	Branch type dominates	Centralized	Weak, but shop-floor role in *Betriebsräte*
N	85.00	11.33	32	LO controls strike funds	Branch type dominates	Centralized	Militant syndicalist
DK	77.15	17.59	51	DsF has few powers	Craft and general	Centralized	*Tillidsman* system
B	65.43	14.29	31	CS has few powers	Branch type emerging	Centralized	Weak
CH	65.05	8.01	21	SGB monopolizes strike calls and funds, but rival Christian	Branch	Centralized	Strong

TABLE 5.2. *Continued*

| | Unions affiliated to main confederation | | | | Dominant types of union | Individual unions | |
| | Membership as % of | | No. | Powers of confederation re affiliates | | Characteristic internal authority structure over local groups, individual members, etc. | Characteristic shop-floor organization |
	known unions	labour force					
D	65.00	12.43	49	GK monopolizes strike calls and funds, but rival Christian confederation	Branch type emerging	Centralized	Weak, except through *Betriebsräte* where these are operative
S	73.45	14.68	34	LO has few powers over affiliates; rival white-collar organization	Craft and general with some growth of branch unions	Centralized	Strong growth of union 'clubs'
NL	38.62	7.11	29	NVV monopolizes strike calls and funds, but rival Christian confederations	Branch type emerging	Centralized	Weak

IRL	85.00	7.18	50	ITUC has few powers	Craft and general	Varied	Shop stewards in some skilled trades
SF	83.00	3.39	20	FL has very little power over affiliates	Craft, general	Varied; all unions very small	Weak
UK	60.60	17.25	205	TUC has few powers	Craft, general	Varied	Shop stewards in many skilled trades
F	51.01	2.34	36	CGT has very little power over affiliates	See note*	Centralized but unstable	Very weak
E	51.36	2.30	n.a.	UGT co-ordinates co-operation with government	Craft, general	Varied	Very weak

Note: Country boundaries as in Table 5.1.

* Signifies a complex pattern of local cells of the confederations alongside individual economic-branch unions, giving a very large number of units, many of which were, however, parts of the confederation itself.

a tenth of the labour force and confronting a highly militant syndicalist shop-floor movement. The Austrian GK's share, more than a quarter of the work-force in membership of unions, is, however, the highest yet achieved in our review.

Only the Danes can be considered to have a movement linking a significant shop-floor presence to an active national level, though DsF still lacked important co-ordinating powers; and for this reason Denmark ranks only slightly ahead of the Belgian, German, Dutch, Swedish, and Swiss movements. These had all acquired some central powers within their dominant confederations, or in the Swiss case within industrial unions, even if the movements in some of these were religiously divided. The Netherlands and Switzerland are those where religious divisions most weakened the leading confederation, reflected in particularly low levels of representativeness.

The remaining countries all had far stronger monopolies than the Netherlands, but the confederations had little power. They are therefore best ranked against each other by the degree of representativeness of organized labour of the main confederation, though it should be noted that the British TUC had somewhat more power than the Finnish federation. French labour stood alone as clearly the least centralized. Spain is difficult to analyse, with a politically centralized UGT possessing a very weak mobilizing base within industry, while Portugal and Italy no longer have autonomous movements and are therefore beyond our analysis.

Employer Organization, 1925

The main changes—or apparent changes—to affect employers organizations (Table 5.3) were in the fascist cases and in the defeated powers (where a position of resistance against working with unions was changed into one of being required to do so by the political settlement in the first years of the post-war republics—a settlement which, by 1925, was beginning to seem increasingly unnecessary to employers as labour's political strength waned and rising unemployment destroyed its base in the labour market). Both sets of cases were affected by the dramatic instability of revolutionary breakdown and regime change, so we should consider them separately from the more stolid developments in northern Europe.

Spain's employers remained no more *autonomously* organized than in the past, but they were being forced into a degree of associative activity by the regime. Italian and Portuguese employers were also orchestrated into corporative structures by the fascist regime. The ambiguity of interpreting these three cases is as problematic as that of labour in Spain. It was not strictly autonomous development, but many employers, especially in Italy, supported the fascist state.

The German and Austrian pattern is distinguished from the southern European cases by the autonomy of the organizational strength of employers, though Spain more resembles the German-speaking countries in the obligation placed on employers to treat with representatives of autonomously organized labour.

In all other countries employers were left more free by government to pursue policies of their own choosing. In the case of Scandinavia this now meant a highly organized, centralized approach to industrial relations, with employers seeking nation-wide deals with unions, which they sought, not to destroy, but to reshape into stabilizing counterparts—often being willing to engage in massive and uncompromising conflict in order to persuade them to do so. The Netherlands and Switzerland were somewhat similar in the importance placed by employers on organization, though it was not being used in those countries with the same drive and determination to press unions into a national system; the unions were after all weaker and more divided than in the Scandinavian countries.

There was an increasing willingness to deal with unions in the United Kingdom, Belgium, and Ireland, but far less change in France, where it is instructive to note the external stimulus of a need to provide an employers' representative to the ILO that led *government* to encourage the CGPF into existence. This was part of the flurry of post-Versailles activity; its significance had subsided by 1925 and in any case had few implications for domestic practice (Lefranc, 1976).

In Finland the initial post-war years saw the growth of a powerful, combative organization on Scandinavian or German lines (Mansner, 1981). However, this went into severe *decline* after the

TABLE 5.3. *Organizations of capital, c.1925*

	Scope[1]	Power[2]	Other associative business activity[3]
DK	Extensive growth under DA auspices	DA strengthens hold on industrial sector and co-ordinates strategy, seeking a centralized system	Trade associations involved in trade regulation and training
N	Considerable growth	NAF rapidly developing co-ordinating role in most sectors	Trade interests involved in advisory councils
S	Extensive growth under SAF auspices; VF joins SAF, 1917	SAF strengthens hold on industrial sector and co-ordinates strategy, seeking a centralized system	'Directors' Club' of export-sector firms co-ordinates export strategy
D	Strong growth; RDI, 1919	RDI presses for highly centralized collective bargaining; strong powers over affiliates	Close involvement of associations in Weimar industrial strategy
A	Strong growth	Strong centralization of bargaining strategy	Close involvement of associations in industrial strategy
CH	Growth	Employers' associations with well-developed strike funds	Trade associations receive state funds for carrying out delegated public tasks; *Genoßenschaften* organize training
NL	Strong growth; VNF, 1917; CO, 1920	Associations strengthen hold and co-ordinate relations with unions at branch level	CIV formed to co-ordinate strategy, 1920

	[1]	[2]	[3]
E	Weak	Weak organizations engaged by government in co-operation with labour	Weak
I		Confindustria, 1919, accepts role in structures of fascist state	
P		Employers organizations (weak) accept role in structures of fascist state	
UK	Moderate; stable; BEC, 1919	Increasing involvement of associations in lock-outs	Wartime role declining; FBI, 1916
B	Continued growth	Very weak; mainly combating social legislation	Weak
IRL		Very little development	
F	Limited	Government encourages formation of CGPF, but with few powers	Weak
SF	Growth, then decline	Co-ordinating role of STK declines after civil war weakens labour	Limited

Note: Country boundaries as in Table 5.1.

[1] Extent of organization of employer interests.

[2] Resources available to employer organizations to co-ordinate action.

[3] Activity directed at trade rather than labour issues.

crushing of the unions in the Civil War rendered it less necessary. Only Belgium saw employers accelerating in organization less rapidly than labour, while Norway was temporarily the most clearly opposite case.

Outside the dictatorships, trade as opposed to employer organization continued to follow patterns similar to those noted for 1914; Austrian and German organizations resumed their pre-war ways despite the upheavals of the collapse of the *Reich*. But in southern Europe industrial organizations were pressed into a new relationship with the state.

Grouping and ranking these diverse cases is particularly difficult, as employers' organizations are not obviously as adversely affected by right-wing dictatorships as are labour's. The Scandinavians probably rank as the most strongly articulated, as their structures were crescive rather than imposed externally, involved clear sanctions over firms and were paralleled by strong trade associations. Austria and Germany are placed in a separate category because of the obligatory nature of their employers' co-operation with labour. Dutch and Swiss employers' organizations were somewhat less elaborate than all these. Spain has been placed alongside the more thoroughgoing fascist cases; in each country essentially weak bodies were being required to play a role. Of the remaining rather poorly organized liberal countries, Finnish and French employers' bodies were particularly powerless.

With the exception of the dictatorships, there was now a clear relationship between relatively articulated labour movements, organized capitalism, and elaborated collective bargaining. In Norway, the Netherlands, and Switzerland employers were distinctly better articulated than labour. Most remarkably, perhaps, we should note how the disruptions of war made in the end so little difference to the general approaches to relations between states and organized employer interests of the main combatants. France and the United Kingdom remained countries in which governments did little to admit organized groups to sharing political space once the wartime emergency had ended; Austria and Germany returned to their old ways of working through such organizations—a continuity that even the fall of both imperial houses and the dismemberment of the Austrian empire did not disturb.

Power of Organized Labour, 1925

Table 5.4 summarizes the state of union strength around 1925. Since 1914 there had been a considerable increase in membership in most countries, and a smaller increase in political strength. Some account should now be taken of unemployment, though this is still rendered difficult by different national counting systems and by low levels of registration of unemployment in countries with large rural sectors. All we can say is that un-employment in Scandinavia and Austria was higher than in the United Kingdom and the Netherlands, which was in turn higher than in Switzerland. Clearly high unemployment did not hamper union recruitment, but it must have reduced the incentive for employers to bother to come to terms with otherwise impressive labour movements.

Over half our cases now have movements with reasonable incipient strength. Denmark and Sweden had labour parties dominating government coalitions at this time, which clearly puts them in a different position from those with higher memberships but less direct political influence. It is difficult to calculate the significance of this, especially when it is compared with the ambiguous 'dependence' of the Austrian and German republics on their labour movements or the similarly ambiguous factor of Christian labour movements in Austria, Belgium, the Netherlands, and elsewhere.

As of 1925, and ignoring what was to follow, the Austrian movement emerges as very strong, especially if we take account of dependent labour only and forget the large remaining peasant population. The movement had suffered some reverses since its immediate post-war dominance, the material situation in the country was appalling, and politically the only state representa-tion of labour was through the highly ambiguous Christian Social Party; but there was simultaneously a curious dependence of the state of *Restösterreich* on the labour movement. It constituted the only element in the society genuinely prepared to commit itself to the new republic—an advantage that rapidly became the opposite when other elements finally became disillusioned with that entity. How do we distinguish between this brittle strength and that of Danish labour, with a poorer mobilization base, but a more secure place in a far more stable polity? Another strong trade-

TABLE 5.4. *Power of organized labour, c.1925*

| | Known union membership as % of | | Major industrial-relations and political developments affecting organized labour within industry | Unem-ployment[2] | Share of popular vote[3] % | Particip-ation in gov't[4] % | Other major political developments affecting wider position of organized labour |
	labour force	dependent labour force[1]					
DK	22.80	35.96	Unions confront series of lock-outs from DA	H	36.6	0.75	
S	19.98	31.03	Unions confront strong action from SAF	H	41.1	0.75	
A	31.06	48.07	Unions' early post-war gains eroded as unemployment rises and employers resume dominance	H	39.6 (44.0)	0.25	Social democracy becoming marginalized but still one of few reliable bases of republic
UK	28.46	31.83	Series of major strikes over wage cuts; general strike, 1926, leads to major union defeat	M	33.3		Labour Party becoming established as main opposition party
B	21.84	30.76	Conflicting pattern of growing union rights and tough employer opposition	?	39.4 (36.1)	0.25	Socialists part of post-war government until 1921; then in opposition until late 1925

D	19.13	28.39	Unions' early post-war gains eroded as unemployment rises and employers resume dominance	H	34.9 (13.6)	0.25	Social democracy becoming marginalized but still one of few reliable bases of republic
CH	12.32	18.95	Employers use recession to dismiss many workers; government withdraws many post-war improvements in union rights	L	23.8 (20.9)	0.25	Labour becoming part of administrative system
NL	18.40	22.99	Employers resist most attempts by unions to extend bargaining	M	22.9 (50.7)		
N	13.33	20.13	Major extensions of union rights after War	H	33.3		Labour Party finds participation in government impossible
IRL	8.45	19.00		?	10.9 (27.4)		Labour Party opts out of alignment over Home Rule conflict
SF	4.09	13.87	Employers reject relations with unions, but some legal rights gained	?	39.4		Labour divided and broken over civil war and Russian revolution
F	4.38	7.60	Employers reject relations with unions	?	9.8		Unions mainly isolated, except during brief period of *cartel des gauches*

TABLE 5.4. *Continued*

Known union membership as % of		Major industrial-relations and political developments affecting organized labour within industry	Unemployment[2]	Share of popular vote[3] %	Participation in gov't[4] %	Other major political developments affecting wider position of organized labour
labour force	dependent labour force[1]					
E						
n.a.	n.a.		?			Socialists and UGT in ambiguous relationship with authoritarian regime
I, P		All levels: autonomous unions banned; fascist dictatorship				

Note: Country boundaries as in Table 5.1.

[1] For Finland, percentage of non-agricultural labour.

[2] H = registered unemployment in excess of 10% of dependent labour force; M = around 10%; L = less than 5%; ? = official figures are low but there are reasons for doubting their reliability.

[3] In most recent general election, secured by labour-movement parties; votes for parties with labour wing but primarily committed to other interests (e.g. Catholic parties) in parentheses. Figures for Denmark, Finland, Germany, Norway, combine social democratic as well as communist parties.

[4] 0.75 = main labour-movement party dominating coalition; 0.25 = party/ies not primarily labour parties but with union wing.

unionism, though caught here one year before its disastrous national strike, was that of the United Kingdom, with a higher overall membership than Denmark (though not if dependent labour only is taken into account). Belgian labour's strength had risen sharply since 1914, as had its political presence.

Among the remaining cases there is no real political argument for changing the order indicated by simple membership strength, except that the partial admission of labour to a role in the unique Swiss political system promotes it above the politically rather isolated Dutch movement. There can therefore be a rank ordering without grouping. One might note that German labour shared the dangerous privilege of its Austrian sister of being the only element fully committed to a new republic that some other powerful forces repudiated. This emerges strongly from accounts of the French occupation of the Ruhr at this time; while the social democrats and unions were suffering the privations of a strike to resist the invaders, German businessmen were secretly negotiating with the French the possible detachment of the Rhineland from the Weimar Republic (Maier, 1975: 390–405).

Norway and the Netherlands, though hardly similar to each other, both had membership levels clearly below the first group but well in excess of the weakest cases. (The Italian and Portuguese movements had effectively ceased to exist.) French labour continued to find it difficult to establish a membership base, and a large part of the movement remained in syndicalist organizations, rejecting political involvement.

Acting within a very rural economy and having no distinctive position on the issues raised by the Civil War that followed the struggle against the British, the Irish unions had to stand aside from the process of nation- and party-building that accompanied independence. They never capitalized on their 'heroic' leadership role in the period before 1918, and were unable to make the state very accessible to them (McCarthy, 1977). There was, however, no repression or even exclusion of the Finnish kind, where the Civil War led to a period of industrial relations hostile to unions from which there was only gradual subsequent recovery. On the other hand, Finnish labour retained its precocious parliamentary strength. A similar precocity was now enjoyed by the UGT in Spain, fragmentary in its membership coverage and internal strength, but vital to the insecure Riveran regime.

Some of these movements, at least those in the first half-dozen countries listed in Table 5.4, had by the 1920s already acquired a membership and political strength greater than would ever subsequently be achieved in France (or beyond Europe, Japan, or the United States), even though they were grappling with levels of unemployment against a context of meagre welfare support that rendered their members very vulnerable to economic disturbance. They were moving from the position of low power in terms of Fig. 2.2 in which they had until now been confined. Of the six, the Danes, Austrians, and Germans appeared to be moving out from low power alongside a move to higher articulation, indicating a shift to social-democratic neo-corporatist quadrant III, though as we have seen this was on a rather brittle basis in the case of the two defeated polities. Swedish developments were possibly going the same way, though institutional growth had been very rapid and recent; this could instead become a case of the unstable dynamic II—a quadrant for which Belgium and the United Kingdom seem destined, unless in the latter case the strength of collective bargaining arrangements *per se* could offset the low articulation of the organizations of employers and employees alike.

As we know, Belgium, Britain, and Sweden (as well as France and Norway) did all move into quadrant II at some stage during the next decade. On the other hand, Denmark's path was not much less rocky, while Austrian and German labour had worse catastrophes with which to contend than could be anticipated.

Economic and Political Development, 1925

Little insight is afforded by evidence of economic growth (Table 5.5). Levels of industrial development or national wealth seem to bear little relationship to forms of industrial-relations system. Detailed suffrage comparisons cease to be of interest given the widespread shift towards universal suffrage after 1918, but we have three dramatic cases of zero suffrage—the dictatorships.

Industrial Conflict, 1925

The conflict data (Table 5.6) suggest some positive relationship between union power and level of conflict: of the four

TABLE 5.5. *Indicators of political and economic development, c.1925*

	Agricultural work-force as % of total work-force	GNP p.c. (1960 US$)	Electorate as % of adult population	Leading economic sectors
A	30.0[1]	655	90.0	Mixed industrial, major steel sector, otherwise many small firms; agriculture still important
B	19.1	985	95.0[2]	Textiles, steel, coal, capital equipment, finance
DK	35.2	845	93.0	Mixed industrial, big tertiary sector, advanced agriculture
SF	71.5	520	88.5	Peasant agriculture
F	41.5	893	87.7[2]	Textiles, mines, engineering, agriculture
D	30.5	712	99.4	Coal and steel dominant; mixed industry, especially capital equipment; agriculture
IRL	51.3	624	99.9	Peasant agriculture, some light industry
I	55.7	480	none	Agriculture, public utilities, textiles
NL	23.6	909	96.5	Mixed industrial, strong tertiary sector, agriculture
N	36.8	863	96.0	Shipping, hydro-electric, mixed industry, agriculture, forest products
P	n.a. (high)	320	none	Agriculture
E	n.a. (high)	426	none	Agriculture, textiles, some industrial development
S	40.4	765	96.3	Industrial, especially capital equipment; textiles, wood, agriculture
CH	27.1	1,020	85.9[2]	Metal industries and watchmaking, financial services
UK	7.6	970	88.9[3]	Textiles, coal, steel, engineering, finance

Note: Country boundaries as in Table 5.1.

[1] Approximate figure.
[2] Adult male population only.
[3] Adult men and women over 30.

TABLE 5.6. *Industrial conflict, 1921–1925*

	Strikes per 1,000		Workers involved per 1,000		Days lost per 1,000	
	dependent labour force	trade-union members	dependent labour force	trade-union members	dependent labour force	trade-union members
A	0.19	0.40	94.19	195.94	878.08	1,826.67
B	0.07	0.23	43.70	142.07	n.a.	n.a.
DK	0.06	0.17	36.89	102.59	1,385.25	3,852.20
SF	0.06	0.43	11.48	82.77	186.95	1,347.87
F	0.07	0.92	26.99	355.13	380.11	5,001.45
D	0.16	0.56	86.20	303.63	1,200.95	4,230.19
IRL[1]	0.18	0.95	25.27	133.00	1,038.70	5,466.84
I[2]	0.06	n.a.	28.05	n.a.	525.30	n.a.
NL	0.11	0.48	17.16	74.64	615.97	2,679.30
N	0.08	0.40	61.22	304.12	2,437.62	12,109.39
S	0.15	0.48	41.39	133.39	1,664.93	5,365.55
CH	0.05	0.26	4.91	25.91	1.30	6.86
UK	0.04	0.13	47.36	148.79	1,649.63	5,182.63

Notes: Country boundaries as in Table 5.1.
Dependent labour force statistics are mainly based on data for 1930, except Austria (1934), Germany (1925), Ireland (1926), Italy (1921).

[1] Conflict data for 1923–5 only.
[2] Conflict data for 1921–4 only.

most powerful movements (Denmark, Sweden, Austria, United Kingdom) only Austria did not rank among the four countries to lose most working days in conflict; Norway's level was precocious. The country with the fifth most powerful movement (Belgium) did not publish these data, but its standing in the table for worker involvements suggests that it was a high-conflict country. Two weak movements (Finland and France) also registered low levels of conflict. Only the Swiss case suggests a link between elaborate industrial-relations institutions and a low level of conflict, the others ranking highly in Table 5.1 having high levels.

It is not easy to see why Austria should have much less conflict than Germany, or Finland than France or Ireland. Moreover, there is nothing in the institutional development of Sweden and the United Kingdom to explain why their level of conflict, even when expressed in relation to union membership, should be higher than that in France—and in 1925 the relatively advanced pluralist system of the United Kingdom was on the brink of its general strike of the following year, the single biggest instance of industrial conflict in the countries and period covered by this study. Meanwhile, the highest conflict is concentrated in Scandinavia, especially Norway, and it is difficult to see why Galenson (1952*b*) once spoke of an association between the Danish 1899 Basic Agreement and a low level of conflict.

THE EVE OF THE SECOND WORLD WAR

During the six years between 1933 and 1938 there were major changes in the industrial-relations systems of most of our countries. Germany (1933), Austria (first as Austro-fascismus in 1934 and then through the *Anschluß* in 1938), and Spain came under fascist/Nazi control and autonomous trade-unionism was destroyed. In all three countries the new regimes embarked initially on a programme of incorporating heteronomous representatives of labour in elaborate authoritarian corporatist structures from plant to state level on the pattern already encountered in Italy and Portugal. But not much of this was seriously intended. The labour wing of the Spanish Falange was soon out-manœuvred by more conservative elements in a manner similar to Italy in

1924. In fact, the Franco regime was never really interested in a national modernization strategy of the kind pursued by Mussolini; its aim was really to keep Spain rural and Catholic, free from the modernizing influences that had eroded traditional authority virtually everywhere else in Europe.

During the period when Hitler was under Mussolini's influence he had also advocated corporatist labour strategies and, as in both Italy and Spain, the Nazi movement had a pro-labour wing that looked forward to the benefits this might bring. As in the other countries it was disposed of early on, in the 'night of the long knives' in 1934. Even with heteronomous labour institutions, corporatist structures contradicted the *Führerprinzip*. The Deutscher Arbeiterfront was maintained in existence and was used as a model (especially in the Netherlands) to encourage labour movements in conquered countries to embrace national socialism, but it had no significance as a representative structure. The anti-corporatist stance of Nazism (as opposed to Catholic-influenced corporatism) is revealed by what happened in Austria at the *Anschluß*. The Austro-fascist regime of Schuschnigg which came to power after a bloody suppression of the social-democratic labour movement in the Civil War of 1934 had erected an elaborate edifice of corporatist institutions around the existing, partly autonomous Catholic wing of the trade unions. After the Germans took control of Austria in 1938 this was entirely obliterated.

Belgium and France (1936) saw major crises in the politics of industrial relations, associated initially with general strikes that threatened regime stability. Denmark (1935), Norway (1936), and Sweden (1938) witnessed the establishment of major central agreements between labour and capital associated with the accession of labour-movement parties to office—and following years of intense conflict. In Switzerland (1937) there was a similar agreement; it was initially limited to the dominant metal and watch industries, but these were of overwhelming importance in both the economy and union movement of Switzerland. The move was accompanied by a certain political development. In the context of events in the bordering nations of Germany, Austria, and Italy, the Swiss government had been admitting organized labour to a far more significant place than hitherto in participa-tion in the boards representative of organized interests that

administer much of Swiss public life in the absence of an elaborate state structure. Similarly in the Netherlands, also under the
shadow of the Nazi threat, elaborate plans were being debated
for the establishment of a tripartite structure (known as PBO) to
run the economy. In the event war and occupation ensued before
they could be implemented.

Beyond our range of countries, these were also the years of the
New Deal in the United States. All these changes took varied
forms and occurred under different circumstances. The only common thread was the need to cope in some way with increasing
industrial conflict and economic difficulty. Conflict was initially
associated with workers' defensive struggles in the Depression,
but in some cases it lasted into the period of recovery, when
labour's strength revived while its awareness of accumulated
grievances was strong.

While several of the developments in democratic countries
were explicitly anti-fascist or carried out in a spirit of national
solidarity against the threat of German invasion, they shared
with fascism a concern for building strong organizations and for
finding new organizational forms for the economy that were
neither free-market nor state-socialist. They also evinced a concern for shoring up national identity in a period of severe tension
and class alienation, though in sharp contrast with the fascist
cases they did not seek part of the solution in violent repression.
There was, however, enough similarity and, it must be stressed,
uncertainty concerning the practices characteristic of fascism
for some confusion between policies, revealed in the careers of
individuals.

Henrik de Man, the Belgian socialist whose *Plan du Travail*
influenced both his own and the Dutch labour movement's
interest in tripartism, came to believe that the German occupying
forces would implement his ideas and so collaborated with them.
Louis Belin, a leader of the French CGT at the time of the Front
Populaire, became Minister of Labour under the Vichy regime,
hoping to put into effect some of his ideas for tripartism that had
made so little headway in the Third Republic, though he ended
by presiding over the dissolution of autonomous trade-unionism
(Lefranc, 1967). Oswald Mosley, the member of the 1929 Labour
government in the United Kingdom who most consistently
supported Keynesian ideas, founded his own fascist party and

supported Hitler even after the outbreak of war. In Denmark, too, social-democratic ideas for a corporate economy overlapped uneasily with fascist ones (Hansen and Henriksen, 1980*a*).

The events of the 1933–8 period left just Finland and Ireland (the two 'new' countries) and the United Kingdom (the oldest industrial society) maintaining a continuity with industrial-relations patterns of the past. (Italy and Portugal had of course already undergone fascist revolutions.) In the Finnish case one can hardly speak of such a past. In Ireland the past was an English one, and we do find in the 1930s an attempt by government (hardly by employers) to persuade the Irish unions to break free from the UK-based organizations that were still important among them and to develop a more distinctly Irish and Catholic orientation. For a period the initiative did lead to a split within Irish labour, but it was not accompanied by a serious attempt to build labour into a Catholic form of corporatism. Was this evidence of the continued English dominance over even Irish nationalist policy-makers, or of the general inability in the 1930s of Catholic social policy to assert itself outside the treacherous fascist embrace?

This really leaves the United Kingdom as the only country to maintain a continuity of *Verbandwesen* since the nineteenth century. The British had been through a system crisis, but in the 1920s, in the wake of the general strike. This had then been comprehensively beaten without recourse to fascist means and labour was no longer in a position to demand a settlement on Scandinavian lines or even to make trouble like its Belgian or French counterparts. The British equivalent of the great Continental agreements of the 1930s was the Mond–Turner talks, a series of discussions between groups of union leaders and major individual employers about the need to rescue some kind of social dialogue out of the thin institutional atmosphere of the aftermath of 1926. Although there were initially simultaneous moves towards a strengthening of national bipartite organizations, once the Depression was clearly under way employers lost their interest, and there was little overall institutional change (Middlemas, 1979).

Institutional Development, 1938

Setting aside the fascist and Nazi cases, the state of overall institutional development in our countries (Table 5.7) mainly demonstrates the distinctive position of the Scandinavian countries, and to a lesser extent Switzerland, which now had systems of bargaining, consultation, mediation, and administration binding the main levels of action, in particular filling out the national (as opposed to state) level, where confederations of unions and employers were the principal actors. In each case the installation of a new system was almost formally registered, which is by no means always the case with change in industrial-relations systems, and followed a major demonstration of labour's enduring strength at a time of increasing international tension. In each of the Scandinavian countries a period of extreme industrial conflict accompanied by major economic crisis led to the formation of political coalitions uniting labour and farm interests (as in the United States at the same time), which led the leading union confederations explicitly to accept a role in maintaining social peace and national order in what they now perceived as 'their' nation.

There were major steps in institutional elaboration in Belgium and the Netherlands, though these remained largely state, as opposed to social-partner, initiatives. The *commissions paritaires* imposed by the Belgian government to encourage both branch-level collective bargaining and a system of interest-group consultation by government nevertheless provided an important structure for the development of a web of relations at various levels (Chlepner, 1956). In 1936, after major industrial conflict, this structure was crowned by the Conseil National du Travail, which played an important formal role in the preparation of labour legislation. But beneath all this many employers remained reluctant to engage in relations with unions. Similarly, though at that stage less formally, the Dutch government had been busy admitting labour to a range of national participation, but again with less response from capital. This followed extensive discussion in the country, embracing socialist, Catholic, and Calvinist circles alike, of the possibility of a participative, consensus-based economy. In some ways these innovations resembled Austrian and German developments in 1918: the political imposition on capital of arrangements for co-operating with labour. However,

TABLE 5.7. *Institutional development of industrial relations, c.1938*

Main pattern of industrial relations	Country	Level				
		Plant	Locality	Branch	Nation	State
Incipient neo-corporatism	DK	Some collective bargaining	Declining	Extensive bargaining	National bargaining between DsF and DA; union involvement in pension schemes	Unions and employers' associations consulted on all major issues
	N		Some bargaining and union involvement in mediation schemes	Extensive bargaining but severe conflict	*Hovedavtalen* between LO and NAF	Unions and employers' associations consulted on all major issues
	S	Some bargaining	Some bargaining and union involvement in mediation schemes	Extensive bargaining but severe conflict	Saltsjöbaden Agreement (LO and SAF); unions and employers seek to avoid	Unions and employers' associations consulted on all major issues

					state role in bargaining and mediation	
State institutions encouraging neo-corporatism	CH	Extensive bargaining	Extensive bargaining	*Friedensab-kommen* to govern relations in metal and watch industry; first GAV		Union involvement in administration of public policy
	B	Collective bargaining		Major growth of *commissions paritaires*		Unions in consultation arrangements
	NL	Spread of consultation schemes	Some bargaining and union involvement in mediation	Some bargaining and union involvement in mediation and pension schemes	PBO discussions	Union involvement in government consultation
Collective bargaining and contestation	UK	Some collective bargaining	Declining bargaining	Extensive bargaining; union involvement in mediation		Unions in small number of consultation schemes

Table 5.7. *Continued*

Main pattern of industrial relations	Country	Level				
		Plant	Locality	Branch	Nation	State
	IRL		Some bargaining	Some bargaining		Some union consultation
Contestation with some state initiatives to reduce conflict	F		Some limited bargaining	Some bargaining	Some growth in CGT–CNPF contact	Temporary concertation of Matignon Agreement, 1936; broken off by 1938
	SF		Some limited bargaining			Some union consultation
Authoritarian corporatism	I, P, E	Autonomous unions illegal; fascist unions of workers and employers have formal consultation role at all levels				
	A	Similar to I, P, E until after *Anschluß*, when all structures abolished				
	D	Deutscher Arbeiter Front replaces unions, but has only token role				

Note: Country boundaries as in Table 5.1.

the degree of engagement offered to labour was far weaker, and Belgian and Dutch labour posed nothing like the threat to capital experienced in the unstable polities of post-1918 Austria and Germany.

A strong growth of collective bargaining distinguishes Ireland and the United Kingdom at this period. Irish developments may, in the light of what was said above, seem somewhat different, but this is illusory. The government was not really interested in industrial development and did not need trade unions for that purpose. If it took an interest in union affairs it was solely to encourage the Republic's unions to separate themselves from the Britain-based unions that still represented about 40 per cent of Irish trade-unionists (McCarthy, 1977). But this mainly took the form of encouraging splits within an already small movement.

The French events of 1936 resembled those in Scandinavia, Switzerland, and Belgium at the same time, particularly the last. However, as we have noted, employers remained far less willing than even the Belgians to co-operate, the changes introduced were limited, superficial, and easily reversed once labour's strength had waned. This change finally took place during 1938 itself. Immediately after 1936 France would have been classified with Belgium and the Netherlands as a case of government imposition of an incipient corporatism on a reluctant capitalism. However, perhaps because they were organizationally far less well established than their counterparts in Scandinavia, French industrialists were not prepared to tolerate such changes. Neither was the political élite sufficiently united to concede an integrated political role to the labour movement. (Among some employers the events of 1936 were enough to encourage political moves similar to those that had taken place in Austria and Germany; indeed, they took advantage of the German invasion of 1940 to establish a pro-German government in the non-occupied part of France in which a fascist corporatist strategy followed the familiar route of an initial but subsequently repudiated incorporation of labour.)

However, enough is left of Popular Front institutions by 1938 to set France apart from Finland, where little change had taken place in the country's limited structures, and where the established right was in any case having difficulty keeping fascists at bay.

Finally, no less than a third of our countries were at that stage under fascist forms of authoritarian corporatism.

Articulation of Labour Movements, 1938

The most significant development between 1925 and 1938 in levels of union articulation (Table 5.8) is the convergence of the Scandinavians on a high level. The similarity of these three countries makes possible a finer comparison than usual, and it is clear that Denmark, the pioneer of the Scandinavian system often consciously imitated by the others, but lacking an industrial-union pattern, was now less *centralized* than the other two, while they had joined it in overall *articulation* through their development of integrated shop-floor presences.

Belgium was less centralized than these cases only because of its socialist–Christian division, though articulation was greatly weakened by the absence of a shop-floor presence. This structure was rather distinctive, and Belgium stands as a case on its own.

The main Swiss confederation now also appears moderately centralized, but because of centralization within individual industry-branch unions. The Dutch were similar but distinctly less articulated because, while their unions resembled those of Belgium and Switzerland in internal structure, the membership was even more fragmented than theirs among ideologically divided confederations.

In the wake of the temporary unity of the Popular Front, the French CGT appeared remarkably centralized; internal union unity persisting for a while after the decline in union strength of the years after 1936.

Individual unions in Britain and Ireland had become somewhat more centralized as high unemployment weakened the usually strong decentralizing forces; had sufficient peacetime years followed 1936 they would probably soon have appeared more centralized than the French. In Finland, on the other hand, the formation of a rival, less radical, confederation reduced labour's slender capacity for articulation even further than before.

Employer Organization, 1938

These developments towards much tighter articulation on the labour side in certain economies were appropriately paralleled among employers (Table 5.9). Scandinavian employers seem to have acquired the centralized bargaining partners they had consistently sought—though this achievement was interestingly associated with political developments unfavourable to employers, rather than the reverse. Swiss employers were similarly well articulated and organized, but with a distinctly lower centre of gravity within the special contours of the Swiss polity. Belgian employers, like their labour counterparts, began to move to a high level of centralized organization, mainly as a result of state prompting through the new *commissions paritaires*, which had been extended to a wider range of industries.

Austrian, German, and Spanish employers joined the fascist mode already established in Italy and Portugal. There were, however, important differences. In Italy and Germany employers' associations were caught up in major state-led strategies for modernization, whereas Portuguese and Spanish fascists were more interested in securing a stable, rural society and kept industrial development in check. During their brief period of rule, Austrian fascists inclined to the Iberian approach, but after the *Anschluß* in 1938 specifically Austrian institutions lost any autonomous identity. I shall keep the fascist countries together as a group, below Belgium (where also the state strongly led the development of organizations, but with considerably less compulsion), but above countries where strong levels of organization were not reached in practice.

In the Netherlands there was considerable talk of moving to a more co-ordinated and constructive response to labour, but not much action; though there was considerable co-ordination for trade purposes in the face of the recession and increasingly threatening world situation. The positions in the United Kingdom and, to a lesser extent, Ireland, were not dissimilar. The role of trade associations in Britain reached an historical peak as they administered the country's reluctantly adopted protectionism.

French employers had largely repudiated the involvement of their leaders in the tripartite negotiations of the Popular Front, rejecting the degree of co-ordination they had proposed. Consequent changes in the constitution of the Patronat gave vigorous expression to this by reducing the organization's power, reinforcing rather than challenging traditional French patterns. In Finland too employers *divested* their organizations of powers; in

TABLE 5.8. *Articulation of trade-union movements, c.1938*

	Unions affiliated to main confederation				Dominant types of union	Individual unions	
	Membership as % of		No.	Powers of confederation re affiliates		Characteristic internal authority structure over local groups, individual members, etc.	Characteristic shop-floor organization
	known unions	labour force					
N	85.00	29.15	c.63	LO monopolizes strike funds and calls	Branch type dominates, but several craft unions survive	Centralized	Union stewards integrated into formal structures
S	84.73	30.51	42	LO acquiring central bargaining powers and monopolizes strike funds and calls	Craft, general with strong growth of branch unions	Centralized	Strong growth of union 'clubs'
DK	92.20	25.16	72	DsF acquiring central bargaining powers	Craft, general	Centralized	*Tillidsman* system
B	61.05	15.46	24	CGTB acquires strike fund and call powers, but does not bargain. Rival Ch...	Branch type	Centralized	Weak

CH	58.18	11.61	21	confederation SGB loses strike call and fund power; rival confederations	Branch	Centralized	Strong
NL	39.69	9.72	29	NVV loses strike call and fund power; rival Christian confederations	Branch type emerging	Centralized	Weak
F	90.95	17.12	38	CGT has few powers	See note*	Centralized	Very weak
UK	77.10	22.14	216	TUC has few powers	Craft, general; some branch	Varied; growing in importance in defensive bargaining climate of recession	Shop stewards in many skilled trades
IRL	71.00	10.67	49	ITUC has few powers	Craft, general	Varied	Shop stewards in some skilled trades
SF	70.00	3.47	20	FL has very little power over affiliates and now faces rival social-democratic SAK confederation	Craft, general	Varied; all unions very small	Weak

Note: Country boundaries as in Table 5.1.

* Signifies a complex pattern of local cells of the confederations alongside individual economic-branch unions, giving a very large number of units, many of which were however parts of the confederation itself.

TABLE 5.9. *Organizations of capital, c.1938*

	Scope[1]	Power[2]	Other associative business activity[3]
DK	Widely established	DA co-ordinates industrial employers in major national bargaining relationship with DsF	Fællesrep co-ordinates business response to severe world economic climate
N	Widely established	NAF co-ordinates industrial employers in major national bargaining relationship with LO	Trade associations co-ordinate business response to severe world economic climate
S	Widely established	SAF co-ordinates industrial employers in major national bargaining relationship with LO	Trade associations co-ordinate business response to severe world economic climate
CH	Continued growth	Metal and watch employers' association co-ordinates employers in key sectoral bargaining	*Verbände* get legal right to organize training and export-risk schemes (both 1931)
B	Continued growth; CCI, 1936	Branch associations are main actors on employers' side in new *commissions paritaires*	Trade associations involved in planning protectionist arrangements
A, D, I, P, E	Employers accept role in structures of fascist and Nazi states		
NL	Continued growth	Associations engage in debate over PBO system, but little action	Trade associations co-ordinate business response to severe world economic climate

	Extent of organization of employer interests[1]	Resources available to employer organizations to co-ordinate action[2]	Activity directed at trade rather than labour issues[3]
UK	Branch-level associations well established	Weak	Trade associations involved in planning protectionist arrangements
IRL	Limited growth; FIM, 1932	FIM mainly lobbies government	Some trade association activity
SF	Decline	STK strike fund and co-ordinating power decline in light of union weakness	Limited
F	Limited	Major advance in CGPF role, 1936, but this repudiated by members; reformed as CNPF, 1938, with weaker powers	Very limited

Note: Country boundaries as in Table 5.1.

[1] Extent of organization of employer interests.

[2] Resources available to employer organizations to co-ordinate action.

[3] Activity directed at trade rather than labour issues.

this case because attacks on the unions by the fascist 'Export Peace' movement had so weakened them that there was no longer any need for vigorous struggle. Finland ranks slightly ahead of France because the degree of power with which employers had earlier equipped their organizations was considerably greater.

Power of Organized Labour, 1938

Table 5.10 shows consolidated union strength in most democratic countries. As we might now expect, the three Scandinavian nations have finally converged from their diverse backgrounds unambiguously to occupy the leading places, each with governing labour or social democratic parties and levels of union membership that in no way are those of infant movements. Belgium can easily be ranked after them. It is difficult to decide whether the industrially strong but politically much-weakened British unions should rank next or those of the Dutch and Swiss whose organization was politically unusual; but all are clearly stronger examples than the rest. It is reasonable to rank union movements in membership order, except that the political strength of the Swiss movement 'promotes' it over the French and Irish; with that exception political and industrial strength seem closely related.

It becomes difficult to measure either industrial or political strength in France at this time. During the peak of the Popular Front period in 1936 union membership had shot up to about 5 million, but it then deteriorated sharply over the following two years, becoming meanwhile an unreliable indicator of any real 'strength'. The political situation is also unclear in that the Socialist Party appears as much more of a labour-movement party than previously (or indeed subsequently); but by April of the year in question the Popular Front had fallen.

Irish labour was politically much weaker than its industrial strength would suggest, but certain factors render the situation more complicated. The country's main party, Fianna Fáil, continued to be 'labour-friendly', though in no sense a labour party, and during the 1930s was finally discovering a national use for the labour movement, or at least part of it.

Labour in Finland had been drastically weakened by attacks from the fascist Lapua movement, but social democracy retained its unusually strong political position.

These were of course years in which labour movements everywhere had been weakened by high unemployment, and it is interesting to note that unions were at their strongest in membership terms where unemployment had begun to decline.

Economic and Social Development, 1938

Table 5.11 shows our usual indicators of development. As in 1925, the suffrage data are now essentially a question of 'everybody or nobody', with a substantial increase in the latter category. The association between dictatorship and industrial-relations system type is unsurprisingly perfect, and with the exception of Germany so is an association between dictatorship and economic underdevelopment. Among the liberal democracies it is notable that the extraordinarily rapid elaboration of industrial-relations institutions throughout Scandinavia followed the equally rapid economic advance of Norway and Sweden. It will be recalled that during the nineteenth century, when Denmark was already a wealthy farming country, Sweden was overall the poorest nation in Europe. Some kind of association between institutional and economic development remains tantalizingly elusive; it is worth noting that Finland and France had been, in the late 1930s, considerably wealthier than were Britain and Denmark when they initially developed fairly strong institutional structures.

Industrial Conflict, 1938

Table 5.12 displays conflict data for the years preceding 1938. These suggest no particular correlations; the highly articulated systems of Scandinavia are associated with very high conflict levels; but these systems were fully installed only towards the end of the period covered, and of course partly in response to the high levels of conflict. The years immediately following cannot be tested, as abnormal procedures of various kinds operated during the War; but there is certainly little evidence of any positive correlation· between institutional development and low levels of

TABLE 5.10. Power of organized labour, c.1938

	Known union membership as % of		Major industrial-relations and political developments affecting organized labour within industry	Unem-ployment[2]	Share of popular vote[3] %	Particip-ation in gov't[4] %	Other major political developments affecting wider position of organized labour
	labour force	dependent labour force[1]					
S	36.01	55.06	Central accord between LO and SAF	D	45.9	0.75	SAP achieves national domination
N	34.29	57.25	Central accord between LO and NAF	D	42.5	0.75	Labour Party achieves national domination
DK	27.29	38.05	Central accord between DsF and DA	D	46.1	0.75	SD achieves national domination
B	25.33	36.98	Involvement in commissions paritaires	D	38.2 (27.1)	0.75	
UK	28.72	36.86		D	38.1	0.75	National government with split Labour Party in opposition
NL	24.49	31.16		H	21.9 (52.7)	0.25	
CH	19.95	28.62	Central accord with watch and metal employers	M	28.0 (20.3)	0.25	Incorporation of social democrats into government

			Temporary significance of Matignon Agreements		Socialist-led Popular Front (until 1938) Government takes interest in labour movement as means of ensuring national unity
F	18.82	33.66	?	35.0	0.50[5]
IRL	15.03	32.60	?	10.0 (51.9)	0.25
SF	4.96	11.64	?	38.6	0.50

Note: Country boundaries as in Table 5.1.

[1] For Finland, percentage of non-agricultural labour.

[2] D = declining from a high peak; H = registered unemployment in excess of 10% of dependent labour force; M = around 10%; ? = relatively low, but there are reasons for doubting reliability of figures.

[3] In most recent general election by labour-movement parties; votes for parties with labour wing but primarily committed to other interests (e.g. Catholic parties) in parentheses. Figures for Belgium, France combine socialist as well as communist parties.

[4] 0.75 = main labour-movement party dominating coalition or combination of labour and quasi-labour parties; 0.5 = labour party as minor coalition partner; 0.25 = participation by Christian, etc. parties.

[5] Only until April, when Popular Front government fell.

T 5.10 SHERRY (11)
P. 170-171

TABLE 5.11. *Indicators of political and economic development, c.1938*

	Agricultural work-force as % of total work-force	GNP p.c. (1960 US$)	Electorate as % of adult population	Leading economic sectors
A	39.0	640	none	Mixed industrial, major steel sector, otherwise many small firms; agriculture still important
B	17.0	1,015	95.3*	Textiles, steel, coal, capital equipment, finance
DK	29.9	1,045	97.0	Mixed industrial, big tertiary sector, advanced agriculture
SF	57.4	913	86.5	Peasant agriculture, forest products, some industry
F	35.6	936	86.9*	Textiles, mines, engineering, agriculture
D	26.0	1,126	none	Coal and steel dominant; mixed industry, especially capital equipment and armaments; agriculture
IRL	47.6	649	97.7	Peasant agriculture, some light industry
I	47.0	551	none	Agriculture, public utilities, textiles and other industrial development
NL	20.6	920	99.4	Mixed industrial, strong tertiary sector, agriculture
N	35.3	1,298	101.3	Shipping, hydro-electric, mixed industry, agriculture, forest products
P	n.a. (high)	351	none	Agriculture
E	n.a. (high)	337	none	Agriculture, textiles, some industrial development
S	28.8	1,097	97.4	Industrial, especially capital equipment; textiles, wood, agriculture
CH	20.8	1,204	89.3*	Metal industries and watchmaking; financial services
UK	6.0	1,181	99.9	Textiles, coal, steel, engineering; finance

Note: Country boundaries as in Table 5.1.

* Adult male population only.

TABLE 5.12. *Industrial conflict, 1934–1938*

	Strikes per 1,000		Workers involved per 1,000		Days lost per 1,000	
	dependent labour force	trade-union members	dependent labour force	trade-union members	dependent labour force	trade-union members
A*	0.00	n.a.	0.51	n.a.	0.31	n.a.
B	0.12	0.32	64.04	173.17	343.30	928.34
DK	0.02	0.05	19.97	52.48	562.22	1,477.58
SF	0.04	0.34	9.75	83.76	119.95	1,030.50
F	0.40	1.19	80.41	238.89	n.a.	n.a.
IRL	0.19	0.58	22.42	68.77	854.28	2,620.49
NL	0.05	0.16	2.98	9.56	49.84	159.95
N	0.19	0.33	18.48	32.28	563.94	985.59
S	0.04	0.07	9.79	17.78	429.61	780.26
CH	0.02	0.14	2.19	7.65	34.32	119.92
UK	0.05	0.14	19.78	53.66	117.91	319.89

Note: Country boundaries as in Table 5.1.

* Conflict for 1934–7 only.

conflict. We are again reminded that major institutional agreements have not been the *result* of national consensus, even if they might have been its precondition.

Conclusions, 1938

By 1938 there was, among countries that had not become fascist, a strong correlation between, on the one hand, the level of national institutional development and, on the other, the degree of union power and articulation, the extent of organization of employers' organizations, and the level of economic development. This is as would be anticipated by most theories of industrial-relations development. The Scandinavian institutions that led the process were in their early stages; it is difficult from this point to determine whether these are elaborate collective-bargaining models or incipient corporatism, though the stress on tight national co-ordination already indicates a departure from the former.

There are, however, a few anomalies. Norwegian and Swedish developments were far more rapid and emerged from a far more conflictual background than either Olsonian or Dunlopian theory would expect. Switzerland is problematic for social-democratic theories of development, with a low level of union power accompanying its high level of institutional development. The United Kingdom is also a problem for social-democratic theory, but not Dunlop's, on account of its low level of union (and business) articulation given the level of union power; it remains the most solid case for seeing unambiguous collective bargaining as the peak achievement of a mature industrial-relations system.

For the rest, the Belgian state seemed to be pushing its organizations to act similarly to the Scandinavians and Swiss; the Dutch were actively discussing a similar policy. Authoritarian corporatism, essentially bogus though that form normally is, was in place in five of our fifteen countries. Of the remaining four, two (the United Kingdom and Ireland) are best described as cases of pluralist collective bargaining, and two (Finland and France) as primarily contestative, with a failed neo-corporatist excursion in the latter for a brief period during 1936.

The degree of change affecting trade unions and industrial-relations systems during the inter-war period was quite remarkable. From essentially fragmented structures outside Denmark, Germany, and the United Kingdom on the eve of the First World War, we now have several elaborate national schemes: well-organized union confederations representing in some cases around a third of the total labour force, and in some countries the completely new system of fascist social organization.

At this stage few people within the social-democratic labour movement had articulated a strategy of overtly seeking neo-corporatism or tripartite co-operation through tightly articulated organizations as their preferred model. The ideology of social-democratic labour remained one of class transformation. Austrian and German labour leaders after 1918 and their Scandinavian counterparts after their political achievements of the 1930s saw tripartite co-operation as a pragmatic way of coming to terms with pressing, indeed desperate, current reality. In their own hearts social-democratic and union leaders possibly did not really envisage that much beyond co-operation would ever happen, but they did not articulate such thoughts as a master strategy for the future. Even non-Marxists like the bulk of British labour saw the future in state-owned production, not in tripartism. And the British, Dutch, and Scandinavian labour leaders who took an interest in Keynesian and Wigforsian ideas saw them principally in terms of aggregate demand management, not as an aspect of organizational co-operation. If they thought of a long-term future for conventional industrial relations (and British unionists certainly did so), they thought in terms of collective bargaining.

Apart from various isolated intellectuals, anyone who wanted to pursue organizational bipartism or tripartism as their ideally preferred political strategy had to do so within Catholic (or just possibly, in the Netherlands and Switzerland, Calvinist) social thought; or—and the two were not mutually exclusive—turn to fascism.

How matters would have developed from there if left to 'normal' economic and political processes we cannot know; the Second World War intervened. Indeed, as in the years leading up to 1914, it is not clear when 'normal' processes stopped: much of what had happened in the 1930s was part of the process of a world girding itself for war and seeking to increase the identification of the working class with the nation for that purpose.

6

The Post-War Years

Si è detto che noi dobbiamo fare tutto il possibile perché
anche l'applicazione di questo Piano risponda al massimo
all'interesse dei lavoratori. Noi abbiamo accettato questo
concetto. Ci siamo rivolti al governo, abbiamo chiesto
di essere ammessi nei due organismi che presiedono
all'applicazione del Piano, ma il governo non vuole
l'intervento della CGIL.

(G. di Vittoria, general secretary of CGIL, on the exclusion of CGIL from the implementation of the Marshall
Plan, 5 October 1948)

Utan tvivel har vi inspirerats av vår ömsesidiga respekt för
styrkan hos motparten, en respekt som kan hāreldas ur
besvärliga erfarenheter i en tidigare period.

(B. Kugelberg, director of SAF, 1963)

The rapid pace of change that characterized European industrial
relations during the 1930s quickened further during the Second
World War. Further increases in repression came from German
occupation and thus exogenously, but in countries not under Nazi
or fascist control (Ireland, Sweden, Switzerland, and the United
Kingdom), and in the unique case of Finland (which fought its
private war against the Soviet Union in the midst of it all),
tendencies similar to those of 1914–18, but far stronger, were
evident. Labour was taken deep into national participation. And
in several of the occupied countries, political élites, leading
employers, and unionists often retained clandestine or exiled
contact, expressing a shared general national interest against the
invaders and often planning together for the future. As in 1914,
the war emergency had strengthened identity. People either
forged institutions to give expression to that, or planned for an
opportunity to do so once Nazi or fascist rule had ended.

As countries were liberated in 1944 or 1945 this latter became
a reality; urgent tasks of reconstruction were planned. This

extended also to Germany, Italy, and Austria as the dictator-ships were removed. For a period there seemed almost complete convergence, outside Iberia, on a model of tight tripartite co-operation, with centralized organizations of capital and labour establishing elaborate industrial-relations institutions and sharing political influence. In the terms of Chapter 2, identity relations were being rapidly and massively strengthened in the light of the shared priorities of rebuilding. At the same time the alliance with the Soviet Union during the war meant a temporary reconcilia-tion with communist parties and unions.

Ireland and Finland were on the margins of all this, experienc-ing only minor mobilization for industrial reconstruction. Indeed, it was not until the late 1950s that Irish governments embarked on a policy of industrialization, preferring until then to keep their country rural and Catholic. However, temporary domina-tion by a Catholic-oriented union confederation extended to Ireland the general characteristics of the period of an assertion of national unity and shared identities. Finland was also primarily a peasant economy at this stage, and as refugees from Karelia were resettled on the land within the remainder of the country, rural and agricultural priorities were reinforced. However, national co-operation was a priority because of the difficult geopolitical situation; communists could not be excluded, but neither could some components of the far right.

The Iberian peninsula differed from elsewhere in that its fascist regimes, which had kept out of the War, were able to survive intact—with the tacit collusion of the Western powers—until the 1970s. Perhaps one similarity with Ireland is important: the Iberian dictatorships also wanted to keep their countries traditional, rural, and Catholic. Very little was left of the old corporatist rhetoric that had implied a degree of mobilization. These were therefore the only countries whose governments and economic élites were not worried about ensuring a work-force geared for economic progress; and they had their own approaches to securing national integration.

A further general force at work, again excluding Portugal and Spain, was a concern by British and American forces of occupa-tion (or liberation) and subsequent reconstruction to favour a pluralist model of both politics and collective bargaining. Strictly speaking of course this contradicted the contemporary striving for increased *identity* of class interests, though no one noticed this at the time because pluralism was the only available model among the victor powers of a democracy that could accommodate organized interests. The Allies were most concerned to promulgate this to dismembered Germany, but also elsewhere.

AFTER THE WAR: 1950

However, this general trend to national integration did not long remain universal. After 1947 and in association with the inception of the Cold War, a sharp divergence set in and became entrenched. We shall therefore, as after 1918, re-examine our countries after the immediate post-war period had settled down, and after identities forged in wartime had relapsed into the patterns of everyday capitalist life. We shall focus on 1950. With the very important exception of Germany (which now became the smaller and more westerly located state, the Federal Republic of Germany) and the smaller case of Finland's loss of Karelia to the Soviet Union, borders were largely the same as they were before the exploits of the Hitler regime and the war.

Institutional Development, 1950

Table 6.1 shows the state of institutional development. In Scandinavia we now see a GPE dynamic clearly in progress, with a ramification of institutional participation since 1938, tightening the web that bound government, employers, and unions together in a diverse mass of relations, reaching out from the central field of wage development to involve matters of economic planning. Centralized actors on both sides of industry not only regulated the industrial-relations system; they were also beginning to share prominently in national public administration. This is not pluralist collective bargaining within boundaries of institutionalized conflict in the Dunlopian mode. As in 1938 the Scandinavian countries form a clear group, but the character of the system has clarified.

There is also evidence of something similar in Austria, though it is in only very early stages following post-war restoration. There is also a difference from Scandinavia in that at plant level there is a union-dominated works-council system rather than union clubs or shop stewards.

Switzerland maintained and strengthened the pattern established in the late 1930s. At governmental level, confederations and other central bodies were integrated in a manner similar to that of Scandinavia or Austria, though across a narrower range of areas. Within industry a more localized pattern prevailed. Like its Alpine neighbour, this country forms a group by itself.

Britain shared with the foregoing countries a close involvement of interest associations in economic policy activities, but virtually always in a consultative, advisory capacity, rarely in administrative, decision-making organs (a point made in a comparison between organizational participation in the three Scandinavian countries and in the United Kingdom and United States by Olsen (1983: 166–71)). If persons associated with interest associations were involved in administrative bodies, they were carefully placed in non-representative roles. For example, the governing boards of nationalized industries would always include trade-unionists. But they would be appointed as individuals, not as representatives; they would always come from another industry. There was now, however, a clear break from the United Kingdom's isolation from European trends in the 1930s; in fact, the decisive change happened in 1940, only two years after the relevant developments in Sweden, but only after the country had fully mobilized for war. While collective bargaining remained the predominant form of industrial relations, the involvement of unions and employers' associations stemming from the War imparted a strong element of incipient corporatism to this case.

In comparison with all the foregoing, for Belgium and the Netherlands, as in the 1930s, government was much more of an active partner in forcing the social partners into forms of co-operation. Pre-war Dutch talk of a system of PBO now became something of a reality, with the erection of tripartite and inter-confessional institutions across the main sectors of the economy and labour market. In particular two institutions symbolized and embodied this new orientation of Dutch political economy. The Labour Foundation (Stichting van de Arbeid) provided a bipartite forum for mediating and arbitrating in labour questions; the Social and Economic Council (Sociaal Economische Raad, SER) provided for tripartite discussion of a far wider area of

TABLE 6.1. *Institutional development of industrial relations, c.1950*

Main pattern of industrial relations	Country	Level				
		Plant	Locality	Branch	Nation	State
Neo-corporatism	DK	Some bargaining		Extensive bargaining	DA and LO set national pay framework	Unions and employer organizations in extensive consultative and administrative arrangements
	N	Some bargaining		Extensive bargaining	NAF and LO set national pay framework	Unions and employer organizations in extensive consultative and administrative arrangements; relaxation of tight, immediate post-war controls

	S	Some bargaining		SAF and LO set national pay framework	Unions and employer organizations in extensive consultative and administrative arrangements
Incipient neo-corporatism	A	*Betriebsräte* with some administrative powers	Extensive bargaining	Early attempts of unions and employer organizations in bargaining, administration and consultation arrangements from state to branch level	
Neo-corporatism with strong local component	CH	Extensive bargaining	Extensive bargaining	Union involvement in administration of policy; GAV spread to wide range of industries	Union and employer organization involvement in administration of public policy; consultation

TABLE 6.1. *Continued*

Main pattern of industrial relations	Country	Level					
		Plant	Locality	Branch	Nation	State
Collective bargaining with incipient neo-corporatism	UK	Growing collective bargaining		Very extensive bargaining; union involvement in mediation		Unions in wide range of consultation schemes
State-supported neo-corporatism	NL	Statutory bipartite works council system		Union involvement in mediation and pension schemes	Government establishes national pay bargaining system and engages in extensive consultation; strong statutory component to policy, alongside elaborate representative	Union involvement in government consultation

Collective bargaining with neo-corporatist elements	B	Statutory bipartite works council system		*Commissions paritaires*	National solidarity pact, 1944	structures; Stichting van de Arbeid, 1943; SER, 1944	Unions and employer organizations in extensive consultation arrangements; pay policy under statutory control
	D¹	*Betriebsräte* with some administrative powers	Regional bargaining	Main bargaining level	Union involvement in pension scheme etc. management		Extensive consultation arrangements; *Tarifvertraggesetz*, 1949
Collective bargaining	IRL		Some bargaining	Extensive bargaining	Some co-ordination of annual pay rounds; unions		Extensive union and employer organization consultation; Labour Court,

TABLE 6.1. *Continued*

Main pattern of industrial relations	Country	Level				
		Plant	Locality	Branch	Nation	State
					involved in mediation schemes	1946
Collective bargaining and contestation	SF[2]		Some limited bargaining	Limited bargaining	Unions involved in mediation schemes	Extensive union and employer organization consultation; state control of income development; centralized bargaining imposed by government
Contestation with minor collective bargaining	I	Statutory bipartite works council system	Some bargaining	Limited bargaining	Some bargaining	Minor consultation of non-communist unions

F	Statutory bipartite works council system	Some limited bargaining	Limited bargaining	Some bargaining	Minor consultation of non-communist unions; law on *conventions collectives*, 1950
Authoritarian corporatism	E, P	Autonomous unions illegal; fascist unions of workers and employers have formal consultation role at all levels			

[1] Germany is now the reduced post-war Federal Republic.
[2] Finland has lost Karelia to the USSR.

policy, and was used by Dutch governments as an essential sounding board to discover whether particular policies commanded general assent (Windmuller, 1969).

The Federal Republic of Germany officially started life only in 1949, so at the time of our snapshot its institutions have hardly taken shape and their character is unclear. Unions were explicitly recognized as constituent bodies of the new state and entitled to considerable consultation by governments. A tight system of industry-wide bargaining was also becoming established, with workers' rights to enjoy such bargaining being established in law. In dispute during 1950, but shortly thereafter to be established, were two central institutions of *Mitbestimmung*, the concept that lies at the heart of the Federal industrial-relations system. First, in all but the smallest companies workers gained the right to elect a third of the company's supervisory board (*Aufsichtsrat*); in the coal and steel industries (*Montanbereich*) this rose to half, with also the right to appoint one member of the top managerial team (*Vorstand*), the labour director. Second, workers won the right to elect works councils (*Betriebsräte*), which unlike the ostensibly similar institutions in Belgium, France, Italy, and the Netherlands, comprised workers' representatives only and enjoyed certain substantive powers over company labour policy and practice. The councils were legally bound to a co-operative approach to relations with employers, and were formally elected by all workers irrespective of union membership.

Very similar conditions attached to the Austrian *Betriebsrat* system, but the unions there were sufficiently strong to ensure that the councils could in practice be dominated by them and serve virtually as a union arm—albeit of a co-operative kind— within the plant, binding unions into a tight web of relationships between workers and employers. The German unions were considerably weaker and feared that the *Betriebsräte* as constituted would be a threat to them. In the event matters turned out to be more complex than this, but in the early 1950s this was not known.

Irish and Finnish unions are drawn somewhat closer into national political discussion than before, but in general these countries predominantly evince a thin collective-bargaining structure, with the level of resistance to union recognition among many Finnish employers more consistent with a contestation model.

France and Italy had both experienced a brief period of national co-operation in the years between liberation from fascism and the onset of the Cold War in 1947. During this period a good deal of legislation was passed on union recognition and works councils at plant level and for union participation in some bodies at national political level. However, by 1950 it was already becoming clear that, at least as far as the communist majority wing of the labour movement was concerned, this was not leading to an elaborated bargaining structure. Both managements and unions kept their mutual dealings to a minimum and avoided compromises or even mutual recognition. These systems remained primarily contestative, with a small element of bargaining.

Meanwhile Portugal and Spain remained under fascist rule, with a comatose authoritarian corporatist structure alongside repression of autonomous union activity, a form of contestation.

Articulation of Labour Movements, 1950

As Table 6.2 shows, the Austrian movement is really in a class of its own for articulation, or at least for its centralizing aspects; but the Norwegian and then the Swedish come close behind, followed at some remove by Denmark.

Rankings then become more difficult to discern. Post-war reconstruction involved a considerable increase in the centralization of the Dutch movement. In terms of the proportion of total union membership represented, the NVV was the weakest confederation in western Europe, but this defect in central control was mitigated by the fact that, partly voluntarily, partly under legal constraint, the Catholic and Protestant confederations co-operated rather than competed with it in wage bargaining and incomes policy. Under Dutch labour law, a collective agreement could come into force only when all recognized unions had signed it; a union that stood aloof from a prospective agreement would therefore be denying its members the right to benefit. (This contrasts interestingly with France, where an agreement could come into force provided any one union signed it, which has

TABLE 6.2. *Articulation of trade-union movements, c.1950*

| | Unions affiliated to main confederation | | | | Individual unions | |
| | Membership as % of | | No. | Powers of confederation re affiliates | Dominant types of union | Characteristic internal authority structure over local groups, individual members, etc. | Characteristic shop-floor organization |
	known unions	labour force					
A	100.00	41.78	16	ÖGB monopolizes strike funds and calls and collective bargaining; dissenting communist minority	Strict branch	Centralized	Weak, but shop-floor role in *Betriebsräte*
N	c.90	36.31	43	LO monopolizes strike funds and calls and bargaining	Branch type dominates	Centralized	Union stewards integrated into formal structures
S	79.08	39.78	44	LO monopolizes strike funds and calls and bargaining; but separate non-manual	Branch type dominates	Centralized	Union stewards integrated into formal structures

							Tillidsman system
DK	84.50	32.15	69	confederation; LO and branch unions together must approve all strikes LO has some control of strike funds and calls and tries to monopolize bargaining	Craft and general	Centralized, but unable to control communist shop-floor action	
NL	32.90	9.87	21	NVV monopolizes strike calls and funds; but separate Christian confederations; however, they all participate in state-co-ordinated bargaining	Branch	Centralized	Weak
D	91.79	22.48	16	DGB seeks co-operation from leaderships of branch unions; small non-manual and *Beamte* confederations	Strict branch	Centralized	Weak

TABLE 6.2. *Continued*

	Unions affiliated to main confederation				Individual unions		
	Membership as % of		No.	Powers of confederation re affiliates	Dominant types of union	Characteristic internal authority structure over local groups, individual members, etc.	Characteristic shop-floor organization
	known unions	labour force					
CH	58.81	16.52	15	SGB seeks co-operation from leaderships of branch unions; rival Christian confederations	Strict branch	Centralized	Strong
UK	84.30	34.63	186	TUC has few powers but seeks some informal co-ordination of bargaining	Craft and general; some branch	Varied	Shop stewards in many skilled trades
B	4245.74	19.31	24	FGTB loses strike call powers; rival Christian confederation; some co-ordination of	Branch	Centralized	Weak

IRL	53.38	13.40	23	Schism; new nationalist CIU larger than ITUC	Craft and general	Varied	Shop stewards in some skilled trades
SF	76.50	15.42	38	SAK has strike call and fund power; rival far-left confederation	Branch type emerging	Varied	Varied
F	75.50	14.21	40	CGT has few powers but co-ordinates many conflict actions; rival confederations	See note*	Centralized	Very weak
I	78.69	18.24	90	CGIL has few powers but co-ordinates many conflict actions; rival confederations	See note*	Centralized	Very weak
E, P	No autonomous trade unions apart from clandestine ones						

Note: Country boundaries as in Table 6.1.

* Signifies a complex pattern of local cells of the confederations alongside individual economic-branch unions.

given French unions an incentive to distance themselves from each other, condemning as inadequate the deals another union signs, without running the risk of their members achieving nothing at all.) *De facto*, therefore, Dutch unions were as centralized as those mentioned above, and probably more so than those of the Danes. The latter had declined considerably in relative centralization during the previous half century, following their continuing refusal to develop an industrial union structure. On the other hand the Danes (as well as the Alpine countries, the other Scandinavians, and the United Kingdom) had developed a shop-floor presence which did not occur in any of the remaining countries.

The German and Swiss cases stand rather apart. In some respects they are highly centralized, but it is really concentration, not centralization, being rooted in a small number of internally centralized industrial unions rather than confederal power as such. When German labour reconstructed itself after its emergence from Nazism it did not re-erect the centralized institutions of Weimar; but it did use its potential centralized power to construct a highly concentrated, homogenous set of industry unions, rather as already existed in Switzerland and was being constructed in Austria—and as had indeed been the *aspiration* of the Weimar labour movement (Müller-Jentsch, 1985). This exceptionally neat and orderly structure, that can result only from considerable acceptance of central direction by individual unions, became and has remained a distinctive feature of the three German-speaking countries. Such a structure might seem relatively easy to achieve in a small country, but West Germany had the largest work-force among the countries under study.

A small number of strong industrial unions, being readily in touch with lower levels and also in straightforward communication on a face-to-face basis through leaders at confederal level, may well be an important form of articulated movement. The German unions, however, lacked a clear presence at shop-floor level. Also lacking the Austrians' high membership, they could not automatically dominate works councils, and at that stage were experiencing as a form of defeat the imposition of such councils by a government under the influence of Catholic social doctrine.

There follows a mixed group of partly articulated movements.

The British TUC, with a very high proportion of members affiliated, was relatively centralized at this time and clearly ranks some way above the similarly structured but, in those years, divided Irish movement. There was a potentially growing co-ordination of wage policies among Irish unions in the newly emerging pattern of national wage rounds, but at this point the degree of articulation was low.

Somewhat higher was that in Belgium, though it should at this time be ranked below the United Kingdom. Although both socialist and Catholic confederations were internally centralized and concentrated—a remarkable change over a quarter of a century—they had not established the kind of co-operation then to be seen in the Netherlands. The Finnish SAK had acquired some central powers and monopoly position, but in other respects it remained internally fragmented as a result of tension between social democratic and communist groups.

The newly reconstructed and even more recently divided Italian movement ranks below the again not dissimilarly structured but more monopolistic French. These are cases of centralization without articulation.

Employer Organization, 1950

Wartime developments induced some changes in employer prac-tices (Table 6.3). The Scandinavians were joined in their commit-ment to centralized bargaining alongside close relations with government by the Austrians, Belgians, and Dutch. As we have seen, in no country does this constitute a radical break in terms of centralized structure, but the willingness to deal systematically with unions at that level was new. The return of Austria to its earlier pattern of organization after the dislocation of fascism, Nazism, and defeat in war is remarkable. The Belgian situation reflects the success of the government strategy of encouraging the formation of *commissions paritaires*.

Neat, orderly, centralized structures with extensive govern-ment involvement are also found in Germany and Switzerland, though here the centre of gravity in industrial relations is, as we would now expect, more in individual industry associations rather than peak bodies. This sets these two apart from the former group. The rapid return of German industry to reliance on strong

TABLE 6.3. *Organizations of capital, c.1950*

	Scope[1]	Power[2]	Other associative business activity[3]
A	Reconstruction of comprehensive *Kammer* system for industrial relations and trade purposes; also voluntary organizations		
DK, N, S	Comprehensive throughout	Central bodies co-ordinate bargaining, etc. and impose sanctions on deviant firms	Some reduction in association role with ending of war
NL	Extensive	Employer associations part of PBO system and derive power from statutory obligations	Trade associations incorporated in post-war economic strategy
B	Extensive	FIB gives central steer to branch bargaining; branch bodies have strike support power	FIB co-ordinates action
CH	Extensive	Metal and watch employers' association co-ordinates employers in key sectoral bargaining; other sectors imitate	Organizations heavily involved in co-ordinating export strategy
D	Extensive; BDA, 1950	Employers' associations play key role in bargaining at regional and branch level, with extensive strike funds; BDA attempts informal co-ordination role	Reconstruction of *Kammer* system of trade representation with new voluntary trade associations (established in advance of new republic); BDI, 1950

E, P Employers accept role in structures of fascist state

	Extent of organization of employer interests[1]	Resources available to employer organizations to co-ordinate action[2]	Activity directed at trade rather than labour issues[3]
SF	Patchy coverage	STK plays role similar to Scandinavian peak associations, but many firms refuse to bargain	Trade associations central to operation of Finno-Soviet trade agreement
UK	Extensive	Branch-level associations a key level of employer bargaining co-ordination, but with few powers	Trade associations important in regulated post-war economy
IRL	Patchy; FUE, 1942	FUE takes lead in co-ordinating pay talks, but few powers	Weak
I	Fairly extensive	Confindustria plays key role in limited bargaining with unions	Associations important in northern industry
F	Fairly extensive	CNPF plays key role in very limited bargaining with unions	CNPF plays weak role; most associations just pressure groups; rival CGPME as radical small-business lobby

Note: Country boundaries as in Table 6.1.

[1] Extent of organization of employer interests.

[2] Resources available to employer organizations to co-ordinate action.

[3] Activity directed at trade rather than labour issues.

organizations is remarkable, after not only all the disruption of the previous decade but also the imposition of Anglo-American models of pluralism since 1945, and the Germans' own shift from a cartellized to a market economy.

The surviving fascist countries should probably be inserted at this point, below those with autonomously developing organizations but above those in which organizations at a nationally aggregated level were not very important at all. Portuguese and Spanish institutions remain similar to those of the post-war years.

In a further three countries (Finland, Ireland, the United Kingdom) there were in varied ways more important steps towards greater central involvement by employers' associations than in the past, but of an unsystematic nature. Northern Italy would also conform to this model, but the country overall appears as less integrated. Employers' organizations in France remained weak.

Power of Organized Labour, 1950

The most powerful labour movements (Table 6.4) remained those of the Scandinavians (particularly the Swedes), now joined by the Austrians, Belgians, and British—all with high union membership and with parties in government which were supportive of the unions and all difficult to rank against each other. The Danes had lost their pre-eminence of earlier in the century; industrial employment remained relatively low, and in October 1950 the Social Democrats lost office, which must for a while place the Danish movement below the Belgian. The strength of the Austrian movement was increased by the fact that its associated party was vital to the stability of the new and still occupied country on the East–West border. In addition, elaborate forms of co-operation had been devised to maintain good relations between socialist trade-unionists and their Catholic (People's Party) colleagues. Austrian and Danish trade-unionists, and probably Belgians as well, had to cope with higher unemployment than their counterparts in other countries with strong unions.

It is unfortunately difficult to rank the large and heterogeneous group of Finland, Ireland, Italy, Germany, the Netherlands, and Switzerland. All had similar levels of union membership and

	Known union membership as % of		Major industrial-relations and political developments affecting organized labour within industry	Unem-ployment[2]	Share of popular vote[3] %	Particip-ation in gov't[4] %	Other major political developments affecting wider position of organized labour
	labour force	dependent labour force[1]					
S	50.30	65.51		L	52.4	1.00	
N	40.34	56.74		L	51.5	1.00	
UK	41.08	45.44		L	46.1	1.00	
A	41.78	64.57	Codetermination-based system of industrial relations established in law	M	43.6 (44.0)	0.50	Country occupied by World War victor powers
B	42.21	58.95	Statutory works council system introduced, excluding unions from plant	M	39.2 (47.7)	0.25	
DK	38.05	53.47		M	44.2	1.00[5]	
NL	30.01	42.33	Employer-dominated system of plant representation introduced; but strong union legal rights	L	33.3 (53.4)	0.75	Coalition regime forged during Nazi occupation

Table 6.4. *Continued*

	Known union membership as % of		Major industrial-relations and political developments affecting organized labour within industry	Unem-ployment[2]	Share of popular vote[3] %	Particip-ation in gov't[4] %	Other major political developments affecting wider position of organized labour
	labour force	dependent labour force[1]					
CH	28.10	39.65		L	31.3 (21.2)	0.75	
IRL	25.11	44.83		M	8.7 (41.9)	0.25	Government tries to use Catholic component of union identity to strengthen national unity
D	24.49	34.58	Codetermination-based system of industrial relations established in law; union role placed on legal basis	H	34.9 (31.1)	0.25	Denazification and division of country strengthen pressure to incorporate labour
SF	20.16	34.70		?	46.3	0.00	Country's difficult geopolitical position strengthens pressure to incorporate labour

| I | 23.18 | 41.43 | Statutory works council system introduced, excluding unions from plant | ? | 31.0 (55.6) | 0.25 | Dominant communist wing of labour movement excluded from national integration after onset of Cold War |
| F | 18.82 | 23.89 | Statutory works council system introduced, excluding unions from plant | ? | 28.6 (26.3) | 0.25 | Dominant communist wing of labour movement excluded from national integration after onset of Cold War |

Note: Country boundaries as in Table 6.1.

[1] For Finland, percentage of non-agricultural labour.

[2] H = registered unemployment in excess of 10% of dependent labour force; M = around 10%; L = less than 5%; ? = reliable figures not available on a broadly comparable basis.

[3] In most recent general election, secured by labour movement parties; votes for parties with labour wing but primarily committed to other interests (e.g. Catholic parties) in parentheses. Figures for all except Ireland and UK combine social democratic as well as communist parties. French socialists count as not primarily a labour-movement party.

[4] 1.0 = straight labour party government; 0.75 = main labour-movement party dominating coalition or combination of labour and quasi-labour parties; 0.50 = labour party as minor coalition partner; 0.25 = participation by Christian etc. parties.

[5] Only until October, when social-democratic government fell.

either various degrees of government involvement by unions or political élites dependent on labour for helping to shore up national unity (in some cases because of the position of the country on the new Cold War boundary). Consociational government participation probably ranks the Netherlands and Switzerland above the others. Also, unemployment was very high in Germany.

While the numerical strength of Italian unionism places it with the above nations, it had, like the French movement, been weakened by deep and bitter divisions and by the expulsion of the majority communist wing of the movement from national respectability. Despite the general spirit of the period and the preference of the United States and the United Kingdom for constitutional industrial relations, the spectre of communism enabled political and business élites in these two countries to return to the exclusionary policies pursued by a number of countries after the passing of the wave of pro-labour euphoria similar to that which had accompanied the end of the First World War. The only other sizeable communist movements—in Finland and to a lesser extent Austria—did not have the same implications, partly because they were not the dominant wings of the national labour movements, and partly because they were located in neutral countries over which the Soviet Union had a good deal of influence.

Economic and Political Development, 1950

Indices of development (Table 6.5) are now mainly of interest for the economic variables, though the continuing existence of two dictatorships should be noted. With the exceptions of the relatively rich agricultural societies of Finland, France, and Norway, we have a fairly straightforward association between industrialism and wealth. This enables us to point out two associations, the first between relative poverty and either low institutional development or fascism (Italy, Portugal, and Spain); and the second between wealth and trends towards GPE (Denmark, Netherlands, Norway, Sweden, Switzerland, and the United Kingdom). However, that leaves as perplexing exceptions Austria and Germany (poor but incipiently corporatist) and France (rich but contestative).

TABLE 6.5. *Indicators of political and economic development, c.1950*

	Agricultural work-force as % of total work-force	GNP p.c. (1960 US$)	Electorate as % of adult population	Leading economic sectors
A	32.3[1]	721	89.3	Mixed industrial; major steel sector; otherwise many small firms; agriculture still important; major economic dislocation following *Anschluß* and war defeat
B	12.1	1,167	93.3	Textiles, steel, coal, capital equipment, finance
DK	25.6	1,277	98.3	Mixed industrial, big tertiary sector, advanced agriculture
SF	46.0	1,027	99.7	Primarily agriculture, also forest products, engineering
F	33.0[1]	1,177	90.4	Mixed industrial, agriculture
D	23.2	834	97.8	Coal and steel dominant; mixed industry, especially capital equipment; economy recovering from post-war dismantling
IRL	39.6	744	97.4	Agriculture, some light industry
I	40.0	590	100.9	Agriculture, public utilities; textiles and other industrial development
NL	18.8	1,019	95.4	Mixed industrial, strong tertiary sector, agriculture
N	25.9	1,652	98.2	Shipping, hydro-electric, mixed industry, forest products
P	n.a. (high)	383	none	Agriculture
E	n.a. (high)	367	none	Agriculture, textiles, some industrial development
S	20.3	1,712	98.1	Industrial, especially capital equipment; forest products
CH	16.5	1,368	92.7[2]	Metal industries and watchmaking, financial services
UK	5.1	1,352	97.8	Coal, steel, engineering, financial services

Note: Country boundaries as in Table 6.1.

[1] Approximate figure.
[2] Adult male population only.

Industrial Conflict, 1950

We now see a relationship between institutional development and conflict consistent with the expectations of neo-corporatist theory (Table 6.6). The countries with thin institutions, the contestative systems (Finland, France, Italy, and to some extent Ireland) have conflict levels not just higher, but considerably higher, than elsewhere. Further, several of the countries that seem set on a path towards neo-corporatism (Sweden, Germany, Switzerland, and Norway) have, in the main, lower conflict levels than those with straightforward collective bargaining. Austria, Denmark, and the Netherlands have rather too much conflict for this thesis, but the main exception is Belgium, which has far too much conflict. It is however notable that the Belgian unions lacked the degree of articulation typical of the other cases that were tending towards corporatism.

Conclusions, 1950

Putting. all these elements of the early post-war years together, we can see that the Scandinavian group and Austria were acquiring both the characteristics and the organizational preconditions for a GPE model of industrial relations. Centralization and political involvement, endangering as they do any institutionalized containment of conflict, clearly make these cases different from pluralist collective bargaining in the terms of Chapter 2. These are the ones that Dunlopian theory cannot explain without classifying them as dynastic or revolutionary. They are also varied among themselves in ways that create difficulties for Olsonian theories about the very gradual way in which dense institutional textures are supposed to become established: Denmark developed in reasonably Olsonian fashion, but Norwegian and Swedish developments were very sudden; and Austria reconstructed its networks very rapidly indeed after years of dislocation and organizational destruction.

Belgium and the United Kingdom are not dissimilar but, albeit for different reasons, lacked well-articulated labour movements and employers' organizations, though they had both moved in that direction since the pre-war years. Germany, the Netherlands and Switzerland are similar to the Austro-Scandinavian group

TABLE 6.6. *Industrial conflict, 1946–1950*

	Strikes per 1,000		Workers involved per 1,000		Days lost per 1,000	
	dependent labour force	trade-union members	dependent labour force	trade-union members	dependent labour force	trade-union members
A[1]	n.a.	n.a.	6.94	10.75	90.31	139.87
B	0.09	0.16	85.90	145.72	694.62	1,178.32
DK	0.02	0.04	9.60	17.95	257.65	481.86
SF	0.10	0.29	53.52	154.24	1,158.81	3,339.51
F[1]	0.12	0.38	256.12	816.97	546.35	1,742.74
D[2]	0.01	0.03	14.98	42.75	35.64	101.71
IRL	0.23	0.51	23.09	51.06	403.52	900.11
I[2]	0.12	0.25	311.73	656.97	1,052.27	2,217.64
NL	0.07	0.17	15.08	35.62	111.25	262.82
N	0.04	0.07	6.17	10.87	68.85	121.34
S	0.03	0.04	5.67	8.38	30.62	45.24
CH	0.02	0.06	3.61	10.29	51.67	147.33
UK	0.09	0.20	23.80	52.38	100.46	221.08

Note: Country boundaries as in Table 6.1.
[1] Worker involvement figures for 1948–50 only.
[2] Conflict data for 1949–50 only.

except that their emerging pattern is taking place with relatively weak labour movements. These cases are not so consistent with the 'social-democratic' interpretation of neo-corporatism, raising the question of why tightly organized employers and states predominantly controlled by right-of-centre forces bothered to incorporate labour in their arrangements. Why did they not behave like their French or Italian counterparts?

It is not unreasonable to speak of some hesitant convergence on a neo-corporatist model at this stage; go back three years to 1947 and one would have included France and Italy as showing symptoms of similar arrangements, leaving only the two fascist corporatist cases (Portugal and Spain) and the two 'new' nation-states (Finland and Ireland) outside the neo-corporatist scope. It is important to note that at this stage Finland is not part of a Scandinavian pattern. If anything it might be said to resemble Belgium or the Netherlands in the state-controlled character of its wage-fixing machinery, but Finnish policy was much more coercive and delegated little to the social partners.

Highly elaborated, incipient GPE systems were at this stage accompanied by highly articulated unions and employers' associations. As we have noted, Belgian labour was 'inadequately' articulated for the institutions within which it was expected to perform; so perhaps was Swiss. However, whereas Belgian dis-articulation took the form of union rivalry and confederal weakness, the Swiss was a case of rather atomized local union groups.

In terms of Fig. 2.2, which relates different configurations of articulation and union power, we are primarily aware of the close positive correlation between these variables in this period. Countries occupy very similar positions in Tables 6.1 and 6.4. The Austro-Scandinavian group is now moving into quadrant III, social-democratic corporatism; the geographically heterogeneous group comprising Finland, France, Ireland, and Italy still has weak dislocated unions (quadrant I). The only cases that seem to stray from that diagonal are possibly the United Kingdom and Belgium (in danger of *possibly* entering unstable quadrant II (powerful unions but relatively unarticulated)) and Switzerland (an articulated system but weak unions, IV). A major change since the pre-war years, however, is that it is the *weak* unions that are producing the major conflict.

POST-WAR STABILITY: THE EARLY 1960S

The years of post-war recovery gradually became those of the prolonged European post-war boom. High unemployment, hitherto the virtually inevitable accompaniment of industrial society, gave way to acute labour shortages. Prosperity became very widespread, and while the border between eastern and western Europe remained fraught with tension, old antagonisms among the western European powers disappeared. Six Continental democracies (all those outside Nordic countries and the two small Alpine states) became joined in the European Economic Community.

But while western Europe was converging in many respects, in industrial relations there was a new divergence. The Austrians, Scandinavians, to a lesser extent the Dutch and Belgians, and in their rather different ways the Germans and Swiss, continued to multiply and deepen the network of relations binding industrial-relations actors and imparting to them public administrative as well as industrial bargaining activities, as anticipated in the model of generalized political exchange. But elsewhere patterns moved differently. Not as strongly as after 1918, but not dissimilarly, a corporatist convergence gave way to new divergences.

By the late 1960s there were signs of new major changes. Taking a new 'snapshot' in the early 1960s enables us to see how industrial relations had developed during the years of relative tranquillity before the disruptions of the later period began.

Institutional Development, 1963

Table 6.7 shows the strong thickening of the texture of institutional relations in certain of those countries that seemed in 1950 to be embarking on the GPE dynamic. In Austria, Sweden, Norway, and Denmark unions and employers' organizations had become deeply engaged in a range of national-level institutions that enabled or required them to participate in economy-wide decision-making on wage movements and in the administration of various labour-related services, moving especially in the Swedish case into aspects of labour-market policy.

Similar institutions existed in Belgium and the Netherlands, though limited to a somewhat narrower range of issues and need-

Table 6.7. *Institutional development of industrial relations, c.1963*

Main pattern of industrial relations	Country	Level					
		Plant	Locality	Branch	Nation	State	
Strong development of neo-corporatism	A	*Betriebsräte* with some administrative powers		Involvement of unions and employer organizations in bargaining, administration and consultation arrangements from state to branch level, formalized at national level in Paritätische Kommission, 1956			
	DK	Collective bargaining		Extensive bargaining	DA and LO set national pay framework	Unions and employer organizations in extensive consultative and administrative arrangements; government seeks pay policy to remedy defects of DA/LO system	
	N	Some bargaining		Extensive bargaining	NAF and LO set national pay framework	Unions and employer organizations	

| S | Some bargaining | Extensive bargaining | SAF and LO set national pay framework | Unions and employer organizations in extensive consultative and administrative arrangements | consultative and administrative arrangements |

TABLE 6.7. *Continued*

Main pattern of industrial relations	Country	Level	Plant	Locality	Branch	Nation	State
Neo-corporatism developing with strong state support	NL		Statutory bipartite works council system		Union involvement in mediation and pension schemes	Government continues to operate statutorily supported tripartite pay bargaining system, also extensive consultation through SER and devolved administration	Union involvement in government consultation
	B		Statutory bipartite works council system	*Commissions paritaires* gain legal powers, 1957	Growing bargaining; 'social peace' clauses exchanged for union advantages	*Programmation sociale* agreements involve social partners in tripartite consultation and administration	

developing with strong decentral component		some administrative powers	bargaining	level	involvement in pension scheme etc. management	involvement of unions and employer organizations in administration; obligation on government to do this, 1958
	CH		Extensive bargaining	Further growth of GAV and *Friedenspflicht* agreements		Unions and employer organizations in extensive administrative arrangements
	UK	Further growth of bargaining		Very extensive bargaining; union involvement in mediation		Government seeking tripartite agreement on wage restraint
Strong collective bargaining	IRL			Extensive bargaining	Attempts at stability through national pay rounds	Government involves social partners in economic development talks

TABLE 6.7. Continued

Main pattern of industrial relations	Country	Plant	Locality	Branch	Nation	State
Growing shop-floor action within contestative bargaining	SF	Intensive autonomous shop-floor action		Growing bargaining	Fragile SAK–STK attempts at agreements	State regulation of wages ends
	I	Statutory bipartite works council system but growing shop-floor militancy	Some bargaining	Growing bargaining in public sector	Some bargaining	Minor consultation of non-communist unions
	F	Statutory bipartite works council system	Some limited bargaining	Some growth of bargaining in public sector	Some bargaining	Government assists non-CGT unions, increasing fragmentation of union movement
Authoritarian corporatism	E	Minor development of collective bargaining and shop-floor representation within fascist system				
	P	Autonomous unions illegal; fascist unions of workers and employers have formal consultation role at all levels				

ing continuing government support. In Belgium this now took the form of *programmation sociale*, a series of national tripartite agreements on incomes development and a broad range of social policies. These would sometimes be incorporated into legislation. Given the deadlocked nature of Belgian party politics over the language issue at this time, legislation was often implemented by the dubiously democratic device of royal decree, prior agreement to a policy in *programmation sociale* enabling the government to bridge this democratic deficit while simultaneously enhancing the acceptance of national responsibility by organizations of employers and employees.

In the Netherlands the institutions of PBO through the SER and the Stichting had continued to develop, though never giving unions the degree of general economic policy influence and administrative participation they had envisaged during the debates of the late 1930s; and the incomes agreements, unlike those in Scandinavia or Austria, continued to need statutory backing. It is worth noting that the increasing resort to government incomes-policy intervention that was coming to characterize Denmark during the early 1960s was rendering that country a possible third candidate for membership of this group.

Similar again were Germany and Switzerland, except that there remained in these countries a split between national-level participation by confederal and union leaders and more localized collective bargaining. The degree of GPE was weaker, so much less being resolved at national level, though the public-policy administrative role by social partner organizations was prominent in these countries.

All the above cases had seen either a rapidly or a gradually intensifying neo-corporatism. In several other countries post-war neo-corporatism had deteriorated. Ireland and the United Kingdom were now pre-eminent cases of strong collective bargaining, the two countries having converged from somewhat different positions in the early 1950s. Irish industrialization had increased the importance of unionized labour. Governments had begun to commit themselves to a modernization policy in the late 1950s and therefore began to interest themselves, employers, and unions in relationships going beyond collective bargaining, though there is no case for defining the system as anything other than straight pluralist bargaining.

Meanwhile the British had diverged from the 'Scandinavian' path of development that they seemed to be following in the early post-war years. The country had reverted to a collective bargaining mould as Conservative governments lost interest in economic co-ordination, to the tacit relief of the unions. Further, collective bargaining was shifting to the unofficial shop-floor level, in a manner quite disarticulated from branch-level official negotiations. (This was to change during the 1960s when there was an increasingly frantic search to re-establish institutions of the kind that had deteriorated during the 1950s.)

Between these countries and Finland, France, and Italy there is a further fault-line separating collective bargaining from contestative systems. In Finland, government control of incomes development was relaxed in 1956, but instead of the hoped-for transition to a centralized Scandinavian model, the system shifted to one of intensive and conflictual bargaining. Until the late 1960s political conflict divided the labour movement in ways that were not conducive to central co-ordination, though governments did continue their efforts to encourage co-operative behaviour through extensive consultation of interest groups. France and Italy remained more or less at the low level of institutionalization that had long characterized them, though with an important growth in collective bargaining, especially in state industries, in the early 1960s. In both cases this was undertaken for political at least as much as industrial-relations reasons; governments were seeking to reinforce national unity in the face of the continuing— and apparently increasingly anachronistic—level of class conflict in these countries.

Another split divides these cases from the authoritarian corporatist group. Portugal and Spain remained dictatorships until the 1970s, though in the latter country there was an interesting revival of genuine worker representation within the bosom of the state system. In response to evidence of growing unrest, the government established a structure of elected shop-floor committees for dealing with local grievances. Although these could have no overt links with autonomous unions, which remained illegal, or with the clandestine political parties, in practice it was activists from these, especially communists, who took advantage of the new institutions and secured election to places on them (Amsden, 1972).

Articulation of Labour Movements, 1963

Articulation is also relatively easy to rank (Table 6.8). There is again a tight Austro-Scandinavian group with strong, wide-membership confederations co-ordinating centralized individual unions but, at least in the Scandinavian cases, delegated task areas for local representatives. Germany is something of a case on its own in that co-ordination was concentrated at the branch-union level, though the small number of these within the DGB rendered this a tight organization. Another notable feature of the German situation by this stage was the growing ability of unions to learn how to make use of works councils, despite their being explicitly non-union bodies (Leminsky, 1965). The DGB unions would put up candidates for office on the councils (achieving up to 80 per cent success in this) and would subsequently co-opt these councillors into their own decision-making structures; a particularly sophisticated form of articulation, and one that indirectly inclined the unions to moderation. Works councillors, being under pressure to take a 'company' view and also wanting to keep some room for manœuvre at company level in wage bargaining, were not likely to support aggressive bargaining demands by the unions.

Next come union movements that tried to secure co-ordination despite ostensibly rival confederations. In the Netherlands and Switzerland the essentially non-competitive relationship between Catholic, Protestant, and social-democratic groupings, plus the encouragement given by political structures to co-operation among these groups, pushed them strongly towards co-operation. The Belgian situation is far less clear, the Christian and social-democratic unions struggling for dominance of the movement. In the early 1960s the Catholic CSC overtook the FGTB, and because the former union was considerably more centralized, this change in leadership led to an overall upgrading of Belgian labour's centralization level.

Following the reunification of the Irish unions during the 1950s, that country rejoined the United Kingdom in a rather special group: movements with extensive, monopolistic confederations which nevertheless lacked any central authority.

Finland, on the other hand, had been beset by a new split as 'moderate' unions formed the SAJ confederation, a rival to the

TABLE 6.8. Articulation of trade-union movements, c.1963

| | Unions affiliated to main confederation | | | | | Individual unions | |
| | Membership as % of | | No. | Powers of confederation re affiliates | Dominant types of union | Characteristic internal authority structure over local groups, individual members, etc. | Characteristic shop-floor organization |
	known unions	labour force					
A	100.00	45.45	16	ÖGB monopolizes strike funds and calls and all collective bargaining	Strict branch	Centralized	Strong shop-floor role in Betriebsräte
N	81.64	40.43	41	LO monopolizes strike funds and calls and bargaining	Branch type dominates	Centralized	Union stewards integrated into formal structures
S	72.50	44.88	43	LO monopolizes strike funds and bargaining; but separate non-manual confederation; LO and branch unions together must approve all strikes	Branch type dominates	Centralized	Union stewards integrated into formal structures

			of strike funds and calls and monopolizes most bargaining		unable to control communist shop-floor action	*Talvshmatt* system
D	81.15	21.77	16	DGB seeks co-operation from leaderships of branch unions; small non-manual and *Beamte* confederations	Strict branch	Centralized	Weak but able to work informally through *Betriebsräte*
NL	36.00	12.69	19	NVV monopolizes strike calls and funds; but separate Christian confederations; however, they all participate in state-co-ordinated bargaining	Branch	Centralized	Weak
CH	56.20	16.84	15	SGB seeks co-operation from leaderships of branch unions; rival Christian confederations	Strict branch	Centralized	Strong but within framework of union discipline

TABLE 6.8. *Continued*

| | Unions affiliated to main confederation | | | | Individual unions | | |
| | Membership as % of | | No. | Powers of confederation re affiliates | Dominant types of union | Characteristic internal authority structure over local groups, individual members, etc. | Characteristic shop-floor organization |
	known unions	labour force					
B	45.87	21.69	34	CSC has overtaken FGTB as leading confederation; both now have strike call powers; government policy necessitates some co-operation	Branch	Centralized	Weak
UK	82.70	34.74	183	TUC has few powers	Craft and general; some branch	Varied	Shop stewards in many skilled trades; growing autonomy of structures at this level

					Craft and general	Mainly decentral	Shop stewards in some skilled trades
IRL	n.a.	n.a.	n.a.	ITUC again sole confederation, but with few powers; some rival individual unions	n.a.		
SF	n.a.	n.a.	n.a.	SAK has strike call and funds power but is internally divided on political lines; also rival 'non-political' confederation (SAJ)	Branch type growing	Varied; communist and social-democratic rivalry within many unions	Strong, autonomous, with powerful communist wing
F	50.67	7.33	n.a.	CGT has few powers but co-ordinates many conflict actions; rival confederations	See note*	Centralized	Very weak
I	61.41	10.03	n.a.	CGIL has few powers but co-ordinates many conflict actions; rival confederations	See note*	Centralized	Very weak
E, P				No autonomous trade unions apart from clandestine ones			

Note: Country boundaries as in Table 6.1.

* Signifies a complex pattern of local cells of the confederations alongside individual economic-branch unions.

SAK, which was in turn split into warring communist and social-democratic factions. This country therefore joins France and Italy as one divided into rival groups.

Given that systems have by this time begun to stabilize, and that the quality of union membership data has also improved, it is now worthwhile considering an aspect of the argument of Chapter 2, which has subsequently been neglected: the role of branch-level unions in the exposed sector of the economy, which, it was argued, contributed to the 'Olson effect' of encompassing-ness. Table 6.9 presents relevant data for the early 1960s for the countries under review. Account is taken, (1) of the proportion of the total unionized labour force that is in unions which are affiliated to the main union confederation and are both of branch type and located in the internationally traded sector of the economy; (2) of the proportion of the total membership of the confederation represented by such members; and (3) of the proportion of the total labour force in membership of such

TABLE 6.9. *Membership of exposed-sector trade unions, c.1963*

	Exposed-sector industry-type union members in main confederation as % of total union members	Exposed-sector industry-type union members as % of	
		main confederation members	total labour force
A	35.30	35.30	15.69
B	23.61	47.59	10.28
DK	16.10	20.10	7.45
SF	18.04	33.71	3.58
F	17.48	29.94	2.29
D	45.52	55.51	13.35
IRL	7.21	7.57	2.26
I	11.22	17.82	2.17
NL	24.45	29.93	8.08
N	28.22	35.19	13.08
S	24.10	31.97	14.64
CH	25.10	42.48	7.06
UK	17.71	21.17	6.94

Note: Country boundaries as in Table 6.1.

unions. The non-traded sector is considered to include the public service (though not state industries), the construction industry and also agriculture which, though internationally traded, is normally subject to some price guarantee arrangement (either the Common Agricultural Policy for members of the European Community or other national arrangements). Data have been collected for the five largest exposed-sector unions in each country, though in most cases that means going down to unions with small relative memberships.

Two factors thus determine the role of such unions within a country: the extent to which its unions take branch form, and the relative size and scope of such unions. In fact, the branch form was normal in the 1960s in the countries being studied: Denmark, Ireland, and the United Kingdom being the only exceptions with a primary pattern of craft and general unions. The exposed-sector factor is not independent of our existing concepts of union power and articulation. The higher the level of union membership, the larger the role within the economy of a large union. Also, as has already been noted, an aspect of the centralized power of a confederation is its ability to group unions into a small number of organizations, and the most rational basis on which to do this has been branch level. It is therefore not surprising that the powerful, highly articulated union movements of Scandinavia and Austria also rank highly on the exposed-sector variable.

However, it is notable that this new variable makes an autonomous contribution to our understanding of Germany and Switzerland, the articulation structures of which were otherwise somewhat anomalous. Single unions (IG Metall and SMUV respectively) in the exposed sector dominated the leading confederations (DGB and SGB) to an extraordinary degree. One also appreciates a divergence from the Scandinavian pattern by the Danish unions resulting from the absence of a branch-union structure.

Employer Organization, 1963

Table 6.10 gives details of employers' associations at this period, showing little change since the 1950s, and it is now clearly a pattern bearing close similarities to that of the unions. There was a tight, strong, national-level role in Scandinavia and Austria—

TABLE 6.10. *Organizations of capital, c. 1963*

	Scope[1]	Power[2]	Other associative business activity[3]
A	Growth of autonomous organizations co-operating with *Kammer*	Role of PK strengthens power of central bodies	Growing importance with economic recovery
N	Comprehensive throughout industrial sector and some tertiary sectors	NAF controls all bargaining strategy	Deep involvement in economic policy
S	Comprehensive throughout industrial sector and some tertiary sectors	SAF controls all bargaining strategy	Deep involvement in economic policy
SF	Extensive	STK takes power to veto agreements, call lock-outs and fine dissenting firms; seeks two-year deals with SAK	Trade associations central to operation of Finno-Soviet trade agreement
DK	Comprehensive throughout industrial sector and some tertiary sectors	DA remains powerful, but losing ability to control decentral tendencies	Deep involvement in economic policy
NL	Comprehensive	Centralized regulation of labour market	Close involvement in economic policy

	[1]	[2]	[3]
B	Extensive	Programmation sociale strengthens role of FIB and branch organizations	FIB co-ordinates action
D	Comprehensive throughout industrial sector and some tertiary sectors	BDA requires all member *Verbände* to have strike funds, 1956, and monitors branch collective agreements	BDI and DIHT administer foreign trade policy
CH	Extensive	Primarily informal, but effective	Organizations heavily involved in co-ordinating export strategy
IRL	Patchy	FIE co-ordinates some wage-round activity	Weak
UK	Extensive	Weak, but attempts at informal co-ordination in co-operation with government incomes policy	Active but not strongly incorporated into policy administration
I	Extensive	Confindustria weakened by departure of state industries to Intersind, 1956; active but reliant on personal rather than representative structures	Associations important in northern industry
F	Limited	CNPF has few co-ordinating powers	Some involvement in state planning
E, P	Fascist structures becoming marginalized in modernization of economy; little modern role for associations		

Note: Country boundaries as in Table 6.1.

[1] Extent of organization of employer interests.

[2] Resources available to employer organizations to co-ordinate action.

[3] Activity directed at trade rather than labour issues.

and here Finnish employers had changed rapidly and considerably in advance of their labour counterparts in developing a
'Scandinavian' pattern. In Denmark, however, the DA was
increasingly ceding authority to government in the control of
incomes, and this country is therefore beginning to conform more
to a 'low countries' (Belgian and Dutch) model of state-assisted
national power for employers in industrial relations. There was a
tight, strong, branch-level role in Germany and Switzerland with
a national role in trade policy almost like an arm of the state. In
the United Kingdom and Ireland there was a looser branch-level
role but with employers' organizations involved in national
economic discussions with government; and in France and Italy a
varied, conflictual role. The authoritarian corporatist structures
of the Iberian regimes were becoming increasingly irrelevant to
those countries' pattern of modernization.

The French and Italian cases, and also the Belgian and British,
are worthy of special comment. In one sense French and Italian
employers' organizations resembled those in Scandinavia, bargaining centrally with union confederations, though through very
different institutional patterns as Table 6.7 showed. The main
difference in internal structure is that the reach of these organizations was much weaker. Employers tried to minimize the extent
of their industrial relations that had to be mediated through
either trade unions or even their own organizations, so the
emphasis was on making minimal central agreements that left
maximum scope for employers' individual decisions. Belgian
employers were in fact rather similar, but for largely political
reasons the Belgian government pulled them into more intricate,
often statutory or at least state-led, relations with unions.

Even if the French and Italian governments had wanted to do
the same, they would have had difficulty making much use of
such organizations as the Patronat or Confindustria. In the former
case the organization was very weak and poorly resourced, and
carried little influence in French business circles (Brizay, 1975;
Lefranc, 1976). Confindustria was considerably stronger, but not
representative of either the biggest firms in the economy or, at
the other extreme, the *mezzogiorno*. And it was more clientilistic
than representative in its relations with firms (Carlini, 1972). It
is interesting to note that when, during the years here under
review, the governments of both France and Italy wanted, for

diverse political reasons, to reduce the level of contestation in the labour market, they did so through policy in the public sector, deliberately avoiding and even challenging the harder-line policies of the private-sector organizations. In the Italian case the formation, in 1956, of Intersind, the association of state industry employers, can clearly be seen as a move towards a pluralist strategy against *both* contestative and neo-corporatist strategies: against the former in its encouragement of bargaining, against the latter in its threatened fragmentation and challenge to the Confindustria monopoly (Collidà, 1972).

Power of Organized Labour, 1963

The measurement of union power is fairly straightforward for this period. The highest memberships were concentrated in the countries with the lowest unemployment and the strongest labour political presence. The rank ordering shown in Table 6.11 is easily comprehensible and shows no great change since the early 1950s. It is interesting to note that a varied mixture of political and macro-economic motives had led several governments to take increasing note of unions or provide new institutions in which they could participate. This even affected Spain, as mentioned above, though that country cannot be included in this table because there was no true autonomous labour movement.

Economic and Social Development, 1963

There is little of interest in these data as our countries, with the exception of Spain and Portugal, converge on a model of liberal democratic industrialism, and Table 6.12 is the last occasion on which we shall consider them. It is notable that Finland and Ireland have ten times the agricultural work-force of the United Kingdom; Sweden is almost twice as rich as fellow neo-corporatist Austria. As before, while the dictatorships are limited to the very poorest European nations, beyond that there is little scope for generalization. France (one of the richest countries) still has one of the least developed institutional systems of industrial relations, while Austria (one of the poorest) has one of the most extensive.

TABLE 6.11. *Power of organized labour, c.1963*

	Known union membership as % of		Major industrial-relations and political developments affecting organized labour within industry	Unemployment[1]	Share of popular vote[2] %	Particip-ation in gov't[3] %	Other major political developments affecting wider position of organized labour
	labour force	dependent labour force					
S	61.90	74.33		VL	52.3	1.00	
N	40.34	56.74		VL	46.8	1.00	
DK	49.83	64.68	Wage restraint becomes government priority	VL	42.1	0.75	
A	45.45	68.27	PK, 1956, confirms centrality of unions	L	44.0 (45.4)	0.75	
B	42.27	64.79	*Programmation sociale* confirms centrality of unions	L	36.7 (41.5)	0.50	Unions gain importance from linguistic deadlock of normal politics
UK	42.00	48.49	Union role in NEDC	VL	43.8		
IRL	37.18	65.70		L	11.6 (43.8)	0.25	
NL	33.40	42.07		VL	28.0 (49.2)	0.75	
CH	28.10	39.52		VL	26.6	0.75	

D	24.49	37.15	(23.4) 36.2 (45.3)	0.25	VL	Cold-War exclusion of communists
I	23.18	24.58	39.1 (44.2)	0.25	L	Geo-political problem of communists
SF	14.75	22.46	41.5		VL	Cold-War exclusion of communists
F	14.47	20.71	21.8 (12.7)		VL	Cold-War exclusion of communists

Note: Country boundaries as in Table 6.1.

[1] H = registered unemployment in excess of 10% of dependent labour force; M = around 10%; L = 2.5–5.0%; VL = less than 2.5%; ? = reliable figures not available on a broadly comparable basis.

[2] In most recent general election, secured by labour-movement parties; votes for parties with labour wing but primarily committed to other interests (e.g. Catholic parties) in parentheses. Figures for Finland, Italy, and Sweden combine social democratic as well as communist and any other labour-movement parties. French socialists count as not primarily a labour-movement party.

[3] 1.00 = straight labour party government; 0.75 = main labour-movement party dominating coalition or combination of labour and quasi-labour parties; 0.5 = labour party as minor coalition partner; 0.25 = participation by Christian, etc. parties.

Table 6.12. *Indicators of political and economic development, c.1963*

	Agricultural work-force as % of total work-force	GNP p.c. (1960 US$)	Electorate as % of adult population	Leading economic sectors
A	22.8	1,232	96.1	Mixed industrial, major steel sector; state-owned large firms and many small private ones
B	7.2	1,484	95.7	Textiles, steel, coal, capital equipment, finance
DK	17.8	1,650	99.4	Mixed industrial, big tertiary sector, advanced agriculture
SF	35.5	1,503	99.6	Growing industrial sector, forest products
F	20.3	1,669	89.4	Mixed industrial, agriculture
D	13.5	1,781	99.5	Coal and steel, advanced industry, especially capital equipment
IRL	35.3	919	100.0	Agriculture, industry developing
I	28.2	978	101.1	Mixed industrial with major state-owned sector
NL	10.7	1,418	97.1	Mixed industrial, strong tertiary sector
N	19.5	2,078	98.8	Shipping, hydro-electric, mixed industry, forest products
P	n.a. (high)	514	none	Agriculture
E	n.a. (high)	529	none	Agriculture, major industrial development
S	13.8	2,263	96.6	Industrial, especially capital equipment; forest products
CH	11.2	1,841	79.6*	Mixed advanced industries, financial services
UK	3.6	1,686	99.2	Mixed industrial, financial services

Note: Country boundaries as in Table 6.1.
* Adult male population only.

System 'Outcomes', 1963

The establishment of better data by the 1960s makes it possible to begin testing whether different kinds of industrial-relations structure are associated with different kinds of economic outcome in addition to the strike statistics we have been considering until now. First, comparison between the conflict data given in Table 6.13 and the institutional material in Table 6.7 suggests a clear association between all neo-corporatist cases and low conflict— with the one exception of Denmark, where we had already noted growing government intervention to prop up the bipartite system. Collective bargaining and contestative systems (Ireland and the United Kingdom; Italy, Finland, and France) do not seem distinguished from each other, *until we consider working days lost per 1,000 union members*; then the three contestative countries appear with considerably higher conflict levels, suggesting that, unlike in the immediate post-war years, it is union weakness that restrains strike activity and makes it possible for employers to 'afford' contestative strategies rather than accept pluralist collective bargaining, as indeed expected in Chapter 2.

Table 6.14 enables us also to compare data on inflation, unemployment, and the additive measure of these two rates that became known during the 1970s as the 'discomfort index' or 'Okun index' after the American economist, Arthur Okun, who first made extensive use of it. Our analysis is unable to make much sense of the separate inflation and unemployment columns, but in the combined index it is notable that the best performances were achieved by the three countries (Germany, the Netherlands, Switzerland) that combined weak trade unions with neo-corporatism. This reminds us of a central argument in Chapter 1 that the achievement of neo-corporatism might be to offset the negative consequences of unionization for the capitalist economy. If this is so, we should expect measures of economic 'bads' to correlate positively with levels of unionization, but with neo-corporatist systems performing better than other types for a given level of unionization. Figure 6.1 plots scores on the combined index against union power as measured solely by proportion of the dependent labour force organized. This does permit a tentative conclusion in support of this hypothesis, but not in a form that distinguishes neo-corporatist from pluralist systems; rather one distinguishing both from contestative ones.

TABLE 6.13. *Industrial conflict, 1959–1963*

	Strikes per 1,000		Workers involved per 1,000		Days lost per 1,000	
	dependent labour force	trade-union members	dependent labour force	trade-union members	dependent labour force	trade-union members
A	n.a.	n.a.	30.30	45.30	81.56	118.61
B	0.02	0.03	16.49	25.46	150.49	232.25
DK	0.02	0.04	24.53	40.25	305.16	452.16
SF	0.04	0.20	29.33	150.70	296.54	1,523.55
F	0.14	0.71	69.78	360.40	201.72	1,000.15
D	0.00	0.01	5.22	13.26	27.68	70.33
IRL	0.11	0.16	21.76	33.12	293.33	446.47
I	0.24	1.09	201.60	938.32	891.23	4,087.36
NL	0.02	0.05	8.17	20.51	33.41	83.88
N	0.01	0.02	6.59	11.27	137.76	235.56
S	0.01	0.01	0.78	1.12	5.48	7.89
CH	0.00	0.01	0.17	0.46	7.88	21.15
UK	0.12	0.25	69.73	147.23	153.31	323.19

Note: Country boundaries as in Table 6.1.

TABLE 6.14. *Economic performance, 1959–1963*

	Inflation[1]	Unemployment[2]	Discomfort[3]
A	3.36	3.12	6.48
B	1.96	3.78	5.74
DK	4.85	1.64	6.49
SF	3.47	1.52	4.99
F	4.29	1.01	5.30
D	2.62	1.06	3.68
IRL	3.01	4.80	7.81
I	3.67	3.56	7.23
NL	1.80	0.76	2.56
N	3.36	1.18	4.54
S	3.09	1.66	· 4.75
CH	2.59	0.45	3.04
UK	3.02	1.94	4.96

Note: Country boundaries as in Table 6.1.

[1] Annual average inflation rate.
[2] Annual average unemployment rate (NB national definitions).
[3] Sum of inflation and unemployment rates.

In general we must conclude that neo-corporatism, at least as defined in the 'Scandinavian' theories, only weakly accounts for the economic outcomes of industrial-relations systems in the 1960s, though there is some support for the stabilizing impact of institutional development of both pluralist and corporatist kinds, and considerable support for the negative association between neo-corporatism and conflict.

Conclusions, 1963

Summarizing the early 1960s overall, the picture has clarified considerably since the early post-war years. Austria and the three Scandinavian countries now present straightforward examples of rapidly developing and stable GPE systems, associated with powerful and articulated organizations on the sides of both capital and labour and thus occupying quadrant III in Fig. 2.2. This outcome is consistent with the Olsonian thesis in both its forms where Scandinavia is concerned and also with the 'social-

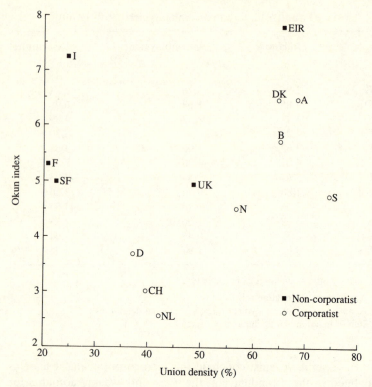

FIG. 6.1. *Economic performance and union strength, 1959–1963*

democratic' thesis, but the Olson theory cannot explain the density of Austrian institutions given the institutional destructions of the Austrian past. Problems continue to be created for Dunlopian theory which can, properly speaking, treat the centralism and politicization found in these societies only in terms of the 'immaturity' of the system or national leadership by either dynastic or revolutionary élites. These should be systems that will 'mature' into collective bargaining. This is hard to reconcile with the growing technical sophistication of these systems, though they are of course all relatively 'new' industrial societies.

A separate group is formed by Germany, Switzerland, and the Netherlands. Here labour's involvement is not so central that one can speak of full GPE in the sense of Chapter 2, but the systems are closer to that pattern than to collective bargaining: unions are *Ordnungsfaktoren*, even *staatstragende Krafte*, albeit of a *junior* kind. The unions in these systems are considerably weaker than in the first group, especially in relation to their well-organized employer counterparts, but they are strongly articulated (especially if one takes account of the exposed-sector variable). This is coherent: an 'Austro-Scandinavian' logic applies, but the weakness of labour leads it to play a concomitantly weaker role in the national system. Particularly with reference to Switzerland, Katzenstein (1984) has spoken of the 'social promotion' of labour; it is accorded by other élites a role in the polity that its numerical strength does not really justify. In exchange for that, labour behaves with exceptional moderation. In terms of the theory set out in Chapter 2, this amounts to a position in quadrant IV of Fig. 2.2, a position of exceptional stability.

Germany surprises the Olsonian theory as does Austria, organizational structures having been rescued so intact following the disruptions of Nazism and war. There is also a major problem for the 'Scandinavian' thesis, which presents growing union power as one of the main motive forces in generating the elaboration of institutions: if unions in these countries are weaker than, say, those in Belgium or the United Kingdom, why have structures of such an elaborate kind been erected? Why, especially perhaps in Switzerland, has labour not simply been marginalized? An association between corporatism and weak unions is of course more compatible with the Dunlop model: these unions simply have not developed a proper collective bargaining strength yet, though Switzerland is hardly a case of 'immaturity'. To resolve this problem fully we must await the final chapters of this book.

Belgium and the United Kingdom were ambiguous cases in the early 1950s; they subsequently moved in different directions and have become more comprehensible. Belgium, with powerful unions but a rather patchy pattern of articulation within both capital and labour, was by the early 1960s being tugged firmly into a distinct neo-corporatism by government policy.

In Britain the opposite happened. While government action had during the 1940s played a similar role with similarly patchy institutions, there was considerable relaxation by government during the 1950s; the centre of gravity of both the industrial-relations institutions and the organization of the two sides of industry shifted downwards. In fact, by the early 1960s government was beginning to nudge gently in a neo-corporatist direction again, but in general the country can be classified as a straight collective-bargaining case, with a structure of interest-group organization appropriate to that. As also the oldest industrial society, it well suits the Dunlop thesis if collective bargaining can be seen to be the most 'mature' system. With a relatively powerfully organized union movement and advanced levels of pluralist institutions, one would place Britain at this stage at the centre of Fig. 2.2: moderate union power, moderate institutionalization and articulation, moderate conflict. Ireland can also be classified as a collective bargaining case, with rather less stability.

As well as in Belgium, Ireland, the Netherlands, and the United Kingdom, governments were becoming interested in 'improving' industrial relations in Finland, France, and Italy; in these cases in an attempt to move from contestation to pluralism. However, the character of the industrial-relations systems is best analysed under the former category. In some respects this corresponds with what we should expect from the structure of the organizations, though there are some differences between the countries.

Finnish governments were trying to move in a Scandinavian direction; Finnish employers were organizing in the way that Scandinavians had been in the early years of the century. In France and Italy the key union characteristic was centralization *without articulation*. This is very consistent with the Dunlop model of an 'immature' industrial-relations system and reinforces the importance of distinguishing between centralization and articulation, a distinction that does not appear in the straight centralization/decentralization contrast of both Dunlopian and most neocorporatist theory. French and Italian unions are also weak, consistent with most theoretical expectation of a contestation model. They are therefore located in quadrant I of Fig. 2.2, but capable from time to time of galvanizing enough power to cause disruption of the kind associated with quadrant II; hence the concern of governments in those countries to seek new forms of stability.

7

Disorganized Capitalism?

The enterprise of the nation appeared to have been lost . . .
The ability of the economy to change and adapt was ham-
pered by the combination of corporatism and powerful
unions. Corporatism limited competition and the birth of
new firms whilst, at the same time, encouraging protectionism and restrictions designed to help existing firms.
Trade unions opposed changes in working practices and fed
the inflationary expectations of their members.

(UK Department of Trade and Industry, 1988: 1)

Freie Gewerkschaften sind Säulen der sozialen Markt-
wirtschaft und eine wichtige Voraussetzung für die Stabilität
unserer Demokratie.

(Helmut Kohl, Christian-Democratic Chancellor of
Germany, on the occasion of the centenary of IG Metall,
5 June 1991, quoted in *Frankfurter Rundschau*, 6 June
1991.)

With the exception of the two Alpine nations, all our countries
saw a resurgence of industrial conflict and institutional instability
sometime between 1968 and 1970; after 1973 the first 'oil shock'
produced a wave of inflation and decline in purchasing power
throughout Western countries that wreaked havoc with expectations and institutions. Virtually everywhere the response of
governments to this crisis, at least until the late 1970s, was to
appeal to central organizations of capital and labour to help
restore stability. There was something of the atmosphere of the
appeals to national identity that we have noted at the time of
World Wars. In some cases these appeals were abrupt, new
interventions—attempts at political exchange in the simple sense.
In others they were rooted in existing generalized political-
exchange models.

However, a further new phenomenon which has to be taken
into account was a shift in the locus of workers' collective action:
disaggregated, localized shop-floor strength of a tenacious kind,

differing considerably from either the conservative defensiveness of traditional skilled craft-workers or the transient eruptions of anger and unsettled grievance that every system had known from the early days of industrial relations. The new form of action was a product of unprecedented full employment, and it began appropriately enough in the United Kingdom, a society that had experienced both sustained full employment and a labour movement already less centralized than most.

THE MID-1970s

Institutional Development, 1975

Taking a new 'snapshot' in 1975 enables us to consider countries in the midst of this process. Table 7.1, on institutional development, reveals a remarkable thickening of the texture of relationships during that short period. In some cases this can be seen as an intensification of the dynamic of an already developing neo-corporatist GPE system. In others there is a new attempt down that road, deliberately in order to try to contain the conflicts of the period. The first group, as before, comprises Austria, Sweden, Norway, and Denmark. As argued in the analysis of Marin (1990*a*) discussed in Chapter 3, once a GPE system is in place the participants in it develop its dynamic, multiplying their interactions, inventing new mechanisms, and also making their relationship increasingly technical. This had been happening in each of these countries since the early 1960s. The Norwegians and Swedes developed the Aukrust (1977) and EFO (Edgren *et al.*, 1973) models of the importance of securing a balance between the exposed and protected sectors of the economy, and used them as benchmarks for bargaining (Flanagan, Soskice, and Ulman, 1983). The Danes adopted a similar practice. Sweden also developed further the role of unions in managing labour-market policy at all levels from nation to local district. But also, in Denmark particularly and increasingly in Sweden, there were several occasions of anxious government intervention to stabilize the price–wage spiral, suggesting strongly that the neo-corporatist system was under strain.

The Austrians further elaborated the mechanisms of the

Table 7.1. *Institutional development of industrial relations, c.1975*

Main pattern of industrial relations	Country	Level: Plant	Branch	Nation	State
Extensive neo-corporatism	A	*Betriebsräte* with some administrative powers	Further elaboration of work of PK		
	DK	Extensive bargaining; new legal co-determination rights	Extensive autonomy of bargaining	Increasing use of technical criteria and agreed models in central bargaining	Growing state intervention and incomes policy; participation of social partners grows further
	N	New legal co-determination rights	Growing autonomy of bargaining	Aukrust Committee sets technical rules for export-sensitive bargaining	Limited state intervention and incomes policy; participation of social partners grows further
	S	Growing bargaining; new legal co-determination rights	Growing autonomy of bargaining	EFO Committee sets technical rules for export-sensitive bargaining	Limited state intervention and incomes policy; participation of social partners grows further
Neo-corporatism	D	*Betriebsrat,* 1972, and worker-	Extensive and stable	*Konzertierte Aktion* system since 1967; increased use of informal government guidelines to steer bipartite	

TABLE 7.1. *Continued*

Main pattern of industrial relations	Country	Level				
		Plant	Branch	Nation	State
		director, 1976, system extended			negotiations; growing involvement of social partners in economic policy
	NL	Works council system extended on German lines, 1976	Growing autonomy of bargaining	Collapse of old incomes policy system, but tripartite co-operation maintained, and growing involvement of social partners in economic policy	
	B	Growth of bargaining autonomy	*Commissions paritaires* continue		Increased state regulation of tripartite agreements; growing involvement of social partners in economic policy
	CH	Stable	Stable	Stable	Stable

UK	Government-led attempts at neo-corporatism on bargaining and contestation base	Further major growth and autonomy of bargaining	Declining	Government encourages national bipartite agreements, but also recourse to statutory intervention; growing involvement of social partners in economic policy
SF		Further major growth and autonomy of bargaining	Extensive bargaining	Statutory incomes policy, encouragement of bipartite national agreements, and major new involvement of social partners in economic policy
IRL		Further growth and autonomy of bargaining	Extensive bargaining	Bipartite attempts to secure centralized national pay deals
I		Massive growth and autonomy of bargaining; major extension of worker and union rights at this level, 1970	Extensive bargaining	Some attempts to achieve limited consensus
				Attempts to promote consensus

TABLE 7.1. *Continued*

Main pattern of industrial relations	Country	Level				
		Plant	Branch	Nation	State
Contestation and collective bargaining	F	Minor growth in bargaining; extension of statutory rights to recognition of *sections syndicales*, 1968	Growth of bargaining	Legal recognition of bargaining at this level	Sporadic and limited tripartite talks
From authoritarian corporatism to contestation	P	Growing demands from workers	Rudimentary bargaining		Revolutionary government seeks to define union role
	E	Growing demands from workers	Rudimentary bargaining		Collapse of dictatorship; no new policy yet in place

Note: Country boundaries as in Table 6.1.

Paritätische Kommission on the lines described by Marin (1982) to produce a tightly woven mesh of negotiations over pay and prices, but extending outwards to incorporate the leaders of functional interest organizations in nearly every aspect of government policy. Austria is, of course, the case at the centre of Marin's (1990*a*) concept of generalized political exchange.

There were also major legislative initiatives in these years for strengthening the role of union representatives at shop-floor level over such matters as health and safety and changes in work organization, especially in the Scandinavian countries, further extending the role of organized interests in the governance of the employment system. A debate began in Denmark and Sweden over the possible introduction of 'wage-earner funds' to provide a means by which workers might share collectively in company profits, these being considered by union policy-makers to be swollen as a result of unions' neo-corporatist co-operation. This would mark a further extension of the process of deepening and widening the role of organizations; however, no changes of substance here had occurred by 1975.

As before, similar but still somewhat less ambitious institutions for national participation by union leaderships existed in Belgium, the Netherlands, and increasingly in Germany; also in Switzerland though with a characteristic emphasis on branch-level action. There is considerable variety of movement among this group, with most new development of a neo-corporatist system taking place in Germany, the least in Switzerland, and with the Dutch needing to rely on more purely organizational arrangements as the *verzuiling* structure that had previously been at the heart of the system began to collapse under the rapid secularization of Dutch society.

Germany showed some signs of converging on the more national (as opposed to branch) pattern of the other neo-corporatist countries with the introduction of the multipartite forum of *konzertierte Aktion* in 1967, though most German observers regard this institution as secondary in importance to the continuing co-operative structures of German neo-corporatist bargaining (Hardes, 1974; Streeck, 1979). Germany and the Netherlands followed Scandinavia with major initiatives in workers' and unions' shop-floor rights and discussions (though no more than that) of wage-earner funds. In German legislation of

1972 the powers of works councils were considerably extended and unions given an explicit role in advising them; in 1976 there was some strengthening of worker directors in the largest companies. Also in 1976 the Dutch replaced their existing consultative, bipartite works councils with powerful unilateral ones of the German kind (Teulings, 1985).

In all these countries except Switzerland, and especially in Belgium, there were, as in Denmark and Sweden, signs of strain in the system as governments resorted to *ad hoc* interventions and occasional statutory controls. But there was no threat to the legitimacy and operation of the neo-corporatist arrangements.

Finland, Britain, Ireland, and increasingly Italy, form a further group of countries whose institutions were clearly venturing down the neo-corporatist road—in the case of Britain this marked a return to the abortive moves of the 1940s. In each instance we find steps towards greatly increased national involvement by central union leaderships, most intensively in Finland but prominent in all these cases. The institutions did not yet have the intricate complexity of constantly growing scope for exchanges typical of GPE as such, so we should speak (as we did of Scandinavia in the 1930s and Austria in the 1950s) of incipient GPE. These countries also resemble many of those already discussed in experiencing frequent government intervention to encourage and support neo-corporatist arrangements, though these should of course be seen as signs of the *weakness*, not the viability, of neo-corporatism.

Finnish governments, faced with a high level of industrial conflict, had been trying for several years to initiate a national policy of this kind, but had been held back by divisions in the labour movement that made union co-operation impossible to achieve. Soon after these divisions were at least formally healed, in 1968, the government launched its incomes-policy initiatives. While these were designed to induce co-operation and were, as the 1970s developed, accompanied by the familiar multiplication of mechanisms for tripartite co-operation, there was much recourse to statutory intervention (Helander, 1982; 1984). Finland was clearly trying to learn from its Nordic neighbours, but was doing so in the difficult years of the 1970s when the Scandinavian systems themselves were showing signs of stress.

Britain had been engaged in a similar but weaker and considerably less ambitious pattern since the early 1960s, with several initiatives for tripartite co-operation being reinforced, and then hopelessly compromised, by statutory intervention. The culmination was the 'social contract' of the mid-1970s, which was eventually broken in 1979 by an upsurge of shop-floor discontent. It involved the now familiar mix: increased restraint traded for influence and participation at various levels (Crouch, 1977). Irish governments engaged in similar initiatives, achieving for much of the decade an informal, primarily bipartite (union and employer) co-operation of a clear neo-corporatist kind. It managed without much government intervention, but its scope was relatively narrow (Hardiman, 1988; McCarthy, 1977).

Italy's experience was not dissimilar, opportunities for overcoming the historic alienation of the labour movement being pursued by a variety of political, union, and industrial forces (Regalia *et al.*, 1978; Regini, 1982). But the degree of institutional development for such integration remained weaker. As Marin has pointed out (1990), Pizzorno's (1978) concept of political exchange, rather than GPE, remains more suitable for describing the large, once-and-for-all deals that unions, governments, and employers in that author's country attempted to form rather than the dense web of deals and shared administration typical of Marin's Austria and the other cases of an established neo-corporatism.

However, preliminary and hesitant though these moves were in Italy during the mid-1970s, that country should no longer be grouped with France, where far less activity of this kind took place outside moments of crisis. One such moment was, of course, the upheavals of May 1968 which, even though they soon produced a conservative political climate, also included a short-lived instance of Pizzornian political exchange (Dubois *et al.*, 1978). As in 1936, unions, government, and employers met to resolve the immediate massive crisis—before returning to their separate camps and beginning to disentangle themselves from each other's embrace. But *les événements* did lead to the introduction of considerable legislation strengthening the role of unions' and workers' rights at company level. This was, similarly to the public-sector initiatives in the early 1960s, almost explicitly an attempt to strengthen pluralism and collective bargaining and move France out of the contestative mode of its industrial relations.

Within a year or so of 1975, Portugal and Spain emerged from dictatorship. Unions and political parties immediately leapt out of their former clandestine existence. Initially this meant a burst of pure contestation as hardly any institutions for conflict regulation existed. There were soon attempts at constructing such. In Spain these initially took the form of measures to construct a collective-bargaining system. In Portugal, under Marxist revolutionary military leadership, there was a more explicit attempt at erecting neo-corporatist institutions, though concentrated at national level with little ramification at the base.

Articulation of Labour Movements, 1975

The articulation of union organizations (Table 7.2) acquires a new complexity at this time, particularly among the strongly neo-corporatist countries, for a reason having far more than methodological importance. The manual labour confederations of Scandinavia were losing their hegemonic role following the rise of independent white-collar groupings. Even where, as very temporarily in Sweden in 1975, these co-operated with the manual union movement, their confederations were themselves only weakly centralized, and therefore the overall impact of the rise of white-collar unions was to fragment the labour movement. Further, the dominance of LO by exposed-sector unions was beginning to decline even in Norway and Sweden, though the strength of these unions within the country as a whole continued to grow as a result of strong overall union growth (Table 7.3).

Although the same decline of the exposed sector was taking place in Austria, general articulation remains virtually unscathed because there was only one confederation. The Norwegian LO temporarily retained its monopoly status as a confederation and a bigger share of organized labour than its Swedish counterpart, though autonomous unions were growing fast. Both countries' movements remained for the present highly articulated, with a central administrative capacity joined to local union work and participation in the structures considered in Table 7.1. The Austrian, Norwegian, and Swedish unions are the only ones to

retain both high centralization and a virtual monopoly of confederal labour representation.

Belgium and the Netherlands form a separate group as articulated but not at all monopolistic. Belgium is more centralized
and better articulated than earlier, partly because there was now
extensive *de facto* co-operation between the CSC and the FGTB,
and partly because the more centralized Catholic CSC had now
clearly overtaken the social democratic FGTB as the majority
confederation. As mentioned, the state-supported Dutch corporatist structure had begun to collapse in the late 1960s as
secularization eroded the relevance of the *verzuiling* system in
which it was rooted. Co-operation among confederations could
no longer be assumed, but a high level of articulation remained
within confederations and the NVV and NKV were close to
merging. The decline of the exposed sector was disguised in
Belgium by the predominance of such unions within the CSC and
of public-service unions within the FGTB. Dutch unions followed
the same exposed-sector decline as most other countries.

The two 'branch-level-co-ordinated' cases, Germany and
Switzerland, remained stable though with some loss of monopoly, especially in Switzerland. But perhaps most striking is the
retention of positions of particular strength by the leading
exposed-sector metal-working union in these countries. It
becomes increasingly difficult to decide whether Germany should
rank above Belgium and the Netherlands for overall central co-
ordinating capacity.

A fourth group comprises those with reasonable monopolies
but only moderate levels of centralization: Finland, Ireland, the
United Kingdom, and Denmark. There had been far-reaching
changes in Finland, with the ending of interconfederal rivalry,
though conflicts between communists and social democrats within
the unions still cause it to be ranked below the countries discussed so far. Ireland and the United Kingdom, which had after
all the two most impressively monopolistic confederations after
the ÖGB, were engaged in major efforts at co-ordination with
employer and government groups on matters of policy; but their
structures remained essentially decentral. Denmark seemed to be
leaving the scope of the 'Scandinavian model' of unionism,
internal decentralization combining with loss of monopoly consequent on the rise of professional and white-collar unions and

TABLE 7.2. *Articulation of trade-union movements, c.1975*

	Unions affiliated to main confederation				Individual unions	
	Membership as % of		No.	Powers of confederation re affiliates	Dominant types of union	Characteristic internal authority structure over local groups, individual members, etc.	Characteristic shop-floor organization
	known unions	labour force					
A	100.00	51.24	16	ÖGB monopolizes strike funds and calls and all collective bargaining	Strict branch	Centralized	Strong shop-floor role in *Betriebsräte*
N	74.71	44.80	35	LO monopolizes strike funds and calls and bargaining but growth of autonomous white-collar unions	Branch type dominates and sometimes challenges LO role	Centralized	Union stewards integrated into formal structures but becoming restless
S	63.13	77.70	25	LO monopolizes strike funds and bargaining; separate non-manual confederation growing in strength but co-operating in EFO system	Branch type dominates and sometimes challenges LO role	Centralized	Union stewards integrated into formal structures but becoming restless

B	51.06	31.31	19	CSC has some control over strike funds and calls and sometimes co-ordinates bargaining in conjunction with FGTB	Branch	Centralized	Weak
NL	74.71	22.10	16	NVV and NKV in process of amalgamating to form FNV; CNV remains autonomous	Branch	Centralized	Weak but gaining role in new works councils
D	82.24	24.13	17	DGB seeks co-operation from leaderships of branch unions; small non-manual and *Beamte* confederations	Strict branch	Centralized	Weak, but role in *Betriebsräte* legally recognized, 1976
CH	50.63	16.84	15	SGB seeks co-operation from leaderships of branch unions; Christian confederations	Strict branch	Centralized	Strong but within framework of union discipline
DK	71.55	43.80	44	LO has lost control of strike funds and calls but continues to try to co-ordinate bargaining; conflict among LO unions and with white-collar confederation	Craft and general	Centralized, but with strong decentral trends	*Tillidsmænd* increasingly restless

TABLE 7.2. *Continued*

	Unions affiliated to main confederation					Individual unions	
	Membership as % of		No.	Powers of confederation re affiliates	Dominant types of union	Characteristic internal authority structure over local groups, individual members, etc.	Characteristic shop-floor organization
	known unions	labour force					
SF	64.32	43.46	28	SAK regains monopoly and tries to co-ordinate bargaining, but has only weak strike controls	Branch	Varied; continuing tension with communist groups	Varied; highly autonomous in several sectors
IRL	97.54	34.85	89	ITUC tries to co-ordinate bargaining, but has only weak strike controls	Craft and general	Varied	Varied; highly autonomous shop stewards' movements in several sectors
UK	91.80	44.14	109	TUC tries to co-ordinate bargaining in co-operation with government incomes policy, but has only	Craft and general; some branch	Varied	Varied; highly autonomous shop stewards' movements in rapidly

				weak powers			growing number of sectors
I	50.72	16.69	38	CGIL has few powers but tries to co-ordinate action; moves towards *de facto* unity with 'rival' confederations	See note* but branch basis predominant	Centralized	Growing autonomy and militancy on extensive scale
F	44.00	7.84	42	CGT has few powers; rival confederations	See note*	Centralized	Usually weak but capable of autonomous action
P	n.a.	n.a.	n.a.	CGTP-IN established; favoured by new regime but has few powers beyond mobilization	Varied	Highly decentral	Weak
E	n.a.	n.a.	n.a.	Rival organizations emerging	Varied	Highly decentral	Weak, but with bases in structures of old regime

Note: Country boundaries as in Table 6.1.

* Signifies a complex pattern of local cells of the confederations alongside individual economic-branch unions.

TABLE 7.3. *Membership of exposed-sector trade unions, c.1975*

	Exposed-sector industry-type union members in main confederation as % of total union members	Exposed-sector industry-type union members as % of	
		main confederation members	total labour force
A	33.14	33.14	16.72
B	22.16	44.67	11.89
DK	14.36	19.54	7.21
SF	24.18	35.08	10.81
F	10.93	24.77	2.22
D	46.71	57.29	14.34
IRL	7.56	8.04	2.43
I	10.54	20.80	2.93
NL	21.85	27.68	7.24
N	26.47	34.81	13.29
S	27.95	34.93	15.00
CH	23.45	42.77	5.94
UK	16.72	18.70	7.39

Note: Country boundaries as in Table 6.1.

the decline of the exposed sector. Of these countries only Finland had an orthodox branch-type union structure, and one which followed the Norwegian and Swedish pattern of the period of exposed-sector unions growing in importance within the economy but declining relatively within union confederations.

Despite the new divergence between their national institutions, the Italian and French union movements remained structurally similar to each other. A few years later the Italian unions were to attempt, abortively, an alliance similar to that achieved by the different parts of the Dutch movement in the post-war years. The emerging new Iberian union movements were, not surprisingly, rather inchoate at this period.

Employer Organization, 1975

Two changes since the early 1960s concerned employers' organizations (Table 7.4). On the one hand even the countries that were weakly developed in 1950 had now experienced some organizational strengthening. On the other hand, however, employers' organizations had been affected by two developments also relevant to unions: the growth of the tertiary sector and of public employment. The former had been a major question for the Scandinavian employers, whose tight organizational unity had previously been possible partly because, like their partner LOs, they were concentrated in manufacturing and mining. The scope of their organizations now occupied a much smaller part of the economy than in 1950 or even in 1963. This was less of an issue for the looser organizations of, say, Britain, France, and Germany, where tertiary firms had long been members of central confederations. The rise of public employment was a problem for all employers' organizations except the Austrian *Kammer* system.

Within these general developments the strengthened position of Finnish employers calls for special note. The salience for the Finnish economy of the major government-negotiated trade relationship with the Soviet Union had rendered Finnish industrial employers dependent on organization and dialogue with the state. This had then become relevant to organization for the labour market, with the Swedish example readily available. The other countries in which neo-corporatist experiments were taking place (Ireland, Italy, and the United Kingdom) had also seen some measures for increased co-ordination among employers, though not to the same extent.

Power of Organized Labour, 1975

The measurement of union power (Table 7.5) is fairly straightforward in this period, membership and political strength being fairly well correlated. Denmark and *a fortiori* Belgium might be ranked below the United Kingdom, as unemployment was higher and in Belgium labour influence on government less secure. Germany is placed above Ireland because of labour's greater political strength in the former country. Italy might be ranked below Switzerland on the grounds of the greater political integration of the main wing of the labour movement in the latter. Overall, Scandinavia, Austria, Belgium, and the United Kingdom continue, as in the 1960s, to have the strongest trade-union movements. However, the most dramatic change is the extra-

Table 7.4. *Organizations of capital, c.1975*

	Scope[1]	Power[2]	Other associative business activity[3]
A, DK, D, N, S, CH		Continuing development of tendencies visible in 1963; but Scandinavian organizations weakened by decline in manufacturing sector in which their co-ordinating power is rooted	
NL	Comprehensive throughout industrial sector and some tertiary sectors	Merger of former denominational associations	Close involvement in economic policy
SF	Extensive	STK committed to seeking detailed national agreements with SAK, and acquires power within industry necessary to do this	Trade associations central to operation of Finno-Soviet trade agreement
B	Extensive	FIB merges with tertiary sector organizations to form FEB	FEB co-ordinates action
IRL	Growing	New IFC, 1969, tries to co-ordinate bargaining strategy of employers and secures informal authority	Increasing involvement in economic policy
UK	Extensive	Merger of BEC and FBI to form CBI, 1965; new body seeks informal co-ordination of	Active but not strongly incorporated into government policy

I	Extensive	employers and co-operation with government incomes policy	Associations important in northern industry
F	Limited	Confindustria reforms internal structure to equip it for a co-ordinating role	Growing involvement of organizations in state planning, but main activity rests with individual firms
		CNPF ready to play more active role, but little scope	
E	Rapid early growth	CEOE establishing co-ordinating role	Too early to determine
P	No clear structure of organizations yet emerging following collapse of fascist regime		

Note: Country boundaries as in Table 6.1.

[1] Extent of organization of employer interests.

[2] Resources available to employer organizations to co-ordinate action.

[3] Activity directed at trade rather than labour issues.

TABLE 7.5. Power of organized labour, c.1975

	Known union membership as % of		Major industrial-relations and political developments affecting organized labour within industry	Unemployment[1]	Share of popular vote[2] %	Participation in gov't[3] %	Other major political developments affecting wider position of organized labour
	labour force	dependent labour force					
S	77.70	84.81	New co-determination, safety, etc. laws	L	48.9	1.00	
SF	67.57	85.64		VL	43.8	0.50	
N	59.96	72.00	New co-determination, safety, etc. laws	VL	35.3	0.75	
A	51.24	65.01		VL	50.4 (42.9)	1.00	
DK	61.21	75.49		VL	34.1	0.75	
B	61.32	75.24		L	26.7 (32.3)	0.25	
UK	48.08	56.37	Major political conflict over attempts at industrial-relations law reform (since 1968); new laws favourable to union powers, 1974–6	L	39.3	1.00	
D	29.34	34.91	Extensions to works council, 1972, and co-determination, 1976, laws favourable to unions	L	45.8 (44.9)	0.75	

				[1]	[2]	[3]	Political left gains from collapse of dictatorships
IRL	35.73	54.30		M	13.7 (46.2)	0.50	
NL	32.34	37.97	New works council law on German pattern, 1976	L	31.8 (31.3)	0.75	
I	32.91	47.04	Statuto dei Lavoratori, 1970, greatly extends union and worker rights	M	27.2 (53.5)	0.25	
CH	29.17	36.36		VL	24.9 (21.1)	0.75	
F	17.83	22.80	New union and worker legal rights following May 1968 upheavals	L	21.3 (18.9)		
P, E	n.a.	n.a.	Reappearance of free trade unions after collapse of dictatorships	?	too early for elections		

Note: Country boundaries as in Table 6.1.

[1] H = registered unemployment in excess of 10% of dependent labour force; M = around 10%; L = 2.5–5%; VL = less than 2.5%; ? = reliable figures not available on a broadly comparable basis.

[2] In most recent general election secured by labour-movement parties; votes for parties with labour wing but primarily committed to other interests in parentheses. Figures for Denmark, Finland, Netherlands, Sweden combine social-democratic with communist etc. parties in labour-movement party total. French socialists count as a party not primarily of the labour movement.

[3] 1.0 = straight labour party government; 0.75 = main labour-movement party dominating coalition or combination of labour and quasi-labour parties; 0.5 = labour party as junior coalition partner; 0.25 = government participation by Christian or other quasi-labour parties.

ordinary growth in Finnish union strength, in the wake of that country's recent industrialization. It now becomes possible to generalize about Nordic rather than Scandinavian union strength, and it is notable that the change in Finnish institutional development from poorly scattered collective bargaining to incipient GPE is associated with this development in union power.

There had been a relative stagnation of union strength in Switzerland and to an extent in Austria. French unions, despite the age and tradition of their movement, now rank above only the newly liberated and as yet unquantifiable unions of the Iberian peninsula, being the only other labour movement bereft of all government representation as well as the weakest in membership.

Assessing Outcomes, 1975

Table 7.6 displays industrial conflict data for the years preceding our snapshot. While it is difficult to account for the very high amount of strike activity in Italy, there does otherwise seem to be a rough association between membership and conflict levels among the countries without settled neo-corporatist arrangements. Strike activity is relatively low among most of the neo-corporatists, especially when conflict is measured in terms of union membership, which, it was established in Chapter 1, is the preferred approach of this study following the logic of Olson's (1982) and Calmfors and Driffill's (1988) arguments. Denmark is something of an exception, but we have already noted a growing dissociation in that country between the development of GPE as an institution and a decreasing capacity of the social partners to provide the kind of organizational infrastructure it required. Low overall conflict levels are notable in France, but again this is readily explained in terms of low union membership.

Table 7.7 confirms a similar pattern for inflation, unemployment, and the combined Okun discomfort index. With the expected exception of France, we find the best performances among the established neo-corporatist systems. Figure 7.1 shows, as did Fig. 6.1, the continuing capacity of the neo-corporatist systems to contain the hypothetically disruptive effects of high union membership; though this time there is little relationship between union strength and 'discomfort'. The poorest levels of

TABLE 7.6. *Industrial conflict, 1971–1975*

	Strikes per 1,000		Workers involved per 1,000		Days lost per 1,000	
	dependent labour force	trade-union members	dependent labour force	trade-union members	dependent labour force	trade-union members
A	n.a.	n.a.	8.10	12.46	10.72	16.48
B	0.07	0.09	27.25	36.22	250.92	333.49
DK	0.06	0.08	57.93	76.76	451.43	598.16
SF	0.73	0.85	230.81	269.51	774.61	904.48
F	0.25	1.03	151.11	622.62	251.66	1,036.92
D	n.a.	n.a.	10.13	26.14	61.29	158.17
IRL	0.25*	0.46*	54.38	100.15	416.55	767.13
I	0.33	0.71	475.83	1,024.83	1,405.98	3,028.17
NL	0.00	0.01	5.71	14.75	40.31	104.13
N	0.01	0.01	5.18	6.99	59.76	80.68
S	0.04	0.04	11.39	12.12	99.64	106.03
CH	0.00	0.01	0.36	1.05	1.17	3.42
UK	0.13	0.23	68.91	122.25	661.27	1,173.09

Note: Country boundaries as in Table 6.1.
*Figure for 1972–5 only.

TABLE 7.7. *Economic performance, 1971–1975*

	Inflation[1]	Unemployment[2]	Discomfort[3]
A	8.1	1.7	9.8
B	10.9	3.9	14.8
DK	9.9	3.0	12.9
SF	14.4	2.2	16.6
F	10.2	3.4	13.6
D	6.7	2.3	9.0
IRL	15.9	7.0	22.9
I	13.9	5.8	19.7
NL	9.8	3.5	13.3
N	8.6	1.8	10.4
S	8.5	2.3	10.8
CH	8.3	0.1	8.4
UK	16.8	3.9	20.7

Note: Country boundaries as in Table 6.1.

[1] Annual average inflation rate.

[2] Annual average unemployment rate (NB national definitions).

[3] Sum of inflation and unemployment rates.

economic performance are consistently recorded by the countries without settled, established routines of GPE but trying desperately to build them at the level of policy, but not in terms of infrastructural support: Ireland, Italy, the United Kingdom, and (but with a good unemployment performance) Finland. Denmark is less deviant here, being able, like Finland, to maintain a good unemployment record.

In terms of Fig. 2.2, Austria, Belgium, Norway, and Sweden seem now clearly to occupy the high articulation/strong labour quadrant III associated with stable neo-corporatism and enviable economic and social outcomes, with a doubt over Belgium's performance. Germany and the Netherlands might also occupy that quadrant, but their *relative* union weakness perhaps steers them, with Switzerland, towards quadrant IV. Denmark's declining articulation is moving that country dangerously towards the unstable quadrant II, which is now clearly occupied by Finland, Ireland, Italy, and the United Kingdom, with France alone—

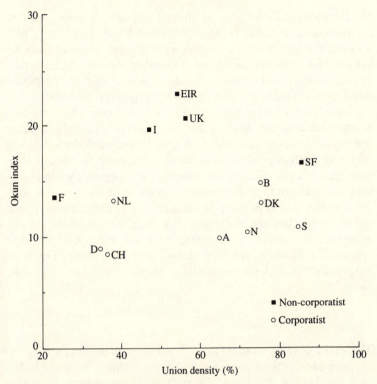

Fig. 7.1. *Economic performance and union strength, 1971–1975*

though perhaps also Portugal and Spain—in quadrant I (with occasional lurches, as in 1968, into II).

It is easy to see why it was the 1970s that brought neo-corporatist cases to the attention of academic observers, as it is then that they were clearly associated with more successful economic and industrial-relations outcomes than in the pluralist cases, in particular with an ability to optimize those successes alongside the maintenance of strong trade unions. It is also there-fore comprehensible that several countries tried to imitate the dynamics of these systems, though as we have seen none did so successfully. The demands of articulation and the role of the exposed sector were generally not perceived by policy-makers. As the examples of Denmark and Finland respectively show, neither a past record that was being undermined by current reality nor a current attempt building on a rickety base were enough to achieve the subtle balancing act of neo-corporatism. Against this, France—setting 1968 aside—stands as a reminder of the possibility of finding success with very weak organized interests.

One also has intimations of the strain being borne by the Scandinavian model. Manual workers' unions, especially those in the exposed sector, had, since the late 1930s, carried the burden of being *Ordnungsfaktoren* in these economies, a burden that they never really planned on assuming so thoroughly; and now they were losing their hegemony as both the tertiary sector and white-collar workers rose in numbers. In Scandinavia these groups were heavily unionized but their organizations rarely accepted any wider socio-political burden than straight representation of their members in collective bargaining. For how long could the LO unions continue to play their historical role alone?

Conclusions, 1975

The main novelty of the 1963–75 period was the emergence of an incipient GPE in the four countries Finland, Ireland, Italy, and the United Kingdom. In each case the pattern followed was one familiar to us from consideration of the Scandinavian cases earlier and consistent with what I have called the 'social-democratic thesis': heightened union industrial and political power, major difficulty in transcending episodes of high conflict, leading to either bipartite or tripartite attempts at forging an agreement on wage development achieved by binding employers' organizations and unions into an intense net of exchanges. However, in each case there were major defects in the articulation of trade-unionism, and in all but one (Finland) employers too were not powerfully co-ordinated.

In Britain, Ireland, and Italy highly autonomous shop-floor movements maintained and indeed strengthened a form of bargaining that led to increased tension between the shop-floor and a union leadership increasingly being dragged in the opposite direction. In Finland the issue was more explicitly political: a wing of the communist shop-steward movement was co-ordinating opposition to a policy that was otherwise being conducted in classic Nordic fashion.

In Britain and Ireland shop-floor autonomy had long been a feature of the union movement. An attempt to tackle it in Britain following the Donovan Report (1968) had been so tied to a classic collective bargaining model that it had not considered means of extending articulation from the shop-floor to a leadership oriented to national economic policy. Developments in that direction in the later 1970s were a case of 'too little too late' to effect major change. The shop-floor movement in Italy was far younger, having developed slowly since the early 1960s before emerging with force and vigour from 1969. As with Denmark, Norway, and Sweden in the 1930s, incipient GPE followed greatly intensified industrial conflict rather than the reverse. Clearly, the expectations of pluralist theory concerning centrally co-ordinated labour movements are not entirely flawed.

While our historical review has suggested something of a drift towards GPE attempts, these last points serve as a reminder of the strict requirements of a fully working GPE model. Union strength, an assertion of union confederal power, a strong employers' organization, and links with friendly governments are not enough. There must be some form of articulation reaching down to labour's roots. Denmark in the 1970s shows how articulation can 'fail'. From the 1930s onwards the refusal of Danish unions to merge into a branch structure had distinguished them from their Scandinavian neighbours as well as from the Germanic movements. It was, as in Britain and Ireland, a mark of dominance by particularist interests, an absence of co-ordination and of commitment to branch- and economy-wide goals. By the mid-1970s it was associated with a return to high conflict and poor economic outcomes.

THE MOST RECENT YEARS

The heady inflation of the 1970s was in many countries associated with the rising power of the labour movement. But, not unlike the precarious power of the Austrian and German movements of the 1920s, though immeasurably less disastrously, it held its perils for those who benefited from it. If one's power is associated with phenomena generally regarded negatively, one should beware. This was of course mainly true in those countries where the move to a GPE model with a powerful labour contribution was not matched by the articulated organizational structures implied by the theory of GPE. In the stable cases, on the other hand, this was, alongside the late 1930s in some countries, neo-corporatism's 'finest hour', as the evidence at the end of the previous section indicates.

In general the inflation of the 1970s ended in recession, and in many countries the political response to the period was a sharp shift to the right. Domestic politics apart, international monetary agencies and powerful international investors looked to deflationary policies to remove the heat from the labour market. In many instances Keynesian demand management, the fundamental prop to workers' power since the 1940s, was abandoned. Even where forces favourable to the labour movement retained political power, they and their policies were affected by these developments; where parties of the right governed, they amplified them. Labour had shown its potency in the decade or so following 1968, leading many conservatives to question the wisdom of their post-war assumptions of seeking to pacify unions by incorporating them. The recession of the early 1980s now led them to question whether such propitiatory policies were even necessary. So much was general; the particular configuration of power relations varied from country to country.

Institutional Development, 1990

Table 7.8 summarizes the state of institutional development at the end of the 1980s. There has been considerable change and diversification. There is however a major, *general* tendency among all our countries for the centre of gravity to shift towards the level of the firm. In some cases (especially in Scandinavia) this was a change of some novelty. Its character varies somewhat. In Britain it took the form of a *collapse* of branch-level agreements; in Scandinavia it was more a matter of employers' associations *deciding* that they wanted a decentralization. This becomes clear when one notes years when the associations pulled back to a central national agreement and were able to do so successfully.

In Belgium and the Netherlands, and to some extent also in Scandinavia, there was a certain amount of government intervention in wage determination through statutory incomes policies. These are to be interpreted as failures of neo-corporatism, not of its presence, since they denote a mistrust by government of the capacity of the bargaining parties.

Government policy becomes, methodologically, generally troublesome at this period, as it was often trying to pull a system in a particular direction which might not correspond to the prevailing underlying structure. This has of course been the case at earlier periods in our study (for example with Belgium in the late 1930s); but this was always being done in the context of thin existing institutions, where the government's action was the major factor of substance to be considered. By the 1990s most countries had strong existing institutional legacies which might contradict recent policy attempts. Thus, the fact that the British government was trying to break up, and the Spanish trying to establish, a settled institutional system should not blind us to the fact that the underlying texture of bargaining remained far richer in the former country.

Classification of countries is further made difficult by the fact that several neo-corporatist cases are beginning to unravel in terms of their effectiveness at binding together the various levels. However, the *structures* are often still in place, doing considerable business, and sometimes indeed still expanding their range of tasks. Braun's (1988) description of the situation in the Netherlands, *Konzertierung ohne Konsens,* could stand as a motto for the period. Our groupings therefore become rather loose.

Although Austria is the only case in which a fully articulated GPE was functioning *relatively* effectively—and even here there were tensions—we can still define a group of countries in which, despite looming disintegration, GPE processes constituted the main way in which business in industrial relations and associated fields of activity was conducted. Norway and Sweden still rank alongside Austria, and it is now possible to include Finland here, which is the only one of the 1975 'aspiring neo-corporatists' to have continued with the full elaboration of institutions typical of GPE systems.

Germany and Switzerland were virtually as stable as Austria,

TABLE 7.8. *Institutional development of industrial relations, c.1990*

Main pattern of industrial relations	Country	Level			
		Plant	Branch	Nation	State
Extensive neo-corporatism	A	Stable	Stable		Essentially stable, but some dislocation as a result of privatization of state industries
	SF	Growing autonomous collective bargaining	Extensive and often autonomous bargaining	Tripartite institutions create 'Scandinavian' system	
	N, S	Growing autonomous collective bargaining	Growing autonomy of bargaining	Recurrent crisis of viability of central bargaining system	Recurrent state intervention in incomes policy; other participative institutions intact
Neo-corporatism with strong branch component	D	Further increases in *Betriebsrat* role, through legislation and employer practice; increasing wage determination at this level	Extensive and stable, with some controlled decentralization to company level	Formal concerted action declines, but *de facto* relations stable	Stable

		Growth of bargaining autonomy			
Declining neo-corporatism	B		Some decline, but *commissions paritaires* continue	Resumption of bargaining after statutory pause, 1987	Strict state control of bargaining for most of 1980s; other tripartite institutions continue
	DK	Extensive	Growing autonomy of bargaining but with bipartite attempt at organized stabilization	Fragmentation of bargaining at this level	Growing state intervention and incomes policy; other participative institutions continue, but decline in union involvement
	NL	Increasing shift to this level, but unions weak and not making use of works council system	Growing autonomy of bargaining	Some decline in importance	Some state intervention in income determination; participative institutions continue, but trend towards technocratic rather than representative advisory networks

TABLE 7.8. *Continued*

Main pattern of industrial relations	Country	Level			
		Plant	Branch	Nation	State
Incipient regional neo-corporatism in limited areas; elsewhere bargaining/contestation	I	Continuing autonomous bargaining	In northern and central regions considerable tripartite administration of labour market, through regional government, unions and employers' groups; bargaining also strong. Lack of development of this kind in south	Unstable; ranging from co-operation to conflict	Sporadic attempts to promote consensus
State-led attempts at neo-corporatism; bargaining/contestation	E	Growing, but unions very weak	Some bargaining	Weak, but series of national accords under government encouragement; increasing difficulty in reaching these in	Government tries to encourage tripartite accords and to construct elementary participative network

IRL	Continuing shift to this level	Declining	Collapse of attempts to secure centralized deals, 1981; revival, 1989	Intermittent encouragement of tripartite co-operation
F	Major rise, through both legal requirement and managerial practice, but mainly with non-union institutions	Growth of bargaining	Some growth in general agreements between employer and worker *syndicats*, usually excluding CGT	Government encourages some participation by representative institutions
P	Weak	Slight growth	Limited tripartite pact, 1987	Limited government interest in encouraging pacts and participation
Disaggregating collective bargaining; contestation — UK	Continuing shift to this level	Collapse of institutions in private sector; government seeks collapse in public sector	Collapse of most arrangements	Government rejects nearly all strategies of tripartite co-operation, reduces contact with unions to a minimum and abandons all incomes policy outside public sector

Note: Country boundaries as in Table 6.1.

though in the former country there was a greater decentralization of bargaining to company level than previously associated with the works-council system. These two keep their place as having a special form of neo-corporatism with particular emphasis on the branch level. There was however a distinct relaxation of, or decline from, a previously high level of corporatist relations in Belgium, Denmark, and the Netherlands, a position where one senses they might be joined by the rest of Scandinavia within a number of years, especially following the major change of government in Sweden in 1991. In each case much of the existing institutional structure was left intact, but there was a move by government and employers towards reliance on different kinds of mechanism for policy stabilization: in Belgium and occasionally in the Netherlands, statutory intervention in bargaining; in the Netherlands increased reliance on technocratic advice from management specialists rather than a search for social consensus through the SER; in Denmark an attempt to move to more *laissez-faire* policies, followed however by an attempted reconstruction of institutions after 1989.

These cases of 'corporatism on the way down' meet some others on the way up—though these all still lacked anything like the GPE infrastructure still active in the former group. Within this set of countries Italy's development has become so unusual that it requires separate classification. Much of the activity that will be described in further countries was to be found there, but in the north and midlands of the country there has been a remarkable growth of branch- and regional-level tripartite administrative agencies as well as bargaining, in particular in association with some regional tiers of government (Regalia, 1988; Regini, 1987). While this is in no way linked to balancing structures at plant level, it otherwise forms an embryonic 'German' system—but in part of a country and therefore not characteristic of a national system. Will something similar occur later this decade in the new Germany?

The uniting characteristic between Italy and the next group of countries is an *intermittent* policy by government, employers' organizations, and unions to erect a national forum for achieving consensus, but on the basis of a disparate and decentralized bargaining system. This is very similar to the 'aspiring neo-corporatism' of the 1970s, and there is some considerable overlap in the countries involved. However, the most striking instance, Spain, was a country which was just emerging from the authoritarian corporatism of fascism at the time of our last snapshot. Since 1979, but particularly since the Socialist Party (PSOE) took control of the government in the early 1980s, there was a strategy of encouraging tripartite social pacts and accords, attempting virtually explicitly to replicate a version of 'northern European' neo-corporatism (Perez-Diaz, 1987; Estivill and Hoz, 1990; Giner and Sevilla, 1984).

Ireland had of course been through all this before, and on the basis of far stronger collective-bargaining institutions. The country had, for most of the 1980s, given up on neo-corporatist attempts and returned to a straight pluralist model; by the time of our snapshot however it had at least temporarily returned to the search for national accord. Portuguese developments were not unlike those in Spain, though pursued less consistently by government—after the collapse of the more rigid corporatism installed by the immediate post-revolutionary government of Marxist military.

France still ranks as the least institutionalized system, apart from Portugal, though in terms of direction of movement it ranks alongside Italy, Spain, and Ireland rather than Belgium, Denmark, the Netherlands, or the United Kingdom. There was, as in the years before our previous snapshot, a bout of legislation designed to encourage bargaining and consultation at company level. This was a continuation of trends since the late 1960s, and fits a well-established French tradition of state intervention. Far less precedented have been moves by both the CNPF and several branch organizations of employers to encourage framework agreements with the unions on a number of issues concerned with economic restructuring, despite the unions' weakness (to be discussed below) and the abstention of the declining but largest confederation, the still-communist CGT, from virtually all the agreements. All this is to be seen as establishing a collective-bargaining system out of contestation though some elements could be said to be neo-corporatist.

It becomes very difficult to rank the United Kingdom. As already remarked, the structure of institutions is in many ways richer than in Spain, but the 1980s did see not only a dismantling of almost all state and national institutions of neo-corporatism but also a virtual collapse of branch-level or any other form of co-ordinated cross-company bargaining (Ingram and Cahill, 1988). The institutions that survived and flourished were those at company level, which makes for a highly disaggregated pluralist model. There was less disaggregation within the public sector, though there was a move by government in favour of fragmentation and the size of the sector was reduced by privatization.

Articulation of Labour Movements, 1990

Union articulation declined everywhere except in Belgium, Finland, the Netherlands, Spain, and Switzerland, but there are important variations (Table 7.9). In Austria, Ireland, the United Kingdom, and Scandinavia the decline took the form of a combined development of a relatively declining exposed sector (Table 7.10), and decentralizing tensions among and within unions (aggravated in Scandinavia by a decline in the hegemony of manual confederations consequent on the rise of white-collar employment and unionization). There was also, as we shall see below, a change in employer strategy. The same is broadly true of Germany, the Netherlands, and Switzerland, with a significant difference. Here the position of exposed-sector unions remained strong because of the extraordinary role of one major union. In the German and Swiss cases this is the historically familiar metal-industry union; in the Netherlands it emerges through the formation of one new cross-branch union defined virtually explicitly as *the* exposed-sector union, following the amalgamation between the Catholic and the social democratic confederations which itself improved the articulation of Dutch unionism.

It becomes difficult to decide whether Norwegian and Swedish unions should now actually rank as less articulated than German, and where Belgium (given *de facto* confederal unity) ranks in relation to them. Denmark has clearly sunk considerably as growing shop-floor disintegration, the rise of extra-LO white-collar unions and the associated decline of the exposed sector took a particularly heavy toll. Finnish articulation is still lower than in these cases because of the evidence of continued factional conflicts at shop-floor level, despite measures to strengthen strategic capacity at national level. Similar attempts in Italy met with even more severe difficulties. Not only were strong moves in the early 1980s to unite the rival confederations disappointing in their outcome, but the decade was marked by the strong growth, especially in the public sector, of autonomous shop-floor unions (known as *comitati della base*, or *Cobas*) quite unrelated to the national unions (Negrelli and Santi, 1990). This is a bigger crisis of articulation than any we have met earlier in this study; even during the peak of the British shop-steward movement in the 1970s there was no disaffiliation from official unions (Batstone, 1979). There was also a diminution of articulation in the United Kingdom consequent on the decline in any state-level role for the TUC and hence in its claim to importance within the movement.

Spain and Portugal have by now developed union structures sufficiently detailed for us to be able to rank their articulation: it is clearly low.

Employer Organization, 1990

There was some change in employers' organization (Table 7.11), though little that made an impact on countries' relative rankings since 1975, apart from a decline in those confederations that depended particularly heavily on the exposed sector for their members. There was almost everywhere a shift in the locus of bargaining from associations to companies, though as has been noted, in some cases (Scandinavia, Germany, and the Netherlands) this was a controlled development planned by the associations and revocable by them; in others, in particular the United Kingdom, it was a result of a collapse of associational activity among employers.

Power of Organized Labour, 1990

Table 7.12 indicates some changes in union power. Membership was markedly down in almost all countries except those where unions retained some role in the administration of unemployment insurance schemes (Rothstein, 1989): Belgium, Denmark, Finland, and Sweden. The decline was most severe in France, Italy, the United Kingdom, and the Netherlands. Unemployment might be considered to have weakened unions further in several

TABLE 7.9. *Articulation of trade-union movements, c.1990*

| | Unions affiliated to main confederation | | | | | Individual unions | |
| | Membership as % of | | No. | Powers of confederation re affiliates | Dominant types of union | Characteristic internal authority structure over local groups, individual members, etc. | Characteristic shop-floor organization |
	known unions	labour force					
A	100	48	15	Stable; some tension between manual and white-collar unions	Strict branch	Centralized	Strong shop-floor role in *Betriebsräte*
N	67	36	33	New rival white-collar federations; also tension between public and private sector unions within LO	Branch type dominates and increasingly challenges LO role	Centralized	Increasing autonomy
S	60	46	24	Deterioration in relations between LO, TCO, and SACO-SR; also tension between	Branch type dominates and increasingly challenges LO role	Centralized	Increasing autonomy

				public- and private-sector unions within LO			
B	53	31	19	Increasing interconfederal co-operation	Branch	Centralized	Weak
D	82	22	17	Relatively stable	Strict branch	Centralized	Growing role of *Betriebsräte*, sometimes in co-operation, sometimes in conflict, with unions
CH	51	13	15	Stable	Strict branch	Centralized	Stable
NL	59	12	15	FNV retains powers, but tension with CNV and MHP	Branch	Centralized	Weak
SF	65	44	26	SAK strengthens role, but continues to confront centrifugal tendencies	Branch	Centralized, but with internal conflict	Considerable autonomy in some sectors
IRL	90	43	78	ITUC secures some authority to co-ordinate action	Craft and general	Varied	Varied

TABLE 7.9. *Continued*

| | Unions affiliated to main confederation | | | | | Individual unions | |
| | Membership as % of | | No. | Powers of confederation re affiliates | Dominant types of union | Characteristic internal authority structure over local groups, individual members, etc. | Characteristic shop-floor organization |
	known unions	labour force					
DK	70	51	33	Growing inter- and intra-confederal conflict, especially between general (SID) and metal unions within LO	Craft and general	Centralized, but with strong decentral trends	Considerable autonomy in some sectors
UK	89	29	98	TUC loses influence as it loses relationship with government; hardly any co-ordination	Craft and general; some branch	Varied	Considerable autonomy in some sectors
I	52	14	21	Interconfederal unity achieved and lost again in	Branch	Varied	Continuing autonomy, often completely

			early 1980s, but continuing informal co-operation			outside union framework
F	31	2	n.a.	Continuing decline of CGT; other confederations active	Branch	Varied	Weak
E	n.a.	n.a.	n.a.	CC.OO and UGT compete for dominance	Varied	Highly decentral	Weak, but with bases
P	n.a.	n.a.	n.a.	CGTP-IN established but has few powers beyond mobilization	Varied	Highly decentral	Weak

Note: Country boundaries as in Table 6.1.

TABLE 7.10. *Membership of exposed-sector trade unions, c.1990*

	Exposed-sector industry-type union members in main confederation as % of total union members	Exposed-sector industry-type union members as % of	
		main confederation members	total labour force
A	29.32	29.32	15.69
B	20.67	26.20	13.10
DK	12.16	17.13	8.16
SF	21.42	22.40	14.15
F	21.44	51.12	3.43
D	44.52	54.18	15.69
IRL	5.55	5.89	2.27
I	14.22	29.52	6.02
NL	23.36	38.17	7.44
N	20.16	29.43	11.31
S	19.13	31.51	15.52
CH	21.04	40.68	5.89
UK	12.33	13.77	5.95

Note: Country boundaries as in Table 6.1. Figures based on mid-1980s data.

countries, especially Ireland and Spain, also Belgium, France, and Italy, and earlier in the decade the United Kingdom.

Political changes, unemployment, and other events sometimes worked in opposed directions. The strength of its institutional position and the political situation probably rank Austria above Denmark, despite the considerable difference in membership levels. Similarly, the institutional stability of German unions, including incidentally through the co-determination system, must rank them above the British and probably the Irish and Italians too; similarly with the Swiss and the British. Political changes were hostile everywhere except France, Italy, Norway, Spain, Sweden, and Switzerland.

The membership strength of Portuguese unions is remarkable, especially when compared with Spain, where unions enjoyed a much stronger politico-institutional position and prominence. Although the unions' cited statistics are regarded as an exag-

TABLE 7.11. *Organizations of capital, c.1990*

	Scope[1]	Power[2]	Other associative business activity[3]
A, D, CH		Continuing stability of existing patterns, but controlled shift to more company-level collective bargaining in	Germany
DK, SF, N, S		Continuing powerful role for organized interests, but central bodies themselves increasingly seek shift to branch or especially company level in relations with labour	
NL		Stable, but operating increasingly through technocratic rather than tripartite forms	
B		Continuing important role, but increasingly reliant on state intervention to stabilize collective bargaining	
I	Varied according to region; increasingly important in north and midlands	Confindustria continues to seek co-ordinating role	Extensive at regional level in north and midlands
F	Increasing	CNPF and branch organizations launch several bargaining initiatives, though with little co-ordinating power	Growing involvement with government
E	Extensive	Weak, though CEOE is very active	Growing involvement with government
IRL		Shift of bargaining to company level weakens role	As 1975
UK		Major uncontrolled shift of bargaining to company level weakens role	As 1975
P		Weak	Weak

Note: Country boundaries as in Table 6.1.

[1] Extent of organization of employer interests.

[2] Resources available to employer organizations to co-ordinate action.

[3] Activity directed at trade rather than labour issues.

TABLE 7.12. *Power of organized labour, c.1990*

	Known union membership as % of		Major industrial-relations and political developments affecting organized labour within industry	Unemployment[1]	Share of popular vote[2] %	Participation in gov't[3] %
	labour force	dependent labour force				
S	76	83		VL	49.1	1.00
SF	68	81		L	43.8	0.50
N	53	61		L	44.4	—[4]
A	48	55		L	42.8 (32.1)	1.00
DK	73	82	Non-social-democratic government minimizes contact with unions	M	45.7	1.00
B	58	62		H	30.5 (27.5)	0.75
D	27	32		M	33.5 (43.8)	0.25
I	27	35		H	39.2 (33.6)	0.50
IRL	32	48		VH	14.5 (44.2)	0.25
CH	26	30		VL	18.4 (20.0)	0.75
UK	27	43	Conservative government minimizes	M	30.0	

NL	21	24	contact with unions; new legislative framework reduces unions' powers and rights	M	32.3 (35.8)	0.50
E	n.a.	10	Union rights established; government dependent on union co-operation for national stability	VH	54.9	1.00
F	6	8	Extension of some union, but mainly worker, rights, 1981	H	11.3 (34.8)	0.25
P	n.a.	30	Union rights established for first time in Portuguese history	M	34.4 (50.2)	0.25

Note: Country boundaries as in Table 6.1.

[1] VH = registered unemployment in excess of 15% of dependent labour force; H = 11–15%; M = around 10%; L = 2.5–5%; VL = less than 2.5%; ? = reliable figures not available on a broadly comparable basis.

[2] In most recent general election secured by labour movement parties; votes for parties with labour wing but primarily committed to other interests in parentheses. Figures for Denmark, Finland, Ireland, Italy, Norway, Portugal, Spain, Sweden combine social democratic with communist and other left parties in labour-movement party total. NB: French socialists count as a party not primarily of the labour movement.

[3] 1.0 = straight labour party government; 0.75 = main labour-movement party dominating coalition or combination of labour and quasi-labour parties; 0.5 = labour party as junior coalition partner; 0.25 = government participation by Christian or other quasi-labour parties.

[4] Labour in sole office from October.

geration, the 30 per cent level is a reduced figure on which Portuguese observers seem agreed (Pinto, 1990).

Outcome Indicators, 1990

Spain and Portugal can now be included in this analysis, though the data on unemployment in Portugal, not unlike those for Switzerland, are difficult to assess. As was common in earlier periods in many countries, people who lose their jobs in the modern sector can often still return to the family home and plot in the countryside, and the real unemployment rate may be much higher. There was also during the 1980s the unusual phenomenon of some state corporations retaining their workers but not paying them any wages.

Table 7.13 gives details of industrial conflict in the late 1980s. The only remaining low-conflict cases were the Alpine countries, Germany and the Netherlands. The other established and stable neo-corporatist countries (the Scandinavians) still have relatively lower levels than the pluralist countries, though considerably higher than in their post-war past. France, however, with one of the least developed bargaining, let alone neo-corporatist, systems, has conflict levels lower than many of these, though this may be related to the low level of union membership.

It is still the case that, when union membership strength is taken into account, conflict in the neo-corporatist countries remains relatively low. However, in assessing this evidence from the 1980s it is important to note a change that has taken place in the relationship between neo-corporatist industrial relations, as displayed in Table 7.8 and the articulation of union movements (Table 7.9). In earlier decades these tended to rise in parallel; and countries (such as the United Kingdom) in which attempts were made to establish neo-corporatism without articulation soon switched back to a collective-bargaining or contestation model more compatible with low articulation. Denmark (perhaps eventually the rest of Scandinavia too) presents a case where the level of generalized political exchange remains high—though noticeably declining—while articulation is collapsing. It seems clear that the neo-corporatist structures by themselves cannot sustain the outcomes associated in theory with neo-corporatism if

TABLE 7.13. *Industrial conflict, 1986–1990*

	Strikes per 1,000		Workers involved per 1,000		Days lost per 1,000	
	dependent labour force	trade-union members	dependent labour force	trade-union members	dependent labour force	trade-union members
A	0.00	0.00	1.38	2.34	1.42	2.40
DK	0.08	0.09	17.95	19.55	41.24	44.92
SF	0.41	0.50	115.46	138.95	401.47	483.13
F[1]	n.a.	n.a.	8.60	94.16	65.06	712.51
D	n.a.	n.a.	4.89	15.05	4.58	14.11
IRL[2]	0.10	0.17	33.21	53.90	282.01	457.69
I[3]	0.11	0.22	298.43	578.57	2,499.70	4,846.16
NL	0.01	0.02	2.85	10.41	12.75	46.65
N	0.01	0.01	29.04	43.78	149.94	226.03
P	0.09	0.39	50.40	210.70	79.78	333.49
E	0.15	1.33	284.51	2,598.79	618.11	5,645.93
S	0.03	0.03	13.83	16.06	132.47	15.38
CH	0.00	0.01	0.05	0.16	0.36	1.14
UK	0.04	0.08	31.78	64.92	141.31	288.67

Notes: Country boundaries as in Table 6.1.
Belgium has ceased to publish strike statistics.

[1] French data on numbers of conflicts are no longer comparable with those of other countries.
[2] Number of strikes figure for 1986–9 only.
[3] Number of strikes figure for 1986–7 only.

TABLE 7.14. *Economic performance, 1986–1990*

	Inflation[1]	Unemployment[2]	Discomfort[3]
A	2.19	4.08	6.27
B	2.13	9.58	11.71
DK	3.92	8.64	12.56
SF	4.83	4.32	9.15
F	3.09	9.84	12.93
D	1.36	5.90	7.26
IRL	3.29	16.04	19.33
I	5.75	10.64	16.39
NL	0.75	8.90	9.65
N	6.27	3.48	9.75
P	11.34	6.46	17.80
E	6.46	18.60	25.06
S	6.25	1.82	8.07
CH	2.52	0.67	3.19
UK	5.96	8.80	14.76

Note: Country boundaries as in Table 6.1.

[1] Annual average inflation rate.

[2] Annual average unemployment rate (standardized OECD definitions except for Austria).

[3] Sum of inflation and unemployment rates.

infrastructural support from the internal structure of participant organizations deteriorates. The Finnish case similarly suggests that the establishment of GPE structures of an advanced level cannot compensate for a continuing absence of appropriate infrastructure.

The evidence on inflation and unemployment (Table 7.14) gives us something new, though not unanticipated in our earlier analyses. The lowest inflation levels are scored by three neo-corporatist cases which do not rank high in terms of union power and where union articulation is supplemented by exceptionally important exposed-sector unions (Germany, the Netherlands, and Switzerland), together with Austria, where labour was considerably more powerful, though less so than in the Nordic countries, and Belgium, where uniquely the dominant union confederation is tied to a Christian-democratic party. In contrast the clearly 'labour-dominated' Nordic neo-corporatisms have

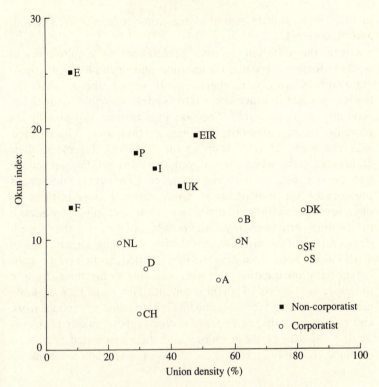

FIG. 7.2. *Economic performance and union strength, 1986–1990*

very indifferent records. They are no better, or are actually worse, than most collective-bargaining or contestational cases. On the other hand, if one sets aside the special case of Switzerland, the countries with the best records on *unemployment* were precisely the 'social-democratic' neo-corporatist countries, including Finland and Austria but not Belgium or the 'decayed' case of Denmark.

On the combined Okun index the first nine rankings are occupied by all nine countries that we have identified as having strong elements of established neo-corporatism, with Denmark appropriately occupying ninth place. As Fig. 7.2 shows, all neo-corporatist countries continue to contain the potential economic consequences of a high level of union membership, though, as in 1975, there is little overall association between union strength and 'discomfort'.

Given the different relative preferences of employers and workers for good records on inflation and unemployment, these main results are comprehensible. It would appear that the leading partner in a neo-corporatist system was able to steer the economy in its preferred direction in a manner not possible in pluralist cases. However, in doing so they were all, in their different ways, clearly straining the high-trust legacy of their corporatist past, when *shared* goals between capital and labour had been easier to find and achieve. Employers' widespread preferences for moving away from national organizations to plant-level bargaining demonstrate their declining confidence in existing arrangements. Meanwhile, unions in the social-democratic corporatist countries with declining organizational articulation were becoming unable to deliver behaviour consistent with low inflation, but were still able to use their strength to secure low levels of unemployment. This cannot be a viable model in the long term. Meanwhile, the decline of manual work and employment in the exposed sector suggests major problems for the capacity of these unions and their associated parties to continue to dominate the character of any national consensus.

Conclusions, 1990

The main overall conclusion for this period is therefore that a long-present division has become increasingly important: that between forms of neo-corporatism dependent on powerful, articulated, and centralized union movements (Austria, Scandinavia, and now Finland), and those built on weaker union movements whose articulation depended more on the strength of one dominant exposed-sector union rather than a centralized confederation, as well as powerful employers' organizations (Switzerland, now the Netherlands, Belgium, and, less conforming to the 'weak' case, Germany). These are countries that can be said to inhabit the quadrant of 'over-determined' social order, IV, in Fig. 2.2. The importance of such a category was not really anticipated by any of the theories of industrial-relations organization we have been following: it is certainly not predicted by

Dunlop, and it causes considerable difficulty for the social-democratic hypothesis, though less for Olsonian theory.

Where unions lost power during the 1980s, incipient corporatisms based mainly on government aspirations of the 1970s that lacked a high articulation base in workers' and employers' own organizations were knocked back into straight collective bargaining (more strongly in the United Kingdom than anywhere else). These countries were sent into unstable quadrant II, unless (as at times appeared to be the case in the United Kingdom) they may have been weakened to the point of returning to I. Very similar was Denmark, where the basis of earlier neo-corporatism has been eroded by the decline in articulation; now clearly a quadrant II case. Inadequate inarticulation has still left Finland on the margins of II and III, and Norway and Sweden threaten to move into II if union and employer articulation continue to decline.

France, for all the political and institutional change of the 1980s, seems still to be located in quadrant I. Despite the attempts at neo-corporatist strategies in Portugal and Spain, the poor articulation level of organizations in these countries leave them too in I, though Spain's ostensibly weak labour movement seems capable of threatening situations more typical of quadrant II.

8

An Overview

Having examined different periods piecemeal, it is now necessary to gain some overview of the era as a whole in order to assess evolutionary theories of development and to determine whether particular points in economic and political change are associated with steps in the growth of unions and employers' organizations. Indicators of industrialization, national wealth, and economic structure have only a very crude relationship with those of system development. There does seem to be a level of per capita GNP (around US$ 400 (1960) in fact) below which no country has developed strong trade unions or a collective-bargaining system. Although for much of this century this has been a 'southern European' matter, an early comparison of Denmark and Sweden bears out the same point: the latter country in no way developed its neighbour's elaborate industrial-relations institutions until it had transcended its earlier poverty. Beyond that basic level however there is scope for very little generalization, as the case of France—rich but not really developing viable institutions until the 1970s—shows.

The French case might be thought to be explained by that country's slow rate of industrialization, but the evidence hardly supports that thesis. Denmark developed elaborate institutions when still highly agricultural, while Belgium was once another opposite case. Again, comparison between northern and southern Europe is instructive. One may progress further by noting an association between, on the one hand, latifundia agriculture and a slow development and, on the other, free farmers and high development. That variable feeds into the *wealth* variable, not directly into level of industrialization, though there might be something about organizational *forms* in the rural economy that has deeper institutional implications.

Different types of economic structure also fail to find much association. Britain, Germany, and Sweden seem to support the case that elaborate industrial-relations systems develop within economies with large firms in the big export sectors (steel and engineering); but Austria, Denmark, the Netherlands, and Switzerland all developed their institutions under small-firm handicraft economies.

There is some support for the Dunlop thesis that the growth of institutionalized relations is most likely to take place under liberal bourgeois regimes; certainly 'dynastic feudal' as well as fascist regimes are associated with very low levels of institutional development, and the curious mix of democracy and authoritarianism that made up the old German and Austrian empires was associated with an equally mixed system of industrial relations. However, it should be noted that the state-level or state-inspired forms of participation that unions enjoyed under these empires stemmed more from their authoritarian than from their liberal components.

More of a puzzle for the Dunlop thesis is the case of France. Dunlop himself resolved this by treating France as having dynastic feudal elements. This is difficult to sustain. True, there was, and to a degree continues to be, a tradition of patronal rights among French employers. But this stems more from the post-1789 system of free peasant proprietorship than from dynastic feudalism. It seems particularly puzzling for the assertively bourgeois republican regime of Third-Republic France to be regarded as essentially feudalistic while Victorian Britain, which still maintained a good deal of aristocratic rule, is regarded as the quintessence of bourgeois liberalism.

It is indeed notable that, throughout the nineteenth century, Britain trailed far behind France (and indeed most other countries) in its level of democracy, while having a powerfully developed trade-unionism. In so much literature that stems from an essentially Anglo-American tradition there is a stereotypical assumption of an association between liberalism, bourgeois dominance, industrialism, and democracy on the one hand and authoritarianism, Catholicism, and ruralism on the other. France, the United Kingdom, and Denmark between them all demonstrate the limitations of this association in the late nineteenth and early twentieth centuries. The Dunlop thesis works well, in a rather simple way, when accounting for the general growth of industrial relations at the purely industrial level. Once it begins to tackle political variables it becomes far less sure.

This point becomes even more evident when we consider the development of neo-corporatist elements. As I have already argued, the Dunlop thesis has no place for the structure of organizations implied by generalized political exchange. Centralized, intellectual union leaderships, non-competing unions, and highly aggregated bargaining arrangements are in his thesis associated with 'revolutionary intellectual' union chiefs. It would be a considerable stretching of definitions to regard the union leaderships and collective-bargaining systems of post-Second-World-War Scandinavia, Austria, and Germany as 'revolutionary', though there may be some power in the rather different observation that in both its democratic and authoritarian forms the socialist tradition is one of strong, rather centralized institutions. What is particularly difficult to accept, however, is the conclusion that one would have to draw from Dunlop's thesis that such arrangements are essentially bogus and fail to provide proper representation for workers. Our discussion in the preceding chapters has suggested the greater possibility of the reverse.

Perhaps one does greater justice to the Dunlop thesis by arguing that neo-corporatism is not simply a form of industrial relations completely outwith the scope of his theory, but that it might be seen as a synthesis of his bourgeois and revolutionary forms. What if, instead of continuing to pursue revolutionary goals, a socialist trade-union movement of the late-nineteenth-century European type comes to terms with capitalist élites, who in turn come to terms with it? Might one then get a combination of a centralized movement and the disaggregation associated with liberal industrial relations? Such a synthesis would correspond to Kjellberg's (1983 and 1990) argument that the most effective union movements usually have points of strength at *both* the centre *and* the shop floor, and that therefore the simple epithet 'centralized', so often used in the literature to describe such cases, is really misleading. It is this insight that I have tried to capture in my distinction between 'articulation' and 'centralization'.

This may be a realistic way of describing what happened to Scandinavian and German labour movements, but it does not accord with the facts of our analysis to associate all pressure for centralization to the labour side. As we have seen, much of the thrust towards the construction of these systems came from employers, either directly as in the case of Sweden or through workers establishing centralized structures in parallel with a centralized and politically important associative structure of business interests on the trade-association side. With the Austrian, German, and Swedish examples in mind one is able to see the variety in forms of organization of modern capitalism so often missed by observers who take as their paradigm either economic theory or Anglo-American experience, rather than European economic history.

The general assertion of established theories of industrial relations, that labour's growing strength, if not suppressed, will lead to increased collective contract relations with employers, is confirmed by our data. We have also seen that continued growth in labour's power will lead to a capacity to act at state level, but also that this is not a simple function of union power, as the cases of the British TUC (high power but, for a long time, poor state capacity) and the Finnish SAK, the Belgian FGTB, the Dutch NVV, and the Swiss SGB (the other way round) show.

A centralized labour movement will begin to engage in GPE rather than persist with pure bargaining alone, but the process has often been very slow and should not be seen as irreversible. There will be change in the cases of a decline in labour's power or a change in its level of decision-making capacity. Examples of the former have been Austria and Germany in the 1920s, and of the latter include the Danish LO and the Dutch FNV, currently losing capacity, and the Finnish SAK, currently gaining it.

There is a paradox in that a mix of centralized political action and localized bargaining seems associated with an instability of GPE structures in Denmark, Finland, Italy, and the United Kingdom, but with extreme stability in Austria, Germany, and Switzerland. The answer lies in the different forms of articulation between the levels. In the former list of countries autonomous and often oppositional shop-steward or similar rank-and-file movements lead decentralized action. In the 'Germanic' coun- tries the lower levels were anticipated, even shaped, by union leaderships, employers, and/or the law. Indeed, rather than representing oppositional forces they have often been focuses for inserting a concern for the fate of individual companies into union calculations. This has been well described in the German literature (e.g. Bergmann *et al.*, 1975; Streeck, 1979). Works councils can, by definition, operate only at the level of the individual company and must therefore do their best for their members within the framework of market constraints faced by that company, especially as they share management responsibility for some aspects of its operation. Rather than leave the works councils as a thoroughly rival form of worker representation, the unions have tried, as discussed in Chapter 6, to incorporate them by including works council members in their branch- and regional-level bargaining commissions. These works councillors are then often a moderating influence on the union when it formulates its demands, since they do not want the union's claims to make their company-level work more difficult. They also do not want those claims to take up all slack in the scope for bargaining, leaving them nothing extra to negotiate at company level. Hence the robustness of German and Austrian (and in different ways Swiss) representative structures at a time when employers everywhere have been pushing for company-level industrial relations.

The role of employers' organizations in the shaping of systems of articulation also provides difficulties for the social-democratic or 'Scandinavian' thesis that stable, encompassing, responsible forms of unionism are forged primarily by powerful labour movements. The form of the thesis developed by Stephens (1979), which uses centralization as well as union power as an explanatory variable, has been shown by the preceding chapters, to have strength—especially of course if articulation is substituted for centralization. However, we need to acknowledge employers, not just in our accounts of 'strong' unionism of the Scandinavian kind, but also and perhaps particularly in the relatively weak but incorporated union movements of Switzerland, and to a certain extent Federal Germany and the Netherlands; or Belgian unions, uniquely dominated by a social Christian confederation. Given that these movements did not 'win' their place at the national table by sheer assertiveness, why have they not been marginalized in the manner of, say, French unions or the Italians in the 1950s?

The answer is partly found in Katzenstein's (1984) concept of 'social promotion', developed specifically for the Swiss case. For political reasons some states have needed to incorporate labour.

This produces a strange problem if labour is poorly organized; it is needed as an interlocutor but is not really up to the task. The solution is to grant it a place rather higher than its true power really merits, and not to call its bluff. Such a movement may not be strictly 'encompassing' in the Olsonian sense because it rarely represents more than a minority of the labour force. However, as part of the social promotion deal such unions have often achieved rights of *Verallgemeinung*: the ability to have an agreement reached between recognized employers' associations and unions made legally binding on the whole branch concerned. Such a provision, found in all four countries as well as in Austria, imposes the state of encompassingness on a minority union in a way that, say, the American bargaining system never achieves. It is an important reason why membership levels are rarely a good predictor of union behaviour. A union obliged to act encompassingly but weak in mobilizing power is likely to be the most co-operative type of trade union.

We are back with the analysis of four types of union set out in Fig. 2.2 in Chapter 2. The straightforward social-democratic corporatist cases (high union power, high union and employer articulation, category III) can provide a high level of Olsonian encompassing stability. These are the classic Scandinavian and Austrian cases. However, even more likely to provide stability, because less vulnerable to unsettling as a result of labour's exercise of power, is category IV, where movements are articulated but weak. In Chapter 2 we asked how such a combination was likely to occur. The answer, we now see, is that articulation may sometimes derive from social promotion, when a labour movement is given national political tasks to fulfil despite its relative weakness; it binds its lower levels into co-operation with this activity because it is unlikely to achieve an autonomous power. This is the Swiss and Dutch, in many respects the German, and occasionally the Austrian, case.

A high level of power and a low level of articulation (quadrant II) may result from an historical development discouraging the transformation of power into politicized strength (Ireland, the United Kingdom, Finland, and Italy), or from a deteriorating articulation (Denmark; possibly by the late 1980s the whole of Scandinavia). This is an exceptionally unstable pattern and is unlikely to survive long without political intervention. Finally, a combination of union weakness and low articulation (quadrant I) will be quite stable for obvious reasons. By the 1970s only France approximated to this pattern, though Portugal and Spain may be there rather than in quadrant II, and outside Europe it would apply also to many parts of the United States of America.

We may also venture an answer to a final question. In the 1930s in Scandinavia, and in some other countries after the Second World War, a desperate, crisis-ridden, political exchange was able to generate what eventually became stable neo-corporatist systems. Why did the spate of similar, slightly less panic-ridden, activity in the 1970s not have a similar outcome? In those earlier years the labour market, except in Finland and Ireland, was dominated by manual work in manufacturing industry. *Ceteris paribus*, this was fertile soil for the erection of country-wide organizations of capital and labour with certain strategic goals. What was often lacking was mutual acceptance by the social partners and the state of each other's long-term survival. In particular, the option of excluding organized labour altogether was always present for the other two actors. As the century has progressed there has been, more or less, an increasing willingness of the two sides to come to terms with each other, but also a decline in both the willingness of workers to be co-ordinated by a solidaristic organization, and, perhaps more important, a collapse of the manual manufacturing model of employment.

'Solidaristic organization' presents us with an interesting irony. Historically in Europe such solidarities focused and concentrated a sense of identity at a level other than the nation-state and therefore worked directly against the generation of national identity—hence a good deal of the persecution that movements representing such solidarities received at the hands of established political forces. These may be class solidarities (as in Scandinavia at one time), religio-cultural ones (as in Belgium, the Netherlands, and Switzerland) or a combination of the two (as in Austria, France, and Italy). But, as we have seen in the foregoing chapters, solidarities that initially undermined national identity subsequently helped construct institutions that became a base for forging national co-operation. Precisely because leaders, especially of labour, were co-ordinating combative organizations, they were able to mobilize loyalty and obedience; which they then used to enter relationships with their 'enemies', the employers, in order to secure co-operation. Neo-corporatist systems eventually became established where such solidarities helped construct centralized organizations able to participate in strategic bargaining—though this was by no means a sufficient condition for effective centralization as the French and Italian cases show.

To complete the irony, in recent decades the once threatening subnational solidarities have atrophied, partly because of the very success of the national institutions. But since the latter have been erected on the base of tamed and incorporated versions of the former, they are in turn weakened. We see the symptoms of this in such phenomena as the secularization of the Netherlands and the eruption in the late 1960s of decentralized industrial militancy impatient with centralized union forces that had come to represent 'bureaucracy' rather than an increasingly unrealistic class solidarity (Streeck, 1982; Visser, 1990).

Either the mid-1930s or the immediate post-war years were moments in various countries when class solidarities, national co-operativeness, and the dominance of the manufacturing economy peaked. Neo-corporatism may have been 'discovered' in the 1970s, but it was being established between 1935 or 1945 and around 1965. The 1970s seem in terms of our model of institutional development the peak of *elaboration* of the mechanisms of GPE, but by then its solidaristic supports had in fact started to crumble.

Since then countries have moved in contrary directions. Where GPE models already existed in the mid 1970s, there was often commitment to keep them working, if with reduced ambitions. Elsewhere, the failure of new 1970s experiments has led to a search for very different solutions—including both mild returns to the repression of organized labour and a new search for means of securing the identity of workers with their companies, or with the capitalist system, that do not require the intermediary of unions performing within GPE.

The future therefore remains rather open. Can labour movements outside Germany and Switzerland replace the hegemony of manual workers' unions in the exposed sector with something more truly encompassing of the late twentieth-century workforce? Meanwhile, we have not yet tracked down our central puzzle of sources of diversity. Olson's theory is too simple and is not really trying to answer this question. Dunlop stops short at collective bargaining. Social-democratic theory does not help with, on the one hand, Germany, the Netherlands, and Switzerland or, on the other, the United Kingdom. Why does an organized industrial politics survive so many regime changes in Austria and Germany when it crumbles so readily in France and the United Kingdom? Why does Switzerland have such a strong version of such politics despite its ostensible economic liberalism? To answer these questions we need to push back beyond the history recounted here to both an earlier past and to a wider range of issues.

PART III

ECONOMIC ORGANIZATIONS AND POLITICAL SPACE

9

Political Space and European State Traditions: The Religious Base

Dabei kommt es heute, anders als für Montesquieu, entscheidend darauf an, daß Hemmung und Balancierung nicht das Zustandekommen gemeinsamen Entscheidungshandelns überhaupt blockieren oder sehr erschweren. Freiheitssicherung und Verhinderung des Mißbrauchs politischer Macht können in der sozial- und leistungsstaatlichen Demokratie nicht mehr primär durch Nichthandeln der Inhaber der politischen Entscheidungsgewalt erreicht werden.

(Böckenförde, 1977: 244)

The historical record displayed in Part II contains cases of both dramatic change and extraordinary persistence. Austrians and Frenchmen have alike been involved in bloody civil strife over the role of organized labour in industrial society, and both have moved through a series of contrasting regime types. But in Austria there has throughout been an abiding continuity in that the state has rooted itself in varying structures of organized interests. In France there has been an equally persistent suspicion of organized groups representing social interests, whoever they might be.

The most frequently compared European state traditions are those of the three major modern European powers: Britain, France, and Germany. Slomp (1990), for example, in an analysis similar to that adopted in this volume but addressed to labour movements rather than industrial-relations systems, makes these three (with the Soviet Union) the prototypical forms. The comparisons take a familiar form. Maurice, Sellier, and Silvestre (1982), comparing French and German industrial behaviour, compare the strong statism of the former with the elaborate role for organized interests found in the latter. Lane (1989), adding the United Kingdom and considering all aspects of the relationship between management and labour, characterizes these two in a similar way and sees the market as generally more dominant in the United Kingdom, alongside rather decentralized organizations. Hall (1986) adopts an approach like that being embarked on in this Part of the present volume, tracing current industrial practices back through a long historical trajectory. His focus on industrial policy concentrates on a statist France and an essentially market-governed Britain, with some discussion of organized Germany.

What are the deeper historical roots of these continuities? Why do states vary so much among themselves but individually persist so long with a recognizable pattern of relations between themselves and organized interests? And can we draw any conclusions concerning the conditions under which major changes take place in these patterns?

The shifts that have occurred during the twentieth century itself in the politics of organized interests mainly concern the balance of power among the different social forces. It is in the means by which, the style in which, various groups have grappled with these changes that the deeper historical continuities may be seen.

'Style' may seem a trivial variable compared with the balance of power; an epiphenomenon if there ever was one. But it is not to be written off in this way. When the active groups in a particular society tackle the latest conflict that has occurred in relations between them, they do not work out *ab initio* how, in some abstract way, a problem of that kind should ideally be resolved. No one has the kind of knowledge needed to answer such questions in complex matters, and in any case only a few component strands are loosened from the historical bale for manipulation at any one time. Usually, therefore, a solution will be sought that involves as little disturbance as possible to known and understood principles of organization, that enables most use to be made of predictabilities from past experience.

This does not mean that striking innovation never happens. To move from having trade-union leaders put in prison to inviting them to ministerial talks, or vice versa, to cite a not uncommon case of policy shift during the period under review, is dramatically innovative. But perhaps precisely because such moves involve a step into the unknown, there will usually be attempts to carry them out in a manner that is, in as many respects as possible, tried and familiar.

The two decades after the European economic crash of 1873 were such a period of institutional innovation. Everywhere industrialism was moving out of its purely competitive phase into the epoch of 'organized capitalism', a development, impelled principally by conditions of international competition, which struck different societies at very different stages of their individual economic progress. At the same time the organization of labour became an issue that all states needed to take seriously. What clues did an earlier age of functional-interest politics bequeath to these industrial or industrializing states? In turn, what relevance did the solutions found in the final quarter of the nineteenth century have for the new organizational politics of the second half of the twentieth?

For the central concept in this discussion I return to that of political space introduced in Chapter 3. It was there encountered as a dimension that was entered as industrial-relations organizations sought to exercise influence beyond the occupational sphere. Our concern was with how the actions of such organizations 'moved out' to occupy such space. We must now consider political space in its own terms and define it more closely. I mean by the term that range of issues over which general, public decisions are made within a given political unit, particularly decisions which are seen by political actors to affect overall social order. The territory so designated is variable, and to that extent its definition may well be a matter of conflict within societies. The articulation of such definitional conflicts is ultimately relevant to the current thesis, but to introduce it as a variable here would make the analysis too complex.

It is a crucial feature of the classic liberal political economy that political space is monopolized by specialized political institutions: legislature, executive, and judiciary. Civil society enters these institutions only through its members adopting formal, specialized political roles, whether as members of one of these institutions or as individual citizen-electors. Functional and other specifically denominated social interests may approach the political institutions as external lobbies and pressure groups, but their entry *within* these institutions is regarded as a form of corruption or (as in the British House of Lords) an odd compromise between liberal and earlier forms of government.

That a form of political monopoly lies at the heart of liberalism may seem paradoxical, but it is part of the important truth that *laissez-faire* is not anarchism. The state has vital functions within liberal market capitalism; if they are not performed by the state, they will be taken over by groups within civil society, which will therefore cease to be the non-political actors that participants in the market system are required to be. On the other hand, if the state steps beyond its vital functions, it will begin to intervene in civil society in a manner that more obviously disturbs market relations. Theoretically, therefore, a pure liberal market economy requires a state that is not only limited and restrained but which is, within its proper sphere, sovereign. It is the *clarity* of state–society boundaries that distinguishes this kind of political economy, not a weakness of the state.

The theory is reflected in history. In most western European states a period of absolutism preceded the development of capitalism as the dominant economic system (Anderson, 1974; Poggi, 1978). In feudalism political authority is too parcellized and mixed with land-holding to enable civil society to function in proper market fashion. The typical urban associations, the guilds, differed from pure associations of interests by carrying out delegated political functions of maintaining order within their craft (Black, 1984). By concentrating and distilling political sovereignty into itself, the absolutist state depoliticized civil society in a manner useful to the development of market relations, though in many cases it 'went too far' and began to use its accretion of power to interfere in civil society itself.

It is important to distinguish these questions from that of 'strong' versus 'weak' states, which refers to the capacity of a state to carry out effectively those functions which it claims to be able to perform; a strong state does not have to be a highly interventionist one, while a weak state may well be interventionist. Although a state that occupies only a fragment of potential political space is likely to be a weak one, a restricted state which nevertheless carries out all the functions needed to secure basic order may well rate as very strong precisely because it concentrates its power and does not try to achieve 'too much'.

Indeed, a need to restrict the state precisely in order to make its strength effective was part of the new right's critique of the arguably over-extended states of the 1970s (e.g. Crozier, Huntingdon, and Watanaki, 1978; Rose and Peters, 1977). Similarly, while it takes a very strong state to act *effectively* as a highly interventionist one, it is quite possible to envisage ineffective states that intervene beyond their means.

Medieval political economies were typically those in which political space was shared. The state, such as it was, *both* left several aspects of social regulation to guilds, *Stände*, and similar corporate bodies, and interfered in economic affairs. During absolutism and also during what Maier (1981) calls 'the parliamentary parenthesis' these essentially organizational forms of regulation were dismantled. Order was typically secured through a combination of direct but external state regulation and market forces, with the state guaranteeing the private property rights necessary for market relations and contract to operate.

Maier uses his term to designate the period, primarily in the mid-nineteenth century, when an older pattern of post-medieval corporatist interest representation had broken down, giving way to a universal and individualistic model. After this period, essentially from the 1870s onwards, organized economic interests of a modern kind became increasingly important. Could the state continue to cope with them through the mixture of market forces and external regulation, or would it interpenetrate them in order to co-opt their organizational resources for the task of securing order, as envisaged in corporatist theory and ideology? Almost everywhere there were moves in the latter direction, but, just as absolutism and parliamentarism penetrated different societies to very different degrees and lasted for differing periods, these moves varied widely in extent, with ramifications in differences between polities that are still with us.

To view the subject theoretically, from the point of view of the Hayekian model of state–society relations, the 'natural' state of affairs is for economic relations to be governed by market processes (Hayek, 1973); it is engagement by collectivity, whether in the shape of the state or interest organizations, that needs special explanation. To view the subject historically is to see it the other way round; states and organizations are enmeshed in the economy from the outset; it is how they were often driven out that needs explanation. The stance adopted here—at the cost of economy of explanation—is that nothing can be taken for granted, everything needs to be explained. How was it that, in some cases, organized interests were driven out from or marginalized within the political economy? How was it that in others they managed to withstand the powerful logic of the liberal process?

We can break the issue down by considering how organized interests fared in their relations with states and political élites during the three great struggles in the emergence of modernity:

1. Their relationship to conflict between church and state in the century 1789–1891 (from the French Revolution to *Rerum Novarum*, the Papal encyclical that accommodated the Catholic Church to social interests and their organization in modern society).
2. Their relationship to processes shaping the 'modern' form of European states, especially during the period between 1848 and 1918.
3. The fate of guild-type organization at the onset of serious industrialization.

To this is added a fourth, more recent, twentieth-century, process:

4. The political power of the labour movement during the twentieth century.

The first two, 'state-forming', processes will be discussed together in this chapter; the third, relating to 'economic organization', in the following chapter; and the fourth in Chapter 11.

We find that some political circumstances of the emergence of the modern state weakened or *inhibited* the role of organized interests. They found themselves on the 'wrong side' in the modernization struggle and either disappeared or became allied with anti-modernizing forces, becoming protectionist and divorced from politico-economic responsibility. This was a fatally determining characteristic. Once it had happened in an unambiguous way, nothing could save them. They lacked central influence and the state was jealous of the political space that they continued, apparently parasitically, to occupy. These factors were then mutually reinforcing, resulting in hopelessly decentralized organizational structures of capital and labour that were likely to be politically favoured only during anti-modernizing periods or as an aspect of an abiding clientelism. Such circumstances inhibited a future strategic or responsible role for these organizations.

The role of the Catholic Church is central in this, since in societies where it had remained the dominant (often sole) church after the Reformation it became the central rallying point for all forces alienated from modernization. The countries affected are France, Italy, Portugal, Spain, and (with some important exceptional points to which we shall return) Belgium. The Hapsburg Empire, which ostensibly should conform to this model, does not do so for reasons that will become clear.

At the opposite pole we have those cases where organized interests, far from being discomfited by the rise of the modern state, were part of its very structure and helped make the state: Germany, Switzerland, and to a certain extent both Belgium and the Netherlands, though with certain problems in the former case because of its membership also of the former group. Such political contexts facilitated a strong role for organized interests.

In the remaining cases the political conditions were broadly neutral. These are Protestant states where the churches (Lutheran and Anglican) made their peace with the state long before the birth of modernizing forces and created few if any challenges to its authority. Guild structures had been taken over and adopted by the new religious dispensations and were not left isolated on those grounds. We are here speaking essentially of the Nordic countries and the British Isles. In northern Germany this factor is added to the 'facilitating' ones already mentioned. 'Neutrality' is evaluated differently depending on whether or not the Hayekian view cited above is adopted. If the 'naturalness' of free markets is accepted, then such continuing forces would amount to no more than historical residues, which will either be bypassed by the naturally more vigorous processes of the free market or will remain as minor encumbrances to such processes. If, however, an agnostic view is adopted, entertaining the possibility that non-market mechanisms may function positively, then the neutral state may sometimes provide a context within which they flourish, as social actors 'naturally' find them useful.

POLITICAL INHIBITORS

The place of guild structures in struggles over the secular state is clearly only a small part of the general struggle over the relationship between state and church. This was the key question affecting state sovereignty and the occupation of political space before the emergence of issues of the market and civil society, and in several societies it remained an issue throughout the subsequent period too. To the extent that the liberal state had to struggle to assert its autonomy from and superiority over an established religion, it became exceptionally 'jealous' of political space, reluctant to share it, and thus exclusive in its claims to sovereignty. Against this, pro-church forces maintained traditions of space-sharing. In the context of the fallen world cut off from the City of God, the Catholic Church was willing to share responsibility with secular powers for the good conduct of human order.

The paradigm case of the exclusive claims of the secular state is of course the French Republic. In their drive to integrate the nation around republican symbols as opposed to the Catholic Church, French republicans from 1789 asserted the sovereignty and inaccessibility of the state, which stood above and outside society and its many claims (Hayward, 1983: 55 ff.). The issue is seen at perhaps its sharpest and most permanent in the struggle over church schools. A major outcome is a long-term confrontation between a jealous secular state and a determinedly active church (Lipset and Rokkan, 1967: 15, 38–40; D. A. Martin, 1978: 40, 118–20). At least in the immediate post-1789 period it is rather difficult to separate this drive by the state from the second theme of the state's autonomy from ancient corporate forms, as so many of these were combined with church power.

At a later stage there was a secondary development: the state rendering itself both inaccessible and dominant, the newly developing labour movement found little chance of influencing it and therefore became highly oppositional, much of it embracing first syndicalism and then communism (Reynaud, 1975: ch. 3). This in turn reinforced the existing tendency of the state, because labour thereby rendered itself increasingly unattractive as a potential 'social partner' for either the state or capital; a process of cumulative mutual hostility was thus set in train.

The fact that much corporatist ideology originated within French Catholicism does not refute this analysis. When the Vatican finally marked its reconciliation with pluralism and industrial society with the publication of the encyclical *Rerum Novarum* in 1891, its doctrine of accepting the organization of labour but rejecting class conflict led, in the context of the period, and in the light of the Church's fondness for medieval guild structures, to a corporatist approach to industrial relations among Catholics. This assisted in both the elaboration of doctrines of corporatist politics and the development of a Catholic minority wing of the labour movement. In fact, in France and elsewhere, corporatism proved a troublesome asset for Catholics, as it could be interpreted to mean a variety of relationships between labour and capital, ranging from employer-controlled syndicates to forms of antagonistic co-operation.

But so long as the republican tradition of suspicion of religion remained central to French state practice, as it did throughout the Third Republic, there was no scope for corporatism becoming a national model. It remained a minority stream to which both the state and its main opponent, the increasingly socialist majority wing of labour, remained impervious. In that context, even if Catholicism had been more influential among French employers, it is unlikely that that would alone have changed politics. The post-revolutionary *lois Le Chapelier* of 1791, which banned all combinations of economic groups, whether of masters or of men, extended their influence throughout most of the nineteenth century. Even though by the 1860s business associations were tolerated far more than labour ones, this amounted only to the state turning a blind eye. It had no use itself for relations with such organizations, preferring to deal directly with individual *patrons*, and was unable to admit formal organizations to any official role (Lefèvre, 1894: 213–50; Brizay, 1975: ch. 1).

A corporatist *Staatslehre* was a highly contentious issue in France as it raised fundamental issues of the autonomy of the republic—a tradition shared by the bourgeois regime and its equally *laïque* socialist and communist opponents. Consequently it could find expression only following a victory of Catholic conservatism over both liberal and socialist republicanism. This eventually happened only with the partial and temporary triumph of the Vichy regime, which suppressed both the republican tradition and its labour antagonists; but then, with labour reduced to shadow front organizations, that state had little need for anything other than a façade of corporatism.

Only in France did the secular state triumph for so long a period after 1789, even if there were temporary interruptions. This marks that country out as decisively distinctive in a number of respects. However, similar forces were at work in the other southern European countries where modernizing forces found it necessary to take an anti-Catholic, militantly liberal-secular form: Italy, Spain, and Portugal (D. A. Martin, 1978: 36–41). While in each case both the economies and the forces of liberalism were far weaker than in France—in Portugal exceptionally so—what liberal regimes there were had still found it necessary to assert a monopoly claim to political space against the Catholic Church (Linz, 1981). Old corporatist groups retained their hold. Unlike their French counterparts they were not driven out: liberal forces were too weak to expel them. But irrespective of which side predominated, the outcome was that interest organizations (other than those which were anarchistic or socialistic) were caught on the anti-modernizing, conservative side at an important formative moment. We shall see this further in Chapter 10.

Italy was perhaps the sharpest case of the state's struggle for autonomy, as for many years the Vatican opposed even the existence of a secular state governing the peninsula. But it is more difficult to understand subsequent Italian history. It is the only one of the four southern European states that has seen Christian democracy installed as the dominant political force since 1945. If the state no longer had its mission of secularizing sovereignty, why was there no sharp reversal of practice? First, the religious question is but one force being considered, and we have yet to examine the others; but second, there are large time-lags in these historical processes. If organizations and state practices have developed in a certain way over many years, they will not easily make rapid adaptations to a changed situation. The pre-fascist legacy of Italian capital and labour was of disaggregated, decentralized action, unrelated to national tasks.

The fascist interlude in these societies did not clear away organizational realities and learned modes of behaviour; in some respects the opposite was the case. The labour movement had been forged within an inaccessible liberal state that wished to develop no relations with it, and had therefore adopted its various *modi vivendi* in response to that. The underground movement's experience of fascism only confirmed and reinforced that response. For any of the major actors to change historical track would have required strong evidence disconfirming their experience of the past. This began to occur, in France as well as Italy, from 1944 to 1947, but the international politics of the Cold War intervened and returned relations to their familiar path before major changes could be implanted. This demonstrates why nineteenth-century patterns of state–society relations have been of such enduring importance.

The emergence of Spain and Portugal from fascism is still too recent to permit easy generalization about their subsequent development. The corporatist structures of fascism were clearly façades (Giner and Sevilla, 1984: 119–20; Williamson, 1985: ch. 7). While there are interesting similarities in the role played by socialist unions as co-operative forces hostile to their communist and anarchist counterparts in Spain today and the brief Riverist episode in the 1920s, Iberian neo-corporatist attempts in the 1980s bear a closer resemblance to Britain and Italy in the 1970s than to any endogenous past. There is some evidence that employers' associations have been able to draw on old guild traditions, though after such a long interval this seems doubtful.

The heartland of the Counter-Reformation, the Hapsburg Empire, presents a paradoxical case. Catholic forces were so strong that even the opposition operated on their terms. Far from liberals seeking a breakdown of institutions, they sought incorporation within them. Most significantly, a central demand of the 1848 reformers was for the establishment of functional representation through the *Kuria* system for the bourgeoisie. The concept of functional representation itself was not challenged. The brief liberal episode of the 1860s itself took place within imperial hegemony. In its turn, the regime encouraged a certain amount of industrialization. The case thus stands at the opposite pole from France. Later in the nineteenth century secularizing forces took Germany as their model, and this too, as we shall see, provided no encouragement for breaking functional representation.

For reasons that go beyond our present scope, the legacy of liberalism in the Hapsburg lands was one of the weakest in the whole of Europe: the short reign of Joseph II in the 1780s; a few months in 1848; and the 1860s which, being followed by the great European crash of 1873 (which indeed started in Vienna), led to a set-back rather than a beach-head for subsequent liberal progress. Beyond that, the assorted lands that were ruled by the Vienna-based state, leader of the Counter-Reformation, remained a stronghold of Catholicism until the challenges from socialism and pan-Germanism at the end of the century. State and church reached their *modus vivendi* with little need for the state to assert its rights. It therefore remained unmodernized and essentially organic; it experienced no difficulty in the idea of sharing space with suitable approved interests; outside the liberal interlude of the 1860s, it had indeed an historical predisposition to base its practice precisely on such arrangements, fashioning them in a highly conservative form (Talos, 1981: chs. 1, 2).

However, as in the Latin Catholic states, a *displaced* social Catholicism was likely to generate an authoritarian corporatism of a fascist kind, and when it was so displaced in the first Austrian Republic, it did so, establishing the *Austrofaschismus* regime of the 1930s. It is important to distinguish this organic, Catholic fascism from the secular Nazism of Germany. This was made dramatically clear by Austrian history following the *Anschluß*, when the whole edifice of *Austrofaschismus* and its corporatism was abolished and replaced by the Nazi system, based on the *Führerprinzip* rather than corporatism (ibid. ch. 6). But the abiding, specifically Austrian tradition remained corporatist and space-sharing. Therefore, while Austria shares the southern European experience of authoritarian, fascist corporatism, it is distinguished from those countries in its more generalized corporatist legacy.

Belgium is the most complex Catholic case. For much of the nineteenth century after the country's independence it was governed by norms heavily influenced by French republicanism, and church–state conflict paralleled much of the French experience. These were the years of clear Walloon dominance. On the other hand, modern Belgium was differentiated from the northern Dutch neighbour from whom it had seceded mainly because of its dominant Catholicism; and it was by then an advancing *industrial* country, much more so than the Netherlands. There was therefore not the same tension between modern nation-building and

Catholicism as in Italy. Furthermore, in the earlier stage of nation-building, when the combined Low Countries had been pursuing their independence from first Spain and then Austria, the guild traditions of the great Flemish cities had been important building blocks of the new polity in a manner similar to the later German experience. It is not at all surprising that Belgium has appeared as a mixed case throughout much of our analysis.

POLITICAL FACILITATORS

While *Ständestaat* and guild structures are conventionally seen as hindrances to the realization of the 'pure' political forms of the modern nation-state, there are instances where, for various reasons, states have been dependent on the existence of such structures for their own strength. The most outstanding instance is Germany. For reasons that we shall consider again in Chapter 10, the emerging German nation of the mid-nineteenth century possessed a rich array of functional economic institutions, based on interest organizations, *before* it achieved state unity under Prussian domination in 1870 (Fischer, 1964).

The Prussian state did not confront guild structures, being part of the Lutheran pattern described below; the Catholic south had experienced an 'Austrian' rather than a 'French' or 'Italian' model of relations between state and traditional institutions; and the Hanseatic towns of the Baltic coast were guild towns that, far from presenting a backward political model, were among the most economically dynamic parts of Germany. Finally, the principalities of the Rhineland had had imposed on them a state-centred Napoleonic system of chamber representation but had 'Germanized' this by making the chambers genuinely representative, on the Prussian model. These institutions made it easy for the growing new German industry to adopt an essentially *organized* form, long before the cartellized, protectivist economy of the Second *Reich* and possibly even as a precondition for that. These interest organizations were prominent among the groups forging the new united Germany and were therefore constituent parts of it and its subsequent economic modernization.

This functionally representative character of the political legacy bequeathed to the Bismarckian state is often forgotten. To

British observers in particular imperial Germany presents the image of the strong state, of the society forged by bureaucracy at a period when British society as such was so strong that it doubted whether it actually needed a bureaucracy. We are inclined to overlook the fact that the apparent display of strength by the Prussian state was necessary precisely because forging a nation-state out of that disparate entity in the centre of Europe was no mean task; that it was economic as well as military strength that built the new Germany.

Even at the level of political thought, the strong state of Hegelian philosophy was rooted in corporate bodies within society, not within its own *potestas publica* alone as was the French republic. Such writers as Gierke saw the state as comprised of essentially moral social groupings (see the discussion in Black, 1984: chs. 17, 18). This became very mystical and reactionary and at one level eventually fed Nazi ideology. If however the 'moral' or publicly oriented character of corporate groups is removed from the world of mystique and interpreted in terms of the logic of collective action for groups with strategic capacity, it can be located in the very rationalism to which that ideology was so antagonistic.

In addition it must be remembered, as Fischer (1964) reminds us, that the 'modernism' of Germany was always based on the 'antiquated' structures of Prussian society, a hitherto backward part of Europe, and that this powerful new-model industrial state came from these rather than from the liberal roots of either England or France. Of course, if organized interests were candidate *staatsträgende Kräfte* it was important to decide which were *Staatsfreunde* and which *Staatsfeinde*; not a matter that needs be decided in a liberal polity.

Another, particularly extreme, case of state dependence on the resources of organized interests was Switzerland. This is strange, because the country is often depicted as positively 'English' in its liberalism, undirected and early industrialization, and lack of centralism. However, while the English state was concerned to establish a monopoly of control over political space, though defining that space narrowly, this was never possible in the Helvetian Confederation. Paradoxically, the Swiss state was so weak, so liberal, that it lacked the capacity to carry out its own basic functions and looked to functional interests—starting from guild structures that again faced no major politico-religious confrontation (Farago, 1986*b*). The result of this has been an indefinite boundary between state and society, leading to many apparently public functions being borne by private groups (Gruner, 1956; Katzenstein, 1984).

This happened in Switzerland because the extreme weakness of the state rendered the burden to be borne by 'gentlemen's agreements' among private-sphere élites peculiarly high. They are of such importance that they acquire a public and therefore political significance—*staatsträgende Kräfte* again. Switzerland thus provides a clear demonstration of that paradox of the liberal state, which must be both confined but *clearly sovereign within its curtailed sphere*. In the Swiss case much administration of what would elsewhere be state functions has been carried out by representative *Selbstverwaltung* groups: the liberal state–society distinction breaks down. Switzerland has had a heavily shared political space, though of a rather distinctive kind. The character of its religious and linguistic settlements was consistent with this conception of a state comprising a limited number of responsible collective social groups.

The Dutch state has been more orthodox than the Swiss, but only partly so, having been similarly dominated for centuries by bourgeois rather than aristocratic groups and therefore experiencing no absolutist phase, and having quite similar religious patterns. Both countries, along with Belgium, have therefore this distinctive legacy of a state dependent on private groups for the management of public affairs. In common also with the German Hanseatic cities, the Low Countries had inherited important guild polities that had become the base of the otherwise troubled and fragile modern political forms (Daalder, 1971; 1974; Hemerijck, 1990).

The widely noted institutions of consociationism (Lijphart, 1975) reinforce this, but several Dutch scholars have corrected the picture Lijphart presents of consociationism being the *origin* of the process. They point instead to this earlier legacy of power sharing bequeathed by the guild traditions of Amsterdam and other cities of the Low Countries. Corporate rights were stressed against the claims of the Enlightenment and absolutism (Daalder, 1971), and the accommodatory *style* was developed in the sixteenth to eighteenth centuries because of the strength of city councils in the absence of a strong central state (Daalder, 1974: 616). In all these cases—Germany, the Low Countries, and Switzerland—liberalism, however important and early, could never make the strong claims for clearly defined state sovereignty found in Britain and France.

POLITICAL NEUTRALS

Lutheran churches have historically been obedient national institutions, accepting something approaching civil-service status within the state and asserting no superior political loyalty as did the Vatican-based Catholic Church (D. A. Martin, 1978: 23). Lutheran states have therefore suffered no major inhibitions on these grounds concerning sharing political space, though this implies a noncommittal neutralism towards organized interests, not the positive organicism of the unreformed Hapsburg state. This lack of 'jealousy' reduced the extent to which these states confronted guilds and subsequently provoked the formation of highly oppositional labour movements; the spiral of mutual rejection of the French case did not apply here.

This pattern is most clearly seen in the Scandinavian countries (Denmark, Norway, and Sweden). Finland was a Grand Duchy of Russia throughout the nineteenth century, and therefore, like Ireland, was strictly speaking not a polity for our purposes, but governed by a state with a different religious base. However, for much of the period the Russians left almost intact the religious organization of Finland and its governmental structures. These were derived from the preceding five centuries of Swedish rule. Both Finland and Norway lack any native central state tradition—Norway being under first Danish and then, in the nineteenth century, Swedish rule until 1905 (Kuhnle, 1975: 7–10); but given the consonance of Lutheranism throughout the Nordic cultures, this does not present any problems for the variable under discussion.

The situation in Bismarckian Germany was somewhat different in that the south German Catholic minority was large and, left to produce its own nation-state, would probably have developed similarly to Austria. But the Prussian-German state did not encounter the same problems as republican France or Italy in relations with the Church; it was after all a Catholic minority and could not threaten to impose a political form on all Germany. The state was therefore unencumbered by a need to guard jealously its hold on political space, giving it a legacy in this regard similar to the Scandinavian.

For purposes of the present discussion the Anglican Church behaved like a Lutheran one. It never subordinated itself to the state in the same way through state bureaucracy, but relied on essentially informal, 'gentlemanly' arrangements in order to keep its peace with the English ruling class—a fact relevant to the structure of British interest organizations, as we shall see in due course. During the period under discussion, the British state had little cause for jealousy over political space on religious grounds. While discussing Britain it is also opportune to mention that Ireland was at that time completely subsumed under British authority. Unlike the Finns under the Russians, the Irish did not have an opportunity to develop a polity consistent with their religious preference.

In this chapter we have identified an initial major parting of the ways in modern European states. In four cases the character of the encounter between guild society and modernity was such as to inhibit any continuing role for organized interests during the modernization process: France, Italy, Portugal, and Spain. Five other cases had broadly neutral experiences: Denmark, Finland, Norway, Sweden, and the United Kingdom (incorporating Ireland). In four others the encounter positively facilitated a continuing role for organizations: Austria, Germany, the Netherlands, and Switzerland. Finally, Belgium is a genuinely mixed case among all forms.

10

Economic Organizations and Political Space: Historical Legacies

> Most people participated in public affairs through guilds and similar associations. But philosophers saw social personality only in terms of family and state, domesticity and formal politics. A whole range of actual socio-political life vanishes into the air whenever we look at a work of political theory.
>
> (Black 1984: 84, on urban life in the 13th and 14th centuries)

There has, since the days of the Webbs, been much debate over the extent to which modern trade-union organization built on guild traditions. The issue here is slightly different. We are interested, not so much in whether workers from guild backgrounds began to construct unions, but in the extent to which modern interest organizations were able to occupy a *political* role similar to that of their pre-modern corporate predecessors. While they did represent interests, late medieval corporate structures also helped secure order and discipline. They acted under state licence and not as purely self-standing autonomous bodies. And our interest is not limited to unions; guild members were also precursors of modern employers. Often the continuities in their organizations are stronger, *laissez-faire* states rarely being even-handed in their treatment of capital and labour and therefore opposing combinations of workers far more ruthlessly. Furthermore, guilds as such are not the sole examples of pre-modern interest organization. The whole concept of the *Ständestaat*, with its functionally arranged collective representation and denial of the bourgeois concept of individual representation, is relevant.

The point at issue is not legal form or ideology, but differing national traditions of how interests are to be dealt with. Is the use of functional organizations as co-opted agents of order something that contradicts fundamental assumptions about the occupation of public space, of legitimate boundaries between public and private, state and society? Or is it something which political élites and dominant groups find familiar and unchallenging?

Considering the matter solely in terms of time, Table 10.1 presents dates for the effective abolition or at least radical amendment of guild structures in the countries of our study, alongside an indication of the timing of the onset of the modern economy. In Austria there never was an effective abolition. In the Scandinavian countries and much of Germany it did not occur until very close to the period of organized capitalism, enabling us to postulate a continuing viability of a guild *Verbandwesen*. This was also the experience of southern Europe (Italy, Portugal, and Spain), but as we saw in Chapter 9, in those countries guild structures had become irrevocably tied to reactionary or at least anti-modern forces and were therefore not part of modernizing coalitions. Indeed, attempts at abolishing them during liberal or Napoleonic interludes happened well *before* the onset of economic modernization. Finally, in France and the United Kingdom there was, for different reasons, a real and successful onslaught on such structures.

Anthony Black (1984: 29, 67, ch. 6, 116) has described the way in which functional representation of urban crafts has remained a curiously undiscussed component of the developing constitutions of medieval and early modern Europe. Aristocratic and military interests being dominant in that history, the most important streams of theoretical writing celebrated politics as a 'pure' power activity. The achievement and maintenance of rule itself, rooted ultimately in the Weberian monopoly of the means of violence, is the central preoccupation of most major political thinkers and of the national symbolism of most states. The material interests of the populace, including matters of trade and manufacture, enter this world as interests clamouring for attention and legislative action, but they are kept at arm's length from rule itself. Craftsmen and traders are entitled to press their causes on courtiers in the lobby; they may not enter the court.

The modern *laissez-faire* tradition, while it asserted the pre-eminence of the economic, did not challenge this order at all; in fact it enhanced it. The separation of polity and economy ordained by classical liberal thought requires each to be sovereign

TABLE 10.1. *The fate of corporate economic organizations during modernization*

	Fate of guild etc. structures	Modernization
Austria	*Genoßenschaften* abolished in 1848 but reconstituted 1860s; *Kammer* never abolished but strengthened during 1860s	Well established in parts of Reich by 1880s
Belgium	Abolition of all interest organizations from 1830s	Early 19th c.
Denmark	Abolition of guilds, 1862, but rapid restoration of regulatory interest-group system that was not subsequently abolished	Late 19th c.
Finland	Abolition by Russian state, 1868	Mid 20th c.
France	Abolition, 1791	Early 19th c.
Germany	Abolition in early 19th c. in French-occupied Rhineland but later reinstituted; *Kammer* persist in Prussia and eventually influence Rhineland forms; continuing *Ständestaat* patterns in south and Hanseatic states throughout period; formal end to guild controls, 1869, but new trade and industry representation structure already in place and pre-dating German state in its scope	Mid 19th c.
Ireland	Completely under UK domination; guilds suppressed late 18th c.; no formal representative structure of business	Mid 20th c.
Italy	Napoleonic suppression followed by recovery of local cameral structures, but not as part of modernizing republican strategies	Early 20th c.
Netherlands	Suppression of guilds as part of economic liberalism, but cameral structures remain as urban basis of the United Provinces	Late 19th c.
Norway	Abolition in 1869, but continuing incorporation of functional interests in structure of government	Early 20th c.

Table 10.1. *Continued*

	Fate of guild etc. structures	Modernization
Portugal	Abolition of guilds, 1877; parts of cameral structures survive, but not part of a modernizing coalition	Mid 20th c.
Spain	Abolition of guilds, 1877; parts of cameral structures survive, but not part of a modernizing coalition	Mid 20th c.
Sweden	Abolition of guilds in 1860s; temporary replacement by formal representative structures until final abolition in 1870s, by which time new national representative structure was developing	Late 19th c.
Switzerland	Functional representation a central component of political order	Early 19th c.
UK	Guilds in decline, pre-1750; abolished, 1835; no formal representative structure of business	Late 18th c.

in its sphere; what was sought was not control of politics by economic interests, but the disentanglement of the two. Neither did nineteenth-century socialism change this approach. It saw its aim as the transcendence of workers' restriction to their economic role by giving a political dimension to their struggle. This was just as true of the Leninist separation of mere trade-unionism from socialism as of social-democratic splits between party and union.

However, beneath the surface some European political traditions also bequeathed a different approach to functional representation. Guilds and crafts governed medieval cities—setting, according to Black, standards of concern for social welfare not found again until the democratic age. These structures came to terms with monarchical rule—often, of course, siding with kings against the landed aristocracy—but nearly always accepting their junior status. In practice as well as in the world of ideas, the real enemy of functional representation was not the conservatism that tolerated its subordinate survival, but liberalism and modernism—or at least modernism in its initial

English and French formulations. Suppression of antiquated guild and cameral structures was an achievement of the spread of *laissez-faire* and of the French Revolution and its Napoleonic successor. Functional structures found themselves arrayed on the side of feudal, parcellized sovereignty and the counter-revolutionary assemblage of kings, lords, and bishops.

When some of these structures are from time to time rediscovered and celebrated it is often as part of a Romantic conservative reaction. Alongside neo-Gothic, rural, and Catholic revivalist nostalgia came the nineteenth-century concept of corporatism—conceived by writers as diverse as Hegel and Durkheim as a communitarian solution to the conflicts and problems of capitalist industrialism.

But in the most important of these writings it is an extraordinarily 'modern', innovative conservatism. Just as the Meistersinger von Nürnberg, from that doyen of guild-controlled cities, have their medievalism celebrated by one of the most revolutionary and innovative composers of the mid-nineteenth century, so Hegel and Durkheim defined a social and political order for the years after rather than before *laissez-faire* industrialism. The age of organized capitalism reached back to before the period of individualistic liberalism for its intellectual inspiration. It is similar to, perhaps even a part of, what Fred Hirsch (1977) called capitalism's dependence on a pre-capitalist moral legacy: unable to generate moral force or organizational discipline (other than cartels) itself, modern capitalism was sometimes able to preserve and build on its inheritance from earlier economic forms.

As with theory, so with reality. The 'modernism' that enabled the new Germany so rapidly to rival England and France was a modernism built on antiquated models. As Fischer (1964) notes in his study of economic interest representation in Wilhelmine Germany, it was precisely the survival of guild and cameral structures beyond the period of Napoleonic modernization that enabled Germany to tackle the tasks of late industrialism.

Our attention is therefore drawn to the connections that exist, or fail to exist, between older representative structures and industrialization. In particular we hypothesize: the greater the extent to which early structures of economic self-government survive the period of *laissez-faire* capitalism and Napoleonic reform, continuing to occupy legitimate political space, the more likely will a society be to produce during late capitalism systems of functional representation that are well organized and accept a share in governance as well as lobby for immediate interests. The facilitators from Chapter 9 perpetuate their role and are joined by those neutrals with continuing guild legacies. Other neutrals lose guild continuity for economic reasons and join the inhibitors in some, though by no means all, respects. With the exception of France the inhibitors experience a sharp discontinuity between an early, if truncated, state modernization and delayed industrialization.

CONTINUING GUILD LEGACIES

While the survival of guild structures is clearly associated with the weakness of liberalism, it is important to recognize that political liberalism came in a variety of forms, not all of them with the same hostile implications for organized functional interests as economic liberalism.

A major example of a mixed liberal and corporatist legacy is Denmark. In contrast to neighbouring Sweden, the Danish monarchy had an extensive suffrage and bore many of the hallmarks of liberalism. But this had not implied the same attack on old corporate forms as had occurred in Britain or France. There had been no large factory development; the basic modernizing thrust was in agriculture and related industries (Milward and Saul, 1977: 514). The rural liberal groups that represented this development did not want an aggressive *laissez-faire* to prosecute their interests. In fact, from the 1840s onwards the crucial unit of Danish agriculture was the co-operative (ibid. 506–9; Christiansen, 1984). And from this base developed the distinctive Danish network of state-subsidized but autonomously organized local institutions, including schools and cultural life; neither market nor state, but organization—a non-state but public arena, or shared political space.

In this context guild structures remained relatively intact (Elvander, 1974a: 366). Right into the 1890s there were major attempts to revive them (Milward and Saul, 1977: 515). As in Britain the union movement developed on a former guild basis, imparting a craft-based character to Danish unionism that today continues to differentiate it from its Scandinavian neighbours. But unlike in Britain, this structure had not been uprooted from its political role by a prolonged period of anti-combination liberalism. When industrial conflict threatened industrial order at the end of the century, Danish employers were easily able to resort to centralized, co-ordinated action at national level— admittedly a far easier thing to do in an economy as small as the Danish, but also evident of the older historical continuity. Their strategy was to engage the unions in centralized action, and persuade them to join in regulating the labour market, a move to which the Danish unions, also close to their guild origins, responded (Galenson, 1952*b*: 58–9, ch. 5). Since that period, centralized organizations of capital and labour have organized the labour market between them, with very few signs of state jealousy at this invasion of political space (ibid. 97 ff.).

This was a development very different from the more coercive forms of involvement that first drew Austrian, German, and Swedish organized capital and labour together, but the Danish Basic Agreement of 1899 that stimulated it was in many ways a precursor of the kind of peaceful neo-corporatism that would develop in those countries once the balance of power and the character of the political regime had changed in labour's favour. As such, Danish neo-corporatism, beginning extremely early, remained in a relatively underdeveloped form, with craft and general unions rather than industrial unions surviving until the present day.

Scandinavian, and sometimes all Nordic, countries are usually bracketed together in discussions of neo-corporatism, and there is some evidence of mutual imitation behind their similarities, first Denmark, then Sweden, and more recently Finland, being the exemplars. But the institutional bases from which their systems originated differed considerably, though all had a state formation that was broadly neutral towards guilds. Whereas Denmark became a liberal state relatively early, the Swedish state remained rather rigid and authoritarian until the end of the nineteenth century (Kuhnle, 1975: 14–19).

Some authors, implicitly contrasting Sweden with Prussia and concentrating on certain aspects of Swedish society, have argued that it was relatively liberal (Berend and Ranki, 1982: 30–2; Jackson and Sisson, 1976). But this neglects the pre-liberal character of the system of interest representation. As Lipset (1983: 4) has pointed out, late-nineteenth-century Sweden rivalled Germany in the rigidity of its class structure and perpetuation of late-medieval organic political forms. Not only was universal suffrage long delayed, but the state showed a marked preference for collective representation. The guilds were abolished in 1846 but were replaced by trade associations with legal powers (Galenson, 1952a: 108). Formal functional *Ständestaat* representation lasted until 1865.

Though the latter 1860s saw a more wholehearted liberalism with the abolition of both legal trade associations and the estates, this was less than a decade before the era of organized capitalism, which in fact coincided with Sweden's rapid if late industrialization. Both institutional legacy and the international economic environment of the industrial economy's *Gründerjahre* therefore favoured organized capitalism. By the early 1870s local employers' associations had started to appear (Hallendorff, 1927: 21), especially in Skåne in southern Sweden, where Danish and German examples were particularly accessible (ibid. 25). By the early years of the twentieth century employers had established a highly centralized organizational system (Ingham, 1974: 50–2; Jackson and Sisson, 1976). The combination of a tough state and organized capital had also stimulated labour's centralized organization, and the two sides of industry embarked on a mutually reinforcing spiral of organization and centralization (Stephens, 1979: 129–40). It should be noted that, in contrast with the central European states we shall consider below, the system developed more rapidly once labour entered as an important actor. This leads us to the discussion in Chapter 11.

If Denmark and Sweden embodied complex and contrasting mixes of liberal and old-corporate institutions, a much simpler case is presented by the Hapsburg territories, where state formation and indeed state maintenance made use of guilds and similar organizations. The backward, ramshackle nature of the empire had itself inhibited any thoroughgoing rationalization of absolutism, and old-corporatist structures therefore played an even greater part here than in other *anciens régimes*. As a result they exercised an extraordinary influence. An important outcome of the liberal uprising of 1848 had been, not the abolition of such structures, but the addition of the new middle classes to them (Traxler, 1982: 2). Where other bourgeoisies sought *laissez-faire*, the Austrian and Czech middle classes sought representation in compulsory *Kammer*, and secured it. Organized labour in its turn therefore made the achievement of *Kammer* representation a key demand, albeit alongside orthodox trade unions. It secured this in republican *Restösterreich* after 1918; retained it (though with radically 'rearranged' political forces) during the brief period of *Austrofaschismus*; lost it under the Nazis; and promptly reconstructed it in the Second Republic after 1945 (Talos, 1981). Austrian business also remained wedded to *Kammer* representation, to this day retaining it as more important than its voluntary employer associations.

After the crash of 1873 the reversal of liberalism meant that industrialism was viewed with suspicion by the returning conservative élite. Whereas in Prussia the state used corporate structures to engineer industrial society, in Austria they were used to control and impede it. Just as in Britain old paternalistic Tory ideas generated a concern for social welfare as a reaction against industrialism, so similar measures were taken in the Hapsburg lands. But while in Britain this occurred in a country irrevocably immersed in a liberal market economy, in Austria much remained of a corporate legacy in which the new measures could be embodied. Compulsory trade associations were introduced in 1879 (ibid. ch. 2); and several *Selbstverwaltung* institutions were established to run early welfare policies, in which it was possible for trade unions to participate (ibid. ch. 3; Traxler, 1982: ch. 1), including the state social insurance institutions set up in imitation of similar German bodies (ibid. 55, 56).

All this was happening in a non-democratic, authoritarian *Obrigkeitsstaat*. While autonomous protest action or campaigns for suffrage were seen as major threats to authority, the incorporation of labour as well as capitalist interests within corporate forms could be accommodated to a long and familiar tradition. Unlike its Danish counterpart, modern Austrian trade-unionism has transcended guild organization and established more or less an industrial pattern of organization, but it has always retained from the guild period the concept of organizational representation as an aspect of public regulation. Even while confronting the late-nineteenth-century Hapsburg state or the increasingly catastrophic First Republic, organized labour's claim remained fundamentally a bid for a share in the management of the state (Talos, 1981: chs. 3, 7). This helps explain the long-recognized paradox of Austrian socialism, which seemed to be at once the most Marxist and the most reformist of the Continental labour movements. The anti-liberal authoritarianism of the old regime predisposed towards a revolutionary strategy; but the curious way in which that same regime provided some space for limited and state-regulated organized-interest representation gave something very different from revolutionary transformation to aim for.

One can contrast this with France, where the state remained highly involved in economic affairs, indirectly and unwillingly encouraging a politicized *ouvriérisme*, but resisted formal incorporation, leading to a more thoroughgoing Marxist rejectionism within the majority wing of labour. One can also contrast it with Britain, where a non-interventionist state tolerated union growth of a non-formal, non-participative kind, making possible a unionism that rarely had to make explicit any real choice between opposition to the system and participation within it. If French labour became the main Western representative of orthodox Marxism, and British labour of its own form of liberal socialism, the distinctive innovation of *Austromarxismus* in the inter-war years was the model of the participatory economy, with proposals for workers' councils governing industry from the plant level to the national economy (Bottomore, 1978: 23–30, 38–41). Acceptance of the need to develop such institutions in a *Junktim* with existing capitalist and managerial forces may have been seen in theory as a temporary pragmatic necessity given the prevailing balance of power, but over the years that changed imperceptibly into a more permanent acceptance.

The state based on Berlin eventually proved far more successful than its older Viennese counterpart in securing domination of Germany, largely because of its own more modernized, rationalized bureaucracy. However, although it was Prussian rationalism that had excited the admiration of French *philosophes* dispirited by the structure of their own *ancien régime*, the Prussian state ironically incorporated apparent anachronisms that disappeared from post-revolutionary France. As we saw in

Chapter 9, initially a state in search of a society, Prussia absorbed existing forms of political order into itself in order to gain a structure and legitimacy; at least within its Protestant lands it had no fear of incorporating older institutions. Thus the aristocracy was incorporated into the bureaucracy in an almost Russian manner, and guild and corporate structures were absorbed rather similarly to the Hapsburg pattern (Rosenberg, 1958).

But if Austrian conservatives sought to restrict industrialization, the Prussians successfully sought to unify Germany through it. As is well known, the country developed a new model of state-sponsored industrialism, using tariffs, cartels, and bank finance to produce it (Milward and Saul, 1977: 28 ff.). A coalition of manufacturers in heavy industry (especially armaments) and bankers gathered around Bismarck's government, making industrial politics central to German public life in a manner not previously known anywhere. This was especially important after the 1873 recession and the onset of a new defensiveness and avoidance of risk. It is important to recognize that this was not a system of pure state direction; much detailed work was left to the cartels as associations of interests (Maschke, 1964). The German state was authoritarian, but it shared political space with approved organized interests.

While liberalism was a slightly stronger force in Prussia than in the Austrian empire, it was far weaker than in France or Britain, and, again as in Austria, was state-dependent. Guild and corporate structures were never fully abolished, and the regime, lacking both a bourgeois conquest of power and a need for assertive secularism, never found it necessary to establish a clear state–society distinction. Here too we therefore find *Kammer* of the new middle classes that eventually became *Kammer* of modern industry and commerce, and a willingness to incorporate functional interest representation provided it was separated from liberal democratic forces. Of course, labour was marginalized within this structure, but even at this early stage one gets some glimpses of how the fact of an organized capitalism encouraged a tightly organized bureaucratic labour movement. The motive for developing in this way was oppositional; if capital and the state thus expressed their strength, labour must too. But once such organizations were developed they were in a position to take advantage of the chinks of representational opportunities presented by the German state. For example, the local sickness funds, established under Bismarckian welfare policy, were run by elected boards. From 1889 the social-democratic trade unions began to run slates of candidates for these, and—thanks to their organizational resources—soon came to dominate them, affording the unions a new and important base within the official structures (Heidenheimer, 1980: 8, 9). This provided a model of formal, organizational incorporation that, similar to and indeed developing mutually alongside the Austrian case, stimulated late Weimar plans for a council-governed economy among German social democrats and eventually the *Mitbestimmung* model of the contemporary German economy. It is not surprising that the German labour movement was second only to the Austrian in the ambiguity of being concurrently Marxist and incorporationist. It is also remarkable that, while somewhat similar institutions were initiated in France (Lorwin, 1952: 337), they developed nothing like the same importance. French labour organizations lacked the resources to exploit them in the same way, and a major reason was that the institutions of the Third Republic had given them little incentive to acquire them.

In Switzerland, in the absence of a state able to carry on the usual range of public functions, business associations of various kinds were formed in order to pursue them, and since this had to happen from early on in the industrialization process, the connection with guild legacies was strong (Gruner, 1956). The facilitative character of Swiss state formation therefore runs neatly into the question of economic organization. Despite their relative decentralization, these organizations could not become mere special-interest lobbies; they simply had to take on public tasks and therefore public responsibility. In so doing, argue several authors, Swiss organizations in practice have acquired an informal and rather exclusive pattern of élite coherence amounting to a *de facto* centralization (Kriesi, 1982). Although an early industrializer and ostensibly an extreme *laissez-faire* case, Switzerland therefore possesses a strong tradition of organized interests—precisely because of, not despite, the state's lack of functions.

The Netherlands is a weaker version of the Swiss or northern German case. As Daalder (1971; 1974) has described, the United Provinces secured their unity and integration by building on a number of political traditions, including those of the great Dutch merchant cities. These had maintained a guild-like polity much like that described by Fischer for the Hanseatic states. Indeed, this is more than an analogy; the northern German and Dutch merchant city states were part of the same urban economic and political world that developed relatively modern patterns of administration within that part of northern Europe where the development of modern nation-states lagged behind. Eventually these guild structures became obsolete and a drag on the production of a modern economy, but by that stage a general *Verbandwesen* had become entrenched in Dutch political practice and was in any case about to inform the combination of *verzuiling* and élite co-operation that was to be the Dutch solution to religious conflict from the mid-nineteenth to the mid-twentieth centuries. As Smith (1988) remarks, and as earlier in Germany, forms of politics that were initially labour-exclusive during the inter-war years could become labour-inclusive once the balance of power had changed. The organizational style remained relatively constant.

EARLY INDUSTRIALIZERS: FREE-MARKET LIBERALISM

The paradigm case in this category is the United Kingdom. That there was a strong continuity between guild and union organization in Britain is, *pace* the Webbs, now well established (Fox, 1985: esp. ch. 1), though links with modern organizations of employers remain relatively unexplored. But our main interest here is in any legacy of the guilds as delegated polities. The situation is not straightforward. On the one hand, much of this role was entirely lost. First, British unions (and, to a far lesser extent, combinations of employers) experienced their equivalent of the Le Chapelier laws in the form of the Combination Acts.

Although the full force of this exclusion lasted only twenty years, the concept of organized interests being essentially outside the Common Law endured, in effect, until the 1970s. A particularly important moment in the development of United Kingdom industrial-relations institutions was the Trade Union Act of 1871, which made the historically important decision to embody trade-union rights in the negative form of immunities rather than as

positive rights, on the grounds that to grant rights to organizations would impugn the essential individualism of the Common
Law. This is significant in demonstrating how alien to English
liberalism was the idea of co-opting organizations as components
of public order. The great Trade Disputes Act 1906 reinforced
the implications of the immunity approach (Wedderburn, 1986:
16–38). Although from that time on British governments began
to consult with industrial interests, including those of labour,
and sought to co-opt them to the support of government objec-
tives, this was by now taking place on the basis of well-founded
decentralized and non-responsible organizations. The main
historian of these events in Britain advisedly and carefully
speaks solely of the 'corporate bias' of policy, not of corporatism
(Middlemas, 1979).

In addition to this essentially ideological component in the
birthplace of *laissez-faire* and liberal individualism, a discontinuity between guilds and both modern employer-association
and union practice was ensured by the exceptionally drawn-out
character of English industrialization. The period of organized
capitalism after the 1870s was widely separated in time from
the high period of guild organization. Therefore, while English
unions as local bodies of craftsmen, or employers' associations
as local groupings of price-fixers, were able to build on guild
traditions and establish an impressive level of *organization*,
these groupings lacked any political role and hence any centrip-
etal tendency in them and in the state itself remained weak
(Vickerstaff and Sheldrake, 1989). This set the pattern for what
has become the most prominent characteristic of British interest
organization: decentralization and reluctance to become involved
with the state.

On the other hand, these organizations were not pure pressure-
groups in the style of American lobbies, nor did they possess
the extreme oppositionalism of many French interest groups,
confronted, as the latter were, by a powerful and inaccessible
state. In Chapter 9 we saw the early British state as neutral rather
than inhibitive towards organized interests. For most of the nineteenth century it retained its oddly informal character, reflected
in such institutions as the voluntary magistrature and the role of
the élite London clubs as private places where public business
was transacted.

This provided a certain mixing of state and society, a phenomenon achieved in many societies through various forms of corporatism, but attained here through informal, personal, 'gentlemanly' arrangements, very different from the formal organizational relationships developed under organized capitalism proper. This gentlemanly code, which enjoined a certain restraint on the maximization of immediate self-interest for the sake of maintaining a wider unity, was eventually opened, at the margins, to the representatives of organized labour. In this way it has been a mild functional equivalent for corporatism, and in the longer term probably served by its very strength to inhibit the development of corporatism of a more formally organizational kind. This constitutes another chapter in the paradoxical story of the emergence of industrial Britain: the nation that invented industrialism but underwent the process more slowly and reluctantly than most of its imitators; the society that first developed contractual, individualistic liberalism but ringed it around with quasi-aristocratic norms and gentlemanly restraints (Wiener, 1981).

As noted earlier in this chapter, the general European guild nostalgia of the 1870–1914 period might be seen as an aspect of this (see such works as Penty, 1906; Hobson, 1914; Cole, 1917 and 1920). But whereas in Germany this was linked to institutions that related to how the modern economy was really working, in Britain it remained a romantic byway, as the fate of Cole's guild socialism within the labour movement quickly showed. There is also an instructive contrast with the Swiss, who placed a similar weight to that of the English on 'gentlemen's agreements', but in a context where these were, as we have seen, required to assume national responsibilities.

Britain is the only case where assertive free-market liberalism appeared unalloyed as the force dissolving pre-modern corporate forms; it is the country where the 'parliamentary parenthesis' was both more early installed and more enduring than anywhere else in Europe. In France and Belgium, as has been noted, this force was *supplemented* by the inhibiting effect of the church–state split. In the other neutral and facilitating countries it was *offset* by corporatist continuities.

French liberalism had somewhat different preoccupations from British, being relatively more concerned with protecting the autonomy of the secular state and its political space from the Catholic Church, as discussed in the previous chapter, than with economic themes. However, abolition of the guilds was also seen as part of the construction of a liberal economic order. The *lois Le Chapelier* of June 1791 discussed in the previous chapter started the process of placing *syndicats* of workmen and, to a lesser extent, capitalists beyond the pale of the law. Such legislation was later reinforced by the Code Napoléon, which imposed a distinctively French state-guided liberalism wherever France exercised authority (Milward and Saul, 1973: ch. 4). While the Empire restored many *ancien régime* institutions, it did not restore the right to associate (Lefèvre, 1894: 215). Even though the law was often only haphazardly applied, especially in the case of employers (ibid. 227 ff.), there could be no question of such organizations sharing authority with the state.

By the 1870s there had been some change: on the labour side the *bourses de travail* were established as odd but imaginative combinations of labour exchange, club, and embryonic trade unions (ibid. 265; Shorter and Tilly, 1974: ch. 2). But these were kept at arm's length where any wider functions were concerned. By the time they formed a national federation they had become fiercely anarcho-syndicalist (Shorter and Tilly: 166–7; Reynaud, 1975: ch. 3). It is indicative of French liberalism that, although the right to strike was recognized in 1864, unions as such remained illegal until 1884; organized interests were even more difficult for the French Republic to accept than overt protest (Lorwin, 1952: 318). Even employers organized only locally and for *ad hoc* purposes, such as opposition to a tax (Reynaud, 1975: 33; Gillet, 1966: 200), and formed no national organization until they did so under government prompting in the wake of the First World War (Shorter and Tilly, 1974: 33–6). Until the exigencies of that war, French governments had little need for capitalist organizations. The country had settled into her long period of relative economic stagnation, a combination of financier liberalism, peasant agriculture, and family businesses. This was not organized capitalism.

Some forms for such organizations had long existed. The original Napoleonic system had installed compulsory chambers of commerce in France and Italy (Maier, 1981: 40–1). But whereas in Austria and Germany such bodies came to play a considerable part in the organization of capital and as intermediaries between state and business (Fischer, 1964), the French state had little use for them, and capitalists did not use them for much beyond local activities. Just as the Crédit Mobilier had been invented in France but was used far more extensively in countries engaged in a more determined industrialization (Landes, 1956), so French interest representation structures remained undeveloped.

There were elements of the French model in Belgium. As we saw in Chapter 9, Catholic doctrines were able to climb to prominence through far more peaceful means here than elsewhere, though it is doubtful whether this provided a genuine continuity of organizational form. Unlike much of Catholic Europe, Belgium was not a backward area. Its economic history more closely resembles that of Britain, and though its liberalism was of the aggressive secular variety, the most important force in eroding its corporate traditions was the great lapse in time between the onset of industrialization and the arrival of organized capitalism. Despite the economic stagnation of much of the nineteenth century, this latter point also applies to France.

LATE INDUSTRIALIZERS WITH LIBERAL MODERNIZERS

The remaining countries whose position after the Reformation, later church–state struggles, and secularization tended to inhibit the growth of modern interest organizations were all late industrializers. In Italy the guilds were not finally abolished until 1864 (Adams, 1952), but their legacy was of little use to the architects of the new nation, being organized not only around Catholic institutions but also within the fragmented polity of pre-unification Italy. The secular state had little interest in or connection with such organizations, a fact reinforced by the discontinuity between this modernization of the Italian polity and the continued backwardness of the economy. By the 1890s the Italian state, unlike the French, was engaged in a determined attempt to induce rapid industrialization with the help of groups of capitalists in the north (Milward and Saul, 1977: 255 ff.; Sellin, 1974). By then, too, Catholicism and the state had effected something of a reconciliation. But it is remarkable how ineffective this was in establishing a model at all resembling the German case discussed above, especially when it is recalled that at this period Germany and Italy, as the two recently unified large European states, had much in common. Partly the explanation lies in the extreme regional differences between the north and the backward south. But also relevant, and contrasting with Germany, is the absence of continuity with the past produced by the abrupt break of Risorgimento liberalism. A turn to corporatism, albeit a false, authoritarian one, had to await the rise of the undemocratic right in the 1920s. Meanwhile workers' organizations acquired their familiar fragmented character and employers' bodies worked clientelistically.

Economic backwardness also helps explain Spanish and Portuguese developments. The brief liberal episodes saw a discontinuity between the modern state and old corporate forms at a period before the representational needs of an industrial economy had made themselves felt (Berend and Ranki, 1982: 35–9). Medieval forms of interest organization were eventually interpreted by authoritarian forces of the right, and the stage was set for the fascist-corporatist period. It is necessary here to distinguish between the Italian and Iberian cases. Mussolini's fascism was in several respects a genuinely modernizing force, and although the fascist corporations were largely bogus, they were aimed at reconciling economic modernization and hierarchical social forms. Salazar and Franco were more concerned with ensuring that any modernization that did take place would be contained within traditional hierarchical forms; but they were in no hurry to assist that modernization (Linz, 1981; Williamson, 1985: 105–6). When advanced industrialism finally began to affect the Spanish economy in the 1960s the corporatist structures proved to be irrelevant (Perez-Diaz, 1987). Some Spanish observers (e.g. Martinez-Alier and Roca (1988) and Giner and Sevilla (1984)) speak of a continuity 'from corporatism to corporatism' between Francoism and late twentieth-century Spanish social democracy. But, apart from ignoring the bogus nature of most of Franco's institutions and the crucial shift from authoritarianism to democracy, such an account fails to notice the absence of any real organizational legacy between the periods.

EUROPEAN NEW NATIONS

Three countries—Ireland, Norway, and Finland—were neither autonomous nation-states nor at all industrial during the crucial decades. Ireland and Finland did not achieve independence until 1921, from Britain and Russia respectively; both had to undergo violent struggle to achieve autonomy, and both subsequently endured civil wars. Norway's path was much easier. Although the country had been a Danish and then a Swedish colony, it enjoyed considerable autonomy in domestic affairs during its final century of Swedish rule, little struggle was needed to secure independence, and the transition was achieved without domestic conflict. How did the institutions eventually established by these states relate to the issues of shared political space discussed here? As new-born states did they provide real examples of institutional *tabulae rasae*?

When Ireland eventually secured independence it did so under a regime that resembled Spain and Portugal in its commitment to maintaining a Catholic, rural society (Brown, 1981: ch. 5)—though in this case within a democratic polity. But Ireland's political, legal, and associational institutions were deeply coloured by the British past, and despite autonomy from Britain being one of the main motivations of Irish political life, very little has been done to disturb that legacy over the years. The crucial Trade Union Act of 1871 remains the origins of Irish trade-union law, supplemented by the other English Acts of 1906 and 1913 (Boyd, 1972: 68). Also, many Irish unions are autonomous local branches of British unions.

Given Catholicism's virtually unchallenged position, one might have expected some development of Catholic corporatism, and there have been attempts at that. During the 1930s the quasi-fascist blue-shirt movement developed the classic corporatist policies and rhetoric, but this had little resonance in the Irish context (Brown, 1981: 160 ff.). Around the same period, and lasting well into the 1940s, Irish governments tried to encourage a nationalist, Catholic union confederation to rival the existing British-linked organization—with some success as we saw in Chapter 6. But this too collapsed. The prevailing reality of British procedures and ways of treating political space proved a far more substantial guide to everyday practice than any idealized but unrehearsed Catholic models.

The institutional inheritance of independent Finland was neither Finnish nor Russian, but Swedish. Apart from some late attempts at Russification, the Tsarist state had allowed the Grand Duchy to retain the administrative system of its previous centuries of Swedish rule. As in Sweden, this included a *Ständestaat* structure that lasted down to 1906, though guilds had been abolished earlier. There was therefore nothing in the Finnish legacy to encourage state jealousy towards political space; and neither the country's extreme economic backwardness nor the need for unity in the independence struggle encouraged any liberal challenge. Not being present on the historical stage during the crucial late nineteenth century, the Finnish state was not endowed with a particularly powerful legacy for dealing with organized capitalism, but one can descry an incipient corporatism waiting in the wings. This has come into its own in far more recent times, as we have seen in previous chapters (Helander, 1982; Helander and Anckar, 1983).

Norway was not dominated by Swedish institutions, but was able to develop autonomously to the extent that it had a more liberal and participative political system than the dominant power. With no local aristocracy and no *Ständestaat*, it had many of the elements of a liberal system. However, as in Denmark, this was the liberalism of small farmers. They were not concerned to develop the *laissez-faire* state; indeed, the partly autonomous local Norwegian state was a symbol of the country's identity. That state was itself, throughout the long 1680–1880 period, an administrative, civil-servant dominated one (Olsen, 1983: 122), with a strong tradition of seeking the advice and administrative participation of various functional interests (Kvavik, 1976: ch. 4). The society itself was a segmented one, its overall unity masking certain structured divisions through institutions not unlike Dutch *verzuiling*: co-operative élites and segregated masses (Eckstein, 1966: 51–63; Kvavik, 1976: 60, 61).

In this context the small firms that developed in the 1880s prior to Norway's later full industrialization easily formed trade associations, and the guilds had not been abolished until 1866 (Galenson, 1949: ch. 4). However, it was not until the extraordinary period of industrial conflict in the 1920s that these institutions were called upon to cope with major problems of organized labour. When they did, Norwegian institutions quickly established a centralized system for regulating the labour market, with few problems of jealousy over political space on the part of this administrative rather than parliamentary state.

Neither a French nor an English model of aggressive anti-corporate liberalism existed in this former dependent territory on the European periphery; nor was there any strong pressure to tight organizational incorporation on Swedish lines. There was a corporate bias in the easy access to past guild traditions and the character of the administrative state, but the eventual establishment of the Norwegian Basic Agreement in industrial relations in 1935 appears as much as a result of the new rise of organized labour as of earlier historical determinacy.

Through this chapter and the previous one, some national institutional legacies have appeared to inhibit the occupancy of political space by organized economic interests; others have either positively facilitated such occupancy or at least have not obstructed it, enabling governments and interests to turn to such a mechanism at moments presenting major problems of social and economic order.

All those countries whose religious legacies were hostile to political space-sharing (France, Italy, Portugal, and Spain) reinforced that state tradition, mainly because of liberal suspicions of guild forms in these countries, but in France and (very ambiguously) Belgium also because of a prevailing liberal economic doctrine. The 'neutrals' have in most cases become positive facilitators (Scandinavia) because of the compatibility of their guild traditions with modernization or have (perhaps in the cases of Finland and Sweden) at least remained neutral. The exceptions are Britain (and by derivation Ireland) where *laissez-faire* policies were so strong. Those with favourable earlier bases saw these reinforced (the Hapsburg and Hohenzollern empires and the Dutch and Swiss republics).

11

Pathways to Twentieth-Century Industrial Politics: The Social-Democratic Contribution

... the apparently growing needs of Western capitalist firms for collective, non-appropriable production factors, like a rich supply of high and broad functional and extra-functional skills, opens up political arenas where corporate self-government of social groups may be a superior mode of regulation compared to both state intervention and the free market. Why else should there be such a widespread interest in almost all Western countries today not only in workplace-based industrial training but also and simultaneously in trade union involvement in the governance of training systems? Democratic corporatism may have a future after all ...

(Streeck, 1989: 103)

The discussion in Chapters 9 and 10 explains why basic patterns of functional representation as they affected employers and industrial interests were, as we discovered in Part II, more or less set before the onset of the First World War. There may subsequently have been dramatic changes through the installation of dictatorial regimes or in wartime, but the general hypothesis can be sustained that, barring crises involving exceptional levels of state activity, the role of organized *business* interests in political space will vary little.

The fascist and Nazi upheavals that have been the main drastic regime shifts affecting western European countries during the twentieth century did not affect the long-term approach of states to such interests. In the fascist cases superficial corporatist structures were erected on top of or in place of weak existing ones, so the eventual decline of fascism simply left behind a legacy of continuing prevailing weakness. Élites in countries occupied by Nazi forces treated the occupation as a kind of historical parenthesis, resuming their earlier patterns after the invaders had left. In Germany itself there was a complex combination of parenthesis and continuity. The Nazi regime was ambiguous towards organized interests: its propaganda both condemned the *de facto* corporatism of the Weimar republic and lauded that of Mussolini's Italy; its practice was to crush representative bodies in favour of the *Führerprinzip*, but also to make use of business organizations.

The more indelible change wrought in the twentieth century has been the role of labour within functional representation in many countries. The period immediately after the Nazi defeat was, at least temporarily, of major importance in this process. But this was only one of several moments during the era under review when major change occurred on this particular variable. Indeed, it is the accommodation of labour to representative structures that comprises the thoroughly new element making itself felt during the twentieth century. In general one can assert that, often after some periods of conflict, some of it extreme, labour organizations join the system of representation along lines already established. Where business representation has been fragmented and more geared to lobbying than to administration, labour has had little incentive or opportunity to be otherwise. Where capital's organizations were strong and disciplined, labour also had to adopt such a pattern if its organizations were to flourish. Where states were already oriented to sharing political space with employer organizations, legitimating labour as a national interest within a democracy usually involved a similar recognition, albeit on a narrower range of issues; where guild traditions extended into the period of organized capitalism, labour's organizations shared the same legacy.

However, in some instances it is possible to see a distinctive new twist being imparted to the whole structure by the organization of labour. Many commentators have observed that employers organize in response to employees, that is, that unions take the lead in organization of the labour market; while employers might find it *easier* to organize than labour, they have less *need* to do so if an individualized labour market is working well for them. Capitalists being *per definitionem* competitive, they combine only under exceptional circumstances.

This conventional account contains important elements of truth. As the account in Part II showed, formalized employers' associations, especially national confederations, usually post-date the development of significant trade unions. However, our account has also shown (1) that capitalists had often organized for trade representation, foreign trade, training arrangements, etc., well before either their own organization for industrial relations or that of trade unions; (2) that these structures often guided the development of subsequent industrial-relations organizations on both sides; (3) that there has been considerable national diversity in the extent and type of this early organization; and (4) that the cases of strong organization that we have encountered remind us that the conventional model of 'non-associative' capitalism is heavily based on British, American, and southern European cases and does not apply to northern Europe or the Alpine countries.

Indeed, Scandinavia, which is where labour's role ended by being the most determinative, started with employer-led organizational drives (Hallendorff, 1927: 25, on Sweden; Lafferty, 1971: 188, on Norway; Lanzalaco, 1989: 74, 75, on the primacy of *trade*-association organization among employers in this part of the world). Fulcher (1987) points to precisely this point in criticizing 'social democratic' explanations of the origins of corporatism.

These explanations are those discussed in Parts I and II under that title or as 'Scandinavian' theories. We need here to set them in perspective. The variable is a secondary one. Where capitalism was already of an organized type, the rise of social democracy—once it had passed the crucial threshold of legitimacy—was likely to lead to a considerable intensification of such trends; where capitalism was more pure *laissez-faire*, social democracy did not make much difference.

In fact, the causal relations are intricate. John Stephens (1979) has already discussed the way in which labour movements often centralized themselves in order to make political progress and develop national electorates and policy-making capacity. He concentrates on the Swedish case and, like so many observers, on the leading role of Swedish social democracy in producing this system. He omits the part played by the employers' confederation, the SAF, in cajoling a reluctant union movement into increased centralization—centralization that eventually served, as Stephens rightly argues, to strengthen the grip of social democracy.

An ironic story, and one with even further twists. A powerfully organized capitalism might well be one that uses both its organizational might and concomitant political influence to exclude labour and break its organizations. In both Sweden and Germany this was the position of heavy industry, in particular steel and metal-working, in the late nineteenth century, while other employers, including those in middle-sized companies, were far more willing to embrace collective bargaining. But once heavily organized capital of the former type concedes labour's place, it is likely to encounter a powerful and integrated labour movement, with which, to return to the logic of Chapter 2, it can integrate only by going the full distance to neo-corporatism, since any institutionalization of conflict on a disaggregated collective-bargaining model is necessarily transcended by capital's own situation. Sweden had reached this position by the early twentieth century, after the metal employer's organization Verkstad had joined SAF and accepted the logic of labour's role. Subsequent strengthening of social democracy intensified these trends. In Germany the steel- and metal-working employers' reluctance lasted considerably longer, eventually with grim consequences, until a not dissimilar set of structures emerged (building on abortive Weimar examples) after the Second World War.

An important distinction that emerged towards the end of Part II was that between Germany, the Netherlands, and Switzerland on the one hand and Austria and, in particular, Scandinavia on the other. Sharing of political space in the former group had initially been determined by the needs of state building: organized interests were valuable in the construction of the polity, and during the crucial period of state formation this meant primarily organizations of industrialists, crafts, and farmers, not modern industrial labour. In the latter cases, especially the 'neutral' Scandinavian states, important initiatives in political space-sharing were launched during the twentieth century as part of an attempt to resolve economic problems that had a major labour component; organizations of labour loomed large in the central political question of these societies. Behind this lies a further point. In the former group nation-building had been rendered difficult by religious and cultural heterogeneity, and it was partly to seek a unity despite this that states had called on the support of organized interests. In Scandinavia, in contrast, there had been (with the exception of the language conflict in Norway) a notable homogeneity.

Austria (along with Belgium and Finland) is a somewhat in-between case. Problems of national integration have been severe, but were eased first by the loss of the non-German lands in 1918 and second by the cultural reconciliation after 1945; Austrian labour has never quite achieved the political dominance once experienced in Scandinavia, though it has become considerably more powerful than in Germany, the Netherlands, and Switzerland.

Belgian labour has long been divided, and in any case the country has an ambiguous corporatist background. A particularly unusual characteristic in the second half of the twentieth century has been the majority status of the Catholic wing of the labour movement, imparting a unique and highly ambivalent form of labour 'strength'. Finland's labour divisions have been essentially political, over the central question of that country's geopolitical relations with the Soviet Union. This has imparted a weakness, though the general desire of Finnish political élites to model their institutions on Swedish patterns has over time considerably ameliorated labour's situation, particularly in very recent years.

There is in Europe only one case of a powerful, long-established, but decentralized unionism—that of Britain. The power of British labour did not follow Stephens's path at all; no powerful national centre developed in order to advance labour's cause. Labour's strength was rooted in the sheer size of the industrial working class, the absence of major religious conflict and the relative tolerance of nineteenth-century bourgeois rule. Disaggregated as both it and its capitalist counterpart were, British labour could only occasionally take advantage of the organizational possibilities normally associated with social democracy. As this became increasingly problematic during the inflationary years of the 1960s and 1970s, and as the industrial working class shrank in size, so British organized labour lost power. By the late 1980s the movement whose early advance and solid strength had long made it the envy of virtually all other European labour move-

ments was now looking anxiously to increased European integration to protect its threatened position. But the fact that the
British political tradition does allocate *a* role to organized labour
has kept the movement in that country largely within the collective-
bargaining tradition. Moves to *contestation à la française* have
been rare and temporary.

As Currie (1979: chs. 1, 2, 6) has shown, despite the apparent
collectivism of the labour movement, the essential individualism
of British liberalism remains a persistent theme in the United
Kingdom, even if by the 1970s that had come to mean the
individualism of small groups rejecting integration with a large
whole. Like Fox (1985), though with a very different evaluation,
Currie's implicit contrast is with Germany. Cox and Hayward
(1983), seeing unusual but accurate similarities in Britain and
France, point to the fragmentation of unions which, although it
takes a very different form in the two countries, prevents any
strong development of corporatist arrangements.

Hall (1986: ch. 4) shows how the great British breakthrough
from *laissez-faire* was Keynesianism, but that this was used
to provide government with a 'hands-off' and narrow policy
instrument that enabled it to avoid becoming entangled with
economic restructuring and other micro-level questions which
would have required a greater involvement with business associations. His main contrast is with France, where the state
worked at the micro level with selected managements, but he
notes (pp. 155–9) that France resembles the United Kingdom in
not giving a prominent role to business associations, and goes on
to contrast Germany with both in this respect (ch. 10).

In a comparison of policy-implementation processes in Sweden
and the United States (which would be similar to the United
Kingdom in most relevant respects), Elmore, Gustafsson, and
Hargrove (1986) draw attention to the importance of policy being
centralized in the hands of strong administrators for the effective
working of the Swedish tradition (and, one might add, the
German *Beamte* tradition too). But (and here we might contrast
France, which also has a strong central administration), in
Sweden interest groups are heavily involved alongside these
administrators in both policy-making and implementation.
This is a system that long antedates the rise of Swedish social
democracy. In addition, much is delegated to local bi- or tri-

partite bodies and administrative agencies (what I have in this volume called 'articulation'). Kvavik (1976) has made similar points about Norway, and there is a literature on the same lines concerning Austria, Germany, the Netherlands, and Switzerland.

Drawing on Kelman (1981), Elmore, Gustafsson, and Hargrove (1986: 225) also contrast the Swedish political tradition with the Lockeian ideal of the protection of the individual. The pre-democratic origins of the strongly administrative and collectivist Swedish *överhet* state mean that democracy takes the form, not of shaking the state free from individuals, but of domesticating it and using it for the needs of individuals. Translate *överhet* as *Obrigkeit* and much the same can be said of Austria. A major aspect of democracy in such a context is admitting unions and similar bodies to *administrative* levels of the state, and not just democratizing parliamentary assemblies.

Before leaving this assessment of relevant variables that have shaped the occupancy of political space by organized interests, it is important to compare this account with the ostensibly very different one of Peter Katzenstein (1985) who emphasizes the *small size* of corporatist cases. Small states, he argues, are at the mercy of world economic forces; to prosper they have to be competitive; and they can improve their competitiveness by concerted action of the kind that we have described as neo-corporatist bargaining and generalized political exchange. Like the present thesis, this argument is a critique of the view that full free-market competition will always be the best strategy for pursuing competitiveness. In treating size as the crucial variable, however, Katzenstein implicitly rejects my claims for the some-what arbitrary allocations of historical legacies in favour of a more functionalist approach: small states have to concert their economies or they will not survive; therefore they concert their economies.

As always with functional arguments, it is difficult to know when they are refuted. For many years Belgium and Finland did not run concerted economies; but eventually they did. Should we be more impressed by the delay, the fact that for several decades functional logic failed to have its effect, or by the fact that in the long run it apparently did? Ireland still does not have a neo-corporatist structure, but it is a very small state. Does this form an exception to the thesis? Or do we argue (1) that one day it will acquire one; (2) that it is at least currently more corporatist than the United Kingdom, the large country which its institutions frequently resemble; or (3) that Ireland is not a successful economy? And what should we say about Portugal?

How, on the other hand, do we account for the considerable evidence of neo-corporatist structures in the largest European country of all, Federal Germany? Katzenstein quite rightly stresses the weakness of its corporatist structures compared with those of the smaller countries; but they are considerably stronger than those of Britain, France, Italy, or Spain—not to mention Ireland and Portugal.

There are, however, ways in which his argument and mine can be reconciled. First, the size variable is closely related to that of centralization (or articulation) on which I have laid such emphasis. The smaller a country's workforce, the shorter the distance, institutionally speaking, from centre to periphery, and therefore *ceteris paribus*, the easier the resolution of problems of central co-ordination. Here it is worth noting the use made by German interest organizations of the country's federal structure. Second, the question of the economic openness faced by small countries and the way in which that affects their economic decision-making is similar to the present argument concerning the role of unions in the exposed sector. Small countries clearly have both an incentive to acquire neo-corporatist structures and means to ease that acquisition. They have not, however, necessarily achieved those structures without trouble or with universal agreement or at similar paces. Functional logic needs assistance from historical inclination; it is variation in the latter that has been demonstrated in the present discussion.

IN CONCLUSION

Social democracy has played a minor but distinct part in the shaping of neo-corporatist systems. Perhaps the most important aspect of the relationship is that social democracy probably depends on neo-corporatist structures for its own success. To the extent that the strength of social-democratic movements is dependent on the strength of trade unions, a social democracy that lacks the incentives for restraint provided by an effective

neo-corporatism is likely to encounter major problems of instability on the labour market. Britain in the 1970s would be the key
instance of this. France and Spain since the 1980s seem to be
examples of social democracies that, untypically, are not based
on strong unions; the absence of neo-corporatism is less troublesome to them, though it is interesting to note that their governments have sought to encourage some of its elements.

Neo-corporatism emerged from the analysis of Part II as a
form of industrial relations associated with certain kinds of
economic success. The tests applied were not rigorous; the nature
of the data being used prevented any sophisticated statistical
testing of variables. The results were however consistent with
those of the economic research cited in Chapter 1, which used
more rigorous econometric material but cruder indices of corporatism. Neo-corporatism therefore appears from the study as a
desirable form of organizing relations among employers, unions,
and governments—at least for policy-makers committed to the
right of employees to form autonomous representative organizations. There are however several important objections to such
a conclusion which need to be considered before we conclude.

First, several economic analyses suggest that neo-corporatism
may be an endogenous variable—that is, successful economies
tend to produce neo-corporatist institutions, and not vice versa.
The grounds for this argument are the common assumption that
corporatism depends on consensus, and the observation that
economic success helps produce consensus. Ill equipped as my
evidence is to tackle detailed econometric arguments, I believe
that to this particular objection I can claim a successful refuta-
tion. First, I have tried to demonstrate that, both theoretically
and historically, neo-corporatism has not depended on the prior
achievement of consensus. Second, the essential institutional preconditions of neo-corporatist systems were, as Part III has shown,
either acquired or not acquired by societies long in advance of
the economic vicissitudes of the past two decades. One can also
point out—since I make no claim that neo-corporatism is the
only system associated with economic success—that there have
been many cases of successful economies that did not subsequently develop neo-corporatist structures; or, perhaps, social
consensus.

A more difficult and serious objection is that, however desirable neo-corporatism might be, it is not easily adopted as a policy goal. Far from rebutting this argument, the evidence of this work has been to substantiate it. Most of the experiments of the 1970s in countries with institutional legacies inhospitable to neo-corporatism foundered, or at least achieved only modest success.

The fascinating exception of local and regional corporatism in parts of northern and central Italy is of the kind that proves the rule: the corporatism of the *distretti industriali* is that of the crescive, unpremeditated kind, building upwards from existing local roots typical of the earlier developments in northern Europe; it was not, by and large, the result of national strategies of political exchange. What seems to have happened is that the establishment of a vital regional tier of government in Italy since the early 1970s made it possible for existing structures of formally and informally organized interests to generate public goods and generalized exchanges, which the character of Italian national political structures had inhibited. The two important lessons of the Italian experience are: first, that we should not look only to national levels for important political initiatives; and second, that, even for essentially private-sector activities, organized interests do require an arena of politically defined public space if they are to develop mechanisms of GPE.

Of more conventional attempts at neo-corporatist imitation, only two, both involving Sweden, merit serious consideration. The first, which is unsurprising, has been Finland; the other, much less likely and extremely interesting, but unfortunately beyond our European scope, has been Australia. Following the election of a Labour Government in the early 1980s, the Australian Council of Trade Unions sent a delegation, sponsored by the government, to tour European countries to find successful models of union co-operation with government (Archer, 1991; Singleton, 1990). Despite the British origins of Australian trade unions and trade-unionists, they spent far less time in London or Glasgow than in Stockholm, returning to propose a Swedish approach to industrial relations and labour market questions (ACTU-TDC, 1987).

Both the Finnish and Australian experiments have tried, in time-honoured fashion, to take advantage of the ability to stand on the shoulders of predecessors. As we saw in Chapter 7 Swedish (or indeed Scandinavian) institutions have recently become bogged down by their dependence on the central role of the export sector and of the manual working class within manufacturing, both of which are becoming small segments of the labour force. Finnish and Australian institutions are attempting to incorporate organizations representing the whole economy within the same bargaining (and generalized political exchange) umbrella. This can of course be achieved only through a certain amount of 'artificiality', that is, of deliberate government encouragement rather than through the pursuit of long-term, self-defined self-interest by labour-market organizations. Will the appropriate institutional supports develop in response to this 'artificial' stimulus, as they once seemed to do in Belgium and the Netherlands? Or will Australia in particular discover the abiding determinism of deeper historical currents?

A third objection to neo-corporatist institutions has been that, dependent as they are on political and usually national structures, they are being made redundant by the growing autonomy of the company as an actor in industrial relations. Closely associated with this argument is the one which states that, while neo-corporatism might have been useful for the macro-level stabilization crises of the 1970s, it is less equipped for the detailed, company-by-company restructuring characteristic of the contemporary economy. These have been particularly dominant British themes, in both actual practice and in the industrial-relations literature. This national specificity is important: the change has been nothing like as radical in Germany; even in France and southern Europe there is evidence of employers wanting to build up their associational structures and relations with unions at the same time that they develop company personnel management. True, Scandinavian employers are restless at the lack of company autonomy that their national systems give them, but it is doubtful that they will want to dismantle their associational structures to the extent that has occurred in the United Kingdom. At times in the mid-1980s it seemed that Germany, the Netherlands, and Denmark were all following the 'British road', but before the end of that decade it had become apparent that these imitations were only partial.

There is however something very serious in these arguments. While it is foolish to claim that macro-economic problems and policies have simply disappeared, as much of the celebratory literature coming out of Britain seemed to imply during the 1980s, there clearly is a move to more prominence for company-level personnel policy, motivated partly by a desire by Western managements to copy Japanese practice. Unions usually dislike this, because it is at this level that employers are most easily able to define the agenda and determine the balance of power. They can also work to secure the loyalty of workers to the management view, or at least force workers to confront the demand elasticities of product markets. Since the changing character of the work-force is making it difficult for broadly based unions to internalize these elasticities at national level, it may be only or largely through workers' recognition of their dependence on market efficiency at company level that its criteria can be channelled through to unions' decision-making. A similar conclusion is reached by Dore (1990*a*) in his account of the lessons of the Japanese model: companies become sources of community—a concept close but not equivalent to identity in the language of Fig. 2.1.

This argument would seem to contradict the Olsonian logic of encompassingness. However, as we have seen from Chapter 1 onwards, the mechanistic logic of encompassingness can be valuably reinforced by such more substantive factors as the role of unions in the export sector. An influence on unions from *both* encompassingness (from above) and workers' company concerns (from below) may be one of the only ways in which unions representing the more heterogeneous work-forces of the next century will be able to participate in concerted economies. This is of course what happens in the German, Austrian, and, somewhat differently, Swiss cases. We have already discussed in Chapters 6 and 7 the complex ways in which works councils mediate between union and company concerns. Of course, German unions often complain of the constraints imposed by the councils, of their *Betriebsegoismus*; but they have accepted them as part of the structure, work closely with them, and as a result have helped build an economy of considerable strength. The Dutch unions have similar institutions at their disposal; Scandinavian labour has remoter but still serviceable analogies. They will probably have to use them if they want to adapt their systems to con-temporary and future challenges.

There is no reason to conclude that neo-corporatist structures will become irrelevant or negative. To the extent that they provide co-operative means whereby economic actors who are otherwise competing in the market can secure certain public goods they will remain of positive interest to those actors. These gains must of course be offset against any detriments to competitiveness produced by elements of cartel behaviour in the conduct of the groups concerned—such elements in turn being held in check by any effective mechanisms for encompassingness.

Less abstractly, as the completion of the European single market limits the ability of countries to improve their competitive position by imposing barriers to trade, they will seek increasing recourse to mechanisms that do not offend against EC rules but which help secure important collective goods; neo-corporatist arrangements will be among such mechanisms. Co-operation in research and development among firms *via* trade associations, where such possess the strength to provide co-ordination, is an example not necessarily involving labour's organizations. The provision of a highly qualified labour force with polyvalent skills is another, already an important component of German and Scandinavian neo-corporatism, including labour. The importance of labour skills in the economy of the future, as, *inter alia*, Piore and Sabel (1984) have discussed, alongside the advantages of inter-firm mechanisms for providing the training and retraining that such skills require (Streeck, 1985 and 1989) argues against accepting the model of 'disorganized capitalism'. It is also an issue that works effectively with a strong linkage from national confederations of employees and employers to lower organizational levels, reaching right down to company-level institutions, engaged in policy-making and administration within the delegated framework of an articulated system.

As Przeworski (1985), Matzner and Streeck (1991a), Scharpf (1990), and Streeck (1991) have argued, there was a strange misconception in economic thought in the 1970s and 1980s. Social-democratic (or more generally, anti-*laissez-faire*) economic policy was assimilated to Keynesian demand management at the macro-level. Supply-side policy was seen as the preserve of the new right and the free market. In fact, as these recent authors argue and as Swedish social democrats had long demonstrated in practice, neo-corporatist mechanisms that work at improving the quality of the labour force, and at the provision of other infrastructural public goods, address supply-side problems, go far beyond the macro-stance of Keynesianism, and can tackle some tasks beyond the reach of the free market. If neo-corporatism is conceived, as it was in the initial literature of the 1970s, as involving only macro-level incomes policy deals between governments, mass unions, and organized employers, then its role in the sophisticated economies and among the fragmented, highly skilled work-forces of the western European future is clearly, as Windolf (1990) has claimed, very limited. If however it is interpreted in the manner of the most recent theories and research—as means by which economic actors may organize themselves to secure collective and public goods not easily delivered by the free market—then it may turn out to be fundamental to the achievement of that future.

Continuity and Change

What does all this imply for the capacity of a country to amend the logic of its history, for its central decision-makers to move it out of its existing trajectory? We encounter much evidence of attempted direct imitation, not all of it by any means unsuccessful. The centralizing, modernizing, secular French state influenced—or indeed imposed its model on—Italy, Spain, Switzerland, the Low Countries, and much of Germany during and after the Napoleonic period. But the longer term impact varied. Where strong *Ständestaat* structures existed but did not resist the construction of the modern nation-state, they were influenced but far from dislodged by the French republican model. Where such structures were embedded in pre-modern economies and either unconcerned with or hostile to modern redefinitions of the nation-state, they continued in running battle with the modernizing forces, often until this day.

Later in the nineteenth century German models began to exercise a greater influence, especially over neighbouring Austria, Netherlands, Sweden, and Denmark. For our immediate purposes the crucial influence was over the role of organized interests and their structure, among both workers and employers. But in each case the German model was being introduced into what we have seen to be fertile soil. More complex was Belgium, where the unions made an explicit attempt to copy German patterns in the early twentieth century. This was, of course, favoured by the Flemish, which happened to be the more conservative, wing of the labour movement. The more radical Walloons preferred to pattern themselves on their linguistic *confrères* in France—as did, ironically, Belgian *employers*, who were at that stage primarily Walloon and who shared the French approach of rejecting relations with organized labour. By the time the Belgian state began to turn to the country's own legacy of functionalist interests, in the latter inter-war years, German examples were hardly in favour in that country, though an indirect influence may be seen in the way in which the unions had organized themselves around such possibilities.

As the original industrial society, Britain has of course been an example for both capitalists and labour organizations. However, with the exception of Ireland which is as much a case of a rather indelible colonial imposition as of genuine imitation, its organizational features have not been widely imitated within Europe. The pattern of strong but fragmented, non-encompassing labour organization was not sought after, even though Continental union movements often saw the general idea of trade-unionism as primarily British. As Sturmthal (1973) has noted, United Kingdom and United States dominance during the reconstruction periods after both World Wars led to an insistence on the primacy of the collective-bargaining approach to industrial relations—for example in the shaping of the International Labour Office in the 1920s and in the institutional recasting of western Europe after 1945. All this in turn derived from Anglo-American political traditions and the jealousy of their liberal states over the invasion of politico-administrative space by organized labour. But its effects were temporary.

Where a model of non-organized capitalism prevailed, it was based on the French pattern. Even after the Second World War when the British, including leaders of the TUC, played an important part in reconstructing institutions in some European countries, there seems to have been little imitation of British organizational forms. This applies most strikingly to Germany, where distinctly German structures quickly reasserted themselves over Anglo-American importations, even if the language of pluralist collective bargaining was adopted by the Germans themselves.

As noted earlier, Hans Slomp (1990) has identified these three main western European countries (France, Germany, and the United Kingdom) alongside the Soviet Union as the main bearers of alternative models of industrial-relations systems within Europe. The point needs some amendment: Scandinavia provides variants of the 'German' system with more powerful labour movements; the French strong state is not really representative of southern Europe as a whole; and Britain's associated cases are, with the exception of Ireland, outside Europe.

During the post-war years attempts at cross-national borrowings have continued: within Europe, French and German examples have attracted attention from time to time, though among labour movements the most prized model has been the Swedish. Looking beyond Europe there were attempts to imitate the United States or, more recently, Japan.

When can such imitation succeed? All the time actors are choosing, and usually trying to do so rationally in the sense of finding means that will bring them towards their acknowledged ends. But choice is heavily influenced by the availability of means: rather obviously, a means already to hand is more likely to be used than one that would have to be fashioned first, even if the latter is considered superior. For example, the leaders of a union movement with an internally fragmented structure may know that in order to pursue their particular chosen ends they really need an articulated structure, but simply have to do their best without it. (This would for example approximate to the position of the British, Finnish, and Italian unions in the 1970s.) Rationality demands, however, that they should be working on changing their structure, and also that if they demonstrably fail at this they should change their goals, give up the imitation of corporatism, and adjust to something attainable with the means to hand. However, the point at which a strategy must be designated a failure is rarely unambiguously discernible, and leaders with a vested interest in a particular strategy will be reluctant to admit failure.

Another constraint on choice in situations of strategic decision-making is the fact that actors rarely have adequate information, nor is it often clear that there is such a thing as adequate information. Crises apart, the best guide to correct action is the pattern that has been used in the past and whose paths are well known and understood. This might seem irrational or at least lazy from the point of view of the canons of science. But real-world policy-making is not science. Strategy X, which is new and unfamiliar, may seem to have more to recommend it than strategy Y, to which the actors in question are more accustomed; but it is doubtful that its superiority can be demonstrated beyond question, particularly in the specific local circumstances where it has never been tried before and where therefore there are unknown risks. Strategy X also carries with it the danger that, inexperienced at it as local actors are, they might make a mess of it, whereas they have a known record with strategy Y. Add to that calculation the fact that leaders will incur more criticism for pursuing a new strategy that fails than a familiar one, and one can see why familiar patterns are reinforced over time.

These arguments all testify to the power of continuity and help explain such otherwise extraordinary features as the persistence of a recognizable 'German' approach to organized interests despite the violent overthrow of three regimes and a major westward shift of geographical location of the German state during the course of the century. We can also see how patterns of behaviour persist even if the balance of power between interests changes drastically: thus Austria, the United Kingdom, and Switzerland in their different and continuingly contrasted ways 'made room' for labour organizations within structures of interest organization that had previously outlawed or ignored labour.

To find changes of style and structure we have to search hard, ignoring such temporary and failed developments as Irish, Italian, or British neo-corporatism in the 1970s. Belgium in the late 1930s is a candidate, especially when compared with the similar but highly temporary events in France at the same time. Spain since the 1980s is possibly a case, though the co-operation is very delicate and it does reproduce some clear features of the pre-Franco period. Finland has to be partly discounted because of the underlying Swedish institutional structure.

To date, despite their homogenizing impact in so many ways, multinational companies have done little to destroy distinctive national styles. If the argument in this book is correct, that differences in industrial-relations systems reflect deeper historical differences in the occupancy of political space, this is not so surprising. Will the 1992 project for a single internal market within the European Community have a more profound effect? It reaches deeper into the political process, and the EC tends to prefer neo-corporatist patterns since these give it a range of *interlocuteurs* who help remedy its popular deficit. But to date there is little sign that systematic differences of approach to the occupancy of political space are even perceived by policy-makers, let alone have become an object of harmonization. Meanwhile it does seem that the end of the road has been reached by models that rely on the shrinking manual working class to bear the burdens of securing organizational self-discipline in the interests of national economies. Any new lease of life for neo-corporatist institutions will depend on either the construction of more broadly-based labour coalitions, or on the initiative in securing the stability of an organized economy moving to the employers. The latter must imply a shift in the balance of systems towards the level of the company.

APPENDIX: SOURCES

Tables before 1990

Labour force and electoral data for all tables on the power of organized labour, 1870–1975, for all countries other than Portugal and Spain, draw heavily on Flora *et al.* (1983 and 1987). Union membership data and material on characteristics of trade-union confederations, 1914–85, for all tables on articulation of union movements and power of organized labour for all countries other than Belgium, Finland, Ireland, Portugal, and Spain draw heavily on Visser (1987), and on Ebbinghaus and Visser (1990). Tables on business organizations draw on Lanzalaco (1989). All tables on indicators of political and economic development use: for agricultural work-force, Flora (1987); for per capita GNP, Bairoch (1976); for suffrage, Flora (1983). Industrial conflict data, 1900–75, for all countries other than Portugal and Spain, draw heavily on Flora *et al.* (1987). Data on economic performance are from OECD statistics. Additional national sources used in individual tables are as follows:

Table 4.1. Institutional development of industrial relations, c.1870

Austria: Traxler (1982), esp. ch. 1; *Belgium*: Chlepner (1956), esp. 90; *Denmark*: Galenson (1952b); Lafferty (1971), ch. 5; *France*: Cerny (1982); Perrot (1974b), 74–80; Shorter and Tilly (1974), chs. 2, 3; *Germany*: Weitbrecht and Berger (1985); *Netherlands*: Windmuller (1969), esp. 8 ff.; *Norway*: Galenson (1949), ch. 2; *Spain*: Abad de Santillàn (1967); Amsden (1972), 10 ff.; *Sweden*: Korpi (1978); *Switzerland*: Gruner (1956); *UK*: Pelling (1987).

Table 4.2. Organizations of capital, c.1870

Austria: Traxler (1982), 1–4; (1986), 78 ff.; *Belgium*: de Leener (1909); *Denmark*: Bruun (1931b); Dybdahl (1982), 182 ff.; *France*: Lefranc (1976), 28–31; Brizay (1975), ch. 1; *Germany*: Berghahn (1988), 110 ff.; Fischer (1964); Leckebusch (1966), 1–35; Simon (1976), 15–20; Stegmann (1980), 195 ff.; *Netherlands*: Windmuller (1969); *Norway*: Kvavik (1976); *Sweden*: Back (1967); Galenson (1952a), 109 ff.; *Switzerland*: Gruner (1956); *UK*: Armstrong (1984).

Table 4.3. Power of organized labour, c.1870

Austria: Traxler (1982), esp. 18 ff.; *Belgium*: Delsinne (1936), ch. 1; Chlepner (1956), esp. 50, 90; *Denmark*: Bruun (1931a); Galenson

(1952), ch. 2; Lafferty (1971), ch. 4; *France*: Perrot (1974*b*), 72–84; Shorter and Tilly (1974), chs. 3, 6; *Germany*: Weitbrecht and Berger (1985), esp. 485; Müller-Jentsch (1985); *Netherlands*: Windmuller (1969), 8 ff.; Harmsen and Reinalda (1975); *Norway*: Galenson (1949), ch. 2; E. Bull (1955), 38 ff.; *Portugal*: da Fonseca (1979); *Spain*: Abad de Santillàn (1967); *Sweden*: Hadenius (1976); Korpi (1978); *Switzerland*: Gruner (1956), ch. 1; Höpflinger (1976); *UK*: Fox (1985), ch. 4; Pelling (1987), chs. 3, 4.

Table 4.5. Institutional development of industrial relations, c.1900

Austria: Traxler (1982); *Belgium*: Chlepner (1956), esp. 112 ff.; *Denmark*: Galenson (1952*b*); Lafferty (1971), ch. 5; *France*: Perrot (1974*a*), 89–97; (1974*b*), 438–46; Shorter and Tilly (1974), ch. 2; *Italy*: Barbadoro (1973*a*), 122–8, 138; (1973*b*), 84–7; *Germany*: Weitbrecht and Berger (1985); *Netherlands*: Windmuller (1969), esp. 24 ff.; *Norway*: Galenson (1949), ch. 2; Lafferty (1971), ch. 5; *Sweden*: Korpi (1978); *Switzerland*: Gruner (1956), 27; *UK*: Pelling (1987), ch. 6; Wigham (1982); Zeitlin (1990).

Table 4.6. Articulation of trade-union movements, c.1900

Austria: Traxler (1982), 63 ff.; *Belgium*: Chlepner (1956), 114 ff.; Delsinne (1936), ch. 28; *Denmark*: Dybdahl (1982), 247 ff.; *France*: Lefranc (1967), Pt. I, ch. 4; Perrot (1974*a*), 93–7; (1974*b*), 434–8; *Germany*: Albrecht (1982); Armingeon (1988*a*), 18–21; Schönhoven (1980); *Italy*: Barbadoro (1973*a*), 139–65; (1973*b*), chs. 8, 9; *Netherlands*: Windmuller (1969), 24 ff.; Harmsen and Reinalda (1975), 59–80; *Norway*: E. Bull (1955), 45–76; *Sweden*: Hadenius (1976); Kjellberg (1983), 78–80, 167–70; (1990); *Switzerland*: Gruner (1956), ch. 1; *UK*: Currie (1979), ch. 2; Fox (1985), ch. 4.

Table 4.7. Organizations of capital, c.1900

Austria: Traxler (1982), 48 ff.; *Belgium*: de Leener (1909); *Denmark*: Bruun (1931*b*); Dybdahl (1982), 182 ff.; *France*: Lefranc (1976), 28–31; Brizay (1975), 19–21; *Germany*: Berghahn (1988), 110 ff.; Fischer (1964); Leckebusch (1966); Maschke (1964), 35–44; Simon (1976), 19–25; Stegmann (1980), 158–61; *Italy*: Barbadoro (1973*b*), 161–5; *Netherlands*: van Noorden (1984); *Norway*: E. Bull (1955), 55–9; Kvavik (1976); Petersen (1950); *Spain*: Amsden (1972); *Sweden*: Back (1967); Galenson (1952*a*), 109 ff.; Hadenius (1976); Heckscher (1946); Kjellberg (1983), ch. 4; (1990); Skogh (1984); *Switzerland*: Gruner (1956), 32–43; *UK*: Armstrong (1984); Zeitlin (1990), 413.

Table 4.8. Power of organized labour, c.1900

Austria: Talos (1981); Traxler (1982), ch. 2; *Belgium*: Delsinne (1936), ch. 1; Chlepner (1956), 116–18; *Denmark*: Dybdahl (1982), 240 ff.; *France*: Lefranc (1967), Pt. I, chs. 1–4; Perrot (1974*a*), 89–97; (1974*b*), ch. 2; *Germany*: Albrecht (1982); Schönhoven (1980); *Italy*: Barbadoro (1973*a*), 122 ff.; (1973*b*), 13–16, 73–99; *Netherlands*: Windmuller (1969), 24 ff.; Harmsen and Reinalda (1975); *Norway*: E. Bull (1955), 45–7; *Portugal*: da Fonseca (1979); *Spain*: Amsden (1972), 21; *Sweden*: Hadenius (1976); Korpi (1978); *Switzerland*: Gruner (1956), ch. 1; Höpflinger (1976); *UK*: Fox (1985), ch. 4; Pelling (1987), chs. 3, 4.

Table 4.11. Institutional development of industrial relations, c.1914

Austria: Lang (1978), esp. 26–7; Talos (1981), ch. 2; Traxler (1982), esp. 48–56, 71; *Belgium*: Chlepner (1956); Delsinne (1936), esp. 306; *Denmark*: Galenson (1952*b*), esp. 97–107, 226–47; Hansen and Henrikson (1980*a*), esp. 85; *Finland*: Knoellinger (1960), esp. 45 ff.; Mansner (1981); *France*: Lefranc (1967), esp. 81–2, 186; Shorter and Tilly (1974), esp. 27; *Germany*: Heidenheimer (1980), 7–11; Ullman (1977); Weitbrecht and Berger (1985), esp. 486–8; *Italy*: Barbadoro (1973*b*), esp. 151–9; *Netherlands*: Harmsen and Reinalda (1975), 105 ff.; Windmuller (1969), esp. 45; *Norway*: Galenson (1949), ch. 7; Lafferty (1971), 188–218; *Sweden*: Korpi (1978); Kjellberg (1990); *Switzerland*: Parri (1987*a*); *UK*: Clegg (1972), ch. 6; Fox (1985), chs. 5, 6.

Table 4.12. Articulation of trade-union movements, c.1914

Austria: Traxler (1982), esp. 63, 72, 90; *Belgium*: Chlepner (1956), esp. 120; Delsinne (1936), esp. 222–54; *Denmark*: Galenson (1952*b*), esp. 24; *Finland*: Knoellinger (1960), esp. 51; *France*: Lefranc (1967), Pt. I, ch. 4; Shorter and Tilly (1974), esp. 164–8; *Germany*: Armingeon (1988*a*), 65; Müller-Jentsch (1985), esp. 375–7; Schönhoven (1980); *Italy*: Barbadoro (1973*a*), 172–81; (1973*b*); *Netherlands*: Harmsen and Reinalda (1975), 92 ff.; Windmuller (1969), esp. 29; *Norway*: Galenson (1949), esp. 15; *Spain*: Linz (1981), 369; *Sweden*: Hadenius (1976), esp. 23–30 and Appendix; Kjellberg (1990); *Switzerland*: Höpflinger (1976); *UK*: Clegg (1972), ch. 2; Fox (1985), chs. 5, 6.

Table 4.13. Organizations of capital, c.1914

Austria: Traxler (1982), esp. 101 ff.; *Belgium*: Chlepner (1956), esp. 120 ff.; Delsinne (1936); *Denmark*: Dybdahl (1982), esp. 247–50; Galenson (1952*b*), ch. 5; Vigen (1950); *Finland*: Knoellinger (1960), esp. 45; Mansner (1981); Sjöberg (1958), 14–23; *France*: Lefranc (1976), Pt. I; Reynaud (1975), esp. 33; *Germany*: Leckebusch (1966), esp. 58–60 and 125–46; Weitbrecht and Berger (1985), esp. 487; Simon (1976),

26–8; *Italy*: Barbadoro (1973*a*), esp. 161–6; (1973*b*), esp. 180; Martinelli and Treu (1984); *Netherlands*: van Noorden (1984); Windmuller (1969), esp. 46; *Norway*: E. Bull (1955), 113–19; Galenson (1949), esp. 80; Lafferty (1971), esp. 189; Petersen (1950); *Sweden*: Back (1967); Hadenius (1976), esp. 21; Kjellberg (1990); Samuelsson (1968), 209; Skogh (1984); *Switzerland*: Gruner (1956), 43 ff., 76, 108–14; Höpflinger (1976); Prigge (1985), esp. 404; *UK*: Clegg (1972), ch. 4; (1979), ch. 3; Zeitlin (1990).

Table 4.14. Power of organized labour, c.1914

Austria: Traxler (1982), esp. 63, 71; *Belgium*: Chlepner (1956), esp. 116–19; Delsinne (1936), esp. 202; *Denmark*: Dybdahl (1982); Hansen and Henriksen (1980*a*), esp. 92; Galenson (1952*b*), esp. 29; *Finland*: Knoellinger (1960), ch. 3; Nousiainen (1971); *France*: Lefranc (1967), esp. 220; Reynaud (1975), ch. 3; *Germany*: Schönhoven (1980); Weitbrecht and Berger (1985), esp. 485; *Italy*: Barbadoro (1973*a*), 172–81; (1973*b*), esp. 304; *Netherlands*: Harmsen and Reinalda (1975), 81–90, ch. 7; *Norway*: Galenson (1949); *Spain*: Amsden (1972), 14–24; Linz (1981), 368 ff.; *Sweden*: Hadenius (1976); Korpi (1978); *Switzerland*: Gruner (1956); Höpflinger (1976), esp. 92; *UK*: Clegg (1972), ch. 2; (1979), ch. 5; Fox (1985), chs. 5, 6.

Table 5.1. Institutional development of industrial relations, c.1925

Austria: Talos (1981), 130, ch. 4; Traxler (1982), esp. 111–30; *Belgium*: Chlepner (1956), esp. 318 ff.; Delsinne (1936), esp. 306–8 and ch. 33; *Denmark*: Andersen (1976); Galenson (1952*b*); *Finland*: Knoellinger (1960), esp. 68–80; Mansner (1981); *France*: Hayward (1966), ch. 2; Lefranc (1967), 271–303; Reynaud (1975), esp. 82; *Germany*: Leckebusch (1900), esp. 70–5; Weitbrecht and Berger (1985), esp. 490–6; *Ireland*: McCarthy (1977); *Netherlands*: Lijphart (1975), 108 ff.; Smith (1988), 171–3; Windmuller (1969), esp. 43 and 63–5; *Norway*: E. Bull (1955), 82 ff.; Hodne (1983), chs. 2, 3; Galenson (1949), 25–30; *Spain*: Ben-Ami (1985), ch. 8; *Sweden*: Korpi (1978); *Switzerland*: Parri (1987*a*); *UK*: Clegg (1972), ch. 6; Middlemas (1979), 68–174; Vickerstaff and Sheldrake (1989), ch. 2; Zeitlin (1990).

Table 5.2. Articulation of trade-union movements, c.1925

Austria: Traxler (1982), esp. 147–60; *Belgium*: Chlepner (1956), esp. 258–66; Delsinne (1936), esp. 222; Spitaels (1967), esp. 15–20; *Denmark*: Hansen and Henriksen (1980*a*), esp. 178–82; Jørgensen (1975); *Finland*: Knoellinger (1960), ch. 5; *France*: Lefranc (1967), 240–60, 276–8, 315; *Germany*: Müller-Jentsch (1985), esp. 376–7; Rauscher (1985), esp. 386; *Ireland*: McCarthy (1977); *Netherlands*:

Windmuller (1969), esp. 53; *Norway*: Galenson (1949); Lafferty (1971), esp. 184–6; *Spain*: Ben-Ami (1985), ch. 8; Linz (1981), 405; *Sweden*: Hadenius (1976), esp. 35–8; Kjellberg (1990); *Switzerland*: Höpflinger (1976); *UK*: Clegg (1972), ch. 2; Fox (1985), ch. 7; Zeitlin (1990).

Table 5.3. Organizations of capital, c.1925

Austria: Traxler (1982); *Belgium*: Chlepner (1956), esp. 255–6; *Denmark*: Galenson (1952b), esp. 102; Hansen and Henriksen (1980a), esp. 178–82; Vigen (1950); *Finland*: Knoellinger (1960), esp. 71–80; Mansner (1981); Sjöberg (1958), 84–8; *France*: Brizay (1975), 23–34; Hayward (1966), ch. 2; Lefranc (1976), esp. 75–95; J.-M. Martin (1983), 16; *Germany*: Leckebusch (1966), 70–5, 110–26; Simon (1976), 30–6; Stegmann (1980), 163 ff.; *Ireland*: W. Cox (n.d.); *Italy*: Martinelli and Treu (1984); *Netherlands*: Windmuller (1969), esp. 45–50; *Norway*: Galenson (1949); Petersen (1950); *Sweden*: Hadenius (1976), esp. 38; Söderpalm (1980), 16–21; *Switzerland*: Prigge (1985); *UK*: Clegg (1972), ch. 4; Zeitlin (1990).

Table 5.4. Power of organized labour, c.1925

Austria: Traxler (1982), esp. 116–31; *Belgium*: Chlepner (1956), esp. 316–18; van Kalken (1950), 175–85; Spitaels (1967), esp. 31; *Denmark*: Hansen and Henriksen (1980a), esp. 178–82; *Finland*: Knoellinger (1960), esp. 4; *France*: Lefranc (1967), esp. 223–36, 280, 315; Prost (1964); *Germany*: Weitbrecht and Berger (1985); *Ireland*: McCarthy (1977), esp. 67–73; *Netherlands*: Windmuller (1969); *Norway*: E. Bull (1955), 82 ff.; Galenson (1949), esp. 25–30; Hodne (1983), chs. 2, 3; *Spain*: Amsden (1972), 45; Ben-Ami (1985), ch. 8; *Sweden*: Hadenius (1976); *Switzerland*: Höpflinger (1976); *UK*: Clegg (1972), ch. 2; Fox (1985), ch. 7.

Table 5.7. Institutional development of industrial relations, c.1938

Belgium: Chlepner (1956), esp. 319–21; Spitaels (1967), esp. 76; Fafchamps (1961); *Denmark*: Galenson (1952b), 103 ff.; Hansen and Henriksen (1980a), 300–10; Vigen (1950); *Finland*: Knoellinger (1960), ch. 5; *France*: Hayward (1966), 13; Lefranc (1967), ch. 7; (1976), Pt. II, ch. 1; Reynaud (1975), esp. 96–7; *Ireland*: McCarthy (1977), esp. 182–3; *Netherlands*: Smith (1988), 185–8; Windmuller (1969), esp. 72–8; *Norway*: E. Bull (1955), 130–4; Galenson (1949), 175–82; Kvavik (1976), esp. 133–43; NOU (1982), 3–97; Olsen (1983), esp. 172; Petersen (1950); *Sweden*: Korpi (1978); Jackson and Sisson (1976); Kjellberg (1990); *Switzerland*: Höpflinger (1976), esp. 96 ff.; Kriesi (1986a); Parri (1987a); *UK*: Clegg (1972), ch. 6; Middlemas (1979), 174–214; Vickerstaff and Sheldrake (1989).

Table 5.8. Articulation of trade-union movements, c.1938

Belgium: Chlepner (1956), esp. 265–6; Ebertzheim (1959); *Denmark*: Hansen and Henriksen (1980*a*), esp. 178–82; Galenson (1952*b*), chs. 3, 4; Jørgensen (1975); *Finland*: Knoellinger (1960), ch. 5; *France*: Lefranc (1967), ch. 6; Prost (1964); *Ireland*: McCarthy (1977), 108–60; *Netherlands*: Windmuller (1969), esp. 84–5; *Norway*: Galenson (1949); *Sweden*: Hadenius (1976), esp. 45–8; Kjellberg (1990); Lewin (1980), esp. 31–8; Stephens (1979), ch. 5; *Switzerland*: Höpflinger (1976); *UK*: Clegg (1972), ch. 2; Fox (1985), ch. 7.

Table 5.9. Organizations of capital, c.1938

Belgium: Chlepner (1956), esp. 239–40; *Denmark*: Galenson (1952*b*), ch. 5; Vigen (1950); *Finland*: Knoellinger (1960), esp. 71–6; Mansner (1981); *France*: Brizay (1975), 39–55; Ehrmann (1957), 24 ff.; Lefranc (1967), ch. 7; (1976), Pt. II, ch. 1; *Germany*: Simon (1976), 42–4; *Ireland*: W. Cox (n.d.); *Netherlands*: Windmuller (1969), esp. 84–5; *Norway*: Olsen (1983), esp. 172; *Sweden*: Korpi (1978); Jackson and Sisson (1976); Kjellberg (1990); Söderpalm (1980); *Switzerland*: Kriesi (1986*b*); Parri (1987*a*); Rusterholz (1986); *UK*: Clegg (1972), ch. 4.

Table 5.10. Power of organized labour, c.1938

Belgium: Chlepner (1956), esp. 240–1; Ebertzheim (1959); *Denmark*: Hansen and Henriksen (1980*a*); Jørgensen (1975); *Finland*: Knoellinger (1960), ch. 5; *France*: Lefranc (1967), ch. 7; Prost (1964); *Ireland*: McCarthy (1977), 125–33, 144–9, ch. 4; *Netherlands*: Windmuller (1969); *Norway*: E. Bull (1955), 130–4; Galenson (1949); *Sweden*: Korpi (1978); *Switzerland*: Höpflinger (1976); *UK*: Clegg (1972), ch. 2.

Table 6.1. Institutional development of industrial relations, c.1950

Austria: Lang (1978), esp. 31; Talos (1981), ch. 7; Traxler (1982), 172–9; *Belgium*: Chlepner (1956), esp. 243–54, 315–20; Fafchamps (1961); Spitaels (1967), esp. 76–8; *Denmark*: Galenson (1952*b*), ch. 7; Hansen and Henriksen (1980*b*), esp. 72; *Finland*: Knoellinger (1960), esp. 94–7; Mansner (1984); *France*: Hayward (1966), 14, 15; Reynaud (1975), esp. 265–9; *West Germany*: Armingeon (1987); Bergmann (1985); Drewes (1958); *Ireland*: W. Cox (n.d.); McCarthy (1977), esp. 536–43; *Italy*: Contini (1985), esp. 191; Turone (1981), 140–68; *Netherlands*: Scholten (1987*a*); Windmuller (1969), esp. 105–76, 338–400, 435 ff., chs. 7, 11; *Norway*: E. Bull (1955), 147 ff.; Kvavik (1976), ch. 3; Olsen (1983), esp. 202–3; *Sweden*: Korpi (1978); Galenson (1952*b*); Heckscher (1946); Micheletti (1984); *Switzerland*: Höpflinger (1976); Parri (1987*a*); *UK*: Clegg (1972), ch. 6; Middlemas (1979), Pt. II; Vickerstaff and Sheldrake (1989), ch. 4.

Table 6.2. Articulation of trade union movements, c.1950

Austria: Traxler (1982), esp. 178–9; *Belgium*: Chlepner (1956), esp. 268–72; Ebertzheim (1959); Spitaels (1967), esp. 78; *Denmark*: Hansen and Henriksen (1980*b*); *Finland*: Knoellinger (1960), esp. 106–39; *France*: Reynaud (1975), esp. 100, 133–7; *West Germany*: Armingeon (1987), and (1988*b*), 30–2; Bergmann (1985); Rauscher (1985), 387 ff.; *Ireland*: McCarthy (1977), ch. 9, 267–78, 536–8; Roche and Larragy (1987); *Italy*: M. Bull (1988), 78–82; Contini (1985), esp. 197; Turone (1981), esp. 180–2; *Netherlands*: Windmuller (1969), esp. 105–67; *Norway*: E. Bull (1955), 147 ff.; Galenson (1952*b*), esp. 131–3; *Sweden*: Hadenius (1976), esp. 56–81, 123 ff.; Kjellberg (1990); *Switzerland*: Höpflinger (1976); Parri (1987*a*); *UK*: Clegg (1972), ch. 2; (1979), ch. 5.

Table 6.3. Organizations of capital, c.1950

Austria: Lang (1978), esp. 31; Talos (1981), esp. 311; Traxler (1986); *Belgium*: Chlepner (1956), esp. 256; Spitaels (1967), esp. 75–8; *Denmark*: Galenson (1952*b*), ch. 5; *Finland*: Knoellinger (1960), esp. 96–7; Mansner (1984); *France*: Brizay (1975), 71–99; Lefranc (1976), esp. 130–1; Ehrmann (1957), 125–57; *West Germany*: Bergmann (1985); Prigge (1985), esp. 400–2; Simon (1976), 47–52; *Ireland*: W. Cox (n.d.); McCarthy (1977), esp. 536–8; *Italy*: LaPalombara (1964), chs. 3, 8, 9; de Carlini (1972), 60–2; Turone (1981), esp. 184–6; *Netherlands*: Windmuller (1969), esp. 232, 258; *Norway*: Olsen (1983); Petersen (1950); *Sweden*: Kjellberg (1990); Korpi (1978); *Switzerland*: Parri (1987*a*); *UK*: Clegg (1972), ch. 4; (1979), ch. 3.

Table 6.4. Power of organized labour, c.1950

Austria: Lang (1978), ch. 5; *Belgium*: Chlepner (1956), esp. 258–91; Ebertzheim (1959); Spitaels (1967), esp. 23–31; *Denmark*: Hansen and Henriksen (1980*b*); *Finland*: Knoellinger (1960), esp. 100–39; *France*: Reynaud (1975); *West Germany*: Armingeon (1987); (1988*b*), 78–81; *Ireland*: McCarthy (1977); Roche and Larragy (1987); *Italy*: Turone (1981); *Netherlands*: Windmuller (1969); *Norway*: Galenson (1952*b*); *Sweden*: Galenson (1952*b*); Korpi (1978); *Switzerland*: Höpflinger (1976); *UK*: Clegg (1972), ch. 2; (1979), ch. 5; Fox (1985), ch. 8.

Table 6.7. Institutional development of industrial relations, c.1963

Austria: Kotthof (1985), 85; Talos (1981), ch. 7; Traxler (1982), 191–253; *Belgium*: Brande (1973); Gevers (1983); (1987); Kerckhove (1979); Spitaels (1967), esp. 76–8; *Denmark*: Hansen and Henriksen (1980*b*), 150–60; Rasmussen (1985), 393–404; *Finland*: Elvander (1974*b*), 431–4; Knoellinger (1960), 168–78; Mansner (1989); Nousiainen (1971); *France*: Hayward (1966), ch. 3; Keeler (1987), ch. 1; Reynaud (1975), ch. 4;

West Germany: Armingeon (1987); Bergmann (1985); J. Hirsch (1966), 155–88; Leminsky (1965), ch. 3; *Ireland*: W. Cox (n.d.); Lee (1989), 401–4; McCarthy (1977); *Italy*: Contini (1985); Turone (1981); *Netherlands*: Scholten (1987a); Windmuller (1969), 435 ff.; *Norway*: Kvavik (1976), ch. 3; *Spain*: Amsden (1972), chs. 5–7; Martinez-Alier and Roca (1988), 129–31; *Sweden*: Korpi (1978); Micheletti (1984); Rothstein (1985); *Switzerland*: Höpflinger (1976); Kriesi (1986a); Parri (1987a); *UK*: Clegg (1972), ch. 6; Crouch (1977), chs. 4, 11; Middlemas (1979), Pt. II; (1990).

Table 6.8. Articulation of trade-union movements, c.1963

Austria: Kotthof (1985), 85; Traxler (1982), esp. 179–83, 213–17, 252–3; *Belgium*: Spitaels (1967), esp. 30–71; *Denmark*: Hansen and Henriksen (1980b), 150–64; *Finland*: Knoellinger (1960), ch. 7; Nousiainen (1971); *France*: Reynaud (1975), ch. 5; *West Germany*: Armingeon (1987); (1988b), 65–70; Leminsky (1965), ch. 3; Bergmann (1985); *Ireland*: McCarthy (1977), ch. 9; Roche and Larragy (1987); *Italy*: Contini (1985); Turone (1981); *Netherlands*: Windmuller (1969); *Norway*: Kvavik (1976); *Spain*: Ariza (1976); Ellwood (1990); Sartorius (1976); *Sweden*: Hadenius (1976); Kjellberg (1990); Olsson (1991), 25–9; *Switzerland*: Höpflinger (1976); Parri (1987a); *UK*: Clegg (1972), ch. 2; (1979), ch. 5; Currie (1979), ch. 5.

Table 6.10. Organizations of capital, c.1963

Austria: Traxler (1986); *Belgium*: Spitaels (1967), esp. 75–8; *Finland*: Mansner (1989); *France*: Brizay (1975), 101–8; Keeler (1987), ch. 1; Lefranc (1976), 159 ff., 191 ff.; *West Germany*: Bergmann (1985); Simon (1976), ch. 6; *Ireland*: W. Cox (n.d.); *Italy*: M. Bull (1988), 78–82; de Carlini (1972), 62–74; Collidà (1972), 93–104; LaPalombara (1964), chs. 8, 9, 11; Martinelli (1980), 71–7; Martinelli and Treu (1984); *Netherlands*: Windmuller (1969); *Norway*: Olsen (1983); *Sweden*: Kjellberg (1990); Korpi (1978); Olsson (1991), 25–9; *Switzerland*: Parri (1987a); *UK*: Clegg (1972), ch. 4; (1979), ch. 3.

Table 6.11. Power of organized labour, c.1963

Austria: Lang (1978), ch. 5; *Belgium*: Spitaels (1967), 30–7, 48–71; *Denmark*: Hansen and Henriksen (1980b), 162 ff.; Rasmussen (1985), ch. 9; *Finland*: Nousiainen (1971); *France*: Reynaud (1975), chs. 4, 5; *West Germany*: Armingeon (1987); (1988b), 78–81; *Ireland*: Lee (1989), 401–4; McCarthy (1977); Roche and Larragy (1987); *Italy*: Turone (1981); *Netherlands*: Windmuller (1969); *Norway*: Kvavik (1976); *Spain*: Ariza (1976); Ellwood (1990); Sartorius (1976); *Sweden*: Korpi (1978); *Switzerland*: Höpflinger (1976); *UK*: Clegg (1972), ch. 2; (1979), ch. 5; Fox (1985), ch. 8.

Table 7.1. Institutional development of industrial relations, c.1975

Austria: Lang (1978), ch. 7; Marin (1982); Traxler (1982), 191 ff.; *Belgium*: Desolre (1981); Molitor (1978); Spitaels (1972); *Denmark*: Hansen and Henriksen (1980*b*), 345 ff.; Rasmussen (1985); *Finland*: Addison (n.d.); Helander (1984); Helander and Anckar (1983); Mansner (1989); *France*: Birsen (1978); Cox and Hayward (1983); Dubois *et al.* (1978); Goetschy (1987); Keeler (1987), ch. 1; Landier (1982); Maurice *et al.* (1982), ch. 3; Moss (1988); Reynaud (1978); Sellier (1978); Wilson (1982); *West Germany*: Armingeon (1988*b*), 165–6; Brand *et al.* (1982); Hardes (1974); Kirkwood and Mewes (1976); Müller-Jentsch and Sperling (1978); Süllow (1982*a* and 1982*b*); *Ireland*: Hardiman (1988), 163–7; *Italy*: Regalia *et al.* (1978); Regini (1981); Treu (1983); Turone (1981), 140–68; *Netherlands*: Akkermans and Grootings (1978); Scholten (1987*a*); Visser (1987); *Norway*: Kvavik (1976), ch. 4; NOU (1982), 93–9; Olsen (1983), 166, 200–5; *Portugal*: Pinto (1990); *Spain*: Amsden (1972), chs. 5–7; Giner and Sevilla (1984), 126–8, 133–6; Martinez-Alier and Roca (1987), 252 ff.; Perez-Diaz (1987), 222 ff.; *Sweden*: Korpi (1978); Micheletti (1984); Rothstein (1985); Pestoff (1983); *Switzerland*: Höpflinger (1976); Katzenstein (1984); Kriesi (1986*a*); Parri (1987*a*); *UK*: Crouch (1977), chs. 5–10, 12–14; (1978); (1982*a*); Middlemas (1990).

Table 7.2. Articulation of trade-union movements, c.1975

Austria: Lang (1978), ch. 9; Marin (1985); Traxler (1982), 191 ff.; *Belgium*: Desolre (1981); Molitor (1978); *Denmark*: Hansen and Henriksen (1980*b*), esp. 162–4, 316–24; Rasmussen (1985); *Finland*: Addison (n.d.); Koskimies (1981); Lilja (1983), esp. ch. 3; *France*: Cox and Hayward (1983); Dubois *et al.* (1978); Landier (1982); Maurice *et al.* (1982), ch. 3, 286–8; Reynaud (1975), ch. 5; *West Germany*: Armingeon (1987); (1988*b*), 42–5, 65–70; Bergmann *et al.* (1975); Bergmann (1985); Brandt *et al.* (1982); Maurice *et al.* (1982), ch. 3, 288–90; Müller-Jentsch and Sperling (1978); Müller-Jentsch (1985); Streeck (1982); *Ireland*: Hardiman (1988); Hillery (1981); Roche and Larragy (1987); *Italy*: Regalia (1986); Regalia *et al.* (1978); Turone (1981), ch. 4; *Netherlands*: Akkermans and Grootings (1978); Visser (1987); *Norway*: Kvavik (1976); NOU (1982); *Portugal*: Pinto (1990); *Spain*: Amsden (1972), 5–7; Roca (1987); *Sweden*: Kjellberg (1990), 6–8; Korpi (1978); Olsson (1991), 29–33; Stephens (1979); *Switzerland*: Höpflinger (1976); Parri (1987*a*); *UK*: Clegg (1979), ch. 5; Cox and Hayward (1983); Crouch (1978).

Table 7.4. Organizations of capital, c.1975

Austria: Lang (1978); Traxler (1986); *Belgium*: Desolre (1981); Molitor (1978); *Denmark*: Hansen and Henriksen (1980*b*); *Finland*: Addison (n.d.); Koskimies (1981); Lilja (1983), esp. ch. 3; Mansner (1989); *France*: Brizay (1975), 119–70, chs. 4, 5; Bunel and Saglio (1979), ch. 3; J.-M. Martin (1983), 3, 4; Moss (1988); Reynaud (1975), ch. 3; *West Germany*: Armingeon (1987); Bergmann (1985); Bunn (1984); Grant (1986); Müller-Jentsch (1985); Simon (1976), 16; Streeck (1983); *Ireland*: W. Cox (n.d.); Hardiman (1986); *Italy*: de Carlini (1972), 76–81; Collidà (1972), 108–26; Martinelli (1980), 77–82; Treu and Martinelli (1984); Turone (1981), ch. 4; van Noorden (1984); *Norway*: Kvavik (1976); NOU (1982); *Portugal*: Pinto (1990); *Spain*: Aguilar and Jordana (1988); Giner and Sevilla (1984), 119; Perez-Diaz (1987), 224; Roca (1987), 250–1; *Sweden*: Skogh (1984); *Switzerland*: Katzenstein (1984), ch. 3; Parri (1987a); *UK*: Armstrong (1984); Clegg (1979), ch. 3; Grant and Marsh (1977).

Table 7.5. Power of organized labour, c.1975

Austria: Lang (1978); Traxler (1982); *Belgium*: Desolre (1981); Molitor (1978); *Denmark*: Hansen and Henriksen (1980b); Rasmussen (1985), ch. 9; *Finland*: Koskimies (1981); Lilja (1983), esp. 225; *France*: Dubois *et al.* (1978); Landier (1982); Reynaud (1975), ch. 5; *West Germany*: Armingeon (1987); (1988b), 78–81; Bergmann (1985); Brandt *et al.* (1982); Müller-Jentsch and Sperling (1978); Müller-Jentsch (1985); *Ireland*: Hardiman (1988); Hillery (1981); Roche and Larragy (1987); *Italy*: Regalia *et al.* (1978); Turone (1981), ch. 4; *Netherlands*: Akkermans and Grootings (1978); Visser (1987); *Norway*: Kvavik (1976); *Portugal*: Pinto (1990); *Spain*: Perez-Diaz (1987); EDIS (1979); *Sweden*: Elder (1988); Korpi (1978); *Switzerland*: Parri (1987a); *UK*: Clegg (1979), ch. 5; Crouch (1978); Fox (1985), ch. 8.

Tables for 1990

Because of the recency of this period, the account leans heavily on the monthly record of the *European Industrial Relations Review*. Other generally useful sources have been: Armingeon (1989a), on institutional development and union power; M. Baglioni (1990), and *Social Europe* (1990) on institutional development; and Visser (forthcoming), on union power.

Table 7.8. Institutional development of industrial relations, c.1990

Austria: Guger (1992); Marin (1982); (1985); (1987); *Belgium*: Pijnenburg (1989), 46–8; Spineux (1990); *Denmark*: Amoroso (1990); Andersen and Risager (1990); Rasmussen (1985); *Finland*: Eriksson, Suvarto, and Vartia (1990); Helander (1984); Mansner (1989); Pekkarinen (1992); *France*: Cox and Hayward (1983); Goetschy (1987); Hayward (1986), 64–7; Keeler (1987); Moss (1988); Segrestin (1990); *West Germany*:

Armingeon (1988*b*), 7–9; (1989), 4; Clasen (1988); Esser (1982); Jacobi and Müller-Jentsch (1990); *Ireland*: Ewing (1991), ch. 7; Hardiman (1988); *Italy*: Negrelli and Santi (1990); Regalia (1984); Regini (1987); *Netherlands*: Braun (1988), 201–26; Foppen (1989); Scholten (1987*a*); Teulings (1984); Visser (1989); (1990); *Norway*: Foss (1991); Pekkarinen (1992); Rødseth and Holden (1990); *Portugal*: Pinto (1990); *Spain*: Espina (1990); Estivill and de la Hoz (1990); Giner and Sevilla (1984), 126–8, 133–6; Martinez-Alier and Roca (1988), 252 ff.; Perez-Diaz (1987), 221–32; *Sweden*: Ahlén (1989); Calmfors and Forslund (1990); Gustafsson (1989); Hedström (1986); Kjellberg (1990); Lash (1985); Olsson (1991), ch. 3; Pekkarinen (1992); Rehn and Viklund (1990); Rothstein (1987); *Switzerland*: Blaas (1992); Ruf (1986), 279–82; Katzenstein (1984); Kriesi (1986*a*); Parri (1987*b*); *UK*: Batstone (1988); Crouch (1990*c*); Ewing (1991); Ingram and Cahill (1989); MacInnes (1987); Metcalf (1989); Middlemas (1991); Millward and Stevens (1986); Vickerstaff and Sheldrake (1989).

Table 7.9. Articulation of trade-union movements, c.1990

Austria: Marin (1985); *Belgium*: Pijnenburg (1989), 35–6; Spineux (1990); *Denmark*: Amoroso (1990); Andersen and Risager (1990); *Finland*: Eriksson, Suvarto, and Vartia (1990); Helander (1984); Lilja (1983), esp. ch. 3; *France*: Cox and Hayward (1983); Segrestin (1990); *West Germany*: Armingeon (1988*b*), 7–9; Jacobi and Müller-Jentsch (1990); *Ireland*: Roche and Larragy (1987); *Italy*: Negrelli and Santi (1990); Regalia (1986); *Netherlands*: Visser (1987); (1990); *Norway*: Foss (1991); Rødseth and Holden (1990); *Portugal*: Pinto (1990); *Spain*: Aguilar and Jordana (1988); Estivill and de la Hoz (1990); Rijnen (1985); Roca (1987); *Sweden*: Calmfors and Forslund (1990); Kjellberg (1990); Olsson (1991), ch. 3; Rehn and Viklund (1990); *Switzerland*: Fluder (1990); *UK*: Cox and Hayward (1983); Crouch (1990*b*); Olsson (1991), ch. 3.

Table 7.11. Organizations of capital, c.1990

Austria: Traxler (1986); *Belgium*: Spineux (1990); *Denmark*: Amoroso (1990); *Finland*: Mansner (1989); *France*: Moss (1988); Segrestin (1990); Wilson (1982), 190; *West Germany*: Esser (1982); Grant (1986); Jacobi and Müller-Jentsch (1990); *Ireland*: W. Cox (n.d.); *Italy*: Negrelli and Santi (1990); Treu and Martinelli (1984); *Netherlands*: Braun (1988); *Norway*: Foss (1991); *Portugal*: Pinto (1990); Rødseth and Holden (1990); *Spain*: Aguilar and Jordana (1988); Estivill and de la Hoz (1990); Perez-Diaz (1985); Rijnen (1985); *Sweden*: Calmfors and Forslund (1990); Hedström (1986); Rehn and Viklund (1990); Skogh (1984); *Switzerland*: Katzenstein (1984), ch. 3; Parri (1987*b*); *UK*: Armstrong (1984); Grant (1986); Ingram and Cahill (1989).

Table 7.12. Power of organized labour, c.1990

Austria: Marin (1985); *Belgium*: Spineux (1990); *Denmark*: Amoroso (1990); *Finland*: Mansner (1989); *France*: Goetschy (1987); Segrestin (1990); *West Germany*: Armingeon (1988b); Jacobi and Müller-Jentsch (1990); *Ireland*: Roche and Larragy (1987); *Italy*: Negrelli and Santi (1990); Regalia (1984); *Netherlands*: Visser (1987); (1990); *Norway*: Foss (1991); *Portugal*: Pinto (1990); *Spain*: Aguilar and Jordana (1988); Estivill and de la Hoz (1990); Rijnen (1985); Roca (1987); *Sweden*: Hedström (1986); Kjellberg (1990); Rehn and Viklund (1990); *Switzerland*: Fluder (1990); *UK*: Beaumont (1989); Claydon (1989); Crouch (1990c).

References

ABAD DE SANTILLÀN, D. (1967), *Historia del Movimento Obrero Español*, i. *Desde sus origenes a la restauracion borbonica* (Madrid: Editorial ZYX).

ACTU-TDC (1987), *Australia Reconstructed* (Canberra: Department of Trade).

ADAMS, J. C. (1952), 'Italy', in Galenson (1952c).

ADDISON, J. T. (n.d.), 'Finnish Incomes Policy' (University of Carolina, mimeo).

AGUILAR, S., and JORDANA, J. (1988), 'Interest Associations in the Spanish Political Transition' (Bonn: Friedrich Ebert Stiftung, mimeo).

AHLÉN, B. (1989), 'Swedish Collective Bargaining under Pressure: Inter-Union Rivalry and Incomes Policies', *British Journal of Industrial Relations*, 27/3, 330–46.

AKKERMANS, T., and GROOTINGS, P. (1978), 'From Corporatism to Polarisation: Elements of the Development of Dutch Industrial Relations', in Crouch and Pizzorno (1978a).

ALBRECHT, W. (1982), *Fachverein—Berufsgewerkschaft—Zentralverband. Organisationsprobleme der deutschen Gewerkschaften, 1870–1890* (Bonn: Verlag Neue Gesellschaft).

AMOROSO, B. (1990), 'Development and Crisis of the Scandinavian Model in Denmark', in Baglioni and Crouch (1990).

AMSDEN, J. (1972), *Collective Bargaining and Class Conflict in Spain* (London: LSE and Weidenfeld & Nicolson).

ANCKAR, D., and HELANDER, V. (1985), 'Public Allocation by Private Organisations: The Case of Finland' (Paris: International Political Science Association, mimeo).

ANDERSEN, T. M., and RISAGER, O. (1990), 'Wage Formation in Denmark', in Calmfors (ed.), 137–81.

ANDERSEN, T. P. (1976), *Staten og Storkonflikten i 1925* (Copenhagen: Selskabet til forkning i arbejderbevægelsens historie).

ANDERSON, P. (1974), *Lineages of the Absolutist State* (London: New Left Books).

ARCHER, R. (1991), 'The Unexpected Emergence of Australian Corporatism', in Pekkarinen, Pohjola, and Rowthorn (1991).

ARIZA, J. (1976), *Comisiones Obreras* (Barcelona: Avance).

ARMINGEON, K. (1987), 'Gewerkschaften in der Bundesrepublik Deutschland, 1950–1985: Mitglieder, Organisation und Aussenbeziehungen', *Politische Vierteljahresschrift*, 28/1, 7–34.

—— (1988a), 'Politische Regulierung industrieller Beziehungen: Vom

Königreich zur BRD', in M. G. Schmidt (ed.), *Staatstätigkeit: Internationale und Historische Vergleichende Analysen* (Opladen: Westdeutscher Verlag), 151–77.

ARMINGEON, K. (1988b), *Die Entwicklung der westdeutschen Gewerkschaften, 1950–1985* (Frankfurt am Main: Campus).

—— (1989a), 'Arbeitsbeziehungen und Gewerkschaftsentwicklung in den achtziger Jahren: Ein Vergleich der OECD-Länder', *Politische Vierteljahresheft*, 30/4, 603–28.

—— (1989b), 'Trade Unions under Changing Conditions: The West German Experience 1950–1985', *European Sociological Review*, 5/1, 1–23.

—— (1990), 'Labour Relations and Union Development in the 1980s' (University of Heidelberg, mimeo).

ARMSTRONG, E. G. A. (1984), 'Employers' Associations in Great Britain', in Windmuller and Gladstone (1984).

AUKRUST, O. (1977), 'Inflation in the Open Economy: A Norwegian Model', in L. B. Krause and W. S. Salent (eds.), *Worldwide Inflation: Theory and Recent Experience* (Washington, DC: Brookings Institution).

BACK, C. (1967), *Sammansslutningarnas roll i politiken 1870–1910* (Skellefteå: Västerbottens tryckeri).

BAGLIONI, G., and CROUCH, C. J. (1990) (eds.), *European Industrial Relations: the Challenge of Flexibility* (London: Sage).

BAGLIONI, M. (1990), 'Organizational Diversity of Employers' Associations in Europe', paper presented at IREC Conference on Employers' Associations in Europe, Trier, mimeo.

BAIN, G. S., and PRICE, R. (1980), *Profiles of Union Growth* (Oxford: Blackwell).

BAIROCH, P. (1976), 'Europe's Gross National Product 1800–1975', *Journal of European Economic History*, 5/2.

BALDAMUS, W. (1961), *Efficiency and Effort* (London: Tavistock).

BANTON, M. (1983), *Racial and Ethnic Competition* (Cambridge: Cambridge University Press).

BARBADORO, I. (1973a), *Storia del sindacalismo italiano dalla nascita al fascismo*, i. *La Federterra* (Florence: La Nuova Italia).

—— (1973b), *Storia del sindacalismo italiano dalla nascita al fascismo*, ii. *La CGdL* (Florence: La Nuova Italia).

BATSTONE, E. (1979), *Shop Stewards in Action* (Oxford: Blackwell).

BEAN, C., LAYARD, R., and NICKELL, S. (1986), 'The Rise in Unemployment: A Multi-Country Study', *Economica*, 53 (supp.).

BEER, S. H. (1965), *Modern British Politics* (London: Faber & Faber).

—— (1982), *Britain against Itself* (London: Faber & Faber).

BEN-AMI, S. (1985), *Fascism from Above: The Dictatorship of Primo de*

Rivera in Spain, 1923–1930 (Oxford: Oxford University Press).

BENDIX, R. (1956), *Work and Authority in Industry* (New York: Wiley).

BEREND, I. T., and RANKI, G. (1982), *The European Periphery and Industrialisation, 1780–1914* (Cambridge: Cambridge University Press).

BERGER, S. D. (1981*a*), 'Introduction', in Berger (1981*b*).

—— (1981*b*) (ed.), *Organizing Interests in Western Europe* (Cambridge: Cambridge University Press).

BERGHAHN, V. R. (1988), 'Corporatism in Germany in Historical Perspective', in Cox and O'Sullivan (1988), 104–22.

BERGMANN, J. (1985), 'Gewerkschaften: Organisationstruktur und Mitgliederinteressen', in Endruweit *et al.* (1985).

—— *et al.* (1975), *Gewerkschaften in der Bundesrepublik Deutschland* (Frankfurt am Main: Campus).

BIRSEN, J. L. (1978), *La Fait syndicale en France* (Paris: Publi-union).

BLAAS, W. (1991), 'The Swiss Model: Corporatism or Liberal Capitalism?' in Pekkarinen *et al.* (1991).

BLACK, A. (1984), *Guilds and Civil Society in European Political Thought from the Twelfth Century to the Present* (London: Methuen).

BLUM, A. A. (1981) (ed.), *International Handbook of Industrial Relations* (London: Greenwood).

BLYTH, C. A. (1979), 'The Interaction between Collective Bargaining and Government Policies in Selected Member Countries' (Paris: OECD).

BÖCKENFÖRDE, E.-W. (1977), 'Die politische Funktion wirtschaftssozialer Verbände und Interessenträger in der sozialstaatlichen Demokratie', in Hennis, Wielmansegg, and Mate (eds.), *Regierbarkeit* (Stuttgart: Banci).

BOTTOMORE, T. H. (1978), 'Introduction', in T. H. Bottomore and P. Goode (eds.), *Austro-Marxism* (Oxford: Oxford University Press).

BOYD, A. (1972), *The Rise of the Irish Trade Unions* (Tralee: Anvil).

BOYER, R. (1984), *Wage Labor, Capital Accumulation and the Crisis, 1968–1982* (Paris, CEPREMAP).

BRANDE, A. VAN DEN (1973), 'Voluntary Associations in the Belgian Political System', *Res Publica*, 15/2, 329–56.

—— (1987), 'Neo-Corporatism and Functional-Integral Power in Belgium', in Scholten (1987*b*).

BRANDT, G., *et al.* (1982), *Anpassung an der Krise: Gewerkschaften in den siebziger Jahren* (Frankfurt am Main: Campus).

BRAUN, D. (1988), 'Der niederländische Weg in die Massenarbeitslosigkeit, 1973–1981' (University of Amsterdam: doctoral thesis).

BRITTAN, S. (1975), 'The Economic Consequences of Democracy',

British Journal of Political Science, 5.

BRIZAY, B. (1975), *Le Patronat: Histoire, structure, stratégie* (Paris: Seuil).

BROWN, T. (1981), *Ireland: A Social and Cultural History, 1922–1979* (London: Fontana).

BRUNETTA, R., and DELL'ARINGA, C. (1990) (eds.), *Labour Relations and Economic Performance* (London: Macmillan and International Economic Association).

BRUNO, M., and SACHS, J. (1985), *The Economics of World-wide Stagflation* (Oxford: Blackwell).

BRUUN, H. (1931*a*), 'Fagbevægelsens Brydningstid, 1871–1873', in Engelstoft and Jensen (1931).

—— (1931*b*), 'Arbejdsgiverforeninger i Danmark: Årene, 1862–1898', in Engelstoft and Jensen (1931).

BULL, E. (1955), *Norsk Fagbevegelse* (Oslo: Tiden Norsk Verlag).

BULL, M. J. (1988), 'From Pluralism to Pluralism: Italy and the Corporatism Debate', in Cox and O'Sullivan (1988).

BUNEL, J., and SAGLIO, J. (1979), *L'Action patronale du CNPF au petit patron* (Paris: Presses Universitaires de France).

—— (1984), 'Employers' Associations in France', in Windmuller and Gladstone (1984).

BUNN, R. F. (1984), 'Employers' Associations in the Federal Republic of Germany', in Windmuller and Gladstone (1984).

CALMFORS, L. (1990) (ed.), *Wage Formation and Macro-Economic Policy in the Nordic Countries* (Oxford: Oxford University Press).

—— and DRIFFILL, D. J. (1988), 'Bargaining Structure, Corporatism and Macro-Economic Performance', *Economic Policy*, 6.

—— and FORSLUND, A. (1990), 'Wage Formation in Sweden', in Calmfors (1990), 63–130.

CAMERON, D. (1984), 'Social Democracy, Corporatism, Labour Quiescence, and the Representation of Economic Interests in Advanced Capitalist Societies', in J. H. Goldthorpe (ed.), *Order and Conflict in Contemporary Capitalism: Studies in the Political Economy of Western European Nations* (Oxford: Oxford University Press), 143–78.

CASTLES, F. G. (1987), 'Neo-Corporatism and the Happiness Index', *European Journal of Political Research*, 15, 381–93.

CERNY, P. G. (1982), 'Introduction: The Role of Protest in Contemporary French Society', in Cerny (ed.), *Social Movements and Protest in France* (London: Frances Pinter).

CHLEPNER, B.-S. (1956), *Cent ans d'histoire sociale en Belgique* (Brussels: Institut de Sociologie Solvay).

CHRISTIANSEN, N. F. (1984), 'Denmark: End of the Idyll', *New Left Review*, 144.

CLASEN, L. (1988), 'Das neue AVE-Verzeichnis', *Bundesarbeitsblatt*, 2, 26–30.

CLAYDON, T. (1989), 'Union Democracy in Britain in the 1980s', *British Journal of Industrial Relations*, 27/2, 214–24.

CLEGG, H. A. (1972), *The System of Industrial Relations in Great Britain* (Oxford: Blackwell).

—— (1975), 'Pluralism in Industrial Relations', *British Journal of Industrial Relations*, 13/3.

—— (1976), *Trade Unionism under Collective Bargaining* (Oxford: Blackwell).

—— (1979), *The Changing System of Industrial Relations in Great Britain* (Oxford: Blackwell).

COI, S. (1979), 'Sindacati in Italia: iscritti, apparato, finanziamento', *Il Mulino*, 262.

COLE, G. D. H. (1917), *Self Government in Industry* (London: Allen & Unwin).

—— (1920), *Guild Socialism Restated* (London: Allen & Unwin).

COLEMAN, J. S. (1986), *Individual Interests and Collective Action* (Cambridge: Cambridge University Press).

COLLIDÀ, A. (1972), 'L'Intersind', in Collidà (ed.), *La patronata italiana* (Bari: Laterza).

CONTINI, G. (1985), 'Politics, Law, and Shop-Floor Bargaining in Post-War Italy', in S. Tolliday and J. Zeitlin (eds.), *Shop-Floor Bargaining and the State* (Cambridge: Cambridge University Press).

COSER, L. (1956), *The Functions of Social Conflict* (London: RKP).

COX, A. (1988), 'The Old and New Testaments of Corporatism: Is It a Political Form or a Method of Policy-Making?', *Political Studies*, 30.

—— and HAYWARD, J. (1983), 'The Inapplicability of the Corporatist Model in Britain and France: The Case of Labor', *International Political Science Review*, 4/2, 217–40.

—— and O'SULLIVAN, N. (1988) (eds.), *The Corporate State: Corporatism and the State Tradition in Western Europe* (Aldershot: Elgar).

COX, W. (n.d.), 'Employers' Associations' (Dublin, mimeo).

CROUCH, C. J. (1977), *Class Conflict and the Industrial Relations Crisis* (London: Heinemann).

—— (1978), 'The Intensification of Industrial Conflict in the United Kingdom', in Crouch and Pizzorno (1978a).

—— (1982a), *The Politics of Industrial Relations*, 2nd edn. (London: Fontana).

—— (1982b), *Trade Unions: The Logic of Collective Action* (London: Fontana).

—— (1983), 'Pluralism and the New Corporatism: A Rejoinder', *Political Studies*, 31, 452–60.

CROUCH, C. J. (1985), 'Conditions for Trade-Union Wage Restraint', in L. N. Lindberg and C. S. Maier (eds.), *The Politics of Inflation and Economic Stagnation* (Washington, DC: Brookings Institution).

—— (1990*a*), 'Trade Unions in the Exposed Sector: Their Influence on Neo-Corporatist Behaviour', in Brunetta and Dell'Aringa (1990).

—— (1990*b*), 'Les Systèmes de relations industrielles: La Théorie de Dunlop trente ans après et dans une perspective européenne', in J.-D. Reynaud *et al.* (eds.), *Les Systèmes de relations professionnelles* (Paris: CNRS).

—— (1990*c*), 'United Kingdom: The Rejection of Compromise', in Baglioni and Crouch (1990).

—— (1990*d*), 'Generalized Political Exchange in Industrial Relations in Europe during the Twentieth Century', in Marin (1990*b*).

CROUCH, C. J., and PIZZORNO, A. (1978*a*) (eds.), *The Resurgence of Class Conflict in Western Europe since 1968*, i. *National Studies* (London: Macmillan).

CROUCH, C. J., and PIZZORNO, A. (1978*b*) (eds.), *The Resurgence of Class Conflict in Western Europe since 1968*, ii. *Comparative Analyses* (London: Macmillan).

CROUZET, F., CHALONER, W. H., and STERN, W. M. (1969) (eds.), *Essays in European Economic History, 1789–1914* (London: Edward Arnold).

CROZIER, M., HUNTINGDON, S. P., and WATANAKI, J. (1978), *The Crisis of Democracy* (Trilateral Commission).

CURRIE, R. (1979), *Industrial Politics* (Oxford: Clarendon Press).

DAALDER, H. (1971), 'On Building Consociational Nations: The Cases of the Netherlands and Switzerland', *International Social Science Journal*, 23/3, 355–70.

—— (1974), 'The Consociational Democracy Theme', *World Politics*, 26/4, 604–21.

DAHL, R. A. (1961), *Who Governs? Democracy and Power in an American City* (New Haven, Conn.: Yale University Press).

—— (1982), *Dilemmas of Pluralist Democracy: Autonomy versus Control* (New Haven, Conn.: Yale University Press).

—— (1985), *A Preface to Economic Democracy* (Oxford: Polity Press).

DAHRENDORF, R. (1959), *Class and Class Conflict in an Industrial Society* (London: Routledge).

DE CARLINI, L. (1972), 'La Confindustria', in A. Collidà (ed.), *La Politica del padronato italiano* (Bari: de Donato).

DAMGAARD, E., GERLICH, P., and RICHARDSON, J. J. (1989) (eds.), *The Politics of Economic Crisis: Lessons from Western Europe* (Aldershot: Avebury).

DELL'ARINGA, C. (1990), 'Industrial Relations and the Role of the State in EEC Countries', in Commission des Communautés Européennes, DG V, and London School of Economics and Political Science, *Salaires et intégration européenne* (Brussels: European Commission, V/908/90, JM/34).

DELSINNE, L. (1936), *Le Mouvement syndicale en Belgique* (Brussels: Castaigne).

Department of Trade and Industry (1988), *The Department for Enterprise* (London: HMSO).

DESOLRE, G. G. (1981), 'Belgium', in Blum (1981).

DONOVAN, Lord (1968), *Report of Royal Commission on Trade Unions and Employers Associations*, Cmnd. 3623 (London: HMSO).

DORE, R. P. (1990a), 'Two Kinds of Rigidity: Corporatist Communities and Collectivism', in Brunetta and Dell'Aringa (1990).

—— (1990b), 'Japan: A Country Made for Corporatism?', in C. Crouch and R. Dore (eds.), *Corporatism and Accountability: The Place of Organized Interests in British Public Life* (Oxford: Oxford University Press).

DREWES, G. (1958), *Die Gewerkschaften in der Verwaltungsordnung* (Heidelberg: Verlagsgesellschaft 'Recht und Wirtschaft').

DUBOIS, P., *et al.* (1978), 'The Contradictions of French Trade-Unionism', in Crouch and Pizzorno (1978a).

DUNLOP, J. T. (1958), *Industrial Relations Systems* (New York: Rinehart and Winston).

DURKHEIM, E. (1893), *De la division du Travail Sociale* (Paris: F. Alcan).

—— (1897), *Le Suicide* (Paris: F. Alcan).

DYBDAHL, V. (1982), *Det nye samfund på vej, 1871–1913* (Copenhagen: Gyldendal).

EBBINGHAUS, B., and VISSER, J. (1990), 'Where Does Trade-Union Diversity Come From?', 12th World Congress of Sociology, Madrid (Barcelona: International Sociological Association, mimeo).

EBERTZHEIM, R. (1959), *Les Syndicats ouvriers en Belgique* (Liège).

ECKSTEIN, H. (1966), *Division and Cohesion in Democracy* (Princeton, NJ: Princeton University Press).

EDGREN, G., FAXÉN, K.-O., and ODHNER, C. E. (1973), *Wage Formation and the Economy* (London: Allen and Unwin).

EDIS (1979), *El Sindicalismo in España* (Madrid: Fundaciòn F. Ebert).

EHRMANN, H. W. (1957), *Organized Business in France* (Princeton, NJ: Princeton University Press).

ELDER, N. (1988), 'Corporatism in Sweden', in Cox and O'Sullivan (1988).

ELLIOTT, J. (1978), *Conflict or Co-operation? The Growth of Industrial Democracy* (London: Kogan Page).

ELLWOOD, S. (1990), 'The Working Class under the Franco Regime', in P. Preston (ed.), *Spain in Crisis* (Hassocks: Harvester).

ELMORE, R., GUSTAFSSON, G., and HARGROVE, E. (1986), 'Comparing Implementation Processes in Sweden and the United States', *Scandinavian Political Studies*, 9/3, 209–34.

ELVANDER, N. (1974a), 'The Role of the State in the Settlement of Labor Disputes in the Nordic Countries: A Comparative Analysis', *European Journal of Political Research*, 363–385.

—— (1974b), 'Collective Bargaining and Incomes Policies in the Nordic Countries: A Comparative Analysis', *British Journal of Industrial Relations*, 12/3, 417–37.

ENDRUWEIT, G., GAUGLER, E., STAEHLE, W. H., and WILPERT, B. (1985), *Handbuch der Arbeitsbeziehungen: Deutschland, Österreich, Schweiz* (Berlin: de Gruyter).

ENGELSTOFT, P., and JENSEN, H. (1931) (eds.), *Bidrag til Arbejder-klassens og Arbejderspørgsmålets Historie i Danmark fra 1864 til 1900* (Copenhagen: Gyldendal).

ERIKSSON, T., SUVANTO, A., and VARTIA, P. (1990), 'Wage Formation in Finland', in Calmfors (1990), 189–230.

ESPINA, A. (1990), *De la Industrialización al Mercado Unico* (Madrid: Centro de Publicaciones del Ministerio de Trabajo y Seguridad Social), ch. 4.

ESPING-ANDERSEN, G. (1985), *Politics against Markets* (Princeton, NJ: Princeton University Press).

—— FRIEDLAND, R., and OLIN WRIGHT, E. (1976), 'Modes of Class Struggle and the Capitalist State', *Kapitalistate*, 4/5.

—— and KORPI, W. (1984), 'Social Policy as Class Politics in Post-War Capitalism: Scandinavia, Austria and Germany', in Goldthorpe (1984) (ed.), *Order and Conflict in Contemporary Capitalism* (Oxford: Oxford University Press).

ESSER, J. (1982), *Gewerkschaften in der Krise* (Frankfurt am Main: Suhrkamp).

ESTIVILL, J., and HOZ, J. M. DE LA (1990), 'Transition and Crisis: The Complexity of Spanish Industrial Relations', in Baglioni and Crouch (1990).

European Foundation for the Improvement of Living and Working Conditions (1990), *Roads to Participation and Technological Change: Attitudes and Experiences* (Dublin: The Foundation).

EWING, K. D. (1991), *The Right to Strike* (Oxford: OUP).

EYRAUD, F., JOBERT, A., ROZENBLATT, P., and TALLARD, M. (1989), 'Classifications d'emploi et individualisation des salaires en France' (Turin: Association Européennes d'Économistes du Travail, mimeo).

FAFCHAMPS, J. (1961), *Les Conventions collectives en Belgique* (Brussels: La Pensée Catholique).

FARAGO, P. (1986a), 'Formen der Organisationen von Unternehmern am Beispiel von Vier Wirtschaftsverbänden', in Farago and Kriesi (1986)

—— (1986b), 'Formen organisierter Intereßenvertretung in der schweizerischen Politik', in Farago and Kriesi (1986).

—— and KRIESI, H.-P. (1986) (eds.), *Wirtschaftsverbände in der Schweiz* (Grüsch: Verlag Rüegger).

FISCHER, W. (1964), *Unternehmerschaft, Selbstverwaltung und Staat* (Berlin: Duncker und Humblot).

FLANAGAN, R. J., SOSKICE, D. W., and ULMAN, L. (1983), *Unionism, Economic Stabilization and Incomes Policies: European Experience* (Washington, DC: Brookings Institution).

FLORA, P., *et al.* (1983), *State, Economy and Society in Western Europe 1815–1975*, i. *The Growth of Mass Democracies and Welfare States* (London: Macmillan).

—— (1987), *State, Economy and Society in Western Europe 1815–1975*, ii. *The Growth of Industrial Societies and Capitalist Economies* (London: Macmillan).

FLUDER, R. (1990), 'Stability under Pluralist Conditions: Trade Unions and Collective Bargaining in Switzerland', 12th World Congress of Sociology, Madrid.

FONSECA, C. DA (1979), *Historia do Movimento Operario e des Ideias Socialistas em Portugal*, i. *Cronologia* (Lisbon: Europa-America).

FOPPEN, J. W. (1989), 'The Netherlands and the Crisis as a Policy Challenge: Integration or Manœuvres?' in Damgaard *et al.* (1989), 89–106.

FOSS, P. (1991), 'Problems of Centralized Collective Wage Bargaining and Incomes Policy in Norway', (Oxford University: D.Phil. thesis).

FOX, A. (1966), *Industrial Sociology and Industrial Relations* (London: HMSO).

—— (1974), *Beyond Contract: Work, Power and Trust Relations* (London: Faber & Faber).

—— (1985), *History and Heritage* (London: Allen & Unwin).

FULCHER, J. (1987), 'Labour Movement Theory versus Corporatist Social Democracy in Sweden', *Sociology*, 21/2, 231–52.

GALENSON, W. (1949), *Labor in Norway* (Cambridge, Mass.: Harvard University Press).

—— (1952a), 'Scandinavia', in Galenson (1952c).

—— (1952b), *The Danish System of Labor Relations: A Study in Industrial Peace* (Cambridge, Mass.: Harvard University Press).

—— (1952c) (ed.), *Comparative Labor Movements* (New York: Russell & Russell).

GERSHENKRON, A. (1962), *Economic Backwardness in Historical Perspective* (Cambridge, Mass.: Belknap Press).

GEVERS, P. (1983), 'Arbeidsverhoudingen in Belgie', *Tijdschrift voor Sociologie*, 4/1–2, 68–79.

Gewerkschaftliche Monatshefte (1974), 'Auf dem Weg zum "Gewerkschaftsstaat"?', 10/74.

GILLET, M. (1966), 'The Coal Age and the Rise of Coalfields in the Nord and Pas de Calais', *Charbon et sciences humaines*, repr. in Crouzet *et al.* (1969).

GINER, S., and SEVILLA, E. (1984), 'Spain: From Corporatism to Corporatism', in A. Williams (ed.), *Southern Europe Transformed* (London: Harper & Row).

GLYN, A. (1991), 'Social Corporatism, Patterns of Employment and Access to Consumption', in Pekkarinen, Pohjola, and Rowthorn (1991).

GOETSCHY, J. (1987), 'The Neo-Corporatist Issue in France', in Scholten (1987*b*), 177–94.

GRANT, W. (1986), 'Why Employer Organisation Matters: A Comparative Analysis of Business Association Activity in Britain and West Germany' (University of Warwick, Politics Working Paper 42, mimeo).

—— and MARSH, P. (1977), *The CBI* (London: Hodder & Stoughton).

GRUNER, E. (1956), *Die Wirtschaftsverbände in der Demokratie: Vom Wachstum der Wirtschaftsorganisationen im Schweizerischen Staat* (Erlenbach and Zurich: Eugen Rentsch Verlag).

GUGER, A. (1991), 'Social Corporatism: Success or Failure? Austrian Experiences', in Pekkarinen *et al.* (1991).

GUINEA, J. L. (1978), *Los Movimentos Obreros y Sindicales en España* (Madrid: Iberico-Europea).

GUSTAFSSON, G. (1989), 'Challenges Confronting Swedish Decision-Makers: Political and Policy Responses 1974–1987', in Damgaard *et al.* (1989), 163–84.

HADENIUS, A. (1976), *Facklig organisationsutveckling* (Uppsala: Raben & Sjögren).

HALL, P. (1986), *Governing the Economy: The Politics of State Intervention in Britain and France* (Oxford: Polity Press).

HALLENDORFF, C. (1927), *Svenska Arbetgivarföreningen 1902–1927* (Stockholm: mimeo).

HANSEN, S. A., and HENRIKSEN, I. (1980*a*), *Sociale Bydninger 1914–1939* (Copenhagen: Gyldendal).

—— (1980*b*), *Velfærdsstaten 1940–1978* (Copenhagen: Gyldendal).

HARBISON, F. H. (1954), 'Collective Bargaining and American Capitalism', in A. Kornhauser, R. Dubin and A. M. Ross (eds.), *Industrial Conflict* (New York: McGraw Hill).

HARDES, H.-D. (1974), *Einkommenspolitik in der BRD* (Frankfurt am Main: Herder & Herder).

HARDIMAN, N. (1988), *Pay, Politics, and Economic Performance in Ireland 1970–1987* (Oxford: Oxford University Press).

HARMSEN, G., and REINALDA, B. (1975), *Voor de Bevrijding van de Arbeid* (Nijmegen: Socialistiese Uitgeverij).

HARRISON, I. (1989), 'State and Labour in the USA' (Oxford University, unpublished doctoral thesis).

HAYEK, F. VON (1973), 'Cosmos and Taxis', in von Hayek, *Rules and Order* (London: RKP).

HAYWARD, J. E. S. (1966), *Private Interests and Public Policy: The Experience of the French Economic and Social Council* (New York: Barnes & Noble).

—— (1983), *Governing France: The One and Indivisible Republic*, 2nd edn. (London: Weidenfeld & Nicolson).

—— (1986), *The State and the Market Economy: Industrial Patriotism and Economic Intervention in France* (Brighton: Wheatsheaf).

HECKSCHER, G. (1946), *Staten och Organisationerna* (Stockholm: KFs Bokförlag).

HEDSTRÖM, P. (1986), 'The Evolution of the Bargaining Society: Politico-Economic Dependencies in Sweden', *European Sociological Review*, 2/1, 20–32.

HEIDENHEIMER, A. J. (1980), 'Unions and Welfare State Development in Britain and Germany: An Interpretation of Metamorphoses in the Period 1910–1950' (Berlin: Internationales Institut für Vergleichende Gesellschaftsforschung, mimeo).

HELANDER, V. (1982), 'A Liberal Corporatist Subsystem in Action: The Incomes Policy System in Finland', in Lehmbruch and Schmitter (1982).

—— (1984), 'Corporatism or Quasi-Corporatism: The Development of Prices Policy Mechanisms in Finland 1968–1978', in H. Paloheimo (ed.), *Politics in the Era of Corporatism and Planning* (Tampere: Finnish Political Science Association).

—— and ANCKAR, D. (1983), *Consultation and Political Culture: Essays on the Case of Finland* (Helsinki: Societas Scientiarum Fennica).

HEMERIJCK, A. (1990), 'The Historical Fragility of Dutch Corporatism' (University of Tilburg, mimeo).

HENNIS, W. (1961), 'Verfaßungsordnung und Verbandseinfluß: Bemerkungen zu ihrem Zusammenhang im politischen System der Bundesrepublik', *Politische Vierteljahresschrift*, 2.

HIBBS, D. A. (1978), 'On the Political Economy of Long-Run Trends in Strike Activity', *British Journal of Political Science*, 8, 153–75.

HILFERDING, R. (1910), *Das Finanzkapital* (Vienna: Wiener Volksbuchhandlung).

HILLERY, B. J. (1981), 'Ireland', in Blum (1981).

HIRSCH, F. (1977), *Social Limits to Growth* (London: RKP).

HIRSCH, J. (1966), *Die Öffentlichen Funktionen der Gewerkschaften* (Stuttgart: Ernst Klett Verlag).

HIRSCHMAN, A. O. (1970), *Exit, Voice and Loyalty* (Cambridge, Mass.: Harvard University Press).

HOBSON, S. G. (1914), *National Guilds* (London: G. Bell).

HODNE, F. (1983), *The Norwegian Economy 1920–1980* (London: Croom Helm).

HÖPFLINGER, F. (1976), *Industriegewerkschaften in der Schweiz* (Zurich: Limmat Verlag).

INGHAM, G. K. (1974), *Strikes and Industrial Conflict: Britain and Scandinavia* (London: Macmillan).

INGRAM, P., and CAHILL, J. (1989), *The Structure and Process of Pay Determination in the Private Sector, 1979–1986* (London: CBI).

JACKSON, P., and SISSON, K. (1976), 'Employers' Confederations in Sweden and the United Kingdom and the Significance of Industrial Infrastructure', *British Journal of Industrial Relations*, 14/3, 306–23.

JACOBI, O., JESSOP, B., KASTENDIEK, H., and REGINI, M. (1986*a*) (eds.), *Economic Crisis, Trade Unions and the State* (London: Croom Helm).

—— —— —— —— (1986*b*) (eds.), *Technological Change, Rationalisation and Industrial Relations* (London: Croom Helm).

—— and MÜLLER-JENTSCH, W. (1990), 'West Germany: Continuity and Structural Change', in Baglioni and Crouch (1990).

JESSOP, R. D. (1978), 'Capitalism and Democracy: The Best Possible Shell', in G. Littlejohn (ed.), *Power and the State* (London: Croom Helm).

JOHANSEN, L. N., and KRISTENSEN, O. P. (1982), 'Corporatist Traits in Denmark', in Lehmbruch and Schmitter (1982).

JØRGENSEN, P. F. (1975), *Den samwirkende Fakforbund: Kompeten-cespørgmål i Mellemkrigstiden* (Copenhagen: LO).

KALKEN, E. VAN (1950), *La Belgique contemporaine* (Paris: Armand Colin).

KATZENSTEIN, P. (1984), *Corporatism and Change: Austria, Switzerland and the Politics of Industry* (Ithaca, NY: Cornell University Press).

—— (1985), *Small States and World Markets* (Ithaca, NY: Cornell University Press).

KEELER, J. T. S. (1987), *The Politics of Neo-Corporatism in France: Farmers, the State, and Agriculture* (Oxford: Oxford University Press).

KELMAN, S. (1981), *Regulating America, Regulating Sweden* (Cambridge, Mass.: MIT Press).

KENDIX, M., and OLSON, M. (1990), 'Changing Unemployment Rates in Europe and the USA: Institutional Structure and Regional Variation', in Brunetta and Dell'Aringa (1990).

KERCKHOVE, J. VAN DE (1979), 'De Opstelling van de Vakbeweging op de Achtergrond van de Industrielle Ontwikkeling in Belgie: Politisiering en Professionisiering' (Antwerp: Vlaams-Nederlands Sociologen-congres, mimeo).

KIRKWOOD, T., and MEWES, H. (1976), 'The Limits of Trade Union Power in the Corporatist Order: The Case of West German Labour's Quest for Co-Determination', *British Journal of Industrial Relations*, 14/3, 295–305.

KJELLBERG, A. (1983), *Facklig organisering ii tolv länder* (Lund: Arkiv förlag).

—— (1990), 'The Swedish Trade Union System: Centralization and Decentralization', 12th World Congress of Sociology, Madrid (Barcelona: International Sociological Association, mimeo).

KNOELLINGER, C. E. (1960), *Labor in Finland* (Cambridge, Mass.: Harvard University Press).

KNUTSEN, P. (forthcoming), 'Corporatism and the Class Struggle: Studies in the Relationship between the Norwegian Employers Confederation, the Trade Union Movement and the State, 1915–1928' (unpublished manuscript).

KOELBLE, T. A. (1988), 'Challenges to the Unions: The British and West German Cases', *West European Politics*, 11/3, 92–109.

KORPI, W. (1978), *The Working Class in Welfare Capitalism* (London: Routledge).

—— (1981), 'Sweden: Conflict, Power, and Politics in Industrial Relations', in P. Doeringer *et al.* (eds.), *Industrial Relations in International Perspective* (London: Macmillan), 185–217.

—— and SHALEV, M. (1979), 'Strikes, Industrial Relations and Class Conflict in Capitalist Societies', *British Journal of Sociology*, 30/2, 164–87.

KOSKIMIES, J. (1981), 'Finland', in Blum (1981).

KOTTHOF, H. (1985), 'Betriebliche Interessenvertretung durch Mitbestimmung des Beirats', in Endruweit *et al.* (1985).

KRIESI, H.-P. (1982), 'The Structure of the Swiss Political System', in Lehmbruch and Schmitter (1982).

—— (1986a), 'Rahmbedingungen verbändlicher Handeln', in Farago and Kriesi (1986).

—— (1986b), 'Die Berufsbildung in Bauhauptgewerbe', in Farago and Kriesi (1986).

KUHNLE, S. (1975), *Patterns of Social and Political Mobilization: An Historical Analysis of the Nordic Countries* (London: Sage).

KVAVIK, R. B. (1976), *Interest Groups in Norway* (Oslo: Universi-tetsforlaget).

LAFFERTY, W. M. (1971), *Economic Development and the Response of Labor in Scandinavia* (Oslo: Universitetsforlaget).

LANDES, D. (1956), 'The Old Banks and the New: The Financial

Revolution of the Nineteenth Century', *Revue d'histoire moderne et contemporaine*, 3.

LANDIER, H. (1982), *Les Organisations syndicales en France* (Paris: Entreprise Moderne de l'Édition).

LANE, C. (1989), *Management and Labour in Europe* (Aldershot: Elgar).

LANG, W. (1978), *Kooperative Gewerkschaften und Einkommenspolitik: Das Beispiel Österreichs* (Frankfurt am Main: Peter Lang Verlag).

LANGE, P. (1987), 'The Institutionalization of Concertation' (Duke University, NC, Programme in International Economics, Working Paper 26).

—— and GARRETT, G. (1985), 'The Politics of Growth: Strategic Interaction and Economic Performance in the Advanced Industrial Democracies', *Journal of Politics*, 47/3, 792–828.

—— ROSS, G., and VANNICELLI, M. (1982), *Unions, Change and Crisis: French and Italian Union Strategy and the Political Economy, 1945–1980* (London: Allen and Unwin).

LANZALACO, L. (1989), 'La formazione delle associazioni imprenditoriali in Europa occidentale', *Rivista italiana di scienza politica*, 19/1, 63–89.

LAPALOMBARA, J. (1964), *Interest Groups in Italian Politics* (Princeton, NJ: Princeton University Press).

LASH, S. (1985), 'The End of Neo-Corporatism? The Breakdown of Centralised Bargaining in Sweden', *British Journal of Industrial Relations*, 23/3, 215–39.

—— and URRY, J. (1987), *The End of Organised Capitalism* (Oxford: Polity Press).

LECKEBUSCH, R. (1966), *Entstehung und Wandlungen der Zielsetzungen, der Struktur und der Wirkungen von Arbeitgeberverbänden* (Berlin: Duncker und Humblot).

LEE, J. J. (1989), *Ireland 1912–1985: Politics and Society* (Cambridge: Cambridge University Press).

LEENER, D. DE (1909), *L'Organisation syndicale des chefs d'industrie en Belgique*.

LEFÈVRE, CH. E. (1894), *Évolution historique des associations professionnelles dans l'industrie et le commerce de France* (Paris: Henri Jouve).

LEFRANC, G. (1967), *Le Mouvement syndical sous la troisième république* (Paris: Payot).

—— (1976), *Les Organisations patronales en France* (Paris: Payot).

LEHMBRUCH, G. (1982), 'Neo-Corporatism in Comparative Perspective', in Lehmbruch and Schmitter (1982).

—— (1991), 'The Organisation of Society, Administrative Strategies, and Policy Networks', in R. M. Czada and A. Windhoff-Héritier (eds.), *Political Choice: Institutions, Rules, and the Limits of Rationality* (Frankfurt am Main: Campus).

—— and SCHMITTER, P. C. (1982) (eds.), *Patterns of Corporatist Policy-Making* (London: Sage).

LEHNER, F. (1987), 'Interest Intermediation, Institutional Structures and Public Policy', in H. Keman, H. Paloheimo, and P. Whiteley, *Coping with the Economic Crisis* (London: Sage).

—— (1988), 'The Political Economy of Distributive Conflict', in F. Castles, F. Lehner, and M. Schmidt (eds.), *Managing Mixed Economies* (Berlin: de Gruyter).

LEMINSKY, G. (1965), *Der Arbeitnehmereinfluß in englischen und französischen Unternehmen: Ein Vergleich mit der Mitbestimmung* (Cologne: Bund Verlag).

LEWIN, L. (1980), *Governing Trade Unions in Sweden* (Cambridge, Mass.: Harvard University Press).

LIJPHART, A. (1968), *The Politics of Accommodation* (Berkeley, Calif.: University of California Press).

—— and CREPAZ, M. M. L. (1991), 'Corporatism and Consensus Democracy in Eighteen Countries: Conceptual and Empirical Linkages', *British Journal of Political Science*, 21/2, 235–46.

LILJA, K. (1983), *Workers' Workplace Organisations* (Helsinki: School of Economics).

LINDBECK, A. (1976), 'Stabilization Policy in Open Economies with Endogenous Politicians', *American Economic Review*, 66, 1–19.

LINDBLOM, C. E. (1977), *Politics and Markets: The World's Politico-Economic Systems* (New York: Basic Books).

LINZ, J. (1981), 'A Century of Interests and Politics in Spain', in Berger (1981*b*).

LIPSET, S. M. (1983), 'Radicalism or Reformism: The Sources of Working-Class Politics', *The American Political Science Review*, 77/1, 1–18.

—— and ROKKAN, S. (1967), 'Cleavage Structures, Party Systems and Voter Alignments', in Lipset and Rokkan (eds.), *Party Systems and Voter Alignments* (New York: Free Press).

LOPES, S. G. M. DE FREITAS (1980), 'Idéologie et mouvements sociaux: Rapport à l'étude des idéologies basé sur quelques aspects du mouvement ouvrier au Portugal' (Paris: École des Hautes Études en Sciences Sociales, mimeo).

LORENZ, E. H. (1990), 'Trust, Co-operation and Flexibility: A Proposed Framework for International Comparisons' (University of Notre Dame, Ind.: mimeo).

LORWIN, V. (1952), 'France', in Galenson (1952*c*).

LÖSCHE, P. (1973), 'Stages in the Evolution of the German Labour

Movement', in Sturmthal and Scoville (1973).

McCALLUM, J. (1983), 'Inflation and Social Consensus in the Seventies', *Economic Journal*, 93.

—— (1986), 'Unemployment in OECD Countries in the 1980s', *Economic Journal*, 96.

McCARTHY, C. (1977), *Trade Unions in Ireland, 1894–1960* (Dublin: Institute of Public Administration).

MAIER, C. S. (1975), *Recasting Bourgeois Europe* (Princeton, NJ: Princeton University Press).

—— (1981), ' "Fictitious Bonds . . . of Wealth and Law": On the Theory and Practice of Interest Representation', in Berger (1981*b*).

MANSNER, A. (1981), *Suomalaista Yhtaiskuntaa Rakentamassa: STK 1907–1982*, i. *1907–1940* (Helsinki: STK) (Swedish summaries by U.-S. Olander, 'Arbetsmarknadssituationen i Finland före självstän-dighetstiden', and 'Fran förhandlingsförbund till Januarikommuniken: Arbetsgivarnas i Finlands Centralförbund 1918–1940').

—— (1984), *Suomalaista Yhtaiskuntaa Rakentamassa: STK 1907–1982*, ii. *1940–1956* (Helsinki: STK) (Swedish summary by U.-S. Olander, 'Fran Januarikommuniken till Generalstrejken').

—— (1989), *Suomalaista Yhtaiskuntaa Rakentamassa: STK 1907–1982*, iii. *1956–1982* (Helsinki: STK) (Swedish summary by C. Makkonen, 'Fran Generalstrejken till den Inkomstpolitiska Eran').

MARIN, B. (1980), 'Neuer Populismus und Wirtschaftspartnerschaft', *Österreichischer Zeitschrift für Politikwissenschaft*, 2, 157–76.

—— (1982), *Die paritätische Kommission: Aufgeklärter Technocor-poratismus in Österreich* (Vienna: Internationale Publikationen).

—— (1983), 'Wie ist die "Wirtschafts- und Sozialpartnerschaft" möglich?', *Österreichische Zeitschrift für Politikwissenschaft*, 5327–40.

—— (1985), 'Austria: The Paradigm Case of Liberal Corporatism', in W. Grant (ed.), *The Political Economy of Corporatism* (London: Macmillan).

—— (1987), 'From Consociationism to Techno-Corporatism: Austria as a Model Generator?', in Scholten (1987*b*).

—— (1990*a*), 'Generalized Political Exchange: Preliminary Consider-ations', in Marin (ed.), *Generalized Political Exchange* (Frankfurt am Main: Campus), 37–66.

—— (1990*b*) (ed.), *Governance and Generalized Exchange* (Frankfurt am Main: Campus).

MARTIN, A. (1979), 'The Dynamics of Change in a Keynesian Political Economy: The Swedish Case and its Implications', in C. J. Crouch (ed.), *State and Economy in Contemporary Capitalism* (London: Croom Helm).

MARTIN, D. A. (1978), *A General Theory of Secularization* (Oxford: Blackwell).

MARTIN, J.-M. (1983), *Le Conseil National du Patronat Français* (Paris: Presses Universitaires de France).

MARTIN, RODERICK (1978), 'The Effects of Recent Changes in Industrial Conflict on the Internal Politics of Trade Unions: Britain and Germany', in Crouch and Pizzorno (1978*b*).

MARTIN, ROSS (1983), 'Pluralism and the New Corporatism', *Political Studies*, 31/1.

MARTINELLI, A. (1980), 'Organized Business and Italian Politics: Confindustria and the Christian Democrats in the Post-war Period', in P. Lange and S. Tarrow (eds.), *Italy in Transition* (London: Frank Cass).

—— and TREU, T. (1984), 'Employers' Organisations in Italy', in Windmuller and Gladstone (1984).

MARTINEZ-ALIER, J., and ROCA, J. (1988), 'Spain after Franco: From Corporatist Ideology to Corporatist Reality', in Cox and O'Sullivan (1988).

MASCHKE, E. (1964), 'Outline of the History of German Cartels, 1873–1914', *Vortragsreihe der Gesellschaft für Westfälische Wirtschafts-geschichte*, repr. in Crouzet *et al.* (1969).

MATZNER, E., and STREECK, W. (1991*a*), 'Towards a Socio-Economics of Employment in a Post-Keynesian Economy', in Matzner and Streeck (1991*b*).

—— (1991*b*), *Beyond Keynesianism* (Aldershot: Edward Elgar).

MAURICE, M., SELLIER, F., and SILVESTRE, J.-J. (1982), *Politique d'éducation et organisation industrielle en France et en Allemande* (Paris: Presses Universitaires de France).

MEISEL, J. H. (1965) (ed.), *Pareto and Mosca* (Englewood Cliffs, NJ: Prentice-Hall).

METCALF, D. (1989), 'Water Notes Dry Up: The Impact of the Donovan Reform Proposals and Thatcherism at Work on Labour Productivity in British Manufacturing Industry', *British Journal of Industrial Relations*, 27/1, 1–31.

MICHELETTI, M. (1984), 'The Involvement of Swedish Labour Market Organisations in the Swedish Political Process' (Stockholm: Studieförebundet Näringsliv och Samhälle, mimeo).

—— (1985), *Organizing Interest and Organizing Protest* (Stockholm: University of Stockholm).

MICHELS, R. (1911), *Political Parties*.

MIDDLEMAS, K. (1979), *Politics in Industrial Society* (London: André Deutsch).

—— (1990), *Power, Competition and the State,* ii. *Threats to the Post-War Settlement: Britain 1961–74* (Basingstoke: Macmillan).

—— (1991), *Power, Competition and the State,* iii. *The End of the Post-War Era: Britain since 1974* (Basingstoke: Macmillan).

MILLWARD, N., and STEVENS, M. (1986), *British Workplace Industrial Relations, 1980–1984* (Aldershot: Gower).

MILWARD, A. S., and SAUL, S. B. (1973), *The Economic Development of Continental Europe 1780–1870* (London: Allen and Unwin).

—— (1977), *The Development of the Economies of Continental Europe, 1850–1914* (London: Allen and Unwin).

MOLITOR, M. (1978), 'Social Conflicts in Belgium', in Crouch and Pizzorno (1978a).

MOSS, B. H. (1988), 'After the Auroux Laws: Employers, Industrial Relations and the Right in France', *West European Politics*, 11/1.

MÜLLER-JENTSCH, W. (1981), 'Vom gewerkschaftlichen Doppelcharakter und seiner theoretischen Auflösung in Neokorporatismus', *Gesellschaftliche Arbeit und Rationalisierung*, Leviathan Sonderheft, 4/81.

—— (1985), 'Berufs-, Betriebs-, oder Industriegewerkschaften', in Endruweit *et al.* (1985).

—— and SPERLING, H.-J. (1978), 'Economic Development, Labour Conflicts and the Industrial Relations System in West Germany', in Crouch and Pizzorno (1978a).

NEGRELLI, S., and SANTI, E. (1990), 'Industrial Relations in Italy', in Baglioni and Crouch (1990).

NEWELL, A., and SYMONS, J. (1987), 'Corporatism, Laissez-Faire and the Rise of Unemployment', *European Economic Review*, 31.

NOORDEN, W. VAN (1984), 'Employers' Associations in the Netherlands', in Windmuller and Gladstone (1984).

NOU (1982), *Maktutredningens Sluttrapport* 3, 93–100 (Oslo Universitetsforlaget).

NOUSIAINEN, J. (1971), *The Finnish Political System* (Cambridge, Mass.: Harvard University Press).

OFFE, C. (1970), *Leistungsprinzip und Industrielle Arbeit* (Frankfurt am Main: Europäische Verlaganstalt).

—— (1987), 'Challenging the Boundaries of Institutional Politics: Social Movements since the 1960s', in C. S. Maier, *Changing Boundaries of the Political* (Cambridge: Cambridge University Press).

—— (1985) *Disorganized Capitalism* (Cambridge: Polity Press).

—— and WIESENTHAL, H. (1980), 'Two Logics of Collective Action: Theoretical Notes on Social Class and Organizational Form', *Political Power and Social Theory*, 1.

OLSEN, J. P. (1983), *Organized Democracy* (Bergen: Universitetsforlaget).

OLSON, M. (1965), *The Logic of Collective Action: Public Goods and the Theory of Groups* (Cambridge, Mass.: Harvard University Press).

—— (1982), *The Rise and Decline of Nations: Economic Growth,*

Stagflation and Social Rigidities (New Haven, Conn.: Yale University Press).

—— (1986), 'An Appreciation of the Tests and Criticisms', *Scandinavian Political Studies*, 9/1, 65–80.

OLSSON, A. S. (1991), *The Swedish Wage Negotiation System* (Aldershot: Dartmouth).

PALOHEIMO, H. (1984), 'Pluralism, Corporatism and the Distributive Conflict in Developed Capitalist Countries', *Scandinavian Political Studies*, 7/1, 17–38.

—— (1990), 'Between Liberalism and Corporatism: The Effects of Trade Unions and Governments on Economic Performance in Eighteen OECD Countries', in Brunetta and Dell'Aringa (1990).

PANITCH, L. (1976), *Social Democracy and Industrial Militancy* (Cambridge: Cambridge University Press).

PARKIN, M. (1975), 'The Politics of Inflation', *Government and Opposition*, 10.

PARRI, L. (1987a), 'Staat und Gewerkschaft in der Schweiz 1873–1981', *Politische Vierteljahresschrift*, 28/1.

—— (1987b), 'Neo-Corporatist Arrangements: "Konkordanz" and Direct Democracy in the Swiss Experience', in Scholten (1987b).

PEKKARINEN, J., POHJOLA, M., and ROWTHORN, B. (1991a), 'Social Corporatism and Economic Performance', in Pekkarinen *et al.* (1991b).

—— (1991b) (eds.), *Social Corporatism and Economic Performance* (Oxford: Oxford University Press).

PELLING, H. (1987), *A History of British Trade Unionism*, 4th edn. (Basingstoke: Macmillan).

PENTY, A. J. (1906), *The Restoration of the Guild System*.

PEREZ-DIAZ, V. (1985), 'Los Empresarios y la Clase Politica', *Papeles de Economia Española*, 22, 2–37.

—— (1987), 'Economic Policies and Social Pacts in Spain during the Transition', in Scholten (1987b), 216–46.

PERROT, M. (1974a), *Les Ouvriers en grève: France 1871–1890*, i. (Paris: Mouton).

—— (1974b), *Les Ouvriers en grève: France 1871–1890*, ii. *La Conduite de la grève: Les Organisations* (Paris: Mouton).

PESTOFF, V. (1983), 'The Swedish Organisational Community and its Participation in Public Policy-Making: An Introductory Review' (Stockholm University, mimeo).

—— (1990), 'Joint Regulation, Meso Games and Political Exchange in Swedish Industrial Relations', in Marin (1990b), 315–46.

PETERSEN, E. (1950), *Norske Arbeidsgiverforening, 1900–1950* (Oslo).

PIJNENBURG, B. (1989), 'Belgium in Crisis: Political and Policy

Responses 1981–1985', in Damgaard *et al.* (1989), 22–49.

PINTO, M. (1990), 'Trade Union Action and Industrial Relations in Portugal', in Baglioni and Crouch (1990).

PIORE, M., and SABEL, C. (1984), *The Second Industrial Divide: Possibilities for Prosperity* (New York: Basic Books).

PIZZORNO, A. (1978), 'Political Exchange and Collective Identity in Industrial Conflict', in Crouch and Pizzorno (1978*b*).

POGGI, G. (1978), *The Development of the Modern State* (London: Hutchinson).

POHJOLA, M. (1991), 'Corporatism and Wage Bargaining', in Pekkarinen *et al.* (1991*b*).

POOLE, M. (1986), *Industrial Relations: Origins and Patterns of National Diversity* (London: Routledge).

PRIGGE, W.-U. (1985), 'Arbeitgeber- und Unternehmensverbände', in Endruweit *et al.* (1985).

PROST, A. (1964), *La CGT à l'époque du Front Populaire, 1934–1939* (Paris: Colin).

PRZEWORSKI, A. (1985), *Capitalism and Social Democracy* (Cambridge: Cambridge University Press).

RASCH, B. H., and SØRENSEN, R. J. (1986), 'Organisational Behaviour and Economic Growth: A Norwegian Perspective', *Scandinavian Political Studies*, 9/1, 51–64.

RASMUSSEN, E. J. (1985), 'Twenty-five Years of Labour Government and Incomes Policy' (Florence: European University Institute, doctoral thesis).

RAUSCHER, A. (1985), 'Richtungs oder Einheitsgewerkschaft', in · Endruweit *et al.* (1985).

REGALIA, I. (1984), 'Le politiche del lavoro', in U. Ascoli (ed.), *Welfare State all'Italiana* (Bari: Laterza).

—— (1986), 'Centralisation or Decentralisation? An Analysis of Organisational Changes in the Italian Trade Union Movement at the Time of Crisis', in O. Jacobi *et al.* (1985*b*).

—— (1988), 'Forma, rappresentatività e democrazia nelle esperienze sindacali verso gli anni 90: problemi e questioni aperte' (Milan: IRES Lombardia, mimeo).

—— *et al.* (1978), 'Labour Conflicts and Industrial Relations in Italy', in Crouch and Pizzorno (1978*a*).

REGINI, M. (1981), *I dilemmi del sindacato* (Bologna: Il Mulino).

—— (1982), 'Changing Relationships between Labour and the State in Italy: Towards a Neo-Corporatist System?', in Lehmbruch and Schmitter (1982), 109–132.

—— (1987), 'Social Pacts in Italy', in Scholten (1987*b*).

REYNAUD, J.-D. (1975), *Les Syndicats en France*, i. (Paris: Seuil).

—— (1978), 'Nature et rôle des conventions collectives dans la France actuelle', *Revue française de sociologie*, 19/2.

RICHTER, I. (1973), *Political Purpose in Trade Unions* (London: Allen and Unwin).

RIJNEN, H. (1985), 'La CEOE como Organización', *Papeles de Economia Española*, 22, 115–21.

ROCA, J. (1987), 'Neo-Corporatism in Post-Franco Spain', in Scholten (1987*b*), 247–68.

ROCHE, W., and LARRAGY, A. (1987), 'The Trend of Unionization in the Republic of Ireland', in T. Murphy *et al.* (eds.), *Recent Trends in Irish Industrial Relations* (Dublin: University College).

RØDSETH, A., and HOLDEN, S. (1990), 'Wage Formation in Norway', in Calmfors (1990), 237–80.

ROKKAN, S. (1966), 'Norway: Numerical Democracy and Corporatist Pluralism', in R. A. Dahl (ed.), *Political Oppositions in Western Democracies* (New Haven, Conn.: Yale University Press).

ROSE, R., and PETERS, G. (1977), *Can Governments Go Bankrupt?* (New Haven, Conn.: Yale University Press).

ROSENBERG, H. (1958), *Bureaucracy, Aristocracy and Autocracy: Prussia 1660–1815* (Cambridge, Mass.: Harvard University Press).

ROTHSTEIN, B. (1985), 'The Success of the Swedish Labour Market Policy: The Organisational Connection to Policy', *European Journal of Political Research*, 13, 153–65.

—— (1987), 'Corporatism and Reformism: The Social Democratic Institutionalisation of Class Conflict', *Acta Sociologica*, 30:3/4, 295–311.

—— (1989), 'Marxism and Institutional Analysis: Working Class Strength and Welfare State Development, the Swedish Case' (Colchester: ECPR, mimeo).

RUF, H. (1986), 'Krise der Sozialpartnerschaft? Die Vertrags-bewegungen in der Basler Chemischen Industrie und Bauhaupt-gewerbe, 1983–1984', in Farago and Kriesi (1986).

RUSTERHOLZ, P. (1986), 'Maschinenindustrie in Außenwirtschaftspolitik: Die Exportrisikoguarantie in der schweizerischen Politik', in Farago and Kriesi (1986).

SAMUELSSON, K. (1968), *From Great Power to Welfare State* (London: Allen and Unwin).

SARTORIUS, N. (1976), *El Resurgir del Movimento Obrero* (Barcelona: Laia).

SCHARPE, F. (1990), 'The Political Calculus of Inflation and Unemployment in Western Europe: A Game-Theoretical Interpretation', in Marin (1990*b*), 117–46.

SCHMIDT, M. G. (1987), 'The Politics of Labour Market Policy:

Structural and Political Determinants of Rates of Unemployment in Industrial Nations', in F. G. Castles, F. Lehner, and M. G. Schmidt (eds.), *Managing Mixed Economies* (New York: Walter de Gruyter).

SCHMITTER, P. C. (1974), 'Still the Century of Corporatism?' *Review of Politics*, Jan. (subsequently repr. in Lehmbruch and Schmitter (1982)).

—— (1981), 'Interest Intermediation and Regime Governability in Contemporary Western Europe and North America', in Berger (1981*b*), 287–330.

SCHOLTEN, I. (1980), 'Does Consociationalism Exist? A Critique of the Dutch Experience', in R. Rose (ed.), *Electoral Participation: A Comparative Analysis* (London: Sage), 329–54.

—— (1987*a*), 'Corporatism and the Neo-Liberal Backlash in the Netherlands', in Scholten (1987*b*).

—— (1987*b*) (ed.), *Political Stability and Neo-Corporatism* (Beverly Hills, Calif., and London: Sage).

SCHÖNHOVEN, K. (1980), *Expansion und Konzentration: Studien zur Entwicklung der Freien Gewerkschaften in Deutschland, 1890–1914* (Stuttgart: Klett-Cotta).

SCOVILLE, J. C. (1973), 'Some Determinants of the Structure of Labor Movements', in Sturmthal and Scoville (1973).

SEGRESTIN, D. (1990), 'Recent Changes in France', in Baglioni and Crouch (1990).

SELLIER, F. (1973), 'The French Workers' Movement and Political Unionism', in Sturmthal and Scoville (1973).

—— (1978), 'France', in J. T. Dunlop and W. Galenson (eds.), *Western Labor in the Twentieth Century* (New York: Academic Press).

SELLIN, V. (1974), 'Kapitalismus und Organisation in Italien', in Winkler (1974).

SHORTER, E., and TILLY, C. (1974), *Strikes in France* (Cambridge: Cambridge University Press).

SIMON, W. (1976), *Macht und Herrschaft der Unternehmerverbände BDI, BDA und DIHT im ökonomischen und politischen System der BRD* (Cologne: Pahli Rugenstein Verlag).

SINGLETON, G. (1990), *The Accord and the Australian Labour Movement* (Melbourne: Melbourne University Press).

SJÖBERG, W. (1958), *För Arbetsfred: 50 År Samarbete mellan Arbetsgivare* (Helsinki: STK).

SKOGH, G. (1984), 'Employers' Associations in Sweden', in Windmuller and Gladstone (1984).

SLOMP, H. (1990), *Labor Relations in Europe: A History of Issues and Developments* (New York: Greenwood).

SMITH, M. L. (1988), 'Some Historical Problems of Corporatist Development in the Netherlands', in Cox and O'Sullivan (1988).

Social Europe (1990), 'Wage Bargaining in Europe', Supplement 2/90, DGV (Brussels: European Commission).

SÖDERPALM, S. A. (1980), *Arbetsgivarne och Saltjsöbadenpolitiken* (Stockholm: SAF).

SOSKICE, D. (1990), 'Wage Determination: The Changing Role of Institutions in Advanced Industrialized Countries', *Oxford Review of Economic Policy*, 6/4, 1–23.

SPINEUX, A. (1990), 'Trade Unions in Belgium: The Difficulties of a Major Renovation', in Baglioni and Crouch (1990).

SPITAELS, G. (1967), *Le Mouvement syndical en Belgique* (Brussels: Université Libre de Bruxelles).

—— (1972), 'L'Action syndicale en Belgique après Mai 1968' (Paris: Association Française de Science Politique, mimeo).

STEGMANN, D. (1980), 'Unternehmerverbände (Geschichte)', in W. and A. Albers (eds.), *Handwörterbuch der Wirtschaftswissenschaft*, viii. (Stuttgart: Vandenhoeck & Ruprecht).

STEPHENS, J. D. (1979), *The Transition from Capitalism to Socialism* (London: Macmillan).

STREECK, W. (1979), 'Gewerkschaftsorganisation und industrielle Beziehungen', in J. Matthes (ed.), *Sozialer Wandel in West Europa* (Frankfurt am Main: Campus).

—— (1982), 'Organizational Consequences of Neo-Corporatist Co-operation in West German Labour Unions', in Lehmbruch and Schmitter (1982).

—— (1983), 'Between Pluralism and Corporatism: German Business Associations and the State', *Journal of Public Policy*, 3, 265–84.

—— (1985), 'Industrial Relations and Industrial Change in The Motor Industry' (Warwick: University of Warwick).

—— (1989), 'Skills and the Limits of Neo-Liberalism: The Enterprise of the Future as a Place of Learning', *Work, Employment and Society*, 3, 90–104.

—— (1991), 'On the Institutional Conditions of Diversified Quality Production', in Matzner and Streeck (1991*b*), 21–61.

—— and SCHMITTER, P. C. (1985), 'Community, Market, State—Association?', in Streeck and Schmitter (eds.), *Private Interest Government: Beyond Market and State* (Beverly Hills and London: Sage).

STURMTHAL, A. (1953), *Unity and Diversity in European Labor* (Glencoe, Illinois: The Free Press).

—— (1973), 'Industrial Relations Strategies', in Sturmthal and Scoville (1973).

—— and SCOVILLE, J. G. (1973) (eds.), *The International Labor Movement in Transition* (Urbana, Ill.: University of Illinois Press).

Süllow, B. (1982*a*), *Korporatistische Repräsentation der Gewerkschaften: Zur Institutuellen Verbandsbeteiligung in öffentlichen Gremien* (Frankfurt am Main: Campus).

—— (1982*b*), *Die Selbstverwaltung in der Sozialversicherung als Korporatistische Einrichtung: Eine politik-soziologische Analyse* (Frankfurt am Main: Campus).

Talos, E. (1981), *Staatliche Sozialpolitik in Österreich* (Vienna: Verlag für Gesellschaftskritik).

Tarantelli, T. (1986), *Economia Politica del Lavoro* (Turin: UTET).

Teulings, A. (1984), *Vakbeweging en Centrale Overheid* (Amsterdam: SORU).

—— (1985), 'A Political Bargaining Theory of Codetermination: Power and Authority of Works Councils in Strategic Managerial Decision-Making', in R. N. Stern (ed.), *The Organized Practice of Democracy* (Chichester: Wiley).

Traxler, F. (1982), *Evolution Gewerkschaftlicher Interessenvertretung* (Vienna: Braumüller).

—— (1986), *Interessenverbände der Unternehmer: Konstitutionsbedingungen und Steuerungskapazitäten, analysiert am Beispiel Österreichs* (Frankfurt am Main: Campus).

—— (1990), 'Political Exchange, Collective Action and Interest Governance: Towards a Theory of Industrial Relations and Corporatism', in Marin (1990*b*), 37–68.

Treu, T. (1983), 'Collective Bargaining and Participation in Economic Policy: The Case of Italy', in C. J. Crouch and F. Heller (eds.), *International Yearbook of Organizational Democracy*, i. *Organizational Democracy and Political Processes* (Chichester: Wiley).

—— and Martinelli, A. (1984), 'Employers' Associations in Italy', in Windmuller and Gladstone (1984).

Turone, S. (1981), *Storia del sindacato in Italia 1943–1980* (Bari: Laterza).

Ullman, P. (1977), *Tarifverträge und -politik in Deutschland bis 1914* (Frankfurt am Main).

Uyl, J. den (1977), 'Die tijd komt nooit meer terug', in Wiardi Beckman Stichting, *En Toch Bewegt Hat . . .* (Deventer: Van Loghum Slaterus).

Vickerstaff, S., and Sheldrake, J. (1989), *The Limits of Corporatism* (Aldershot: Avebury).

Vigen, A. (1950), *Rigsdagen og Erhvervsorganisationern: Den danske Rigsdag, 1848–1949*, iii. (Copenhagen).

Visser, J. (1987), 'In Search of Inclusive Unionism' (University of Amsterdam, doctoral thesis).

—— (1990), 'Continuity and Change in Dutch Industrial Relations', in Baglioni and Crouch (1990).

—— (forthcoming), 'The Strength of Union Movements in Advanced Capitalist Democracies', in M. Regini (ed.), *Labour Movements towards the Year 2000* (London: Sage).

Webb, B. and S. (1897), *Industrial Democracy* (London: Longmans).

Weber, M. (1919), *Wirtschaft und Gesellschaft*, 3/6, 650–78.

Wedderburn, Lord (1986), *The Worker and the Law*, 3rd edn. (Harmondsworth: Penguin).

Weitbrecht, H., and Berger, G. (1985), 'Zur Geschichte der Arbeiterbewegung', in Endruweit *et al.* (1985).

Wetenschappelijke Raad voor het Regeringsbeleid (1977), *Externe Adviesorganen aan de Centrale Overheid* (The Hague: de Staatsuitgeverij).

Wetenschappelijke Raad voor het Regeringsbeleid (1980), *Plaats en Toekomst van de Nederlandse Industrie* (The Hague: de Staatsuitgeverij).

Wiener, M. J. (1981), *English Culture and the Decline of the Industrial Spirit, 1850–1980* (Cambridge: Cambridge University Press).

Wigham, E. (1982), *Strikes and the Government* (London: Macmillan).

Wilensky, H. (1976), *The New Corporatism, Centralization and the Welfare State* (Beverly Hills, Calif.: Sage).

—— and Turner, L. (1987), *Democratic Corporatism and Policy Linkages* (University of Berkeley, Calif.: Institute of International Studies).

Williamson, P. J. (1985), *Varieties of Corporatism* (Cambridge: Cambridge University Press).

Wilson, F. L. (1982), 'Alternative Models of Interest Intermediation: The Case of France', *British Journal of Political Science*, 12, 173–200.

Windmuller, J. P. (1969), *Labor Relations in the Netherlands* (Ithaca, NY: Cornell University Press).

—— and Gladstone, A. (1984) (eds.), *Employer Associations and Industrial Relations: A Comparative Study* (Oxford: Oxford University Press).

Windolf, P. (1990), 'Productivity Coalitions and the Future of Unionism: Disintegration of Generalized Political Exchange?', in Marin (1990*b*), 289–314.

Winkler, H. A. (1974) (ed.), *Organisierter Kapitalismus* (Göttingen: Vandenhoeck & Ruprecht).

Zeit, Die (1974), 'Marsch in den Gewerkschaftsstaat', 6 Dec., 13.

Zeitlin, J. (1990), 'The Triumph of Adversarial Bargaining: Industrial Relations in British Engineering, 1880–1939', *Politics and Society*, 18/3, 405–26.

Index

pre-1914 67–8, 69, 80, 81, 84,
102, 105; between the wars
131, 135, 159, 161; post-war to
1963 179, 182, 209, 211–12,
231–2; 1975–1990 237,
240–1, 260, 265, 267
liberalism 321, 325–6, 332
as market-governed prototype
295–6
power of organized labour
337–8, 341; pre-1914 72, 73,
75, 94–5, 96, 115, 116, 118,
120; between the wars 145,
146, 149–50, 169, 170, 174;
post-war to 1963 196, 197,
200, 224; 1975–1990 249, 252,
269–70, 276
see also Anglo-American
tradition of industrial relations
United States:
and corporatism 7, 37, 48–9
industrial relations 10, 14, 18,
72, 289, 290
New Deal 155
see also Anglo-American

tradition of industrial relations

verzuiling system, Netherlands
239, 243, 324, 331
Vorort, Austria 93, 114

wage-earner funds 41, 48, 239
Webb, B. and S. 21, 312, 324
Weber, M. 78, 313
white-collar trade unions 242, 243,
258, 268
Whitley Councils, United
Kingdom 126, 128, 135
worker–directors 42, 186, 240
works councils 213, 261–6, 287–8,
321, 344
Austria 80, 178–9, 186, 192, 321
Germany 80, 186, 192, 213, 240,
261–6
Netherlands 80

'yellow' trade unions 105, 118, 135

zero-sum games 32–3, 36, 39